# WEBSTER'S
# NOTEBOOK
# ENGLISH
# THESAURUS

This edition published 2006 by Geddes & Grosset,
David Dale House, New Lanark, ML11 9DJ, Scotland

© 2006 Geddes & Grosset

ISBN 10: 1 84205 580 1
ISBN 13: 1 84205 580 9

Printed and bound by REPRO, Mumbai, India

# A

**abandon** vb 1 (*abandon his wife and children*) desert, leave, forsake, depart from. 2 (*abandon the attempt*) give up, drop, discard, (*inf*) scrap.

**abate** vb (*The storm abated*) die down, lessen, ease, decrease, diminish, moderate, wane.

**abbreviate** vb (*abbreviate a word or phrase*) shorten, reduce, cut, cut short, cut down, contract.

**abdicate** vb 1 (*The king abdicated in 1936*) give up, resign, stand down, retire, quit. 2 (*abdicate responsibilities*) give up, renounce, relinquish.

**abdomen** n (*a pain in the abdomen*) stomach, belly, (*inf*) tummy, (*inf*) insides, intestines.

**abduct** vb (*abduct someone else's child*) kidnap, carry off, seize, hold as hostage, (*inf*) snatch.

**ability** n (*a performer of great ability*) talent, skill, expertise, cleverness, competence.

**able** adj (*an able pupil*) clever, talented, capable, competent.

**abnormal** adj (*an abnormal thing to do*) unusual, strange, odd, peculiar, queer, extraordinary.

**abolish** vb (*abolish smoking in public*) do away with, put an end to, end, stop, eliminate.

**abridge** vb (*abridge the book for children*) shorten, cut down, condense, compress.

**abroad** adv (*go abroad on vacation*) overseas, to a foreign country, to a foreign land, out of the country.

**abrupt** adj 1 (*come to an abrupt end*) sudden, quick, hurried, hasty, swift, rapid, unexpected, unforeseen. 2 (*an abrupt reply*) curt, blunt, brusque, short, rude. 3 (*an abrupt slope*) steep, sheer, sudden, precipitous.

**absent** adj (*absent from school*) not present, away, off, missing, truant.

**absent-minded** adj (*so absent-minded that she didn't hear what people were saying to her*) distracted, preoccupied, absorbed, vague, inattentive.

**absolute** adj (*absolute trust*) complete, total, utter, out and out, outright, perfect, unqualified, sheer.

**abstain** vb (*abstain from voting/ abstain from drinking*) refrain, desist, hold back, keep from.

**absurd** adj (*absurd plan*) ridiculous, foolish, silly, idiotic, stupid, nonsensical, senseless, crazy, ludicrous, harebrained.

**abundance** n (*there was food in abundance*) plenty, profusion, (*inf*) heaps, (*inf*) bags, (*inf*) oodles.

**abundant** adj (*an abundant supply of fresh food*) plentiful, ample, large, great, copious, lavish, profuse.

**abuse** vb 1 (*abuse children*) mistreat, maltreat, ill-treat, ill-use, injure, hurt, harm. 2 (*abuse power*) misuse, misapply, misemploy, mishandle. 3 (*abuse the person who ran into his car*) swear at, curse, insult, rebuke.

**abuse** n 1 (*child abuse*) mistreatment, maltreatment, ill-treatment, ill-use, injury, hurting, harming. 2 (*the abuse of power/ the abuse of alcohol*) misuse, misapplication, misapplying, mishandling.

**abysmal** adj 1 (*abysmal ignorance*) utter, extreme, complete, thorough, profound. 2 (*an abysmal performance*) dreadful, appalling, very bad, worthless.

**accelerate** vb 1 (*The car accelerated*) speed up, go faster, go quicker, pick up speed. 2 (*accelerate the process of change*) speed up, hasten, hurry along, expedite, spur on.

**accent** n 1 (*a southern accent*) way of speaking, pronunciation, inflection, enunciation. 2 (*The accent is on the first syllable*) stress, emphasis, force, accentuation. 3 (*the accent must be on efficiency*) emphasis, stress, importance.

**accept** vb 1 (*accept the gift*) receive, take, take receipt of. 2 (*accept their decision*) agree to, consent to, comply with, acquiesce in, concur with, endorse.

**acceptable** adj 1 (*a very acceptable gift*) welcome, agreeable, delightful, pleasing, pleasant, desirable. 2 (*work that is not acceptable*) satisfactory, good enough, adequate, passable, tolerable.

**access** n (*no direct access to the building from the main road*) entry, entrance, way in, admittance, approach.

**accessible** adj (*accessible sources of information*) attainable, available, reachable, obtainable.

**accessory** n 1 (*accessories for an electric drill*) attachment, extra, addition, adjunct. 2 (*accessories to the crime*) accomplice, associate, confederate, abettor.

**accident** n 1 (*people injured in the mining accident*) casualty, disaster, catastrophe, calamity, mishap. 2 (*old friends who met by accident*) chance, fate, good fortune, luck, (*inf*) fluke.

**accidental** adj (*accidental death/an accidental meeting*) chance, unintentional, unintended, unexpected, unforeseen, unplanned, unpremeditated.

**accommodation** n (*find accommodation for the homeless*) housing, lodging, shelter, board, quarters.

**accompany** vb (*accompany her to the prom*) partner, escort, go with, go along with.

**accomplice** n (*an accomplice in crime*) confederate, accessory, collaborator, abettor, ally, helper, henchman, (*inf*) sidekick.

**accomplish** vb (*accomplish a task*) finish, complete, do, perform, execute.

**accomplished** adj (*an accomplished pianist*) skilled, skillful, expert, gifted, talented, masterly.

**accomplishment** n (*person of many accomplishments*) talent, gift, ability, skill, attainment, achievement.

**account** n 1 (*give a full account of the accident*) statement, report, description, record, story, tale. 2 (*send in the account for the work done*) check, bill, invoice, charges.

**accumulate** vb 1 (*garbage accumulating in the streets*) gather, collect, pile up, build up. 2 (*accumulate many books over the years*) gather, collect, amass, stockpile, hoard.

**accredited** adj (*an accredited representative of the company*) official, authorized, legal, approved, certified.

**accurate** adj 1 (*accurate measurements*) correct, precise, exact, right, errorless. 2 (*an accurate description*) correct, exact, close, true, faithful, strict.

**accusation** n (*deny the accusations*) charge, allegation, imputation, incrimination.

**accuse** vb 1 (*accuse her of murder*) charge, indict, arraign. 2 (*accuse the boys of breaking windows*) blame, put the blame on, lay the blame on, hold responsible for, hold accountable for.

**accustom** vb (*accustom herself to her new surroundings*) adapt, adjust, acclimatize, get used to.

**accustomed** adj 1 (*our accustomed route home*) usual, normal, customary, regular, habitual, routine. 2 (*accustomed to public speaking*) used to, in the habit of, familiar with, acquainted with.

**ache** vb (*My head aches*) hurt, be sore, be painful, throb.

**ache** n (*an ache in his back*) pain, soreness, throbbing, twinge, pang.

**achieve** vb (*achieve one's aim*) accomplish, reach, attain, gain, obtain, acquire.

**achievement** n (*proud of his achievements on the sports field*) accomplishment, attainment, deed, act, effort, feat.

**acid** adj 1 (*an acid taste*) sour, tart, sharp, bitter, vinegary. 2 (*acid remarks*) sharp, sarcastic, caustic, trenchant, acerbic.

**acknowledge** vb 1 (*acknowledge a letter*) answer, reply to, respond to. 2 (*acknowledge defeat*) admit, accept, recognize, grant, concede.

**acquire** vb (*acquire enough money*) obtain, get, come by, gain, procure.

**acquit** vb (*the judge will acquit the accused*) clear, set free, release, discharge, pardon, absolve, exonerate.

**act** vb 1 (*act like a fool*) behave, do, operate. 2 (*act quickly to put out the fire*) take action, move, be active, perform. 3 (*act the part of Peter Pan*) play, perform, enact. 4 (*act in a new play*) be an actor, play a part, perform.

**act** n 1 (*a brave act*) action, deed, undertaking, feat, exploit. 2 (*enjoy the magician's act*) performance, show, turn, routine. **3** (*an act to forbid smoking*) law, ruling, rule, regulation, order, bill, decree, statute.

**acting** *adj* (*the acting principal*) temporary, interim, substitute.

**action** *n* **1** (*His action saved their lives*) act, deed, move, behavior,-undertaking, feat, exploit. **2** (*a movie full of action*) activity, movement, liveliness, energy, vitality.

**active** *adj* **1** (*active children tiring their mothers/ lead active lives*) energetic, full of energy, lively, busy, nimble, (*inf*) on the go. **2** (*sports clubs which are still active*) in action, working, operating, in operation, functioning.

**activity** *n* **1** (*city streets full of activity*) movement, bustle, hustle and bustle, liveliness. **2** (*activities enjoyed after school*) pastime, interest, hobby, pursuit, project.

**actual** *adj* **1** (*The actual cost was far less than the newspapers reported*) real, true, genuine, authentic. **2** (*no actual evidence of burglary*) existing, definite, certain, positive, concrete.

**actually** *adv* (*The boy seems unhealthy but he is actually quite well*) really, in fact, in reality, in truth, truly.

**adapt** *vb* **1** (*adapt the scheme to suit younger children*) adjust, alter, change, convert, modify, vary, reshape, remodel. **2** (*find it difficult to adapt to a new way of life*) adjust, fit in, accustom oneself, become accustomed to, acclimatize.

**add** *vb* **1** (*add some more details to the report*) put in, include, append. **2** (*add the rows of figures*) add up, count, count up, (*inf*) tot up, total. **3** (*Money problems added to his worry*) increase, augment, amplify, intensify, aggravate.

**addicted** *adj* (*be addicted to alcohol*) dependent on, (*inf*) hooked on.

**addiction** *n* (*try to cure his drug addiction*) dependence, dependency, craving, habit.

**additional** *adj* (*require additional supplies*) more, extra, further, supplementary.

**additive** *n* (*additives listed on food labels*) supplement, preservative.

**address** *n* **1** (*find out his address*) where one lives, home, house, residence. **2** (*the address of the company's head office*) location, place, whereabouts. **3** (*unable to read the address on the parcel*) label, directions, inscription. **4** (*the President's address to Congress*) speech, talk, lecture.

**address** *vb* **1** (*address a parcel*) write the address on, label, write the directions on, direct, inscribe. **2** (*How do you address a bishop?*) name, call, speak to, write to, describe. **3** (*address one's remarks to the manager*) direct, communicate, convey, send.

**adequate** *adj* **1** (*adequate supplies for the week*) enough, sufficient, ample. **2** (*work-*

ers who are not adequate) fit, able, competent, qualified, (*inf*) up to scratch.

**adhesive** *n* (*an adhesive to stick the tiles to the wall*) glue, cement, gum, fixative.

**adjacent** *adj* (*living in the adjacent house*) adjoining, next, next door, neighboring, bordering.

**adjourn** *vb* (*adjourn the meeting till the next day*) break off, discontinue, defer, postpone, put off, shelve.

**adjudicate** *vb* (*adjudicate at the singing contest*) judge, arbitrate, referee, umpire.

**adjust** *vb* **1** (*unable to adjust to the new situation*) adapt, become accustomed to, accustom oneself to, get used to, acclimatize. **2** (*adjust the saddle of the bike*) alter, change, modify, rearrange.

**administration** *n* (*in hospital administration*) management, direction, government.

**administrator** *n* (*business administrators*) manager, director, executive, controller.

**admire** *vb* **1** (*admire her hat/admire the view*) express admiration of, approve of, like, compliment, praise. **2** (*admire their courage*) approve of, respect, think highly of, appreciate, applaud, praise, esteem.

**admit** *vb* **1** (*admit his guilt/admit that she could be wrong*) acknowledge, confess, own up, reveal, make known, declare, disclose, divulge. **2** (*a ticket that admits only one person*) let in, allow in, allow entry, permit entry.

**admittance** *n* (*no admittance to the private building*) entry, right of entry, entrance, access.

**adolescence** *n* (*a young person just reaching adolescence*) teenage years, (*inf*) teens, growing up.

**adopt** *vb* **1** (*adopt a child*) take as one's own, take in, take care of, be adoptive parents to. **2** (*adopt a political candidate*) select, choose, pick, vote for. **3** (*adopt modern customs/adopt a foreign style of dress*) assume, take on, take over, affect, embrace, espouse.

**adorable** *adj* (*an adorable little baby*)-lovable, sweet, dear, darling, delightful, appealing, charming, enchanting, winsome.

**adore** *vb* **1** (*They adore their children*) love dearly, be devoted to, dote on, cherish, idolize. **2** (*adore ice cream*) like very much, love, be fond of, enjoy, relish. **3** (*adore God*) worship, praise, glorify, revere, venerate.

**adorn** *vb* (*flowers adorning the room/ adorn the Christmas tree with lights*) decorate, embellish, ornament, beautify.

**adroit** *adj* (*her adroit handling of the situation*) skillful, skilled, deft, expert, clever, able, adept.

**adult** *adj* **1** (*adult people*) grown-up, (*fml*) of age. **2** (*adult trees*) mature, fully grown, developed.

**advance** *vb* (*The armies advance*) move forward, go forward, proceed, press on, forge ahead, make progress.

**advance** *adj* **1** (*the advance party*) leading, first, in front. **2** (*advance warning*) early, previous, prior, beforehand.

**advanced** *adj* **1** (*advanced technology*) progressive, modern, up-to-date, ultramodern, sophisticated, avant-garde. **2** (*advanced studies/ schoolwork that is more advanced*) higher-level, complicated, difficult.

**advantage** *n* **1** (*one of the advantages of being tall*) benefit, asset, good point, blessing, boon. **2** (*have an advantage over his rivals*)-superiority, ascendancy, supremacy, upper hand. **3** (*There is little advantage in going into business with her*) benefit, profit, gain, good.

**advantageous** *adj* **1** (*an advantageous position*) favorable, helpful, beneficial, useful. **2** (*advantageous to his hopes of promotion*) of benefit, beneficial, of assistance, useful, valuable.

**adventure** *n* **1** (*tell her grandchildren of her adventures at sea*) exploit, escapade, deed, feat, experience. **2** (*a journey full of adventure*) risk, precariousness, danger, hazard, peril, uncertainty.

**adventurous** *adj* (*an adventurous life*) risky, precarious, dangerous, hazardous, perilous.

**adversary** *n* (*their adversaries in the battle/her adversary in the tournament*) opponent, enemy, foe, antagonist, rival.

**adversity** *n* **1** (*a homeless person leading a life of adversity*) misfortune, ill-luck, bad luck, trouble, hardship, distress, misery. **2** (*many adversities in his life*) misfortune, mishap, setback, trial, disaster, catastrophe, calamity.

**advertise** *vb* (*advertise a new product*) promote, give publicity to, publicize, (*inf*) push, (*inf*) plug.

**advice** *n* (*give careers advice/get advice on a personal problem*) guidance, counseling, counsel, help, suggestions, hints, tips.

**advisable** *adj* (*Such action is not advisable*) desirable, wise, sensible, prudent, suitable, appropriate, recommended.

**advise** *vb* **1** (*advise them on future careers*) give advice to, give guidance on, guide, counsel, give recommendations, offer suggestions, give hints. **2** (*advise carefulness*) recommend, suggest, urge, commend, advocate.

**advocate** *vb* (*advocate spending less money*) advise, recommend, suggest, urge, press for, favor, support.

**affable** *adj* (*an affable neighbor/in an affable mood*) friendly, amiable, genial, cordial, pleasant, agreeable, good-natured, sociable, courteous.

**affair** n **1** (*It's my affair*) concern, business, matter, responsibility. **2** (*The loss of their home was an unfortunate affair*) event, happening, occurrence, incident, episode, state of affairs.

**affect** vb **1** (*a tragedy which affected all of us*) have an effect on, influence, have an influence on, act on, work on, change, alter. **2** (*a disease affecting his stomach*) attack, infect. **3** (*We were deeply affected by the orphan's sad story*) move, touch, upset, disturb, trouble, stir.

**affected** adj (*an affected way of speaking*) pretentious, artificial, false, pretended, unnatural, assumed.

**affection** n (*feel affection for his children*) love, fondness, caring, devotion, liking, warmth.

**affectionate** adj (*an affectionate farewell*) loving, fond, devoted, tender, warm.

**afflict** vb (*people afflicted by a terrible disease*) trouble, distress, torment, plague.

**affliction** n (*the afflictions associated-with old age*) trouble, disorder, disease, ailment, pain, suffering, hardship.

**affluent** adj (*affluent people living in-expensive houses*) wealthy, rich, well-off, prosperous, well-to-do, (*inf*) well-heeled.

**afford** vb (*unable to afford a new car*) buy, purchase, pay for, pay the price of, meet the expense of.

**affront** n (*sexist remarks that are an affront to women*) insult, offense, slight, snub, indignity.

**afraid** adj **1** (*afraid of the wild animal/afraid to enter the haunted house*) frightened, scared, nervous, terrified, apprehensive, fearful. **2** (*I'm afraid that I cannot help you*) sorry, regretful, apologetic, unhappy.

**age** n **1** (*the wisdom that comes with age*) old age, maturity, seniority, advancing years. **2** (*in the Elizabethan age*) era, period, epoch, time.

**agency** n (*an advertising agency*) organization, business, firm, company, office, bureau.

**agenda** n (*on the agenda for tonight's meeting*) program, schedule, timetable, list.

**agent** n **1** (*an insurance agent/a travel agent*) representative, negotiator, operator, (*inf*) rep. **2** (*an enemy agent*) spy, (*inf*) mole, (*inf*) spook.

**aggravate** vb **1** (*aggravate the situation/aggravate the illness*) make worse, worsen, exacerbate, intensify, increase. **2** (*inf*) (*children aggravating their mother with their noise*) annoy, irritate, anger, exasperate, provoke, get on someone's nerves.

**aggravate** should be used in the meaning of 'annoy' only in informal situations, such as in speech or personal letters between friends. Many people regard this as a wrong use of the word and it should be avoided in formal writing, such as essays.

**aggressive** adj **1** (*people getting aggressive when they get drunk*) quarrelsome, argumentative, belligerent, pugnacious. **2** (*aggressive salesmen/aggressive young workers seeking rapid promotion*) assertive, forceful, dynamic, thrusting, (*inf*) pushy.

**aghast** adj (*aghast at the decision to close the factory*) horrified, appalled, astounded, shocked, flabbergasted.

**agile** adj (*old people still agile/agile young gymnasts*) active, nimble, lithe, supple, sprightly.

**agitate** vb **1** (*The news agitated her*) upset, work up, fluster, perturb, ruffle, disconcert, flurry, excite. **2** (*demonstrators agitating for greater-welfare provision*) campaign, argue.

**agonizing** adj (*an agonizing pain*) excruciating, painful, unbearable, insufferable, piercing.

**agony** n (*accident victims in agony*) suffering, pain, torture, torment, distress, anguish.

**agree** vb **1** (*agree with your suggestions*) concur, comply, accord. **2** (*agree to your demands*) consent to, accept, assent to, acquiesce in. **3** (*accounts of the accident that do not agree with each other*) match, accord, correspond, coincide, tally, (*inf*) square.

**agreeable** adj **1** (*We are agreeable to your coming with us*) willing, amenable, compliant, consenting, assenting, accommodating. **2** (*an agreeable occasion*) pleasant, delightful, enjoyable, pleasurable. **3** (*an agreeable young man*) pleasant, likable, amiable, friendly, nice, affable.

**agreement** n **1** (*all in complete agreement*) accord, assent, concurrence, harmony, unity. **2** (*sign an agreement to purchase*) contract, compact, covenant, pact, pledge, deal.

**aid** vb **1** (*aid the rescue workers*) assist, help, support, lend a hand. **2** (*medicine to aid his recovery*) assist, help, speed up, hasten, expedite, facilitate.

**aid** n **1** (*stop to give aid to a driver whose car had broken down*) assistance, help, support, a helping hand. **2** (*give aid to developing countries*) assistance, help, contributions, subsidy, gift, donation.

**aide** n (*a nurse's aide*) helper, assistant.

**ailment** n illness, complaint, disease, disorder.

**aim** vb **1** (*aim a gun at*) point, direct, train, level. **2** (*aim to get there before dark*) plan, intend, propose, try.

**aim** n (*their aims in life/Their aim is to make a lot of money*) goal, ambition, objective, object, target, purpose, intention, plan, aspiration, design, desire.

**aimless** adj **1** (*lead an aimless life*) pointless, purposeless, futile, undirected. **2** (*aimless young people roaming the streets*) unambitious, drifting, wandering.

**air** n **1** (*fly through the air*) atmosphere, sky. **2** (*an air of loneliness about her*) impression, appearance, atmosphere, mood, quality, look, feeling. **3** (*playing a sad air on the piano*) tune, melody, song, theme.

**air** vb **1** (*air clothes/air a room*) ventilate, freshen. **2** (*air one's views*) make known, make public, publicize, voice, express, vent, communicate, reveal.

**aisle** n (*the aisles in planes/trains*) gangway, passageway, passage, corridor.

**alarm** vb (*alarmed by a loud bang in the night*) frighten, scare, startle, terrify, unnerve, disturb, upset.

**alarm** n **1** (*a burglar alarm/a fire alarm*) alarm signal, alarm bell, danger signal, siren, warning. **2** (*a burglar causing alarm in the neighborhood*) fear, fright, apprehension, terror, panic, disturbance, anxiety, upset, disquiet.

**alert** adj (*stay alert when on sentry duty*) awake, wide awake, aware, attentive, watchful, wary, observant, vigilant.

**alien** adj **1** (*alien lands*) foreign, overseas. **2** (*find themselves in an alien environment*) strange, unfamiliar, unknown.

**alien** n **1** (*aliens deported from the country at the start of the war*) foreigner, non-native. **2** (*aliens from another planet*) extraterrestrial, (*inf*) little green man.

**alight** vb **1** (*alight from the bus*) get off, dismount, descend. **2** (*butterflies alighting on leaves*) land, come down, come to rest, settle, touch down.

**alike** adj (*sisters who are very much alike*) like, similar, the same, identical, indistinguishable.

**alive** adj **1** (*soldiers wounded but still alive*) living, live, breathing, (*inf*) in the land of the living. **2** (*streets alive with shoppers*) crowded, packed, teeming, swarming, overflowing, thronged, (*inf*) crawling.

**allegation** n (*deny their allegations that he was a thief*) claim, charge, accusation, declaration, assertion, statement.

**allergic** adj (*allergic to cows' milk*) hypersensitive, sensitive.

**alley** n (*attacked in a dark alley leading off the main street*) alleyway, lane, passage, passageway.

**alliance** n (*foreign countries forming an alliance against the enemy*) union, association, league, coalition, federation, partnership, affiliation.

**allot** vb (*allot work to each of the students/allot grants of money to those in need*) allocate, distribute, give out, share out, dispense, apportion.

**allow** vb **1** (*allow them to use her swimming pool*) let, permit, give permission to, authorize, (*inf*) give the go-ahead to. **2** (*allow half a roll of wastepaper for wastage*) plan for, make provision for, provide for, take into account, take into consideration.

**allowance** *n* (*a dress allowance*) money, payment, remittance, contribution, grant, subsidy.

**allude** *vb* (*He alluded to the history of the town in his speech*) refer to, mention, mention in passing, touch upon, make an allusion to.

**alluring** *adj* (*a woman of alluring beauty*) attractive, fascinating, charming, enchanting, captivating, bewitching, beguiling, tempting.

**ally** *n* (*their allies in the war*) confederate, associate, collaborator, partner, friend.

**almost** *adv* (*almost four o'clock/ almost two miles long*) nearly, close to, just about, around, not quite, practically, approximately.

**alone** *adj* **1** (*go to the party alone*)-by-oneself, unaccompanied, unescorted, companionless. **2** (*left all alone by her father's death*) solitary, lonely, isolated, desolate, deserted, forlorn. **3** (*He alone can answer those questions*) only, solely, just.

**aloof** *adj* (*people who are aloof do not have many friends*) distant, remote, unresponsive, unapproachable, standoffish, unsociable, unfriendly, cold.

**aloud** *adv* (*cry aloud*) out loud, audibly, clearly, distinctly.

**also** *adv* **1** (*buy a bed and a table also*) too, as well, besides, in addition, into the bargain. **2** (*He's poor; also he's ill*) furthermore, besides, moreover, in addition.

**alter** *vb* **1** (*alter the dress*) change, adjust, modify, convert, reshape, remodel, vary, transform. **2** (*The town has scarcely altered*) change, become different, vary.

**alteration** *n* **1** (*make alterations to the dress/ make alterations to the letter*) change, adjustment, modification, amendment, revision, variation. **2** (*the alteration of his appearance after his illness*) change, difference,-variation, transformation, metamorphosis.

**alternative** *n* (*offer an alternative on the menu for vegetarians*) choice, option, possibility, preference.

**altitude** *n* (*the altitude of the ski resort*) height, elevation.

**altogether** *adv* **1** (*six of us altogether*) in all, all told, in total. **2** (*not altogether sure*) completely, quite, entirely, totally, thoroughly, absolutely, fully, perfectly.

**always** *adv* **1** (*We always shop there*) regularly, invariably, consistently, unfailingly, repeatedly, without exception. **2** (*She's always cheerful*)-continually, continuously, constantly, incessantly, perpetually. **3** (*pro-*

*mise to love her always*) forever, forever and ever, evermore, eternally, endlessly, everlastingly.

**amaze** *vb* (*His sheer stupidity amazed us*) astonish, astound, surprise, dumbfound, flabbergast, daze, shock, stun, (*inf*) stagger, nonplus.

**amazing** *adj* (*have an amazing memory*) exceptional, extraordinary, remarkable, phenomenal.

**ambiguous** *adj* (*Her message was ambiguous*) unclear, uncertain, doubtful, dubious, vague, obscure, puzzling, perplexing, enigmatic, abstruse.

**ambition** *n* **1** (*young members of the firm full of ambition*) aspiration, drive, striving, force, enterprise, enthusiasm. **2** (*Her ambition is to go on the stage*) aim, goal, objective, purpose, intent, dream, hope.

**ambitious** *adj* (*ambitious people seeking promotion*) aspiring, forceful, purposeful, enterprising, go-ahead, assertive.

**ambush** *n* **1** (*terrorists waiting in ambush for the soldiers*) hiding, concealment, cover. **2** (*lay an ambush for the enemy soldiers*) trap, snare, pitfall.

**amiable** *adj* (*in the company of amiable people*) friendly, pleasant, agreeable, charming, good-natured, sociable, genial.

**amnesty** *n* (*declare an amnesty for all political prisoners*) general pardon, pardon, reprieve, forgiveness, absolution.

**among** *prep* **1** (*a house among the trees/live among enemies*) in the midst of, amid, amidst, surrounded by, in the thick of. **2** (*divide it among you*) between, to each of.

**amount** *n* (*a small amount of wood/a large amount of attention*) quantity, mass, measure, volume, extent.

**amount** *vb* (*The bill amounted to hundreds of pounds*) add up to, total, come to, run to.

**ample** *adj* **1** (*ample food for everyone*) enough, sufficient, plenty, adequate, more than enough. **2** (*an ample supply of money*) plentiful, abundant, copious, liberal, generous, lavish. **3** (*her ample bosom*) large, big, substantial.

**amplify** *vb* **1** (*amplify the sound level*) make louder, increase, boost, augment. **2** (*amplify your suggestion*) expand, enlarge on, elaborate on, develop.

**amputate** *vb* (*The surgeon had to amputate his leg after the accident*) cut off, remove, sever, excise.

**amuse** *vb* **1** (*try to amuse the children on a cold, rainy day*) entertain, occupy, interest, divert. **2** (*The comedian's jokes amused everyone*) make laugh, entertain, cheer up, delight.

**amusement** *n* **1** (*various forms of amusement in the beach resort*) entertainment, diversion,

fun, interest, pastime, hobby, recreation. **2**-(*smile with amusement at the comedian's jokes*) laughter, mirth, hilarity, pleasure, enjoyment.

**amusing** *adj* (*an amusing story*) funny, humorous, comical, entertaining, hilarious.

**analyze** *vb* (*analyze the election results*) examine, study, investigate, inquire into, dissect.

**anarchy** *n* **1** (*The fall of the government was followed by a period of-anarchy*) absence of government, lawlessness, revolution. **2**-(*anarchy on the streets when the police went on strike*) lawless- ness, disorder, chaos, confusion, mayhem.

**ancestor** *n* (*trace his ancestors back to the time of the Pilgrim Fathers*) forebear, forefather, progenitor, forerunner, predecessor.

**ancestry** *n* (*She is of Scottish ancestry*)-descent, extraction, origin, derivation, parentage, blood, family tree.

**ancient** *adj* **1** (*ancient customs*) very-old, age-old, time-worn. **2** (*in ancient times*) earliest, early, primeval, prehistoric. **3** (*His ideas on fashion are ancient*) antiquated, old-fashioned, out-of-date, outdated, outmoded, obsolete.

**and** *conj* (*my family and I*) along with, with, together with, as well, in addition to, plus.

**angel** *n* **1** (*angels in heaven*) seraph, cherub, archangel, guardian angel. **2** (*My kind neighbor is an angel*) saint, dear, darling.

**anger** *n* (*feelings of anger at cruelty to animals*) annoyance, rage, fury, indignation, wrath, irritation, ire.

**anger** *vb* (*They were angered by his rudeness*) annoy, infuriate, enrage, irritate, incense, madden, provoke, rile.

**angry** *adj* (*angry mothers scolding their children*) annoyed, cross, furious, infuriated, indignant, irate, livid, enraged, wrathful, incensed, (*inf*) mad.

**anguish** *n* (*The children were in anguish when their pet died*) agony, suffering, pain, torment, torture, distress, misery.

**animated** *adj* (*an animated discussion*) lively, spirited, excited, enthusiastic, passionate, fiery, dynamic, energetic.

**annex** *n* (*add an annex to the house*) extension, wing.

**annihilate** *vb* (*annihilate the enemy army*) destroy, wipe out, exterminate, eliminate, obliterate, eradicate.

**announce** *vb* (*announce that the president was dead*) make known, make public, proclaim, publish, broadcast, report, state, declare, reveal, disclose.

**announcement** *n* (*an announcement of the president's death*) report, statement, notice, proclamation, declaration, bulletin, communiqué, intimation.

**announcer** n (a CNN announcer) commentator, presenter, newscaster, broadcaster, reporter.

**annoy** vb 1 (Her attitude annoyed her parents) anger, infuriate, enrage, irritate, incense, madden, provoke, rile. 2 (Don't annoy your mother while she is working/children annoying the dog) bother, disturb, pester, worry, torment, tease.

**annul** vb (annul the marriage/annul the agreement) declare null and void, nullify, invalidate, cancel, rescind, revoke.

**anomaly** n (anomalies in the tax system) abnormality, irregularity, deviation, aberration, oddity, peculiarity, inconsistency.

**anonymous** adj (The money for the-charity was from an anonymous donor) unnamed, nameless, unknown, unidentified, incognito.

**another** adj 1 (another cup of tea) additional, second, further. 2 (go another time/get another car) different, some other.

**answer** vb 1 (answer the question) reply to, give a response to, respond to, retort. 2 (answer our requirements) meet, satisfy, fulfill, fill, serve. 3 (a man answering the description issued by the police) fit, match, correspond to, be like.

**answer** n 1 (receive no answer to his question/waiting for an answer to his letter) reply, response, acknowledgement, retort, rejoinder. 2 (the answer to the puzzle) solution, explanation.

**antagonism** n (a great deal of antagonism between the two sides) hostility, opposition, animosity, antipathy, enmity, dissension, conflict, friction.

**anthology** n (an anthology of poetry) collection, selection, miscellany, compendium.

**anticipate** vb 1 (The organizers are anticipating a large audience for the concert) expect, foresee, predict, forecast, look for, await. 2 (anticipate his opponent's move) forestall, intercept, prevent, (inf) beat someone to it.

**anticipation** n 1 (buy champagne in anticipation of victory) expectation, prediction. 2 (full of anticipation before the party) expectancy, hopefulness, hope.

**anticlimax** n (After all the fun of planning the actual vacation was rather an anticlimax) disappointment, letdown, disillusionment.

**antiquated** adj (children thinking that their parents have antiquated ideas/an antiquated television set) out-of-date, old-fashioned, outmoded, outworn, obsolete, archaic, passé.

**antique** adj (antique furniture) old, antiquarian, vintage, early.

**antisocial** adj 1 (antisocial people who dislike parties) unsociable, reserved, aloof, withdrawn, retiring, uncommunicative, unfriendly. 2 (playing loud music late at night is an example of antisocial behavior) disruptive, disorderly, lawless, unruly, obstreperous.

**antithesis** n (The antithesis of good is bad) opposite, reverse, converse, inverse, other extreme.

**anxiety** n (full of anxiety about the lateness of her husband) worry, concern, uneasiness, disquiet, nervousness, apprehension, tenseness.

**anxious** adj 1 (anxious parents out looking for their children) worried,-concerned, uneasy, nervous, apprehensive, fearful, tense. 2 (anxious to learn) eager, keen, longing, avid.

**apart** adv 1 (blow the place apart) to pieces, in pieces, to bits, asunder. 2 (a couple living apart) separated, separately, divorced. 3 (a man standing apart at the party) to one side, aside, separately, by oneself.

**apathy** n (Because of apathy many people did not vote) lack of interest, indifference, unresponsiveness, unconcern, lethargy.

**apex** n 1 (the apex of the triangle) top, tip, pinnacle, vertex, peak. 2 (the apex of his career) peak, summit, top, zenith, acme, apogee.

**apologetic** adj (feel apologetic for the trouble which they caused) sorry, regretful, contrite, remorseful, repentant, penitent, rueful.

**apologize** vb (apologize for his error) say one is sorry, express regret, ask forgiveness, (inf) eat humble pie.

**apology** n (accept his apology for his wrongdoing) regret, regrets.

**appalling** adj 1 (an appalling accident) shocking, frightful, horrifying, terrible, dreadful, awful, ghastly. 2 (a piece of work that is quite appalling/appalling behavior) very bad, unacceptable, unsatisfactory, intolerable.

**apparent** adj 1 (It was apparent that she was unwell/problems that were apparent from the start) obvious, clear, plain, evident, discernible, perceptible, manifest. 2 (He eventually saw through her apparent sincerity) seeming, ostensible, outward, superficial.

**apparition** n (They thought they saw an apparition in the graveyard) ghost, specter, phantom, spirit, wraith, (inf) spook.

**appeal** n 1 (make an appeal for help) request, call, plea, entreaty, supplication. 2 (a possibility that holds little appeal for her) attraction, attractiveness, charm, allure, interest. 3 (He has been convicted of the crime but the case is going to appeal) review, reconsideration, re-examination.

**appear** vb 1 (A figure appeared out of the mist) come into view, come into sight, emerge, materialize, surface. 2 (The visitors were very late but they finally appeared) come, arrive, make an appearance, turn up, (inf) show up. 3 (She appeared rather thoughtful) seem, look, have the appearance of, have the air of, give the impression of. 4 (He once appeared in a production of 'Hamlet') act, perform, play, take part.

**appearance** n 1 (the sudden appearance of the police) arrival, advent, materialization, surfacing. 2 (having an appearance of sadness) look, air, expression, impression, manner. 3 (His statement had the appearance of truth but it was a lie) semblance, outward appearance, guise, show, pretense.

**appease** vb (try to appease his angry wife by giving her flowers) calm down, placate, make peace with, pacify, soothe, conciliate, mollify, propitiate.

**appetizer** n (serve smoked salmon as an appetizer) starter, hors d'oeuvre, antipasto.

**appetizing** adj 1 (an appetizing dish) tasty, mouth-watering, flavorsome, delicious. 2 (appetizing smells coming from the kitchen) tempting, inviting, enticing, alluring.

**applaud** vb 1 (The audience applauded) clap, give a standing ovation to, (inf) to give a big hand to. 2 (Everyone applauded his courage) praise, admire, compliment on, commend, acclaim, extol, laud.

**appliance** n (electrical appliances in the kitchen) gadget, tool, implement, apparatus, device, machine.

**applicant** n (applicants for the job) candidate, entrant, competitor, interviewee.

**apply** vb 1 (apply for a job) put in an application for, ask, put in for, try for. 2 (apply ointment to the sore) put on, rub in, cover with, spread, smear. 3 (have to apply force to open the box) use, employ, administer, utilize, exercise, bring to bear. 4 (These regulations do not apply) be applicable, be relevant, be pertinent, be apposite, be appropriate.

**appoint** vb (appoint a new manager) name, select, choose, pick, elect, designate, nominate.

**appointment** n 1 (have a business appointment this afternoon/a dinner-appointment) meeting, engagement,-date, rendezvous, assignation. 2 (take up his new appointment as manager) job, post, position, situation, place.

**appreciate** vb 1 (appreciate offers of help) be grateful for, be thankful for, be appreciative of, give thanks for. 2 (appreciate the urgency of the situation) recognize, acknowledge, realize, know, be aware of, be conscious of, understand. 3 (appreciate good wine) value, prize, treasure, respect, hold in high regard, think highly of, enjoy, take pleasure in. 4 (a *house that has appreciated in value over the years*) increase, gain, grow, rise.

**apprehensive** *adj* (*apprehensive at the thought of being hospitalized*) frightened, fearful, scared, nervous, anxious, worried, uneasy, concerned.

**apprentice** *n* (*find work as an apprentice*) trainee, learner, beginner, probationer, novice.

**approach** *vb* 1 (*visitors approaching the house*) come/go near, draw near, move towards, advance towards. 2 (*panhandlers approaching strangers to ask for money*) go up to, speak to, talk to, engage in conversation, address, hail. 3 (*approach the task with energy*) set about, tackle, begin, start, commence, embark on, make a start on. 4 (*temperatures approaching freezing point*) come close to, come near to, approximate.

**approach** *n* 1 (*the approach to the house*) driveway, drive, access, entrance, entry, way in. 2 (*a new approach to education*) method, system, technique, procedure, style, mode, way. 3 (*make approaches to the government for money*) application, appeal, advances, overtures.

**appropriate** *adj* (*an appropriate time/an appropriate reply*) suitable, fitting, proper, right, apt, apposite, opportune.

**approval** *n* 1 (*The audience showed its approval by applauding*) favor, liking, admiration, appreciation, approbation, regard. 2 (*The committee gave its approval to their plans*) acceptance, agreement, consent, assent, sanction, authorization, (*inf*) the go-ahead, the green light, (*inf*) the OK.

**approve** *vb* 1 (*unable to approve of their actions*) think well of, think highly of, think favorably of, look upon with favor, like, admire, hold in high regard. 2 (*The committee approved her plans*) accept, pass, agree to, consent to, assent to, sanction, authorize, (*inf*) give the go-ahead to, give the green light to.

**approximately** *adv* (*a distance of approximately five miles*) about, just about, around, roughly, nearly, close to, almost, more or less, in the neighborhood of, in the region of, circa.

**apron** *n* pinafore.

**apt** *adj* 1 (*apt to lose his temper*) inclined, given, likely, liable, ready, disposed, prone. 2 (*an apt comment*) appropriate, suitable, fitting, applicable, relevant, apposite. 3 (*an apt pupil*) clever, bright, intelligent, quick, able, smart.

**aptitude** *n* (*have an aptitude for word games*) talent, gift, flair, skill, ability, capability, bent, knack.

**arbitrary** *adj* 1 (*a purely arbitrary decision/The choice of players seemed arbitrary*) personal, subjective, discretionary, unreasoned, unsupported, random, chance, whimsical, capricious, erratic. 2 (*an arbitrary ruler*) despotic, tyrannical, absolute, autocratic, dictatorial, domineering.

**arbitrate** *vb* (*asked to arbitrate in the dispute between union and management*) adjudicate, judge, adjudge, umpire, referee.

**arc** *n* (*the arc of a rainbow*) curve, bow, arch, bend, crescent, semi-circle.

**arch** *vb* (*a cat arching its back*) curve, bend, bow, arc.

**archaic** *adj* (*archaic language/archaic attitudes*) old, out-of-date, oldfashioned, outmoded, antiquated, passé, obsolete, (*inf*) old-hat.

**architect** *n* 1 (*the architect of the new church*) designer, planner, building consultant. 2 (*the architect of the new scheme*) author, originator, planner, creator, founder, instigator, prime mover.

**archives** *npl* (*study the archives of the firm*) records, annals, chronicles, register, documents.

**arctic** *adj* (*arctic temperatures*) freezing, frozen, frigid, icy, glacial, frosty, chilly, cold.

**ardent** *adj* (*an ardent supporter of the local football team*) passionate, avid, fervent, zealous, eager, enthusiastic, keen.

**arduous** *adj* (*an arduous task*) difficult, hard, taxing, laborious, strenuous, tough, onerous, burdensome, tiring, exhausting, grueling, Herculean.

**area** *n* 1 (*live in a pleasant area of the city*) district, part, region, quarter, neighborhood, locality, sector, zone, territory. 2 (*a specialist in the area of computing*) field, sphere, department, discipline, realm, sector. 3 (*measure the area of the room*) dimensions, extent, size, expanse. 4 (*the changing area of the swimming pool*) section, part, portion, space.

**arena** *n* (*the sports arena*) ground, field, stadium, ring.

**argue** *vb* 1 (*Brother and sister are always arguing*) quarrel, disagree, bicker, squabble, wrangle, fight, dispute, (*inf*) fall out. 2 (*He argued that his method was the best*) assert, declare, maintain, hold, claim, contend.

**argument** *n* 1 (*children having an argument over toys*) quarrel, disagreement, squabble, wrangle, fight, dispute. 2 (*the argument against the new scheme*) reasoning, line of reasoning, reasons, grounds, case, defense, evidence, proof.

**argumentative** *adj* (*argumentative people/an argumentative mood*) quarrelsome, belligerent, disputatious, contentious, combative, litigious.

**arid** *adj* 1 (*arid areas of the world*) dry, dried up, desert, waterless, parched, barren. 2 (*an arid discussion*) uninspiring, uninter-

esting, dull, dreary, dry, colorless, lifeless, boring, monotonous, tedious.

**arise** *vb* 1 (*deal with any problems that arise*) appear, make an appearance, come to light, crop up, turn up, emerge, occur. 2 (*matters arising from our discussion*) result, proceed, follow, stem, originate, emanate, ensue.

**aristocracy** *n* (*a member of the British aristocracy*) nobility, peerage, gentry, upper class, high society, (*inf*) upper crust.

**arm** *n* 1 (*have an arm amputated*) upper limb. 2 (*an arm of the terrorist organization*) branch, offshoot, section, department, division, sector.

**arm** *vb* (*arm oneself with a gun/arm oneself with a stick to protect oneself against attack*) provide, supply, equip, furnish.

**armaments** *npl* (*a military armaments store*) arms, weapons, firearms, munitions.

**armistice** *n* (*the armistice that ended the war*) truce, cease-fire, peace.

**armor** *n* (*knights wearing armor*) armor plate, chain-mail, coat of mail, mail, protective covering.

**arms** *npl* 1 (*soldiers laying down their arms*) weapons, firearms, guns, armaments. 2 (*the family arms*) coat of arms, emblem, crest, insignia, heraldic device.

**army** *n* 1 (*the invading army*) military force, troops, soldiers. 2 (*armies of tourists on the island in the summer*) horde, crowd, host, multitude, swarm, throng, mob.

**aroma** *n* (*the aroma of freshly baked bread*) smell, scent, fragrance, perfume, odor, bouquet.

**aromatic** *adj* (*aromatic spices*) fragrant, sweet-smelling, scented, perfumed, piquant, spicy, pungent.

**around** *adv* 1 (*turn around*) in the opposite direction, in reverse. 2 (*around nine o'clock/around five-miles away*) approximately, roughly, close to, near to, nearly, circa. 3 (*flowers planted around the tree*) about, on all sides of, on every side of, surrounding, circling, encircling. 4 (*newspapers scattered around the room*) about, here and there in, all over, everywhere in, in all parts of.

**arouse** *vb* 1 (*The noise aroused the neighbors*) rouse, awaken, waken, wake, wake up. 2 (*behavior arousing suspicion/actions arousing panic*) cause, induce, stir up, provoke, call forth, whip up.

**arrange** *vb* 1 (*arrange the books*) put in order, set out, order, sort, organize, group, classify, categorize. 2 (*arrange a meeting*) fix, fix-up, organize, settle on, plan, schedule.

**arrangement** *n* (*make an arrangement to meet tomorrow*) preparations, plans, provisions, agreement, deal, contract.

**arrest** *vb* 1 (*police arrested the thieves*) take

into custody, take prisoner, detain, seize, capture, catch, (inf) run in. 2 (try to arrest the spread of the disease) stop, halt, bring to a halt, end, check, nip in the bud.

**arresting** adj (her arresting appearance) striking, noticeable, conspicuous, impressive, remarkable, extraordinary, unusual.

**arrival** n 1 (the arrival of winter)-coming, advent, appearance, occurrence. 2 (several new arrivals in town) newcomer, immigrant.

**arrive** vb 1 (arrive at their destination) reach, come to, attain. 2 (when mother arrives) come, get here, appear, put in an appearance, turn up, come on the scene, (inf) show up.

**arrogant** adj (a very arrogant young woman/ have a very arrogant manner) haughty, proud, conceited, vain, self-important, egotistic, overbearing, condescending, disdainful, snobbish, supercilious, imperious, presumptuous, bumptious, boastful, (inf) cocky, (inf) stuck-up.

**art** n 1 (studying art at college) painting, drawing, visual arts. 2 (the art of conversation) skill, craft, aptitude, knack, technique, facility, talent, flair, gift.

**artful** adj (get his own way by artful means) cunning, crafty, wily, sly, deceitful, scheming, shrewd, ingenious, clever.

**article** n 1 (a range of articles going on sale) thing, object, item, commodity. 2 (an article in the newspaper on violence) item, piece, story, feature, report, account, write-up.

**artificial** adj (artificial flowers/an artificial beard) manmade, synthetic, imitation, simulated, ersatz, mock, sham, fake, bogus, counterfeit, (inf) phony.

**ashamed** adj (She was obviously ashamed of what she had done) sorry, shame-faced, abashed, repentant, penitent, remorseful, sheepish.

**ask** vb 1 (We asked where they were going) inquire. 2 (They asked a favor from her/ You should ask-for more money) request, demand, apply for, beg for, plead for. 3 (The-police asked him about his movements on the night of the-murder) question, interrogate, cross-examine, give the third degree to, pump, (inf) grill.

**assault** vb (They assaulted the old man to get his wallet) attack, set upon, strike, hit, (inf) mug.

**assemble** vb 1 (The children assembled in the school hall to hear the news) gather, come together, congregate, convene. 2-(He is assembling the evidence for the prosecution) get together, gather together, collect, accumulate, amass. 3 (furniture that you have to assemble yourself) put together, fit together, construct, build, erect.

**assist** vb (He assisted the doctor to care for the accident victims) help, aid, give assistance to, lend a hand to, support.

**associate** vb 1 (She associates home with security) connect, link, relate. 2 (The clubs are associated in some way) connect, link, join, attach, affiliate. 3 (He associates with crooks) mix, keep company with, socialize, fraternize.

**astonish** vb 1 (Their boldness astonished us) amaze, astound, dumbfound, stun, surprise.

**attach** vb 1 (They should attach luggage labels to their suitcases) fasten, tie, secure, stick, affix. 2 (We attach no importance to that) place, lay, put, apply, ascribe.

**attend** vb 1 (He is unable to attend the meeting) be at, be present at, put in an appearance at, be there/here. 2 (She promised to attend to the matter immediately) deal with, see to, cope with, handle. 3 (You should attend to what your teacher says) pay attention to, pay heed to, heed, listen to, take note of.

**attitude** n 1 (I don't like her attitude to people from other countries) view, point of view, opinion, outlook, thoughts, ideas. 2 (She stood in an attitude of thought) stance, pose, position.

**attorney** n (I have an appointment with my attorney) lawyer, legal adviser.

**attractive** adj 1 (She is a very attractive girl) good-looking, pretty, beautiful, handsome. 2 (That is an attractive idea) appealing, pleasing, tempting.

**authentic** adj (He is the authentic heir to the estate) real, genuine, rightful, lawful, legal, valid.

**authority** n 1 (He does not have the authority to stop us going) power, right, control, force, influence. 2 (We have the authority of the governor to be present) permission, sanction, authorization, (inf) say-so. 3 (He is an authority on local history) expert, specialist, pundit.

**available** adj 1 (have to make do with the material that is available) obtainable, handy, to hand, accessible, ready. 2 (There are still tickets available) free.

**average** adj 1 (She was of average height for her age) normal, typical, ordinary, common. 2 (Her work was just average) run-of-the-mill, mediocre, unexceptional.

**awful** adj 1 (She has an awful cold) dreadful, nasty, unpleasant, troublesome, bad. 2 (in the awful presence of God) awesome, awe-inspiring.

**awkward** adj 1 (They arrived at an awkward time) inconvenient, difficult, problematic. 2 (She is a very awkward child and keeps bump-ing into things) clumsy, ungainly, inelegant, gauche. 3 (It is an awkward piece of furniture) clumsy, unwieldy.

# B

**baby** n (babies in their cribs) infant, child, toddler.

**babyish** adj (older children acting in a babyish way) childish, immature, infantile, juvenile.

**back** n 1 (the back of the building) rear, far end. 2 (the back of the envelope) reverse, other side. 3 (break his back in the accident) spine, backbone.

**back** adv (without looking back) backwards, behind, to the rear.

**back** vb 1 (back the plan) support, give support to, help, assist, encourage, favor. 2 (look for someone to-back the theatrical production)-finance, subsidize, sponsor. 3 (back the horse) bet on, place a bet-on, gamble on. 4 (back the car out of the garage) reverse, drive backwards.

**backer** n (the backers of the theatrical production) sponsor, promoter, financier, benefactor, (inf) angel.

**background** n 1 (people from a wealthy background) upbringing, family circumstances, environment, experience. 2 (photographed against a white background) setting, backdrop, scene. 3 (in the background of the photograph) rear, distance.

**backlog** n (a backlog of work) accumulation, stockpile, arrears, (inf) mountain.

**backward** adj 1 (a backward look) to-the rear, rearward. 2 (a backward area of the world) underdeveloped, slow, retarded, unprogressive.

**bacteria** npl (bacteria from rotting food) germs, microorganisms, microbes, (inf) bugs.

**bad** adj 1 (bad people) wicked, evil, immoral, wrong, sinful, dishonest, dishonorable, criminal, (inf) crooked, naughty, mischievous. 2 (a bad accident) serious, severe, terrible, shocking, appalling. 3 (a bad performance) poor, unsatisfactory, inadequate, inferior, substandard, defective, shoddy, (inf) lousy. 4- (Smoking is a bad habit) harmful, damaging, dangerous, unhealthy. 5- (bad food/food gone bad) rotten, decayed, moldy, tainted, putrid, (inf) off. 6 (bad weather) unpleasant, nasty, dreadful, terrible, disagreeable. 7 (feel bad about hurting her) sorry, regretful, apologetic, guilty, sad. 8 (an invalid feeling bad today) ill, unwell, sick, poorly, under the weather, (inf) below par.

**badge** n (wear the club badge on their blazers) crest, emblem, symbol.

**badly** adv 1 (do the work badly) poorly, unsatisfactorily, inadequately,-shoddily.

**2** (*Things worked out-badly*) unsuccessfully, unfortunately, unfavorably, unluckily, unhappily. **3** (*want something badly*) greatly,-very much, enormously to-a-great degree. **4** (*behave badly*)-wrongly, naughtily, improperly,-wickedly, immorally, sinfully, criminally.

**baffle** *vb* (*police baffled by the crime/students baffled by the exam question*) puzzle, perplex, mystify, nonplus, stump, bamboozle, bewilder.

**baggage** *n* (*collect one's baggage at the airport*) luggage, bags, suitcases, things, belongings, paraphernalia.

**baggy** *adj* (*wear baggy clothes*) loose, slack, roomy, floppy, ballooning.

**bake** *vb* **1** (*bake cakes*) cook. **2** (*earth baked by the sun*) scorch, burn, parch, dry, harden.

**balance** *n* **1** (*weigh the substance on a balance*) scales, weighing machine. **2**-(*trip and lose one's balance*) steadiness, stability, equilibrium. **3** (*pay the balance of the account*) remainder, rest, residue, difference, surplus, excess.

**bald** *adj* **1** (*men going bald*) baldheaded, hairless, (*inf*) thin on top. **2** (*a bald statement*) direct, forthright, blunt, plain, unadorned.

**ball** *n* **1** (*a glass ball*) sphere, globe, orb. **2** (*be invited to a ball*) dance, formal dance, prom.

**ballot** *n* (*choose the new leader by ballot*) vote, poll, election.

**ban** *vb* (*ban smoking in the hall*) prohibit, forbid, debar, bar, veto, make illegal.

**ban** *n* (*impose a ban on smoking*) prohibition, veto, embargo, interdict.

**band** *n* **1** (*the jazz band playing at the wedding celebrations*) group, ensemble, orchestra. **2** (*a band of thieves*) group, troop, company, gang, pack, bunch, mob, team. **3**-(*a metal band/a rubber band*) binding, cord, tie, link, ring, hoop, ligature. **4** (*a band of blue on the white sweater*) strip, stripe, steak, line, bar. **5** (*a band round her hair*) ribbon, braid.

**bang** *n* **1** (*a loud bang when the bomb went off*) boom, crash, blast, explosion, report. **2** (*get a bang on the head*) blow, knock, bump, hit, smack.

**bang** *vb* **1** (*the door banged shut*) slam, crash. **2** (*bang the table with his fist*) strike, hit, beat, thump, rap, whack, (*inf*) bash.

**bang** *adv* (*bang in the middle of his speech*) right, exactly, precisely, absolutely, directly, (*inf*) smack.

**banish** *vb* **1** (*banish them from their native land*) exile, deport, cast out, send away, expel. **2** (*banish the child's fears*) drive away, dispel, dismiss, get rid of, cast out.

**bank** *n* **1** (*borrow money from the bank*) financial institution. **2** (*a child's bank*) piggy bank, savings bank, cash box. **3** (*a bank of information*) store, stock, reserve, reservoir, repository. **4** (*children sliding down grassy banks*) slope, rise, incline, hillock. **5** (*the river bank*) edge, side, shore.

**bankrupt** *adj* (*bankrupt after the failure of his business*) ruined, insolvent, penniless, impecunious, (*inf*) in the red, (*inf*) on the rocks, (*inf*) broke.

**banner** *n* (*banners flying for the inauguration*) flag, standard, pennant, streamer.

**banquet** *n* feast, dinner, dinner party, (*inf*) spread.

**baptize** *vb* (*baptize a baby*) christen, name.

**bar** *n* **1** (*an iron bar*) rod, pole, rail, girder. **2** (*a bar of soap*) block, cake, lump, wedge. **3** (*drinking in the bar/eating in the bar*) pub, snack bar, tavern.

**bar** *vb* **1** (*bar the door*) bolt, lock, padlock, fasten, secure. **2** (*bar them from joining the club*) debar, prohibit, forbid, preclude, ban. **3** (*fallen trees barring their way*) block, hinder, impede, obstruct.

**bare** *adj* **1** (*sunbathing bare*) nude, naked, stark naked, undressed, unclothed, without clothes, unclad. **2** (*a bare room*) empty, vacant, unfurnished, unadorned. **3** (*a bare landscape*) barren, bleak, desolate.

**barely** *adv* (*barely enough food*) hardly, scarcely, only just, just.

**bargain** *n* **1** (*make a bargain not to quarrel*) agreement, pact, contract, deal. **2** (*this coat is a real bargain*) good buy.

**barge** *vb* **1** (*people barging into each-other in crowded stores*) bump, collide, cannon, crash. **2**-(*barge into-a private meeting*) interrupt, intrude on, burst in on, (*inf*) butt in-on.

**barn** *n* outbuilding, shed.

**barrel** *n* (*a barrel of beer*) cask, keg,-vat.

**barren** *adj* **1** (*barren fields*) infertile, unproductive, arid, desert, waste. **2**-(*barren women*) infertile, sterile, childless. **3** (*barren discussions*) fruitless, worthless, useless, valueless, purposeless.

**barricade** *n* (*barricades keeping back the crowds*) barrier, blockade, obstacle, bar.

**barrier** *n* (*a barrier to keep the spectators off the football pitch*) barricade, bar, fence, railing, blockade.

**base** *n* **1** (*the base of the statue*) foundation, support, prop, foot. **2**-(*paints with an oil base*) basis, essence, source. **3** (*climbers setting up a base*) headquarters, depot, center, camp, starting-point.

**base** *vb* **1** (*base his statement on the facts available*) found, build, establish, ground. **2** (*base the novel on his childhood memories*) locate, situate, station.

**bashful** *adj* shy, reserved, diffident, retiring, modest, self-conscious.

**basic** *adj* (*the basic facts/the basic principles*) fundamental, elementary, rudimentary, primary, essential, chief.

**basin** *n* (*a pudding basin*) bowl, dish, container, receptacle.

**basis** *n* **1** (*the basis for his conclusions*) grounds, foundation, base. **2** (*issues that form the basis of the discussion*) starting-point, foundation, base.

**batch** *n* (*a batch of new pupils/a batch of old magazines*) group, quantity, collection, set.

**bathe** *vb* **1** (*bathe the wound*) clean, cleanse, wash. **2** (*bathe in the sea*) swim, go swimming, (*inf*) take a dip.

**batter** *vb* (*batter the door*) bang, beat, strike, knock, pound, thump.

**battle** *n* (*a battle to prevent the enemy army invading*) conflict, fight, clash, skirmish, engagement, encounter, struggle, contest.

**bawl** *vb* (*bawl in order to attract attention*) shout, cry out, yell, roar, bellow, scream.

**bay** *n* (*ships anchored in the bay*) inlet, cove, gulf, basin, bight.

**bay** *vb* howl, bark, yell, cry, growl.

**bazaar** *n* (*tourists at an eastern bazaar*) market, market-place.

**beach** *n* (*pull the boat on to the beach*) seaside, coast, shore, sands.

**beam** *n* **1** (*roof beams*) board, timber, plank, joist, rafter, support. **2**-(*a beam of light*) ray, shaft, steam, streak, flash, gleam, glint.

**bear** *vb* **1** (*bearing gifts*) carry, bring, take, convey. **2** (*bear the weight*) carry, support, hold up, sustain. **3**-(*unable to bear the pain*) put up with, stand, suffer, endure, tolerate. **4** (*bear a son*) give birth to, produce. **5** (*bear a grudge*) have, hold, harbor.

**bearded** *adj* (*a bearded man*) unshaven, whiskered, stubbly, hirsute.

**bearings** *npl* (*lose our bearings on-the mountain*) location, position, whereabouts, way, course, direction.

**beast** *n* **1** (*the beasts of the jungle*) animal, creature, mammal. **2** (*He was a beast of a man*) brute, monster, savage, pig, ogre.

**beat** *vb* **1** (*beat the drum*) bang, hit, strike, pound. **2** (*with hearts beating*) throb, pound, thump, pulsate, pulse, palpitate. **3** (*They beat their children*) hit, strike, batter, thump, wallop, thrash, slap. **4** (*birds with their wings beating*) flap, flutter, vibrate. **5** (*beat the butter and sugar*) mix, blend, whisk, stir. **6**-(*beat the opposition*) defeat, conquer, vanquish, rout, trounce, crush, overwhelm, (*inf*) lick. **7**-(*beat the record*) outdo, surpass, exceed, excel, transcend.

**beat** n 1 (*the beat of the music*) rhythm, time, measure, pulse, throb. 2 (*the policeman's beat*) round, circuit, course, route.

**beautiful** adj 1 (*a beautiful woman*) lovely, pretty, attractive, handsome, glamorous, gorgeous. 2 (*a beautiful view*) lovely, attractive, picturesque, charming, delightful, magnificent, splendid.

**beauty** n 1 (*a woman of great beauty*) loveliness, prettiness, attractiveness, handsomeness, glamour. 2 (*the beauty of the scheme*) advantage, benefit, asset.

**becoming** adj 1 (*a becoming dress*) flattering, attractive, elegant. 2 (*behavior that was hardly becoming*) fitting, suitable, appropriate, apt, proper, seemly, decorous.

**before** adv (*We had met before*) previously, earlier, formerly, in the past.

**beg** vb 1 (*homeless people begging in the streets*) ask for money, cadge, scrounge. 2 (*beg for mercy*) ask for, require, plead for, entreat, beseech, implore.

**beggar** n panhandler, vagrant, downand-outer, tramp, mendicant.

**begin** vb 1 (*begin work*) start, commence, set about, embark on. 2 (*when the trouble begins*) start, commence, get going, arise.

**beginning** n 1 (*the beginning of the relationship*) start, starting-point, commencement, outset, onset, inception. 2 (*the beginning of the book*) start, commencement, first part, introduction, opening, preface.

**begrudge** vb (*begrudge him his success*) grudge, envy, be envious of, resent, be jealous of.

**behave** vb (*behave in a responsible way*) act, conduct oneself.

**behavior** n (*criticize the behavior of the boys*) actions, conduct, manners.

**being** n 1 (*the reason for our being*) existence, life, living. 2 (*beings from another planet*) creature, living thing, individual.

**belief** n 1 (*It is her belief that he is still alive*) opinion, feeling, impression, view, viewpoint, way of thinking, theory. 2 (*religious beliefs*) faith, creed, doctrine, credo. 3 (*have no belief in their ability*) faith, trust, reliance.

**belligerent** adj (*a belligerent man who started a fight*) aggressive, quarrelsome, argumentative, pugnacious.

**belong** vb 1 (*The coat belongs to me*) be owned by, be the property of. 2 (*She belongs to the tennis club*) be a member of, be associated with.

**belongings** npl (*lose all her belongings*) possessions, things, property, personal effects.

**beloved** adj (*her beloved husband*) dearest, darling, loved, adored.

**beloved** n (*wish to marry her beloved*) sweetheart, boyfriend/girlfriend, fiancé/fiancee.

**belt** n 1 (*wear a plastic belt round her waist*) girdle, sash, strap, cummerbund. 2 (*a belt of green fields between the towns*) area, region, tract, zone. 3 (*a belt of blue across the white walls*) strip, stripe, streak, line, band.

**bench** n 1 (*pupils sitting on a bench*) seat. 2 (*a carpenter's bench*) workbench, worktable, table, counter.

**bend** vb 1 (*try to bend the iron band*) curve, flex, loop, arch, twist, contort, warp. 2 (*The road bends to the left*) curve, turn, twist, swerve, veer, incline. 3 (*She bent down to pick up the letter*) stoop, crouch down, lean down, bow down.

**bend** n (*a bend in the road*) curve, turn, twist, corner, angle.

**beneficial** adj (*a climate beneficial to her health*) of benefit, advantageous, favorable, helpful.

**benefit** n 1 (*one of the benefits of living near the sea*) advantage, gain, good point, asset, boon. 2 (*things that are of benefit to all*) advantage, good, profit, use, value, help, service.

**benevolent** adj 1 (*a benevolent old man*) kind, kindly, kind-hearted, generous, helpful. 2 (*benevolent associations*) charitable, nonprofit.

**bent** adj 1 (*a bent iron rod*) curved, crooked, angled, twisted, contorted, warped. 2 (*with bent backs*)-bowed, arched, stooped, hunched.

**bent** n (*of a musical bent*) inclination, leaning, tendency, predisposition, talent, aptitude, flair.

**bequest** n (*receive a bequest in her employer's will*) legacy, inheritance.

**bereavement** n (*Their grandfather has died—we must sympathize with them on their bereavement at this sad time*) loss, death, decease.

**bereft** adj (*bereft of speech*) deprived of, robbed of, devoid of, lacking.

**berserk** adj (*He went berserk when he saw the damage to his car*) mad, insane, frenzied, out of one's mind, wild, enraged, raging, amok, (*inf*) bananas.

**besides** adv (*I do not want to go—besides it is too late*) also, in addition, additionally, moreover, furthermore.

**besides** prep (*four people besides us*) as well as, apart from, in addition to, not counting.

**besiege** vb (*a city besieged by the enemy*) lay siege to, blockade, surround, encircle, beleaguer.

**best** adj 1 (*the best player*) top, foremost, leading, finest. 2 (*the best thing to do*) right, correct, most suitable, most fitting.

**bet** vb (*bet $100 on a horse*) gamble, wager, stake, risk, venture.

**bet** n 1 (*place a bet on a horse*) wager, stake. 2 (*one's best bet*) choice, option, alternative, course of action.

**betray** vb 1 (*betray his friend to the police*) be disloyal to, break faith with, inform on, double-cross, (*inf*) blow the whistle on, sell down the river. 2 (*betray her secret*) reveal, disclose, divulge, let slip, give away.

**beware** vb (*advised to beware of thieves*) be careful, be wary, be on one's guard, guard against, watch out.

**bewilder** vb (*bewildered by all the traffic signs*) confuse, muddle, puzzle, perplex, baffle, nonplus, bamboozle, bemuse.

**bewitch** vb 1 (*bewitched by the pianist's performance*) captivate, enchant, entrance, beguile, charm. 2 (*The wizard bewitched the prince*) put a spell on, cast a spell over, enchant.

**biased** adj (*accuse the referee of being biased/a biased attitude*) prejudiced, one-sided, influenced, partial, bigoted, unfair, unjust.

**bid** vb 1 (*bid $100 for the vase at the auction*) offer, tender, proffer, put forward. 2 (*bid them farewell*) wish, greet, tell, say.

**big** adj 1 (*a big house/a big car*) large, sizeable, great, substantial, huge, enormous, vast, colossal, gigantic. 2 (*a big man*) large, tall, heavy, burly, thickset. 3 (*a big decision*) important, significant, major, serious, grave, weighty.

**bigotry** n (*religious bigotry*) prejudice, intolerance, bias, partiality, narrowmindedness, fanaticism.

**bilious** adj 1 sick, nauseated, queasy. 2 (*walls of a bilious color*) garish, violent, nauseating.

**bill** n (*send them the bill for the work*) account, invoice, check, (*inf*) tab.

**bin** n (*a bin for flour*) container, receptacle, box, can.

**bind** vb 1 (*bind the sheaves of wheat together*) tie, tie up, fasten, secure, attach, truss. 2 (*bind the wound*) bandage, dress, cover. 3 (*bind the seams*) edge trim, hem, finish.

**birth** n 1 (*present at the birth*) delivery, childbirth, confinement. 2 (*of humble birth*) origin, descent, family, parentage, extraction, ancestry. 3 (*the birth of civilization*) origin, beginning, start, creation.

**bit** n (*a bit of chocolate/a bit of cheese*) piece, section, segment, lump, chunk, scrap, sliver, morsel, grain, speck, particle.

**bite** vb 1 (*bite into the apple/biting her nails*) chew, munch, crunch, nibble at, gnaw at, eat. 2 (*The dog bit the man*) sink one's teeth into, snap at, nip. 3 (*bitten by mosquitoes*) sting, puncture.

**bite** n 1 (*a bite of the apple/a bite of food*) mouthful, piece, morsel, bit. 2 (*The dog gave her a bite*) snap, nip. 3 (*insect bites*) sting, prick, puncture. **4** (*food with a bite*) sharpness, spiciness, piquancy, pungency.

**bitter** *adj* **1** (*a bitter taste*) acid, tart, sour, acrid, harsh, pungent, vinegary. **2** (*a bitter old man*) embittered, resentful, sour, acrimonious, spiteful, vindictive. **3** (*a bitter wind*) biting, sharp, raw, penetrating, stinging, freezing. **4** (*from bitter experience*) painful, distressing, unhappy, sad, tragic.

**black** *adj* **1** (*black clothes/black horses*) jet-black, pitch-black, inky, sable, dusky. **2** (*black nights*) dark, pitchblack, inky, murky, unlit, starless. **3** (*in a black mood*) depressed, gloomy, pessimistic, melancholy, sad.

**blame** *vb* **1** (*blame her for the crime*) hold responsible, hold accountable, accuse, charge, find guilty, condemn. **2** (*blame the crime on her*) attribute, ascribe, lay at the door of, (*inf*) pin on.

**blame** *n* (*put the blame for the crime on her*) responsibility, accountability, liability, fault, accusation, guilt, condemnation (*inf*) rap.

**bland** *adj* **1** (*bland food*) tasteless, flavorless, insipid, mild. **2** (*a bland manner*) smooth, suave, urbane, gracious.

**blank** *adj* **1** (*a blank piece of paper*) empty, unfilled, unwritten on, unmarked, bare. **2** (*a blank tape*) clean, empty, unfilled, unused. **3**-(*a blank face*) expressionless, vacant, empty, deadpan, impassive.

**blast** *n* **1** (*hear the blast several streets away*) explosion, bang, report, eruption. **2** (*a blast of cold air*) gust, rush, draft, wind, gale. **3** (*a blast of loud music*) blare, boom, roar.

**blatant** *adj* (*a blatant crime*) glaring, flagrant, obvious, conspicuous, unmistakable, brazen.

**blaze** *n* **1** (*people killed in the blaze*) fire, flames, conflagration, inferno. **2** (*a sudden blaze of light*) flash, flare, beam, streak.

**blaze** *vb* **1** (*logs blazing in the fire*) burn, be ablaze, flame. **2** (*lights blazing*) shine, beam, flash, flare.

**bleak** *adj* **1** (*a bleak countryside*) bare, barren, desolate, dismal, exposed. **2** (*a bleak future*) gloomy, depressing, miserable, dismal, grim, dark.

**blemish** *n* **1** (*blemishes on the fruit*) mark, spot, blotch, bruise, imperfection. **2** (*a blemish in his character*) flaw, fault, defect. **3** (*a blemish on her reputation*) stain, blot.

**blend** *vb* **1** (*blend the ingredients for the cake*) mix, combine, mingle.

**blessing** *n* **1** (*The pastor said a blessing*) benediction, grace, prayer, dedication. **2** (*The rain is a blessing for the driedout farms*) boon, advantage, benefit, asset, help.

**3** (*give the scheme his blessing*) approval, support, sanction, endorsement.

**blind** *adj* **1** (*a blind person with a guide dog*) sightless, unseeing, visually impaired, visually challenged. **2** (*blind to the problems*) unmindful of, heedless of, oblivious to, indifferent to, unaware of, unconscious of, ignorant of.

**blind** *n* (*The blind kept out the sunlight*) screen, shade, shutters, curtain, Venetian blind.

**blink** *vb* **1** (*people blinking in the bright light*) screw up one's eyes, wink, squint. **2** (*with eyelids blinking*) flicker, wink, bat. **3** (*Christmas trees blinking*) flicker, twinkle, wink, glimmer, glitter.

**bliss** *n* (*the bliss of being in love*) ecstasy, elation, euphoria, joy, rapture, happiness, delight.

**block** *n* **1** (*a block of chocolate*) bar, cake, brick, slab, chunk, lump, hunk, wedge. **2** (*a block in the pipe*) blockage, obstruction, stoppage.

**block** *vb* **1** (*leaves blocking the drains*) clog, choke, stop up, obstruct. **2** (*fallen trees blocking the flow of traffic*) bar, halt, obstruct, hinder, impede, hold back.

**bloodshed** *n* (*a battle which resulted in great bloodshed*) killing, murder, slaughter, massacre, carnage.

**bloom** *vb* **1** (*flowers which bloom in the summer*) flower, be in flower, come into flower, blossom. **2** (*children blooming in their new environment*) flourish, thrive, blossom, get on well, prosper, succeed.

**blot** *n* **1** (*ink blots/blots of grease*) blotch, spot, smudge, splotch, smear. **2** (*a blot on her character*) stain, blemish, flaw, fault, defect, taint.

**blot** *vb* **1** (*paper blotted with ink spots*) spot, smudge, blotch, smear, mark. **2** (*blot their reputation*) sully, blacken, stain, tarnish, besmirch. **3** (*blot out memories of the past*) wipe out, rub out, erase, obliterate, destroy.

**blow** *n* **1** (*a blow on the head*) hit, knock, bang, thump, smack, slap, rap, (*inf*) clout. **2** (*It was a blow when her friend went away*) shock, upset, jolt, setback, disappointment, misfortune, disaster, catastrophe.

**blue** *adj* **1** (*blue skies*) azure, indigo, sapphire, ultramarine, navy, navy blue, skyblue, powder-blue, royal blue. **2** (*feeling blue*) depressed, gloomy, miserable, downcast, glum, sad, unhappy, melancholy. **3** (*blue jokes*) obscene, indecent, improper, dirty, smutty.

**bluff** *vb* (*She believed him but he was only bluffing*) pretend, sham, fake, feign, put it on, lie, deceive, fool, hoax, hoodwink.

**bluff** *n* (*He said that he would report her but it was only a bluff*) pretense, sham, fake, deception, subterfuge, hoax.

**bluff** *adj* (*a bluff manner*) outspoken, plainspoken, blunt, direct, frank, candid.

**blunder** *n* (*make a blunder in the calculations*) mistake, error, slip, inaccuracy, (*inf*) slip-up.

**blunder** *vb* **1** (*discover that someone had blundered and had forgotten to reserve a table*) make a mistake, err, (*inf*) slip up, screw up. **2** (*blundering about in the dark without a flashlight*) stumble, lurch, stagger, flounder.

**blunt** *adj* **1** (*a blunt knife*) dull, dulled, unsharpened. **2** (*a blunt statement*) abrupt, curt, brusque, outspoken, plainspoken, direct, frank, straightforward, candid.

**blur** *vb* **1** (*Tears blurred her vision*) obscure, dim, make hazy, make misty, make fuzzy, cloud. **2** (*Grease blurred the windshield*) smear, smudge. **3** (*Time had blurred her memory*) dim, make hazy, make vague, dull, confuse.

**blur** *n* (*When she did not have her glasses on everything was just a blur*) haze, mist.

**blurred** *adj* (*blurred vision*) hazy, misty, fuzzy, indistinct, unclear.

**blush** *vb* (*She blushed with embarrassment*) redden, go red, turn red, go scarlet, go crimson, flush, color.

**board** *n* **1** (*a bridge made of wooden boards*) plank, slat, beam. **2** (*charge her for her board*) food, meals.

**board** *vb* **1** (*board the plane*) get on, enter, go on board, mount, embark. **2** (*board up the windows*) cover up, shut up, seal. **3** (*He boards with a friend of his mother*) lodge, live, have rooms.

**boast** *vb* (*She was always boasting about how well she could sing*) brag, crow, blow one's own trumpet, show off, swagger, (*inf*) swank.

**boastful** *adj* (*a boastful person always telling people about her fine house*) bragging, swaggering, conceited, vain, (*inf*) bigheaded, (*inf*) swanky.

**boat** *n* vessel, craft, dinghy, yacht, ship, rowing-boat.

**body** *n* **1** (*healthy bodies*) physique. **2** (*pains in his body and in his limbs*) trunk, torso. **3** (*bodies in the mortuary*) dead body, cadaver, carcass, corpse. **4** (*the ruling body in the organization*) group, party, band, company, bloc. **5** (*a large body of water*) mass, expanse, extent.

**bodyguard** *n* (*the president's bodyguard*) guard, protector, defender.

**bog** *n* (*The walkers got stuck in the bog*) marsh, marshland, swamp, mire, quagmire.

**bogus** *adj* **1** (*The man in the hospital turned out to be a bogus doctor*) fraudulent, fake, sham, (*inf*) phony. **2** (*pay for the goods with bogus $10 bills*) counterfeit, forged, fake, fraudulent, sham, (*inf*) phony.

**boil** vb (soup boiling on the stove) bubble, cook, simmer.

**boisterous** adj 1 (boisterous children) lively, active, spirited, noisy, loud, rowdy, unruly. 2 (a boisterous wind) blustery, gusting, stormy, wild.

**bold** adj 1 (a bold adventurer) brave, courageous, valiant, gallant, daring, adventurous, intrepid, fearless, heroic, determined. 2 (a bold young woman/so bold as to invite themselves to the party) brazen, impudent, forward, audacious. 3 (bold colors) striking, bright, vivid, eye-catching, showy.

**bolt** n 1 (bolts on the door) bar, catch, latch, fastener, lock. 2 (nuts and bolts) rivet, pin, peg.

**bolt** vb 1 (They bolted the door) bar, lock, fasten, secure. 2 (bolt from the room in fear) dash, run, sprint, dart, rush, hurtle, flee. 3 (The children bolted their food) gulp, gobble, wolf, guzzle.

**bomb** n (a building blown up by a bomb) incendiary device, incendiary, explosive, shell.

**bombard** vb 1 (The enemy bombarded the military stores) bomb, shell, torpedo, blitz, attack. 2 (bombard them with questions) assail, attack, besiege, subject to.

**bond** n 1 (the bond between mother and child) tie, link, connection, attachment. 2 (prisoners escaping from their bonds) chains, fetters, shackles, rope.

**bonus** n 1 (The good food on vacation was a welcome bonus) extra, addition, (inf) plus, benefit, gain, boon. 2 (staff getting a Christmas bonus) gift, tip, gratuity, (inf) perk, reward.

**bony** adj angular, scraggy, gaunt, skinny, skeletal.

**book** vb (book theater seats/book hotel rooms) reserve, make reservations for.

**book** n (borrow a book from the library) volume, tome, publication.

**bookish** adj (She is rather a bookish child) studious, scholarly, academic, intellectual, learned, highbrow.

**boom** vb 1 (hear guns booming) bang, banging, blast, roar, rumble. 2 (a boom in the number of tourists) increase, growth, upsurge, upswing, upturn, boost.

**boor** n (boors with bad manners) lout, oaf, hoodlum, hood.

**boost** vb (boost the morale of the troops) raise, increase, heighten, improve, encourage, help, assist.

**booth** n 1 (a market booth) stall, stand, counter, kiosk. 2 (a telephone booth) cubicle, compartment.

**booty** n (the booty hidden by the burglars) loot, spoils, plunder, haul, (inf) swag.

**border** n 1 (sew a colorful border on the skirt) edging, edge, fringe, trimming. 2 (a flower border) bed. 3 (the borders of the lake) edge, verge, perimeter, margin. 4 (show one's passport qt the border) frontier, boundary.

**bore** vb 1 (bore into the wood/bore a hole in the wood) drill, pierce, perforate, penetrate, puncture. 2 (an audience bored by the comedian) weary, tire, fatigue, be tedious to, bore to tears, bore to death.

**boring** adj (a boring speech) dull, tedious, monotonous, unexciting, uninteresting, wearisome, tiring.

**borrow** vb (borrow money from someone/borrow someone's pen) ask for the loan of, take as a loan, use temporarily, (inf) scrounge, (inf) cadge.

**boss** n (The workers asked the boss for a wage rise) employer, manager, director, owner, (inf) honcho.

**bossy** adj domineering, bullying, overbearing, dominating, dictatorial.

**bother** vb 1 (The children were told not to bother their mother when she was resting) disturb, trouble, worry, pester, annoy, harass, (inf) hassle. 2 (please don't bother to wait for me) take the trouble, trouble oneself, inconvenience oneself, make the effort. 3 (It bothers me that she is not here yet) concern, worry, trouble, upset.

**bother** n 1 (please don't go to any bother over dinner) trouble, inconvenience, effort, fuss. 2 (There was a bit of bother at the game) trouble, disturbance, commotion, disorder, fighting.

**bottle** n 1 (a bottle of milk/a bottle of wine) container, flask, carafe.

**bottom** n 1 (at the bottom of the hill) foot, base. 2 (the bottom of the sea) floor, bed, depths. 3 (the bottom of the street) the far end, the farthest point.

**bound** vb (bound into the room/bound over the fence) leap, jump, spring, vault, spring.

**bound** adj (She thought that she was bound to win) certain, sure, very likely, destined.

**boundary** n 1 (the boundary between the countries) border, frontier, dividing line. 2 (the boundary of the ranch) bounds, border, perimeter, periphery, confines, limits, margin.

**bouquet** n (the bride's bouquet/a bouquet of roses) bunch of flowers, bunch, spray, posy.

**bout** n 1 (a boxing bout) combat, contest, match, round, fight. 2 (a bout of coughing) fit, attack, turn, spell.

**bow** vb (bow his head) incline, bend, nod, stoop.

**bowl** n (a bowl of cereal) dish, basin, container.

**bowl** vb (bowl a ball) pitch, throw, fling, hurl, toss.

**box** n container, receptacle, carton, case, pack, chest, bin, crate.

**box** vb 1 (He used to box for his country) fight. 2 (box a person on the ears) strike, hit, cuff, slap, smack, wallop, (inf) belt.

**boy** n (when he was a boy) youth, lad.

**boycott** vb 1 (boycott goods from that country) bar, ban, black, blacklist, embargo, place an embargo on, prohibit. 2 (boycott their company) shun, avoid, spurn, ostracize, eschew.

**boyfriend** n (She has a new boyfriend)-sweetheart, young man, lover, partner.

**bracing** adj (a bracing climate) invigorating, refreshing, stimulating, exhilarating, reviving, health-giving.

**brag** vb (He brags about having a lot of money) boast, crow, blow one's own trumpet, show off, (inf) talk big.

**brain** n (have a good brain) intellect, mind, intelligence, powers of reasoning, head.

**branch** n 1 (the branch of a tree) bough, limb. 2 (the local branch of the business) division, subdivision, section, department, part.

**brand** n 1 (a brand of breakfast cereal) make, kind, variety, type, sort, line, label, trade name, trademark. 2 (her brand of wit) kind, variety, type, sort, style.

**brandish** vb (a criminal brandishing a knife) wave, flourish, swing, wield, shake.

**brash** adj (a brash young man) bold,-cocky, self-confident, self-assertive, insolent, impudent, cheeky, brazen.

**brave** adj courageous, valiant, intrepid, fearless, plucky, gallant, heroic, bold, daring.

**brawl** n (a brawl in a bar) fight, affray, wrangle, rumpus, row, quarrel, argument, squabble, free-for-all, scrap.

**brawny** adj (brawny lumberjacks) burly, muscular, hefty, powerful, strong, strapping.

**bray** vb (donkeys braying) whinny, neigh, hee-haw.

**brazen** adj (It was brazen of her to kiss a complete stranger on the lips) bold, audacious, forward, brash, impudent, insolent, impertinent, immodest, shameless.

**breach** n 1 (a breach in the sea wall) break, split, crack, gap, hole, opening. 2 (a breach of the legal agreement) breaking, violation, infringement.

**breadth** n 1 (measure the breadth of the room) width, wideness, broadness, span. 2 (discover the breadth of her knowledge of the subject) extent, range, scope, scale, degree.

**break** vb 1 (break a cup) smash, shatter, crack. 2 (break the handle of the bag) snap, split, tear. 3 (The machine broke) break down, become damaged, stop working, cease to operate, (inf) be kaput. 4 (break the law) violate, contravene, breach, infringe, disobey, disregard, defy. 5 (break his arm) fracture, crack. 6 (break the news) tell, impart, announce, communicate, reveal, disclose.

**break** n 1 (*a break in the water pipe*)-crack, hole, gash, split, fracture, chink, tear. 2 (*a break in her career-to care for her children*)-interruption, discontinuation, pause, hiatus. 3 (*She worked for-four-hours-without a break*) recess, rest-period,-interval, intermission, timeout, breathingspace. 4-(*take a-weekend break*) vacation, time off.

**breakthrough** n (*a breakthrough in cancer research*) advance, step forward, development.

**breathe** vb 1 (*breathe in/breathe out*) inhale/exhale, inspire/expire, puff, pant. 2 (*as long as he breathes*) be alive, live, have life.

**breathless** adj (*breathless after running to catch the train*) out of breath, gasping, panting, puffing.

**breed** n (*a breed of cattle*) variety, kind, strain.

**breed** vb 1 (*Rabbits breed very rapidly*) reproduce, multiply, give birth. 2 (*He breeds horses*) raise, rear. 3 (*poverty which can breed crime and violence*) cause, bring about, give rise to, create, produce, stir up.

**breeze** n (*a cool breeze on a hot day*) puff of wind, gust of wind, current of air, draft, zephyr.

**bribe** vb (*try to bribe a member of the jury*) buy off, corrupt, give an inducement to, (*inf*) grease the palm of, (*inf*) give a sweetener to.

**bridge** n (*a bridge over the freeway*)-overpass, viaduct, suspension bridge.

**brief** adj 1 (*a brief statement*) short, concise, succinct, to the point, compact, terse. 2 (*a brief friendship*) short, short-lived, fleeting, passing, transient, transitory, ephemeral.

**brief** vb (*brief a lawyer*) instruct, give instructions to, direct, give directions to, inform, give information to, prime.

**bright** adj 1 (*a bright light*) shining, brilliant, dazzling, blazing, gleaming, radiant. 2 (*bright colors*) vivid, brilliant, intense, glowing, bold, rich. 3 (*bright children*) clever, intelligent, sharp, quick, quickwitted, (*inf*) smart, brilliant, (*inf*) brainy, gifted, talented. 4 (*a bright future*) promising, favorable, hopeful, optimistic, encouraging, fortunate, good.

**brilliant** adj 1 (*a brilliant light*) bright, shining, dazzling, gleaming, radiant. 2 (*brilliant children*) bright, clever, intelligent, sharp, quick, quickwitted, (*inf*) smart, (*inf*) brainy, gifted, talented.

**brim** n (*glasses full to the brim*) rim, lip, top, edge.

**brim** vb (*glasses brimming with wine/eyes brimming with tears*) be full, be filled with, overflow, run over.

**bring** vb 1 (*bring food home*) carry, take, convey, transport, fetch. 2 (*famine which brought disease*) cause, produce, create, result in, give rise to.

**brink** n 1 (*on the brink of the lake*) edge, verge, boundary, border, margin. 2 (*on the brink of the disaster*) edge, verge, threshold, point.

**brisk** adj 1 (*walk at a brisk speed*) quick, fast, rapid, swift, speedy, energetic, lively. 2 (*Business was brisk*) busy, active, hectic.

**brittle** adj (*Glass is a brittle material*) hard, crisp, breakable, splintery.

**broad** adj 1 (*a broad street*) wide. 2 (*a broad range of subjects*) wide, wideranging, broad-ranging, general, comprehensive. 3 (*a broad statement of their plans*) general, non-detailed, imprecise, vague.

**brochure** n (*an advertising brochure*) booklet, leaflet, pamphlet, circular, notice, bill.

**brooch** n (*She wears a silver brooch on her lapel*) pin, clip.

**brow** n 1 (*wipe the sweat from his brow*) forehead, temple. 2 (*the brow of the hill*) top, summit, crown, peak.

**brown** adj (*go brown in the summer*)-tanned, sun-tanned, bronze, bronzed.

**brush** vb 1 (*brush the yard*) sweep, clean. 2 (*brush her hair*) groom, tidy. 3 (*brush her cheek with his lips*) touch, flick, glance.

**brusque** adj (*a brusque reply*) abrupt, blunt, curt, sharp, gruff, rude.

**brutal** adj (*a brutal attack*) savage, cruel, vicious, callous, ruthless.

**bubble** vb 1 (*champagne bubbling*) fizz, effervesce, sparkle, foam, froth. 2 (*a sauce bubbling on the stove*) boil, simmer.

**bucket** n (*need a bucket of water to wash the floor*) pail, container.

**buckle** n (*the buckle of the belt*) clasp, catch, fastener, fastening, clip.

**bug** n 1 (*bitten by bugs when sitting on the grass*) insect, mite. 2 (*He caught a bug and is off work*) infection, virus, germ, bacterium, microbe, microorganism.

**build** vb 1 (*build a new school*) construct, put up, erect. 2 (*build model planes*) make, construct, assemble, put together. 3 (*build his own business*) found, set up, establish, start, begin, develop, institute.

**building** n (*old buildings which are tourist attractions*) edifice, structure.

**bulge** n (*The bag of candy made a bulge in her pocket*) swelling, bump, lump, protuberance.

**bulk** n 1 (*The chest was difficult to move because of its sheer bulk*) size, mass, extent, largeness, hugeness. 2 (*The bulk of the people voted against the proposal*) majority, most, preponderance, mass.

**bulky** adj (*bulky furniture*) large, big,-massive, substantial, heavy, unwieldy, cumbersome, awkward.

**bully** vb (*older boys bullying the younger ones*) browbeat, domineer, intimidate, threaten, persecute, torment, tyrannize, (*inf*) push around.

**bump** vb (*The car that bumped into ours was not insured*) knock, hit, strike, crash into, bang, collide with, ram.

**bump** n 1 (*The child fell out of the tree with a bump*) thud, thump, bang, jolt, crash. 2 (*He has a bump on the head from the accident*) lump, swelling, bulge.

**bumpy** adj (*bumpy roads*) uneven, rough, rutted, pitted, potholed.

**bunch** n 1 (*a bunch of flowers*) bouquet, spray, posy, sheaf. 2 (*a bunch of grapes*) cluster, clump. 3 (*a friendly bunch of people*) group, band, crowd.

**bundle** n (*a bundle of old clothes*) pile, heap, stack, bale.

**burden** n 1 (*the pony's burden*) load, pack. 2 (*the burden of being head of the family*) responsibility, obligation, onus, worry, weight, strain.

**burglar** n (*catch a burglar breaking into the house*) housebreaker, cat burglar, thief, robber.

**burglary** n (*He was sent to prison for burglary*) house-breaking, breaking in, forced entry, theft, robbery, larceny.

**burly** adj (*the burly figure of the lumberjack*) muscular, powerful, thickset, strapping, hefty, beefy, stout.

**burn** vb 1 (*The house was burning*) be on fire, be ablaze, blaze. 2 (*burn the garbage*) set on fire, set alight, ignite. 3 (*burn the shirt with the iron*) scorch, singe, sear.

**burst** vb 1 (*The water pipes have burst*) crack, split, fracture, rupture. 2 (*They burst into the room*) push one's way, barge. 3 (*burst into tears*) break out, explode, erupt, begin suddenly.

**bury** vb 1 (*bury the body*) inter, lay to rest. 2 (*bury her head in her hands*) hide, conceal, cover, put, submerge.

**business** n 1 (*She owns her own business*) company, firm, concern, organization, establishment. 2 (*We don't know what business he is in*) occupation, line, work, profession, job, career. 3 (*It was none of their business*) concern, affair, problem, responsibility. 4 (*an odd business*) affair, situation, matter, circumstance, thing.

**busy** adj 1 (*Don't disturb your mother—she's busy*) occupied, engaged, working, at work. 2 (*have a busy day*) active, energetic, full, hectic.

**buy** vb (*buy a new house*) purchase, make a purchase of, pay for, invest in.

**bypass** n (*the city bypass*) detour, alternative route.

# C

**café** n (*They stopped for a snack at a café*) diner, coffee bar, coffee shop, cafeteria, snack bar, restaurant.

**cajole** vb (*Try to cajole him into coming with us*) wheedle, coax, inveigle, persuade.

**cagey** adj (*They seemed rather cagey about where they were going*) secretive, guarded, non-committal.

**cake** n (*a cake of soap*) bar, block, slab, lump.

**calculate** vb (*calculate the cost*) work out, count, estimate, gauge, figure out, reckon.

**call** vb 1 (*She called out in fear*) cry, shout, yell, scream. 2 (*They called their son Peter*) name, christen. 3 (*The vegetables are called zucchini/That is called wind-surfing*) name, style, designate, term, describe, dub, label. 4 (*She called you from her mobile*) telephone, phone, ring. 5 (*He will call tomorrow to do his aunt's shopping*) pay a call, pay a visit, stop by, stop in, drop by, drop in. 6 (*If the child is ill you had better call a doctor*) send for, ask for, summon. 7 (*They called a meeting of the committee*) call together, convene, summon. 8 (*I call it shocking that he got away with the crime*) think, consider, regard, judge.

**calm** adj 1 (*She remains calm even in an emergency*) cool, composed, selfpossessed, unruffled, tranquil, quiet. 2 (*The sea was calm when the boat set out*) still, smooth. 3 (*It was a calm day for their sail on the lake*) still, windless, mild.

**camouflage** n (*The polar bear's coat is a camouflage in the snow*) protective coloring, disguise, cover, screen, concealment.

**camp** n 1 (*the soldier's camp*) encampment, campsite, camping ground. 2 (*He is in the left-wing camp of the party*) group, set, faction, clique.

**can** n (*a can of soup*) tin, container.

**cancel** vb 1 (*They had to cancel the meeting because of bad weather*) put off, call off. 2 (*They canceled the order because it was late*) call off, retract, declare void, declare null and void, revoke.

**candid** adj (*He was quite candid with them about his reasons for leaving*) frank, open, honest, direct, forthright, blunt, plainspoken.

**cap** n 1 (*He wore a cap to hide his baldness*) hat, baseball cap. 2 (*I can't get the cap off the bottle*) top, lid, stopper, cork.

**capable** adj 1 (*She is a very capable person*) able, competent, efficient, effective. 2 (*He is quite capable of cheating*) likely to, liable to.

**capital** n 1 (*Ottawa is the capital of Canada*) first city, chief city, seat of administration. 2 (*He does not have enough capital to buy the company*) money, finance, funds, cash, means, resources, wherewithal, assets. 3 (*write the title in capitals*) capital letter, upper case letter, (*inf*) cap.

**capsize** vb 1 (*The boat capsized in heavy seas*) overturn, turn over, up-end, keel over, turn turtle. 2 (*The child capsized the bucket of water*) upset, overturn, up-end.

**captivity** n (*enjoy freedom after months in captivity*) imprisonment, custody, confinement, incarceration.

**capture** vb (*The police have captured the escaped prisoners*) catch, take prisoner, take captive, take into custody, arrest, apprehend, seize.

**card** n 1 (*She sent a card to her mother on her birthday*) greetings card, postcard. 2 (*The salesman handed them his card*) business card, identification, ID. 3 (*He was asked to deal the cards*) playing card.

**care** n 1 (*The children were told to cross the road with care*) carefulness, caution, heed, heedfulness, wariness, attention, vigilance, prudence. 2 (*She iced the cake with care*) carefulness, conscientiousness, accuracy, meticulousness, punctiliousness. 3 (*The child is in the care of his grandparents*) protection, charge, keeping, custody, supervision. 4 (*They show no care for other people*) concern, regard, interest, solicitude, sympathy. 5 (*She looked older than she was after a life full of care*) worry, anxiety, trouble, distress, hardship, stress.

**careful** adj 1 (*The children were told to be careful crossing the road*) cautious, heedful, wary, attentive, vigilant, prudent. 2 (*You must be careful of your belongings at the airport*) mindful, heedful, protective. 3 (*You must be careful what you say to the lawyer*) mindful, attentive, heedful, thoughtful. 4 (*They are all careful workers*) conscientious, painstaking, accurate, meticulous, punctilious. 5 (*They do not earn much and so they have to be very careful with money*) thrifty, economic, frugal, cautious, canny.

**careless** adj 1 (*a careless pedestrian who walked out in front of the moving truck*) unthinking, inattentive, thoughtless, forgetful, remiss, negligent. 2 (*The student's work is very careless*) inaccurate, slapdash, disorganized, slipshod, (*inf*) sloppy.

**carpet** n 1 (*They laid a new carpet in the bedroom*) rug, floor covering, mat. 2 (*a carpet of fallen leaves on the grass*) covering, layer.

**carry** vb 1 (*She was asked to carry the bag home*) bring, take, transport, convey, lug. 2 (*Will the bridge carry the weight of the car?*) take, support, bear, sustain. 3 (*The store carries a wide range of goods*) sell, stock, offer.

**case** n 1 (*put the cases in the trunk*)-suitcase, briefcase, baggage, piece-of-luggage. 2 (*a silver cigarette case*) container, box, receptacle.-3 (*a display case for ornaments*) cabinet, cupboard. 4 (*It was the case that she had been ill*) situation, position, circumstance. 5 (*They decided that it had been-a-case of misunderstanding*) instance, occurrence, occasion, example. 6-(*He has been accused of murder and the case comes up next week*) lawsuit, trial, legal proceedings. 7 (*the cardiac cases in the ward*) patient, sufferer, victim, invalid.

**cash** n 1 (*He earns quite a lot but he never seems to have any cash when we go out*) money, wherewithal, funds, (*inf*) dough. 2 (*They want us to pay in cash but we have only credit cards*) money, ready money.

**cast** vb 1 (*snakes casting their coats*) shed, slough, discard, throw off. 2 (*The street lamps cast a yellow light*) give off, send out, shed, emit, radiate. 3 (*The children were casting stones in the river*) throw, fling, pitch, toss, hurl, heave. 4 (*She cast him a glance of contempt*) send, throw, bestow.

**casual** adj 1 (*She wears casual clothes at the weekend*) informal, leisure. 2-(*He is a casual acquaintance not a-close friend*) slight, superficial. 3-(*casual hotel work in the summer*) irregular, temporary, part-time. 4-(*He just made a casual remark about the state of the business*) spontaneous, offhand, impromptu.-5 (*They have a very casual attitude to the dangers of the-journey*) unconcerned, nonchalant, blasé, indifferent. 6 (*I did not-arrange to meet her—it was just a casual meeting*) chance, accidental, unintentional, unforeseen, unexpected.

**catch** vb 1 (*He failed to catch the ball*) get hold of, grasp, grab, seize, snatch, grip. 2 (*The police are determined to catch the escaped prisoner*) capture, take captive, seize, apprehend, arrest. 3 (*Did you catch what he said?*) get, understand, follow, grasp, make out, comprehend, fathom. 4 (*Something bright caught his attention*) attract, draw, capture. 5 (*The child has caught a cold*) contract, develop, get, become infected with.

**catch** n 1 (*The catch of the bag is broken*) lock, fastener, fastening, clasp. 2 (*There is no catch on the door*) lock, latch, bolt.

**cause** n 1 (*What was the cause of the accident?*) origin, source, root, agent. 2 (*The patient's condition gives cause for concern*) reason, justification, grounds, call. 3 (*the cause of animals' rights*) ideal, principle, belief.

**cautious** adj (be cautious about trusting strangers) careful, wary, watchful, guarded, chary, heedful, attentive, alert, vigilant.

**cease** vb (The firm has ceased to operate/It ceased operating) stop, halt, finish, leave off, suspend, quit, desist from.

**celebrated** adj (the celebrated painter) famous, renowned, well-known, notable, noted, distinguished, eminent, illustrious.

**central** adj 1 (occupying a central position in the town) middle. 2 (central New York) middle, inner. 3 (That is the central issue of the discussion) main, chief, principal, key, core, focal.

**center** n 1 (The town hall is in the center of the town) middle, heart. 2 (at the center of the quarrel) middle, hub, core, focus, focal point, hub, kernel.

**certain** adj 1 (They are certain that-he will arrive) sure, positive, confident, assured. 2 (Failure is certain)-sure, assured, inevitable, inescapable, (inf) in the bag. 3 (It is-certain that-they have already left) sure, definite, unquestionable, beyond question, indubitable, undeniable, incontrovertible. 4 (There is no certain remedy for the disease) sure,-definite, definite, unfailing, dependable, reliable, foolproof, (inf) surefire. 5 (There were certain people who did not believe him) particular, specific.

**chain** n (a chain of events) series, succession, string, sequence, train, progression.

**chance** n 1 (They took a chance when they crossed the bridge—it is very rickety) risk, gamble, hazard. 2 (There is a good chance that we will get there on time) prospect, possibility, probability, likelihood. 3 (You will not get another chance like that again) opportunity, opening. 4 (We haven't been in touch for years—we met again quite by chance) accident, coincidence, luck, fortuity.

**change** vb 1 (We have had to change the arrangements for the meeting) alter, modify, vary, reorganize, transform. 2 (She has changed completely since I last saw her) alter, be transformed, metamorphose. 3 (She has changed jobs) switch.

**character** n 1 (He seems to have changed in character since I first knew him/The character of the town has altered) nature, disposition, temperament, temper, personality, makeup, ethos. 2 (We need a person of character in the job) strength, backbone, integrity, uprightness, honesty. 3 (His former teacher gave him a letter saying he was of good character/The incident damaged his character) reputation, name, standing. 4 (one of the characters in Shakespeare's 'Hamlet') role, part, persona. 5 (one of the village's characters) eccentric, individual.

**characteristic** adj (He treated the occasion with characteristic arrogance) typical, distinguishing, individual, particular.

**charge** vb 1 (The accused has been charged with murder) accuse, indict. 2 (The French forces charged the enemy army) attack, rush, assault, storm. 3 (The soldier charged the cannon) load, fill. 4 (What did they charge for the apartment?) ask, levy. 5 (Tell them to charge it to my account) debit, put down to, bill.

**charge** n 1 (The charge was one of murder) accusation, indictment, arraignment. 2 (He has charge of the accounts) responsibility, care, protection, custody. 3 (What is the charge for hiring the boat?) cost, price, fee, rate, amount, payment.

**charm** n 1 (She had a great deal of charm/They were taken with the charm of the village) attractiveness, attraction, appeal, allure, fascination. 2 (She has a tiny horseshoe as-a lucky charm) amulet, talisman. 3 (She has a bracelet with charms on it) trinket, ornament. 4-(the sorcerer's charm) spell, magic.

**chart** n (record the information in the form of charts) table, graph, diagram.

**chase** vb 1 (The hunters were chasing the deer) run after, pursue, follow. 2 (They chased away the burglar) put to flight, drive away.

**chatter** vb (The girls were chattering about their boyfriends) chatter, babble, prattle, jabber.

**cheap** adj 1 (Fruit is very cheap in-the summer there) inexpensive,-low-cost, low-priced, reasonable, economical. 2 (She wears cheap and gaudy jewelry) inferior,-shoddy, tawdry, trashy, (inf) tacky.

**cheat** vb 1 (He cheated the old lady into giving him her savings) deceive, trick, swindle, dupe, hoodwink. 2 (His brother cheated-him out of his inheritance) deprive of, deny, thwart, prevent from.

**check** vb 1 (The police checked the man's ID) examine, inspect, look at, scrutinize, test. 2 (You must check that the door is locked) confirm, make sure, verify. 3 (They had to find some way to check the vehicle's progress) stop, halt, slow down, delay, obstruct, impede.

**cheeky** adj (He was scolded for being cheeky to the teacher) impertinent, impudent, insolent, disrespectful, forward.

**cheer** vb 1 (The crowds began to cheer) applaud, shout hurray. 2 (The arrival of her friends cheered her) brighten up, buoy up, perk up, enliven, hearten, exhilarate, gladden, elate.

**cheerful** adj 1 (They were in a cheerful mood when the sun shone) happy, merry, bright, glad, light-hearted, carefree, joyful. 2 (She was wearing a dress in cheerful colors) bright.

**cherish** vb 1 (She cherishes memories of her father) treasure, prize, hold dear, revere. 2 (The children cherish their pets) look after, care for, tend, protect. 3 (They cherish hopes of success) have, entertain, cling to, harbor.

**chest** n 1 (He was wounded in the chest) breast, sternum. 2 (The miser kept his treasure in a chest) box, trunk, casket, coffer, container, receptacle.

**chew** vb (children told to chew their food thoroughly) munch, crunch, champ, masticate.

**chief** adj 1 (the chief man of the tribe) head, leading, foremost, principal. 2 (We must discuss the chief points in the report) main, principal, most important, essential, prime, key, central.

**child** n 1 (when he was a child) young one, little one, youngster, young person, (inf) kid. 2 (parents and their child) offspring, progeny, son/daughter.

**choice** n 1 (You have some choice in the matter—the meeting is not-compulsory) option, selection, preference. 2 (There is a wide choice of fruit and vegetables in the supermarket) selection, range, variety. 3 (We have little choice but to go) option, alternative, possibility.

**choke** vb 1 (The murderer choked her to death) strangle, throttle. 2 (He choked to death on the smoke from the fire) suffocate, smother, stifle, asphyxiate. 3 (The drains are choked and had to be cleared) block, clog, obstruct.

**choose** vb 1 (The child chose some candy at the store) pick, select, settle on, opt for, decide on. 2 (He always does just as he chooses) like, wish, want, prefer, fancy, desire.

**chop** vb 1 (They began to chop the old trees down) cut down, fell, hew, hack down. 2 (They chopped up the vegetables for the soup) cut up, dice, cube.

**chronic** adj 1 (She suffers from a chronic illness) long-standing, longterm, persistent, lingering. 2 (They are chronic liars) habitual, hardened, inveterate.

**circle** n 1 (The children were asked-to draw a circle) ring, round,-ball, globe, sphere, orb, loop, disk. 2 (She has a large circle of friends) group, set, crowd, ring, clique.

**circuit** n (They had to run three circuits of the track) round, lap, turn, loop, ambit.

**circulate** vb 1 (They circulated information to the club members) spread, distribute, issue, give out, disseminate, advertise. 2 (blood constantly circulating) flow, move round, go round, revolve, rotate.

**circumstances** npl (The family lives in poverty-stricken circumstances) state, situation, conditions.

**civil** adj 1 (There had been a civil war in the

country) internal, domestic, home. 2 (*The army were in control but there is now a civil government*) civilian, non-military. 3 (*She might have asked in a more civil way/They are very civil people*) polite, courteous, mannerly, well-mannered, refined, civilized, cultured.

**civilized** *adj* 1 (*peoples of the world who were not then civilized*) enlightened, educated, socialized. 2 (*She is a very civilized person*) cultivated, cultured, educated, sophisticated, refined, polished.

**claim** *vb* 1 (*He wrote in to claim his prize*) lay claim to, request, ask for, demand. 2 (*They claim that they had nothing to do with the crime*) assert, declare, maintain, profess, allege.

**clash** *vb* 1 (*The child clashed the cymbals*) strike, bang, clang, clatter, clank. 2 (*I have another appointment which clashes with my proposed meeting with you*) coincide, conflict. 3 (*One group of the committee clashed with the other*) be in conflict, have a disagreement, argue, quarrel, fight. 4 (*The curtains clashed horribly with the carpet*) jar, be incompatible, be discordant.

**class** *n* 1 (*what appeals to the working class*) social division. 2 (*The awards are divided into four classes*) grade, rank, level, classification, category, set, group. 3 (*a lot consisting of one class of objects*) category, group, set, order, sort, type, variety, species, genre, genus. 4 (*The two pupils are in the same class*) study group, grade.

**clean** *adj* 1 (*The children had no clean clothes*) unsoiled, spotless, laundered. 2 (*The village is in need of a clean water supply*) pure, clear, unpolluted, untainted, uncontaminated. 3 (*The student asked for a clean piece of paper*) unused, blank. 4 (*people who live clean lives*) good, virtuous, upright, honorable, righteous.

**clear** *adj* 1 (*It was clear that she was ill*) obvious, evident, plain, apparent, unmistakable. 2 (*You must try to give a clear account of what happened*) plain, explicit, lucid, coherent, intelligible. 3 (*We had a clear day for our flight*) bright, fair, fine, cloudless. 4 (*a door made of clear glass*) transparent. 5 (*You have to stay five clear days*) whole, complete, entire.

**clever** *adj* 1 (*He is a very clever student*) intelligent, bright, smart, gifted. 2 (*It was clever of them to open a new restaurant at that time*) smart, shrewd, astute, ingenious. 3 (*They are not very academic but they are clever with their hands*) skillful, deft, handy, dexterous.

**climate** *n* 1 (*a cold climate*) weather, weather pattern. 2 (*an unstable political climate*) atmosphere, feeling, mood, spirit.

**climb** *vb* (*The boy climbed the ladder*) go up, ascend, mount, scale, clamber up.

**cling** *vb* 1 (*She began to cling to her mother's hand*) hold on to, grip, clutch, grasp, clasp. 2 (*They tried to change her mind but she clings to her old beliefs*) stick to, hold to, stand by, adhere to.

**clip** *vb* (*She clipped her son's hair*) cut, trim, snip, crop, shear, prune.

**cloak** *n* 1 (*She wore a black evening cloak*) cape, mantle, shawl, wrap. 2 (*There was a cloak of secrecy surrounding the whole affair*) cover, screen, mask, mantle, veil, shield.

**clog** *vb* 1 (*They thought that it was leaves that were clogging up the drains*) block, obstruct, stop up. 2 (*The sheer volume of correspondence has clogged up the system*) obstruct, impede, hinder, hamper.

**close** *vb* 1 (*They were asked to close the gate*) shut, fasten, secure, lock, bolt. 2 (*They closed the meeting with the chairperson's speech*) end, bring to an end, conclude, finish, wind up. 3 (*The gap between the two runners closed*) narrow, lessen, grow less, dwindle. 4 (*They finally closed the bargain*) conclude, complete, settle, seal, clinch.

**close** *adj* 1 (*The houses were very close to each other*) near. 2 (*They have been close friends for years*) intimate, devoted, close-knit, bosom. 3 (*You must pay close attention to what she says*) careful, attentive, intense, assiduous. 4 (*She was able to give a close description of the man who attacked her*) exact, precise, accurate. 5 (*The weather was very close*) humid, muggy, stuffy, airless, oppressive. 6 (*The whole family is extremely close with money*) mean, miserly, parsimonious, stingy.

**clothing** *n* (*They washed all their clothing*) clothes, garments, attire, apparel.

**cloudy** *adj* 1 (*under cloudy skies*) overcast, hazy, gray, leaden, heavy. 2 (*The liquid in the glass was cloudy*) opaque, milky, murky, muddy. 3 (*Her vision is rather cloudy*) unclear, blurred, hazy.

**clumsy** *adj* 1 (*The antique chest is a clumsy piece of furniture*) awkward, unwieldy, hulking, heavy, solid. 2 (*The child is clumsy and is always bumping into things*) awkward, ungainly, uncoordinated, blundering, maladroit, (*inf*) klutzy.

**coarse** *adj* 1 (*The coat was made of a very coarse fabric*) rough, bristly, hairy, shaggy. 2 (*She prefers to bake with a coarse flour*) unrefined, unprocessed, crude. 3 (*They all have rather coarse features*) heavy, rugged. 4 (*He tells coarse jokes*) crude, vulgar, smutty, blue, dirty, bawdy, earthy, obscene, pornographic.

**coffee shop** *n* (*They met at the coffee shop*) diner, coffee bar, cafe, cafeteria, snack bar, restaurant.

**cold** *adj* 1 (*It was a cold winter's day*) chilly, cool, freezing, icy, raw, frosty, glacial.

2 (*The children were feeling cold*) chilly, freezing, frozen, frozen to the marrow, shivery. 3 (*She seems rather a cold woman/She received them with rather a cold manner*) frigid, unresponsive, unemotional, indifferent, apathetic, distant, remote, reserved, detached.

**collect** *vb* 1 (*The children were collecting firewood for a bonfire*) gather, accumulate, amass, pile up, stockpile, store, hoard. 2 (*They are collecting money for a children's charity*) gather, raise. 3 (*She collected the books from the library*) fetch, call for, go and get. 4 (*A crowd collected round the speaker*) gather, assemble, converge, congregate.

**collide** *vb* (*The cars collided*) crash, smash, bump.

**color** *n* 1 (*She has sweaters in several colors*) shade, hue, tint, tone. 2 (*people of different color*) skin-coloring, skintone, complexion, coloring. 3 (*The children were told to add a bit of color to their stories*) vividness, life, animation.

**combine** *vb* 1 (*They combined the ingredients*) mix, blend, amalgamate, bind. 2 (*They have combined their resources to open a restaurant*) join, put together, unite, pool, merge. 3 (*They have combined to form one team*) get together, join forces, team up, club together, cooperate, associate, amalgamate, merge.

**comfort** *n* 1 (*They were poor but they now live in comfort*) ease, coziness, snugness, well-being, affluence. 2 (*They tried to bring some comfort to the widow*) solace, consolation, condolence, sympathy, support. 3 (*The children were a comfort to their mother*) solace, help, support.

**comic** *adj* (*It was a comic situation*) funny, amusing, entertaining, diverting, droll, hilarious, farcical.

**command** *vb* 1 (*The king commanded them to go*) order, direct, instruct, bid. 2 (*He commands the force*) be in command of, be in charge of, control, rule, govern, direct, preside over, head, lead, manage.

**comment** *n* (*He made comments on how ill she was looking*) remark, observation, statement, view.

**commercial** *adj* 1 (*He has undertaken a commercial training*) business, trade, marketing. 2 (*The seaside village is becoming too commercial*) money-oriented, profit-oriented, mercenary, materialistic. 3 (*His business idea was not a commercial one*) profit-making, profitable.

**commitment** *n* 1 (*She has a great commitment to her job*) dedication, devotion, involvement. 2 (*He had many financial commitments*) responsibility, obligation, undertaking, duty, liability.

**common** *adj* 1 (*Fighting in the street is com-*

mon there) usual, ordinary, everyday, regular, frequent, customary, habitual, standard, routine, commonplace, run-of-the-mill, traditional. **2** (*There is a common belief that the place is haunted*) widespread, universal, general, prevalent, popular. **3** (*things that appeal to the common people*) ordinary, normal, average, typical, run-of-the-mill. **4** (*It was a very common type of watch*) ordinary, commonplace, unexceptional, undistinguished. **5** (*The politicians said that they were working for the common good*) communal, collective, public. **6** (*They regard her as a very common girl*) vulgar, coarse, uncouth, low.

**communicate** *vb* **1** (*They were unable to communicate the information back to headquarters*) pass on, convey, make known, impart, report, relay. **2** (*We do not communicate with them any more*) be in touch, be in contact, have dealings with. **3** (*In order to get a job in some industries it is important to be able to communicate*) be articulate, be fluent, be coherent, be eloquent.

**compatible** *adj* **1** (*The couple are just not compatible*) suited, well-suited, like-minded, in tune, having rapport. **2** (*The two accounts of the incident are not at all compatible*) in agreement, consistent, in keeping.

**compel** *vb* (*They plan to compel him to go*) force, make, coerce, oblige, dragoon, pressure.

**compete** *vb* **1** (*Will they all compete in the race?*) take part, participate, go in for, be a competitor, be a contestant. **2** (*The two brothers are competing against each other in the final*) vie, contend.

**competent** *adj* (*They are very competent workers*) capable, able, proficient, efficient, skillful.

**complaint** *n* **1** (*They made a complaint about the standard of the food*) protest, criticism, grievance. **2** (*Nothing ever pleases them—they are full of complaints*) grumble, (*inf*) grouse, (*inf*) gripe. **3** (*He has a stomach complaint*) illness, disease, disorder, ailment.

**complete** *vb* (*They failed to complete the job on time*) bring to completion, finish, conclude, accomplish, fulfill, achieve, execute, perform.

**complete** *adj* **1** (*He has the complete set of books*) whole, entire, full, total, intact, unbroken. **2** (*They think that she is a complete fool*) absolute, utter, thorough, thoroughgoing, total, outand-out.

**complicated** *adj* (*It is a very complicated problem*) difficult, involved, complex, puzzling, perplexing.

**compose** *vb* **1** (*The children were asked to compose a poem*) make up, think up, create,

concoct, invent, produce. **2** (*She was upset but tried to compose herself*) calm, calm down, quiet, control.

**comprehend** *vb* **1** (*The young students were unable to comprehend the scientific information*) understand, grasp, fathom, take in. **2** (*We cannot comprehend how they could behave like that*) understand, imagine, conceive, fathom, perceive, get to the bottom of.

**comprehensive** *adj* (*His knowledge of the subject is quite comprehensive*) inclusive, thorough, extensive, exhaustive, full, broad, widespread.

**compulsory** *adj* (*Attendance at the meeting is compulsory*) obligatory, mandatory, forced, essential, de rigueur.

**conceal** *vb* **1** (*She concealed the papers under her mattress*) hide, keep hidden, cover up, secrete, tuck away. **2** (*They tried to conceal their fears*) hide, cover up, disguise, mask.

**conceited** *adj* (*She is so conceited that she spends ages looking in the mirror*) vain, proud, arrogant, haughty, immodest, egotistical, (*inf*) bigheaded.

**concern** *n* **1** (*We were full of concern for the safety of the missing children*) worry, anxiety, distress, apprehension. **2** (*The news was of concern to all parents*) interest, importance, relevance. **3** (*They were told that it was none of their concern*) business, affair, interest, responsibility, job, duty. **4** (*They are partners in a manufacturing concern*) business, firm, company, establishment.

**concise** *adj* (*a concise report that gave all the main points*) brief, short, succinct, terse, crisp, to the point.

**conclude** *vb* **1** (*We concluded the talks at midnight*) finish, end, close. **2** (*We were unable to conclude an agreement with the other side*) negotiate, bring about, pull off, clinch. **3** (*We were forced to conclude that the witness was lying*) come to the conclusion, deduce, gather, assume, suppose.

**condemn** *vb* **1** (*We condemned them for injuring children*) blame, censure, criticize, disapprove of, upbraid. **2** (*The murderer was condemned to death*) sentence.

**condition** *n* **1** (*housing conditions*) state, situation, circumstances, position. **2** (*The horses were in good condition*) form, shape, order, fitness, health. **3** (*They were allowed to rent the land but with certain conditions*) restriction, proviso, provision, stipulation, prerequisite, stipulation. **4** (*The old lady has a heart condition*) complaint, disorder, disease, illness, ailment, problem.

**conduct** *n* **1** (*The teacher reported the child's conduct to his parents*) behavior, actions. **2**

(*Their conduct of the economy was criticized*) direction, organization, management, control.

**confess** *vb* **1** (*She confessed when she heard that her friend was being blamed for the crime*) own up, admit guilt, plead guilty, accept blame, make a clean breast of it. **2** (*I must confess that I know nothing about it*) admit, acknowledge, concede, allow, grant.

**confidence** *n* **1** (*The people have no confidence in the government*) trust, faith, reliance. **2** (*competitors full of confidence*) self-confidence, self-assurance, poise, aplomb. **3** (*The girls exchanged confidences*) secret, private affair.

**conflict** *n* **1** (*There has been conflict between the neighbors for years*) disagreement, discord, dissension, friction, strife, hostility, ill will. **2** (*the conflict between love and duty*) clash, friction. **3** (*There were many killed in the military conflict*) battle, fight, war, clash.

**confuse** *vb* **1** (*All the questions confused the child*) bewilder, puzzle, perplex, muddle. **2** (*His remarks just confused the situation*) muddle, mix up, jumble, obscure, make unclear. **3** (*The old man became confused in old age*) muddle, disorient, befuddle. **4** (*She confused the two books which looked alike*) mix up, mistake.

**congratulate** *vb* (*We congratulated them on the birth of their son*) wish joy to, offer good wishes to, compliment, felicitate.

**connect** *vb* **1** (*The gardener connected the hose to the faucet*) attach, fasten, join, secure, clamp, couple. **2** (*Only a path connects the two mountain villages*) link, join, unite. **3** (*The child connects his mother with security*) associate, link, equate, identify.

**connection** *n* **1** (*There is no connection between the crimes*) relationship, link, association, correspondence. **2** (*They had a meeting in connection with staff redundancies*) reference, relation. **3** (*one of her husband's connections*) relative, relation, kindred.

**conscientious** *adj* (*conscientious workers*) careful, diligent, painstaking, hard-working, assiduous, meticulous, punctilious.

**consequence** *n* **1** (*unable to foresee the consequences of their actions*) result, effect, upshot, outcome, repercussion. **2** (*It was a matter of no consequence*) importance, significance, note.

**considerate** *adj* (*She has very considerate children*) thoughtful, attentive, concerned, solicitous, obliging, kind, sympathetic.

**consistent** *adj* (*keep the room at a consistent temperature*) uniform, steady, constant, unchanging.

**conspicuous** *adj* **1** (*There had been conspicuous alterations to the city*) obvious, clear, noticeable, evident, apparent, discernible, visible. 2 (*Her clothes were conspicuous by their bright colors*) obvious, striking, obtrusive, blatant, showy.

**constant** *adj* 1 (*keep it at a constant temperature*) uniform, even, regular, steady, stable, unchanging, invariable. 2 (*We have had a constant stream of inquiries*) continuous, uninterrupted, unbroken. 3 (*tired of her constant complaints*) neverending, nonstop, endless, unending, incessant, continual, perpetual, interminable. 4 (*He was constant in his love for her*) faithful, devoted, staunch, loyal, true.

**contact** *vb* (*They tried to contact her parents*) get in touch with, communicate with, be in communication with.

**container** *n* (*containers to transport the food*) receptacle, vessel.

**content** *adj* (*He is quite content with his life*) contented, satisfied, pleased, happy, comfortable.

**contest** *n* (*the competitors in the contest*) competition, tournament, match, game.

**continual** *adj* 1 (*tired of their continual questions*) frequent, regular, repeated, recurrent, persistent, habitual. 2 (*There was continual noise from their apartment*) continuous, endless, nonstop, incessant, constant, interminable.

**continue** *vb* 1 (*The road continues beyond the village*) go on, extend, keep on, carry on. 2 (*He may continue as chairman*) go on, carry on, stay, remain, persist. 3 (*We continued the search all night*) maintain, sustain, prolong, protract. 4 (*They continued looking for the ring*) go on,-carry on, keep on, persist in, persevere in. 5 (*They stopped the search overnight but continued it at dawn*) resume, renew, recommence, carry on with.

**continuous** *adj* (*They have a continuous supply of fuel/upset by the continuous traffic noise*) constant, uninterrupted, unbroken, nonstop, endless, perpetual, incessant, unceasing, interminable, unremitting.

**contract** *n* (*a business contract*) agreement, arrangement, deal, settlement, pact, bargain, transaction.

**contrast** *n* 1 (*the contrast between the two styles of government*) difference, dissimilarity, distinction, disparity. 2 (*He is a complete contrast to his father*) opposite, antithesis.

**contribute** *vb* 1 (*They were all asked to contribute to the charity*) give, give a contribution, donate, give a donation to, subscribe to, help, give assistance to, assist, aid, support. 2 (*His leadership contributed to the success of the company*) add to, help, assist, have a hand in, be conducive to, be instrumental in.

**control** *vb* 1 (*It is she who controls the budget of the company*) be in control of, be in charge of, manage, administrate, direct, govern, head. 2 (*The firefighters could not control the fire*) contain, keep in check, curb, limit.

**convenient** *adj* 1 (*select a time convenient for both of us*) suitable, appropriate, fitting, favorable, advantageous. 2 (*houses convenient for schools*) handy, within-reach, within easy reach, accessible.

**convert** *vb* 1 (*We converted the attic into another bedroom*) alter, adapt, make into, turn into, change into,-transform. 2 (*convert pounds into dollars*) change, exchange. 3-(*The missionary converted the tribesmen to Christianity*) cause to change beliefs, reform, convince of.

**convict** *n* (*The convict escaped*) prisoner, jailbird, criminal, felon, (*inf*) crook.

**convincing** *adj* 1 (*Her argument seemed very convincing*) persuasive, plausible, credible, cogent, powerful. 2 (*Our team had a convincing victory*) decisive, conclusive.

**cool** *adj* 1 (*The weather was rather cool*) cold, chilly, fresh. 2 (*They wanted a cool drink*) cold, refreshing. 3 (*people who can remain cool in an emergency*) calm, composed, selfpossessed, unexcited, unruffled, unperturbed. 4 (*She was rather cool when we went to see her*) aloof, distant, remote, offhand, unfriendly, chilly, unresponsive, apathetic. 5 (*They were amazed at the cool way she stole the goods from the store*) bold, audacious, brazen, impudent.

**cope** *vb* 1 (*He found it difficult to cope when his wife died*) manage, carry on, get by, get along. 2 (*He had to cope with the money problems*) deal with, handle, contend with, manage.

**copy** *n* 1 (*give out copies of the report at the meeting*) duplicate, facsimile, photocopy, xerox (*trademark*), photostat (*trademark*). 2 (*It was not the original vase but a clever copy*) reproduction, replica, fake, sham, counterfeit. 3 (*buy several copies of the newspaper*) issue, example.

**correct** *adj* 1 (*That is not the correct answer*) right, accurate, true, precise, exact. 2 (*What is the correct behavior on such an occasion?*) proper, suitable, fitting, seemly, appropriate, apt, accepted, usual.

**cost** *vb* 1 (*How much does a car like that cost?*) be priced at, sell for, come to, fetch. 2 (*You should get the mechanic to cost the repairs for you*) price, put a price on, estimate, evaluate.

**count** *vb* 1 (*students asked to count the row of numbers*) count up, add up, total, calculate, compute. 2 (*Could you count the people as they enter the hall?*) keep a count of, keep a tally of, enumerate. 3 (*What he thinks does not count*) matter, be important, be of account, mean anything. 4

(*They counted themselves fortunate to have somewhere to live*) consider, deem, regard, look upon, think, judge.

**counterfeit** *adj* (*counterfeit bills*) fake, forged, fraudulent, sham, bogus, (*inf*) phony.

**country** *n* 1 (*all the countries of the world*) nation, state, realm. 2 (*He would do anything for his country*) native land, homeland, fatherland, mother country. 3 (*They left the city to live in the country*) countryside, rural area. 4 (*The government should listen to what the country thinks*) public, general public, people, nation, population. 5 (*The country around there is very flat*) land, terrain, territory.

**courage** *n* (*the courage of the soldiers in battle*) bravery, valor, gallantry, heroism, boldness, daring.

**course** *n* 1 (*in the course of a varied career*) progress, progression, development. 2 (*The ship was a bit off course*) route, way, track, direction, path, tack, orbit. 3 (*You should try a different course of action*) method, procedure, process, system, technique. 4 (*The car disappeared in the-course of a few minutes*) duration, passage, lapse, period, interval, span. 5 (*The race was canceled as the course was flooded*) track, circuit.

**courtesy** *n* (*She showed a lack of courtesy towards elderly people*) politeness, civility, good manners, respect, deference.

**cover** *n* 1 (*There was a cover of snow over the ground*) covering, layer, coat, blanket, carpet, mantle, film. 2 (*They sought cover from the storm*) shelter, protection, refuge, sanctuary. 3 (*His business is just a cover for his drug-dealing*) smoke screen, cover-up, concealment, disguise, pretext, camouflage, mask, cloak, veil. 4 (*The insurance policy provides cover against fire and theft*)-insurance, protection, compensation. 5 (*the design on the cover of the book*) dust jacket, wrapper. 6 (*pull up the covers over the sleeping child*) bedclothes, blankets, quilt.

**cowardly** *adj* (*He is too cowardly to complain*) timid, timorous, fearful, fainthearted, lily-livered, (*inf*) yellow, (*inf*) chicken.

**cozy** *adj* (*a cozy room*) snug, comfortable, homely, secure.

**crack** *n* 1 (*There is a crack in this cup*) chip, chink. 2 (*There are several cracks in the wall*) fracture, split, crevice, slit. 3 (*The crack on the head made him pass out*) blow, knock, bump, smack, whack, thump, wallop. 3 (*They heard the crack of a pistol*) report, bang.

**crash** *vb* 1 (*The cymbals crashed*) clash, clang, clank, clatter, bang. 2 (*The car crashed into the wall*) bang into, bump into, hit, collide with. 3-(*His son crashed his car*) smash, wreck, write off. 4 (*The chimney crashed* on to the sidewalk) topple, fall, plunge, tumble. **5** (*They listened to the sea crashing against the ship*) dash, batter, smash, break. **6** (*Their business crashed*) fail, collapse, fold, go under, go to the wall.

**credit** *n* **1** (*He received little credit for a fine performance*) praise, commendation, acclaim, tribute, applause, recognition. **2** (*The famous artist was regarded as being a credit to the town*) honor, asset, glory. **3**-(*His credit is not good*) financial standing, solvency.

**creep** *vb* **1** (*creatures that creep along the ground*) crawl, slither, wriggle. **2** (*They began creeping up on the burglar*) steal, sneak, slink, tiptoe.

**crime** *n* **1** (*He was convicted of the crime of theft*) offense, misdeed, wrong, misdemeanor, felony. **2** (*Crime is on the increase*) law-breaking, wrongdoing, felony, evil, vice.

**criticize** *vb* (*She is always criticizing him*) find fault with, blame, censure, pick holes in, (*inf*) nitpick.

**crooked** *adj* **1** (*a crooked stick*) bent, curved, twisted. **2** (*The old man had a crooked back*) deformed, misshapen. **3** (*That picture is crooked*) tilted, at an angle, askew, slanted, sloping. **4** (*They think that he is a crooked salesman*) dishonest, dishonorable, unscrupulous, fraudulent.

**cross** *adj* **1** (*Their mother was cross at the children's naughtiness*) angry, annoyed, irritated, vexed. **2** (*She is-a-cross old woman who is always-shouting at the neighborhood children*) irritable, short-tempered, bad-tempered, ill-humored, disagreeable, surly, crotchety, cantankerous.

**crush** *vb* **1** (*The workers crushed the grapes*) squash, squeeze, compress. **2** (*They crushed the stones*) break up, smash, pulverize, ground, pound. **3** (*Sitting so long had crushed her dress*) crease, crumple, rumple, wrinkle, crinkle. **3** (*The army crushed the rebellion*) quell, quash, suppress, subdue, put down, stamp out, overpower.

**cry** *vb* **1** (*The children began to cry-for their mothers*) weep, shed tears, sob, wail. **2** (*She cried out in pain*) call out, shout out, yell, scream.

**cure** *n* (*trying to find a cure for cancer*) remedy, treatment, panacea.

**curious** *adj* **1** (*We are curious to hear-what happens at the meeting*) interested. **2** (*She is always curious about the affairs of her neighbors*) inquisitive, prying, meddlesome, snooping, (*inf*) nosy. **3** (*It was a curious sight*) odd, strange, unusual, peculiar, weird, bizarre, mysterious.

**current** *adj* **1** (*the current fashion for-pale-colored clothes*) present, present-day, contemporary, existing, modern. **2** (*Those*

traditions are no longer current) around, prevalent, common, general, popular.

**curved** *adj* (*a curved stick/a curved back*) bent, arched, bowed, crooked, rounded, humped.

**custom** *n* **1** (*The local customs are dying out*) tradition, practice, convention, ritual. **2** (*It was his custom to go for a walk before breakfast*) habit, practice, routine, wont, way. **3** (*He is grateful for their custom*) trade, business, patronage.

**customer** *n* (*stores trying to attract new-customers*) client, patron, buyer, shopper, consumer.

**cut** *vb* **1** (*cut the meat into cubes*) cut up, chop, divide, carve, slice. **2** (*He cut his finger with a razor blade*) wound, gash, slash, pierce. **3** (*She cut her son's hair*) trim, clip, crop, snip, prune, shear. **4**-(*The firm must cut its expenditure*) cut back on, reduce, decrease, curtail, slash. **5** (*The essay is too long—you must cut it*) shorten, abridge, condense, abbreviate. **6** (*She cut some paragraphs from the article*) cut out, delete, excise. **7** (*The driver cut the engine*) switch off, turn-off.

**cynical** *adj* (*She is cynical about our chances of success/They are very cynical people*) pessimistic, skeptical, doubting, distrustful, suspicious.

# D

**dagger** *n* (*He killed his enemy with his dagger*) stiletto, poniard, dirk, knife.

**dainty** *adj* **1** (*a dainty little girl*) petite, neat, graceful. **2** (*dainty china cups*) delicate, fine, exquisite.

**damage** *n* **1** (*There was a great deal of damage to his car*) harm, destruction, accident, ruin, impairment. **2** (*The incident caused damage to his reputation*) harm, injury, hurt, detriment, loss, suffering.

**damp** *adj* **1** (*They hung up their damp clothes to dry*) wet, soaking, sopping. **2** (*The ground was damp*) wet, soggy. **3** (*It was a damp day*) wet, rainy, drizzly, humid, muggy.

**danger** *n* **1** (*There was an element of danger in the job*) peril, jeopardy, risk, hazard. **2** (*pollution is a danger to lives*) risk, menace, threat, peril.

**dangerous** *adj* **1** (*They were in a dangerous situation*) risky, perilous, hazardous, precarious, insecure. **2** (*The police say that he is dangerous*) threatening, menacing, alarming, nasty.

**dare** *vb* **1** (*He did not dare climb the high tree*) have the courage, pluck up courage, have the nerve, risk, venture. **2** (*His friends dared him to jump from the high wall*) challenge, throw down the gauntlet. **3**

(*They dared their father's anger to go to the nightclub*) defy, brave, face, confront.

**daring** *adj* (*a daring deed/a daring fellow*) bold, adventurous, brave, courageous, plucky, reckless, rash.

**dark** *adj* **1** (*It was a very dark night*) black, pitch dark, pitch black, inky, dim, murky, unlit. **2** (*She has dark hair*) dark brown, black, jet-black, sable. **3** (*They lived in the dark ages*) unenlightened, ignorant, uneducated, uncultivated, uncultured. **4** (*dark, dingy rooms*) gloomy, dismal, drab, dim, dingy, bleak, dreary, cheerless. **5** (*She was in a dark mood*) gloomy, depressed, morose.

**dawdle** *n* (*They dawdled on their way to school*) dally, loiter, linger, delay, tarry.

**day** *n* **1** (*She doesn't mind driving during the day*) daylight, daytime. **2** (*in this modern day*) time, age, era, epoch.

**dead** *adj* **1** (*Her father is dead/the dead man*) deceased, departed, lifeless, gone. **2** (*dead village traditions*) extinct, gone, perished. **3** (*dead matter*) without life, lifeless, inanimate. **4** (*Her fingers were dead with cold*) numb, benumbed, without feeling. **5** (*The small town is dead at-night*) boring, dull, uneventful, unexciting.

**deadly** *adj* **1** (*He drank a deadly poison*) fatal, lethal, toxic, poisonous. **2**-(*He was struck a deadly blow*) fatal, mortal, lethal, dangerous, death-dealing, terminal. **3** (*They were deadly enemies*) fierce, hostile, grim, hated.

**deaf** *adj* **1** (*The accident left him deaf*) with impaired hearing, stone deaf, as deaf as a post. **2** (*They were deaf to her pleas*) indifferent, unmoved by, oblivious to, heedless of.

**deal** *vb* **1** (*She was unable to deal with the problem*) cope with, handle, attend to, sort out, tackle, manage. **2** (*They need a book that deals with the early history of the town*) be about, have to do with, concern, discuss. **3** (*He does not know how to deal with children*) act towards, behave towards, cope with, manage. **4** (*He was asked to deal the cards*) distribute, give out, share out, divide out, dole out. **5** (*They dealt him a fatal blow*) give, deliver, administer.

**deal** *n* **1** (*a business deal*) arrangement, agreement, transaction, contract, pact. **2** (*He did not get a fair deal*) treatment, usage.

**dear** *adj* **1** (*He lost his dear wife*) beloved, loved, darling, cherished. **2** (*She was a dear child*) sweet, adorable, lovable, darling, attractive, winning, enchanting. **3** (*It was a dear car*) expensive, costly, high-priced, valuable, exorbitant.

**death** *n* **1** (*Death was caused by strangling*) dying, demise, decease, loss of life, passing away, killing, murder, slaughter. **2**

(*There were many deaths in the flu epidemic*) fatality, dead people. **3** (*The close of the firm marked the death of his hopes*) end, finish, cessation, destruction, ruin, annihilation.

**decay** *vb* **1** (*The food had begun to decay*) go bad, rot, decompose, putrefy, spoil. **2** (*The Roman empire decayed*) decline, degenerate, deteriorate, wane, ebb.

**deceitful** *adj* **1** (*She is a very deceitful-child*) lying, untruthful, dishonest,-false, insincere, untrustworthy, underhand. **2** (*He got into the house-by deceitful means*) underhand, fraudulent, crooked, dishonest, cheating, crafty, sneaky.

**deceive** *vb* (*His friends did not realize that he was deceiving them*) delude, mislead, take in, hoodwink, pull the wool over (*someone's*) eyes, swindle, dupe.

**decent** *adj* **1** (*He seemed a decent enough fellow*) honest, honorable, trustworthy, worthy, civil. **2** (*Her behavior was not considered decent*) seemly, proper, appropriate, decorous, pure. **3** (*He earns a decent salary*) reasonable, ample, good, adequate, sufficient.

**decide** *vb* **1** (*They decided to stay*) come to a decision, reach a decision, make up one's mind, resolve, commit oneself. **2** (*That decided the matter*) settle, resolve, determine. **3** (*The judge will decide the case*) judge, make a judgment on, make a ruling on, give a verdict.

**decision** *n* **1** (*They finally reached a decision*) resolution, conclusion, determination, settlement. **2** (*The judge will announce his decision*) judgment, verdict, ruling. **3** (*He is a man of decision*) decisiveness, determination, resolution, resolve, firmness.

**decisive** *adj* **1** (*Her personality was the decisive factor in her getting the job*) deciding, determining, conclusive, critical, crucial. **2** (*They need someone decisive in charge of the firm*) determined, resolute, firm, forceful.

**decline** *vb* **1** (*They declined the invitation*) turn down, refuse, say no to. **2** (*The influence of the leader has declined*) get less, lessen, decrease, diminish, dwindle, fade. **3** (*The Roman empire was declining then*) deteriorate, degenerate.

**decorate** *vb* **1** (*They decorated the Christmas tree*) adorn, ornament, embellish, trim. **2** (*They have begun to decorate the house*) paint, paper, renovate. **3** (*The soldier was decorated for bravery*) honor, give a medal to, cite.

**decrease** *vb* **1** (*The number of the pupils at the school is decreasing*) grow less, lessen, diminish, dwindle, drop, fall off, decline. **2** (*They have decreased the number of places available at the school*) reduce, lower, lessen, cut back, curtail. **3**-(*The

storm finally decreased*) die down, abate, subside.

**deed** *n* **1** (*a dishonest deed*) act, action, feat, exploit, undertaking, enterprise. **2** (*The deeds to the house*) document, contract, title deed.

**deep** *adj* **1** (*They dug a deep hole in the sand*) yawning, cavernous. **2** (*They have a deep affection for each other*) intense, fervent, ardent, heartfelt. **3** (*He has a deep distrust of doctors*) profound, extreme, intense, great. **4** (*He has a very deep voice*) low, low-pitched, bass, booming, resonant. **5** (*She always wears clothes in deep colors*) rich, strong, vivid, intense, dark.

**defeat** *vb* **1** (*The army finally defeated the enemy*) beat, conquer, vanquish, win a victory over, get the better of, overcome, rout. **2** (*The motion in the debate was defeated*) reject, overthrow, throw out, outvote.

**defect** *n* **1** (*a defect in the material*) fault, flaw, imperfection, blemish. **2** (*They tried to find the defects in the system*) deficiency, weakness, shortcoming, failing, inadequacy, snag.

**defense** *n* **1** (*Walls built as a defense for the house*) protection, safeguard, guard, security, cover, fortification,-barricade. **2** (*a report in defense of the system*) justification, vindication, argument, apology, exoneration.

**defer** *vb* (*They had to defer the date of the meeting*) put off, postpone, delay, hold over, adjourn.

**deficiency** *n* **1** (*She suffers from vitamin deficiency*) lack, want, shortage, dearth, insufficiency, scarcity, deficit. **2** (*It was the only deficiency in the system*) defect, flaw, fault, imperfection, failing, shortcoming, drawback, snag.

**definite** *adj* **1** (*They have no definite plans*) clear-cut, fixed, established, precise, specific, particular. **2** (*It is not definite that he is leaving*) certain, sure, settled, decided, fixed.

**defy** *vb* **1** (*They decided to defy their parents and go to the movies*) disobey, disregard, ignore. **2** (*The army defied the enemy*) withstand, resist, stand up to, brave, confront.

**degree** *n* **1** (*There was a marked degree of improvement in her work*) extent, amount, level, measure. **2**-(*The dancers reached a high degree of expertise*) level, stage, grade, point.

**dejected** *adj* (*She was feeling dejected after her friends left*) miserable, wretched, downcast, depressed, sad, despondent.

**delay** *vb* **1** (*We have had to delay our vacation*) postpone, put off, put back, defer, adjourn, put on ice. **2** (*They were delayed by heavy traffic*) hold up, hold

back, detain, hinder, impede, hamper, obstruct.

**deliberate** *adj* (*His murder was quite deliberate*) intentional, on purpose, planned, calculated, prearranged, premeditated.

**delicate** *adj* **1** (*She was very delicate as a child*) weak, frail, sickly, unwell, infirm. **2** (*cups made of delicate china*) fine, exquisite, fragile, thin. **3** (*It was a very delicate matter*) difficult, sensitive, tricky. **4** (*The situation required delicate handling*) careful, tactful, discreet, diplomatic.

**delicious** *adj* (*They serve delicious food at the restaurant*) tasty, flavorful, flavorsome, appetizing, luscious, (*inf*) scrumptious.

**delight** *n* (*She was filled with delight at seeing her friend again*) joy, pleasure, gladness, happiness.

**delightful** *adj* **1** (*We had a delightful evening at the theater*) pleasant, enjoyable, entertaining, amusing, diverting. **2** (*She is a delightful person*) charming, engaging, attractive, nice.

**deliver** *vb* **1** (*He delivers morning newspapers*) distribute, bring, take round. **2** (*They delivered the little girl to her mother*) hand over, convey, present. **3** (*She delivered a moving speech/deliver a sigh of relief*) give, give voice to, utter, speak, express, pronounce. **4** (*They were able to deliver the prisoners*) free, set free, liberate, release.

**demand** *vb* **1** (*The workers demanded a wage rise*) call for, ask for, request, press for, insist on, clamor for. **2** (*The work demanded patience*) call for, require, need, take, involve.

**demanding** *adj* (*They have very demanding jobs*) difficult, taxing, exacting, hard, tough.

**demolish** *vb* (*They began to demolish the old buildings*) knock down, tear down, pull down, level, flatten, raze, dismantle.

**demonstrate** *vb* **1** (*She demonstrated how to change an electric plug*) show, illustrate, teach, explain. **2** (*Her expression demonstrated how she was feeling*) show, indicate, display, exhibit, manifest. **3** (*The documents demonstrated that she was telling the truth*) show, establish, prove, confirm, verify. **4** (*They planned to demonstrate against the new road*) protest, stage a protest.

**dense** *adj* **1** (*They were lost in a dense forest*) thick, close-packed, impenetrable. **2** (*He was too dense to follow the instructions*) stupid, thick, dim, slow.

**deny** *vb* **1** (*He began to deny that he had said it*) contradict, refute, retract, negate, disagree with. **2** (*The committee might deny their request*) refuse, reject, turn down, decline, dismiss.

**depart** *vb* **1** (*We have to depart at dawn*) leave, go, take one's leave, take oneself off, set out, start out, (*inf*) make tracks. **2** (*results that depart from the norm*) deviate, diverge, differ, vary.

**depend** *vb* **1** (*The firm depends on him to look after the place*) rely on, count on, bank on, lean on, put one's faith in. **2** (*The success of the business will depend on the order*) be dependent on, hinge on, turn on, hang on, rest on, revolve around.

**deport** *vb* (*They decided to deport the refugees*) banish, expel, exile, evict, transport, extradite, expatriate.

**depreciate** *vb* (*The houses have depreciated in value*) decrease, lessen, lower.

**depressed** *adj* (*He was feeling depressed having lost his job*) miserable, downcast, low in spirits, melancholy, gloomy, glum, dejected, sad, unhappy.

**depth** *n* **1** (*measure the depth of the water*) deepness. **2** (*It was a book of great depth*) profundity, wisdom, insight, understanding, weight, importance.

**deprived** *adj* (*deprived children brought up in poverty*) poor, needy, in want, disadvantaged.

**derelict** *adj* (*derelict farmhouses*) dilapidated, tumbledown, run-down, ramshackle, broken-down, abandoned, forsaken.

**descend** *vb* **1** (*She descended the stairs gracefully*) come down, go down, climb down. **2** (*The hot air balloon descended*) go down, come down, drop, fall, sink, plummet. **3** (*They descended from the train with their baggage*) get off, get down, alight, dismount.

**describe** *vb* **1** (*He was asked to describe the incident*) give a description of, give an account of, give details of, recount, relate, report, explain, tell about, narrate. **2** (*They have described her as beautiful*) call, label, designate.

**desert** *vb* **1** (*a man who had deserted his family*) abandon, forsake, leave, turn one's back on, leave in the lurch, throw over. **2** (*The army are looking for the soldiers who deserted*) abscond, run away, quit, defect.

**deserve** *vb* (*He deserves reward*) merit, be worthy of, warrant, rate, be entitled to, have a claim on.

**design** *n* **1** (*The architect showed the committee the designs for the new building*) plan, blueprint, sketch, drawing, outline. **2** (*The fabric designs are very modern*) pattern, motif, style. **3** (*It was a cunning design to break into the building*) plan, scheme, plot, stratagem, aim. **4** (*They did it with the design of stealing money*) aim, intention, goal, objective, purpose.

**desire** *vb* **1** (*She desires some comfort in her old age*) wish, want, long for, yearn for, crave, covet, hanker after, (*inf*) have a

yen for. **2** (*They desire to leave at once*) wish, want, feel like.

**desolate** *adj* **1** (*on the edge of a desolate territory*) bare, barren, bleak, wild. **2** (*an area full of desolate farms*) deserted, forsaken, solitary, lonely, isolated. **3** (*She was desolate when he went away*) miserable, wretched, sad, unhappy, dejected, forlorn, lonely.

**despair** *vb* (*He has despaired of ever getting a job*) lose hope, give up hope, lose heart, be discouraged, give up, throw in the towel.

**desperate** *adj* **1** (*It was a desperate attempt to save the town*) daring, risky, hazardous, wild, reckless, rash, imprudent. **2** (*Some desperate criminals have escaped*) wild, violent, lawless, reckless. **3** (*They are in desperate need of more food*) urgent, pressing, critical, crucial, serious, dire, great. **4** (*They are desperate for money*) in great need of, in want of. **5** (*The family is in a desperate state*) dreadful, shocking, appalling, deplorable, intolerable. **6** (*help required for desperate people*) despairing, hopeless, despairing, distressed, wretched.

**despise** *vb* (*She despises people who tell lies*) scorn, look down on, shun, disdain, sneer at, mock, hate, loathe.

**despondent** *adj* (*The pupil was despondent when she heard that she had failed the exam*) downcast, cast down, low in spirits, disheartened, discouraged, disappointed, gloomy, melancholy, wretched, miserable.

**destroy** *vb* (*The bridge was destroyed in the war*) demolish, knock down, pull down, tear down, wreck, smash, shatter, blow up, wipe out.

**detach** *vb* **1** (*She detached the hood from her coat*) unfasten, remove, separate, uncouple, free. **2** (*She detached herself from her group to join us*) move away from, separate, dissociate.

**detail** *n* **1** (*The police try to notice every detail at the scene of the crime*) particular, point, circumstance, feature, aspect. **2** (*draw up a general plan and not bother with the details*) particular, fine point, minutiae.

**detect** *vb* **1** (*They thought that they detected a smell of gas*) notice, note, make out, spot, identify, distinguish, sense, observe. **2** (*The police were detecting the crime*) investigate, probe.

**deter** *vb* (*They hope the stiff sentence will deter others from committing such a crime*) put off, prevent, stop, discourage, restrain, scare off.

**determined** *adj* **1** (*He is a very determined person and will probably win*) firm, resolute, tenacious, singleminded, strong-willed, dogged, persistent, stubborn, inflexible.

**2** (*They are determined to leave*) set on, intent on, bent on.

**detest** *vb* (*The rivals detest each other*) hate, loathe, abhor, feel aversion to, feel hostility to.

**detrimental** *adj* (*The incident was detrimental to his reputation*) injurious, harmful, damaging, hurtful, disadvantageous, destructive.

**develop** *vb* **1** (*children quickly developing into adults*) grow, turn, mature. **2** (*modern cities developing rapidly*) grow, expand, enlarge, spread, progress, evolve. **3** (*They are trying to develop a scheme for expansion*) originate, set in motion, establish, form, institute. **4** (*They have the beginnings of a plan but they have to develop it*) elaborate, work out, enlarge on, amplify, flesh out. **5** (*The child has developed a cough*) acquire, get, contract. **6** (*A quarrel developed between the two women*) begin, start, commence, happen, come about, break out.

**device** *n* **1** (*a handy device for use in the kitchen*) gadget, appliance, utensil, implement, tool, apparatus, contrivance, contraption. **2** (*They thought of a cunning device to get into the building*) ploy, ruse, trick, stratagem, scheme, dodge, plan.

**devil** *n* **1** (*a story about the devil and hell*) Satan, Beelzebub. **2** (*She dreamt that she was being pursued by devils*) demon, evil spirit, fiend. **3** (*The slave's master was a devil*) brute, savage, monster, beast, fiend, scoundrel, villain. **4** (*The child is a little devil*) imp, scamp, rascal, rogue.

**devious** *adj* (*They are very devious people/ They will get what they want only by devious means*) underhand, cunning, sly, crafty, wily, deceitful.

**devoted** *adj* **1** (*the religion's devoted followers*) loyal, faithful, true, staunch, dedicated, committed, constant. **2** (*time devoted to hobbies*) set aside, allocated, assigned, allotted.

**devout** *adj* **1** (*devout Christians*) pious, religious, godly, holy. **2** (*It was their devout hope that he would be present*) sincere, deep, profound, earnest, heartfelt, fervent, genuine.

**diagnose** *vb* (*The doctor diagnosed mumps*) identify, recognize, distinguish, detect, pronounce.

**dialogue** *n* (*a dialogue between the presidents*) conversation, talk, exchange of views, discussion, conference, tête à tête.

**die** *vb* **1** (*The doctors think that he is going to die*) pass away, breathe one's last, lose one's life, meet one's end, (*inf*) give up the ghost, (*inf*) kick the bucket, expire. **2** (*All hope died when they heard the news*) end, come to an end, vanish, disappear, pass, fade. **3** (*The car's engine died*) stop, fail, break down, peter out.

**differ** vb **1** (*Their tastes differ completely*) be different, be dissimilar, be unlike, vary, diverge. **2** (*The two sides still differ on the best course of action*) disagree, dissent, be at variance, be in dispute, be in conflict, clash, argue, quarrel. **3** (*The scientist's results differ from the norm*) vary, diverge, deviate, depart from, contradict.

**difference** n **1** (*There was marked difference between the two sisters*) dissimilarity, distinction, variation, contrast, disparity, incongruity. **2** (*They have had several differences over the years*) difference of opinion, disagreement, dispute, clash, argument, quarrel, row, altercation.

**different** adj **1** (*Their tastes in clothes-are very different*) dissimilar, unlike, at variance, contrasting. **2** (*With her new hairstyle she looks completely different*) changed, altered, transformed. **3** (*She wears a different sweater every day*) another, fresh. **4** (*The dress is available in different colors*) various, several, varied, assorted. **5** (*She was looking for something a bit different to wear to the wedding*) unusual, out of the ordinary, uncommon, distinctive, special, singular, extraordinary, rare.

**difficult** adj **1** (*Working on the building site was very difficult work*) hard, strenuous, arduous, demanding, taxing, laborious, tiring. **2** (*It is a difficult problem to solve*) hard, complicated, complex, involved, intricate, problematic, tough. **3** (*I felt that we had arrived at a difficult time*) inconvenient, ill-timed, unfavorable. **4** (*The family has gone through a difficult period*) hard, tough, distressing, grim. **5**-(*She has always been a difficult child*) troublesome, unmanageable, recalcitrant, intractable.

**dig** vb **1** (*dig the earth before planting potatoes*) break up, work, turn over, loosen. **2** (*The prisoners dug a tunnel to try to escape*) dig out, excavate, hollow out, gouge out, scoop out, burrow, mine. **3** (*She dug her friend in the ribs at the lecture to wake him up*) prod, jab, poke, push, elbow. **4** (*The newspaper reporter is trying to dig up facts about the politician's private life*) search, probe, investigate, research, delve.

**dignity** n **1** (*She was anxious not to lose her dignity in front of people*) pride, self-esteem, self-respect. **2**-(*the dignity of the procession*) stateliness, ceremoniousness, formality, decorum, majesty, grandeur, nobility.

**dilapidated** adj (*an area full of dilapidated houses*) run-down, tumbledown, broken-down, ramshackle, crumbling, in disrepair, decaying, neglected.

**diligent** adj (*diligent pupils studying hard in school*) conscientious, industrious, hard-working, assiduous, painstaking, studious, zealous.

**dim** adj **1** (*The light from the street lamps was dim*) faint, feeble, weak. **2** (*people frightened to walk along the dim corridors*) dark, gloomy, badly lit, dingy. **3** (*They saw a dim shape in the mist*) vague, indefinite, ill-defined, blurred, shadowy, fuzzy. **4** (*They have only a dim recollection of the incident*) vague, indistinct, hazy, blurred, confused. **5** (*He failed to understand because he is a bit dim*) stupid, dense, dumb, dull, slowwitted. **6** (*His prospects of getting a job are rather dim*) gloomy, unpromising, depressing, discouraging.

**dingy** adj (*They live in run-down dingy houses*) dim, dark, gloomy, dull, drab, murky, dirty, discolored, shabby.

**direct** adj **1** (*the direct route to the city*) straight, shortest. **2** (*a very direct manner/a direct statement*) frank, straightforward, blunt, forthright, clear, plain, candid, open.

**direction** n **1** (*They complained about his direction of the project*) administration, management, government, leadership, supervision, conduct, handling, control, guidance. **2** (*You must obey the teacher's directions*) order, command, instruction, directive, bidding. **3** (*The climbers have gone in the wrong direction*) route, way, course, path.

**dirt** n **1** (*They cleaned the dirt from their boots*) grime, mud, muck, filth, dust. **2** (*piles of dirt in the yard*) soil, earth, loam. **3** (*She complained about the dirt in some of the videos*) filth, obscenity, indecency, smut, pornography, bawdiness, lewdness, ribaldry. **4** (*She is given to spreading dirt about her neighbors*) scandal, slander, gossip.

**dirty** adj **1** (*Their boots were dirty*) unclean, soiled, grubby, grimy, muddy, mucky, filthy, dusty, messy, stained, polluted. **2** (*The toilets are dirty and are never cleaned*) filthy, unhygienic, unhealthy, contaminated, polluted. **3** (*He embarrassed her by telling dirty jokes*) filthy, obscene, indecent, blue, smutty, pornographic, bawdy, lewd, ribald. **4** (*That was a dirty trick*) nasty, unfair, dishonest, dishonorable, deceitful, underhand, fraudulent.

**disability** n (*help for people with some form of disability*) incapacity, learning difficulty, learning disability, infirmity, handicap.

**disadvantage** n **1** (*discover the disadvantages of the system*) drawback, snag, weak spot, weakness, flaw, defect, fault, handicap, obstacle, minus. **2** (*children who suffer from financial disadvantage*) deprivation, hardship. **3** (*The incident turned out to be to their disadvantage*) detriment, disservice, harm, damage, injury, hurt, loss.

**disadvantageous** adj (*The circumstances were disadvantageous to them*) unfavorable, adverse, unfortunate, detrimental, prejudicial, deleterious, damaging, injurious.

**disagree** vb **1** (*The two sides had talks but they still disagreed*) differ, diverge, be at variance, be at odds. **2** (*The police said that the stories of the witnesses disagreed*) differ, be dissimilar, be unlike, be different, vary, clash, conflict, diverge. **3** (*The children were always disagreeing*) argue, quarrel, bicker, wrangle.

**disagreeable** adj **1** (*It was a very disagreeable experience*) unpleasant, nasty, horrible, foul, dreadful, revolting. **2** (*He is a disagreeable old man*) bad-tempered, ill-natured, cross, irritable, surly, churlish, rude, nasty, unpleasant.

**disappear** vb **1** (*The sun disappeared behind the cloud*) vanish, recede, fade, retire, retreat. **2** (*traditions which have now disappeared*) die out, be no more, end, pass, fade, perish, become extinct.

**disappoint** vb **1** (*We hated to disappoint the children by canceling the picnic*) let down, dishearten, upset, sadden. **2** (*We had to disappoint their hopes*) thwart, frustrate, foil, baffle, hinder, obstruct, hamper, impede.

**disapprove** vb (*She disapproves of the young people's behavior*) find unacceptable, dislike, be against, be displeased by, frown on, blame.

**disaster** n **1** (*earthquakes and other natural disasters*) catastrophe, calamity, tragedy, mishap, setback, reversal. **2** (*The play was a disaster*) failure, flop.

**discard** vb (*discard old newspapers*) throw away, throw out, dispose of, jettison, scrap, dump.

**discharge** vb **1** (*The pipe was discharging a foul-smelling liquid*) give off, send out, emit, exude, excrete, ooze, leak. **2** (*Several workers were discharged*) dismiss, sack, get rid of, declare redundant, (*inf*) fire, (*inf*) axe. **3** (*She did not discharge her duties*) carry out, do, perform, execute. **4** (*He discharged a firearm*) let off, fire, shoot. **5** (*The prisoner has been discharged*) set free, free, release, let go, acquit, clear, reprieve.

**disclose** vb (*She finally disclosed her reasons for leaving*) make known, reveal, divulge, tell, communicate, impart.

**discomfort** n **1** (*She experiences some discomfort in her eye*) ache, pain, soreness, twinge, irritation, throbbing. **2** (*the discomfort of traveling long journeys in a very small car*) inconvenience, difficulty, trouble, bother, drawback.

**discordant** adj (*She has a discordant voice/discordant sounds*) harsh, strident, shrill, grating, jarring.

**discourage** vb **1** (*The young man was discouraged by failing his driver's test*) dishearten, dispirit, deject, depress, disappoint, demoralize. **2** (*They tried-to discourage* the girl from applying for the job) deter, dissuade, talk out of, advise against, restrain.

**discover** vb 1 (*The police discovered a new clue*) uncover, find, come across, bring to light, turn up, unearth. 2 (*The scientists have discovered a new cancer drug*) invent, devise, originate. 3 (*We discovered that he was very ill*) learn, find out, come to realize.

**discreet** adj (*behavior that was far from being discreet/a few discreet remarks*) careful, cautious, prudent, tactful, diplomatic, wise.

**discriminate** vb 1 (*Children should be taught to discriminate between right and wrong*) distinguish, differentiate, separate. 2 (*She said that her employers discriminated against women*) show prejudice towards, show bias towards, be biased towards.

**discuss** vb (*The committee discussed the problem*) talk about, confer about, debate, consider, deliberate.

**disease** n (*The old man is suffering from a brain disease*) illness, disorder, complaint, condition, malady, ailment.

**disgrace** n 1 (*He found it difficult to endure the disgrace of being in prison*) shame, humiliation, dishonor, degradation, ignominy. 2 (*The pupil is in disgrace for playing truant*) disfavor, discredit, disrepute.

**disgraceful** adj 1 (*Their behavior was disgraceful*) shameful, shameless, dishonorable, shocking, outrageous, unseemly, improper. 2 (*The pupil's work is disgraceful*) very bad, appalling, dreadful, terrible, shocking.

**disguise** vb 1 (*They disguised themselves as police officers*) dress up, camouflage. 2 (*He tried to disguise the scar on his face*) conceal, hide, cover up, mask, screen.

**disgust** vb 1 (*The thought of eating snails disgusts them*) revolt, repel, put off, sicken, nauseate, (*inf*) turn off. 2 (*They were disgusted by the behavior of the teenagers*) scandalize, shock, appall, outrage, offend.

**disheveled** adj (*They felt disheveled after their long journey*) untidy, unkempt, bedraggled, messy, tousled, (*inf*) mussed up.

**disinterested** adj 1 (*The judges of the competition must be disinterested*) unbiased, unprejudiced, impartial, detached, objective, neutral, fair.

**dismal** adj 1 (*feeling dismal because he was ill and had to stay in bed*) miserable, wretched, despondent, gloomy, sad, unhappy. 2 (*They plan to redecorate the dismal room*) dark, dim, dull, dingy, drab, dreary, bleak, cheerless.

**dismiss** vb (*He was dismissed from his job*) sack, give notice to, discharge, lay off, declare redundant, (*inf*) fire.

**disobey** vb (*They disobeyed the rules*) defy,

disregard, flout, contravene, infringe, violate.

**disorderly** adj 1 (*They tried to tidy the disorderly office*) untidy, messy, cluttered, disorganized, out of order, chaotic. 2 (*The police tried to control the disorderly crowds*) unruly, rowdy, boisterous, rough, wild, lawless, rebellious.

**display** vb 1 (*They displayed the goods in the store window*) exhibit, put on show, show, present, set out. 2 (*The young gymnasts displayed their expertise*) demonstrate, exhibit, show, show off, flaunt. 3 (*The accused displayed no emotion as he was sentenced by the judge*) show, exhibit, indicate, manifest, show evidence of, demonstrate.

**dispose:—dispose of** vb (*They disposed of the garbage by burying it*) get rid of, throw away, throw out, discard, jettison, scrap, dump.

**dispute** n (*The two friends had a dispute over money*) argument, quarrel, row, wrangle, clash, altercation, feud.

**disrupt** n (*The protesters disrupted the meaning*) disturb, interrupt, interfere with, obstruct, impede, hamper.

**dissolve** vb 1 (*Salt dissolves in water*) liquefy, melt. 2 (*They both dissolved in tears*) break into, be overcome by. 3 (*They have decided to dissolve their partnership*) end, terminate, break up, discontinue, wind up. 4 (*The crowds dissolved when the police arrived*) break up, split up, disband, separate, go their separate ways.

**distance** n 1 (*measure the distance between the two trees*) space, gap, interval, span, stretch. 2 (*They were concerned about the distance of the house from the town*) remoteness.

**distant** adj 1 (*The children like to hear stories of distant places*) far-off, remote, out of the way, outlying, farflung, faraway. 2 (*in distant times*) long ago, far-off. 3 (*The two villages are ten miles distant from each other*) away, apart, separate. 3 (*I have only a distant recollection of what happened*) dim, vague, faint, hazy, indistinct. 4 (*She is rather a distant person*) aloof, detached, remote, reserved, unfriendly, unsociable, uncommunicative, standoffish, unapproachable.

**distinct** adj 1 (*There was a distinct resemblance between the two crimes*) clear, clear-cut, plain, obvious, marked, definite, unmistakable, manifest, patent. 2 (*There are two distinct issues to be discussed*) separate, individual, different, disparate.

**distinguish** vb 1 (*He found it difficult to distinguish some colors from others*) tell apart, tell the difference between, differentiate, discriminate. 2 (*They thought that they could distinguish a dim shape in the mist*)

make out, detect, discern, notice, see, observe. 3 (*The soldier distinguished himself in the battle*) make famous, bring fame to, bestow honor on.

**distress** n 1 (*the child's distress on being separated from her parents*) suffering, pain, agony, misery, wretchedness, heartache, sorrow, sadness. 2 (*homeless people in distress*) hardship, adversity, misfortune, need, want, poverty, deprivation.

**distribute** vb 1 (*They distributed advertising leaflets on the street*) issue, pass out, pass round, circulate. 2 (*The teacher distributed books to the children*) give out, hand out, allocate, issue, allot, dispense.

**district** n (*They live in a district at the edge of the city*) area, region, place, locality, neighborhood, sector.

**disturb** vb 1 (*They don't like being disturbed when they are at work*) interrupt, distract, bother, trouble, pester, intrude on, interfere with, harass, (*inf*) hassle. 2 (*The cleaner was asked not to disturb the documents on the desk*) disarrange, disorganize, muddle, confuse. 3 (*The news of the closure of the school disturbed them*) concern, worry, upset, fluster, perturb.

**dive** vb (*He dived into the water to save the drowning child*) jump, leap, dip, drop, nose-dive, submerge.

**diverge** vb (*The roads diverge at the end of the village*) separate, divide, split, part, fork, branch off.

**divide** vb 1 (*You should divide the rope in two*) sever, cut, split, separate. 2 (*The road divides suddenly*) diverge, separate, divide, split, part, fork, branch off. 3 (*They divided the cake out among the children*) distribute, deal out, share out, allocate, allot, apportion.

**divine** adj 1 (*divine beings*) godly, heavenly, celestial, holy. 2 (*Taking part in divine worship*) religious, holy, spiritual. 3 (*The bride looked divine*) lovely, beautiful, charming, wonderful, marvelous.

**doctor** n (*They called a doctor when the child was ill*) medical practitioner, general practitioner, GP, physician, hospital doctor, consultant, specialist, pediatrician.

**document** n (*the documents relating to the business deal*) paper, official paper, certificate, record, deed.

**dogged** adj (*They admired her dogged determination*) determined, resolute, stubborn, obstinate, tenacious.

**dominant** adj 1 (*He is the dominant member of the group*) supreme, controlling, influential, authoritative, domineering. 2 (*It was the dominant issue on the agenda*) chief, main, principal, leading, predominant.

**domineering** adj (*He is so domineering that everyone is afraid of him*) overbearing, arrogant, dictatorial, masterful, tyranni-cal, bullying, (*inf*) bossy.

**doom** *n* (*people who are always predicting doom*) catastrophe, disaster, destruction, ruin, downfall.

**door** *n* (*stand at the door of the house*) door-way, entrance, entry.

**doting** *adj* (*doting parents*) indulgent, ador-ing, devoted, fond.

**double** *adj* 1 (*I saw the double of that dress last week*) duplicate, pair. 2-(*a-double thick-ness of cloth*) twofold, folded, two-ply. 3 (*His words had a double meaning*) dual,-am-biguous, ambivalent, two-edged.

**doubt** *n* 1 (*They are having doubts about his efficiency as a leader*) misgiving, mis-trust, distrust, reservations. 2 (*They are full of doubts about what they ought to do*) uncertainty, indecision, hesitation, irresolution.

**doubtful** *adj* 1 (*It is doubtful that he will be present*) uncertain, in doubt, unsure. 2 (*The genuineness of the signature is doubtful*) open to question, questionable, uncer-tain, dubious, debatable, disputable, inconclusive. 3 (*The meaning ofthe-word is doubtful*) dubious, unclear, ambiguous, obscure. 4 (*His parents thought that he was associating with doubtful people*) dubious, questionable, suspicious, suspect.

**down** *adj* 1 (*They were feeling down at the end of the vacation*) downcast, dejected, depressed, gloomy, miserable, sad, unhappy. 2 (*The computer system is down*) malfunctioning, inoperative, not work-ing.

**downright** *adv* (*She was downright rude*) utterly, completely, totally, absolutely, thoroughly, positively.

**drab** *adj* (*They live in very drab surroundings*) dingy, dull, dismal, dreary, gloomy, cheerless, dim, dark.

**drag** *vb* 1 (*They dragged the fallen trees from the forest*) haul, pull, draw, tug, yank, tow. 2 (*Time dragged*) move slowly, crawl.

**drastic** *adj* (*a drastic remedy*) extreme, severe, rigorous, harsh, radical, dire.

**draw** *vb* 1 (*draw a house*) sketch, make a picture of, make a diagram of, portray, depict, design. 2 (*draw a chair up to the table*) pull, drag, haul, tow, tug, yank. 3 (*He drew a sword from its sheath*) take out, bring out, withdraw, extract, produce. 4 (*Her hat drew a lot of attention*) attract, catch, captivate. 5 (*draw the curtains*) pull, close, shut. 6 (*They drew level with the other car*) move, go, proceed.

**dreadful** *adj* 1 (*It was a dreadful accident*) ter-rible, frightful, horrible, grim, awful, shocking, appalling, ghastly, gruesome. 2 (*What a dreadful man!*) nasty, unpleas-ant, disagreeable, horrible, frightful, odious.

**dream** *vb* 1 (*The child seems to dream every night*) have dreams, have nightmares. 2 (*He said that he saw a ghost but he must have been dreaming*) see things, halluci-nate, imagine things. 3 (*She was dream-ing instead of concentrating on her work*) daydream, be in a reverie, be lost in thought. 4 (*He would not dream of upset-ting her*) think, consider.

**dreary** *adj* (*They live in dreary surroundings*) dismal, drab, dingy, dull, gloomy, cheer-less, gloomy, dark.

**dress** *vb* 1 (*They were all dressed in black*) clothe, attire, array, garb. 2 (*She was late and had to dress quickly*) get dressed, put on clothes. 3 (*The nurse dressed the wound*) cover, bandage, bind up. 4 (*The children dressed the Christmas tree*) decorate, adorn, ornament, trim, deck.

**drink** *vb* (*She drank the water quickly*) swallow, gulp down, partake of, quaff, (*inf*) swig.

**drip** *vb* (*Water began to drip from the faucet*) trickle, dribble, plop, leak, splash, ooze, exude.

**drive** *vb* 1 (*young people learning to drive a car*) operate, steer, handle, direct, manage. 2 (*They came by train but we drove here*) go by car, come by car, travel by car, motor. 3 (*They drove the cattle to the milking parlor*) press, urge, push, prod, goad, spur. 4 (*poverty drove them to steal*) force, compel, oblige, make, pressure, coerce. 5 (*They began to drive posts into the ground to make a fence*) hammer, ram, bang, plunge, sink.

**drop** *vb* 1 (*The hot air balloon dropped out of the sky*) drop down, descend, fall, plum-met, plunge. 2-(*Water dropped from the branches*) fall, drip, trickle, dribble, plop. 3 (*She dropped her baggage and fell into a chair*) let fall, let go. 4-(*He has decided to drop piano lessons*) give up, stop, abandon, discontinue, cease, end, finish, quit. 5-(*She has dropped her latest boyfriend*) leave, forsake, abandon, jilt. 6 (*House prices have dropped*) fall, lessen, decrease, decline, dwindle, plummet, plunge.

**drowsy** *adj* (*people often feel drowsy after a heavy meal*) sleepy, tired, weary, lethar-gic, sluggish.

**drug** *n* 1 (*Medical scientists have discovered a new cancer drug*) medical drug, medi-cine, medication, medicament, cure, remedy. 2 (*concern over young people who are addicted to drugs*) addictive drug, nar-cotic, opiate, barbiturate, (*inf*) dope.

**drunk** *adj* (*drunk people staggering down the road*) intoxicated, inebriated, under the influence, tipsy.

**dry** *adj* 1 (*the dry regions of the world*) arid, parched, scorched, dehydrated, desic-cated. 2 (*dry fallen leaves*) withered, shriv-eled, wilted, desiccated. 3 (*The cheese has grown very dry*) dried out, hard, stale. 4-(*The lecture was very dry and the audience was bored*) boring, dull, uninteresting, tedious, monotonous, tiresome.

**dual** *adj* (*He plays a dual role in the firm*) dou-ble, duplicate.

**dubious** *adj* 1 (*He is dubious about going to the meeting*) doubtful, unsure, uncertain, hes-itant, irresolute, wavering. 2 (*The result is still-dubious*) doubtful, uncertain, unsure, unsettled, up in the air. 3-(*He seems rather a dubious character*) suspicious, suspect, questionable, untrustworthy.

**dull** *adj* 1 (*It was a dull day*) overcast, cloudy, dark, gloomy, dismal, bleak. 2 (*She always wore dull colors*) drab, dreary, dark, somber. 3 (*We heard the dull thud of some-thing falling*) muffled, muted, indistinct. 4 (*The professor gave a very dull talk*) bor-ing, uninteresting, dry, tedious, monot-onous.

**dumb** *adj* 1 (*He has been dumb since birth*) without speech, mute. 2 (*They were struck dumb at the beauty of the view*) speechless, silent, wordless, mute, inarticulate, at a loss for words. 3 (*He is so dumb that he did not get the job*) stupid, unintelligent, dense, thick, slow-witted.

**duplicate** *vb* 1 (*She was asked to duplicate the documents*) copy, photocopy, reproduce, photostat (*trademark*). 2 (*There does not seem to be work around and workers are duplicating tasks*) repeat, do over again.

**duplicity** *n* (*his duplicity in swindling the old lady*) deceit, deceitfulness, double-deal-ing, trickery, guile, dishonesty.

**durable** *adj* 1 (*the durable effects of the drug*) long-lasting, lasting, persisting, perma-nent. 2 (*The boots must be durable*) long-lasting, lasting, hardwearing, sturdy, strong, tough.

**dust** *vb* 1 (*dust the furniture*) wipe, brush, clean, mop. 2 (*She dusted the cake with powdered sugar*) sprinkle, dredge, scatter.

**duty** *n* 1 (*He has a sense of duty towards his parents*) responsibility, obligation. 2 (*He failed to carry out his duties and was fired*) job, task, chore, assignment. 3 (*They had to pay duty on the goods which they brought into the country*) tax, levy, tariff, excise.

**dwindle** *vb* (*Their hopes are dwindling as time goes on*) grow less, lessen, decrease, diminish, fade.

# E

**eager** *adj* 1 (*eager students*) keen, enthusi-astic, avid, earnest, zealous, fervent. 2 (*people eager to learn/ eager for information*) avid, anxious, longing for, yearning for, desirous of.

**early** adv 1 (*get up early*) at dawn, at daybreak, with the lark, at cockcrow. 2 (*visitors who arrived early*) too soon, ahead of time, prematurely. 3 (*It is very important that you arrive early for your interview*) in good time, ahead of schedule.

**early** adj 1 (*an early reply*) prompt, speedy, quick, rapid, fast, without delay. 2 (*an early crop*) advanced, forward, premature, precocious. 3-(*early man*) primitive, prehistoric, primeval.

**earn** vb 1 (*earn an extremely high salary*) make, get, receive, obtain, draw, clear, take home. 2 (*earn the respect of his colleagues*) gain, win, attain, secure, merit, deserve.

**earnest** adj 1 (*an earnest young man who studies hard*) serious, solemn, grave, intense, staid, studious, diligent. 2 (*make an earnest plea for mercy*) fervent, ardent, passionate, intense, heartfelt, sincere, urgent.

**earnest:—in earnest** adj 1 (*They were in earnest about walking all the way home*) serious, sincere, not joking. 2-(*They set to work in earnest*) zealously, wholeheartedly, with a will, with commitment, determinedly.

**earnings** npl (*She tries to save part of her earnings*) income, salary, wages, pay.

**earth** n 1 (*earth, moon and stars*) globe, world, planet. 2 (*the earth and the sky*) land, ground. 3 (*children getting covered in earth from playing in the yard*) soil, dirt.

**earthenware** n (*a store selling local earthenware to the tourists*) pottery, crockery, stoneware, ceramics.

**earthly** adj 1 (*a book about creatures that were not earthly*) terrestrial. 2-(*earthly pleasures*) worldly, nonspiritual, secular, temporal, material, fleshly, carnal. 3 (*They have no-earthly chance of success*) feasible, possible, conceivable, likely, realistic.

**earthy** adj 1 (*the earthy smell of a newly dug garden*) soil-like, dirt-like. 2 (*tell jokes which were rather earthy*) bawdy, crude, coarse, ribald, indecent, blue.

**ease** n 1 (*wealthy people leading a life of ease*) comfort, contentment, affluence, wealth, prosperity, luxury. 2 (*do the job with ease*) effortlessness, facility, no difficulty, deftness, adroitness. 3 (*Ease of manner is important in his job*) naturalness, composure, affability.

**ease** vb 1 (*receive some pills to ease the pain*) lessen, reduce, diminish, relieve, soothe, alleviate, mitigate. 2 (*The storm finally eased*) lessen, grow less, abate, moderate, slacken off. 3 (*A letter would ease his mother's mind*) comfort, give comfort to, calm, soothe, give solace to. 4 (*try to ease the part of the machine into the right posi-*

tion) guide, maneuver, inch, edge, steer, slide.

**easy** adj 1 (*an easy task*) simple, effortless, uncomplicated, straightforward, undemanding. 2 (*She had an easy mind when she knew her family were safe*) at ease, untroubled, unworried, at peace, calm, tranquil, composed. 3 (*an easy manner*) natural, relaxed, easygoing, composed, unreserved, affable, (*inf*) laid-back.

**easygoing** adj (*He is too easygoing to get upset about anything*) relaxed, placid, happy-go-lucky, tolerant, understanding, undemanding, patient, (*inf*) laid-back.

**eat** vb 1 (*eat candy*) consume, devour, chew, swallow, gulp down, bolt, wolf, (*inf*) tuck into. 2 (*What time do you eat?*) dine, have a meal, take food. 3 (*Acid had eaten away the material*) erode, corrode, wear away, rot.

**eavesdrop** vb (*The child tried to eavesdrop on her parents' conversation*) listen in on, overhear.

**ebb** vb 1 (*when the tide ebbed*) go out, flow back, retreat, draw back, recede. 2 (*The popularity of the president ebbed*) decline, lessen, decrease, dwindle, fade away, peter out.

**eccentric** adj (*The villagers think he is eccentric/She has an eccentric way of dressing*) strange, peculiar, odd, weird, outlandish, bizarre, zany, freakish, unconventional, (*inf*) offbeat, (*inf*) way-out.

**echo** vb 1 (*The sound echoed round the hall*) resound, reverberate, ring. 2 (*She simply echoed what her father said*) repeat, reiterate, reproduce, copy, imitate, parrot.

**economical** adj 1 (*have to be economical with fuel so that it will last the winter*) sparing, thrifty, careful, frugal. 2 (*an economical form of transport*) inexpensive, reasonable, low-cost, low-price, cheap.

**economize** vb (*Since prices have gone up we will have to economize*) cut back, spend less, cut expenditure, tighten one's belt, draw in one's horns.

**ecstasy** n (*Her idea of ecstasy was to-lie on a beach all day*) bliss, rapture, joy, elation, delight, happiness, pleasure.

**ecstatic** adj (*They were ecstatic when their team won the championship*) elated, exultant, in raptures, overjoyed, joyful, jubilant, jumping for joy, on cloud nine, in seventh heaven.

**edge** n 1 (*the edge of the road*) side, verge. 2 (*the edge of the town*) border, boundary, perimeter.

**edgy** adj (*feel edgy when her children were late home*) on edge, anxious, nervous, tense, uneasy, worried, (*inf*) uptight.

**edible** adj (*food that is scarcely edible*)-eatable, consumable, digestible, palatable.

**edict** n (*by edict of the emperor/obey the offi-*

cial edicts) order, decree, command, law, rule, act, statute.

**edit** vb 1 (*They edited the manuscript which he had written*) revise, correct, alter, adapt, emend. 2 (*He edits the daily newspaper*) be the editor of, be in charge of, direct.

**edition** n (*last week's edition of the magazine*) issue, number, publication.

**educate** vb (*children who were educated at the little local school*) teach, instruct, school, train.

**educated** adj (*the kind of books that educated people might read*) wellread, knowledgeable, literate, cultivated, cultured.

**education** n (*receive a good education*) schooling, teaching, instruction, training, tuition.

**eerie** adj (*hear an eerie noise in the middle of the night*) strange, unnatural, uncanny, ghostly, frightening, (*inf*) scary.

**effect** n 1 (*It is difficult to say what the effect of the changes will be*) result, consequences, outcome, influence, impact. 2 (*I like the general effect of-the color scheme*) impression, impact.

**effect, take effect** vb 1 (*new regulations taking effect from next week*) come into force, come into operation, begin, become law, become valid. 2 (*when the sleeping pills take effect*) work, be effective.

**effective** adj 1 (*an effective government*) successful, competent, capable, efficient, productive. 2-(*an effective color scheme*) striking, impressive, attractive. 3 (*rules which will be effective from next year*) valid, in force, in operation, operative.

**effects** npl (*her personal effects*) belongings, possessions, goods, things, baggage, luggage.

**effervescent** adj (*effervescent soft drinks*) sparkling, fizzy, bubbly, carbonated.

**efficient** adj 1 (*a very efficient worker*) capable, competent, able, effective, productive, skillful, organized. 2 (*an efficient system*) effective, wellorganized, well-run, streamlined.

**effigy** n (*effigies of ancient kings*) likeness, image, statue, bust.

**effort** n 1 (*work requiring a great deal of effort*) exertion, power, energy, work, force, application, struggle, strain, (*inf*) elbow grease. 2 (*She passed her driver's test at her second effort*) attempt, try, endeavor, (*inf*) shot, (*inf*) go.

**effortless** adj (*He made lifting the heavy weights seem effortless*) easy, simple, uncomplicated, no trouble, unexacting, undemanding.

**effrontery** n (*She had the effrontery to go ahead of everyone standing-in line*) impudence, impertinence, cheek, audacity, temerity, (*inf*) nerve.

**effusive** adj (*When she pays people compliments*

she is so *effusive*) gushy, demonstrative, extravagant, lavish.

**egg, egg on** *vb* (*His friends egged him on to steal the apples*) encourage, urge, spur, goad, prod, prompt.

**eject** *vb* **1** (*He was ejected from the club for trying to start a fight*) throw out, remove, banish, evict, (*inf*) kick out, (*inf*) turf out, (*inf*) chuck out. **2**-(*She was ejected from the plane*) thrust out, throw out, propel.

**eke:—eke out** *vb* **1** (*eke out the lamb stew by adding a lot of vegetables*) stretch out, increase, supplement. **2** (*We must try to eke out our fuel supplies*) be economical with, be sparing with, economize on. **3** (*The poor peasants eke out a living from the soil*) scrape, scratch.

**elaborate** *adj* **1** (*elaborate carvings/ elaborate patterns*) detailed, intricate,-complex, ornate, fancy, showy, fussy,-(*inf*) flashy. **2** (*draw up-an elaborate plan*) complicated, detailed, complex, involved, intricate.

**elaborate** *vb* (*asked to elaborate on his suggestion*) expand, enlarge, amplify, flesh out.

**elapse** *vb* (*A long time elapsed before they met again*) pass, go by, roll by, slip by.

**elastic** *adj* **1** (*elastic materials*) stretchy, springy, pliant, flexible, rubbery. **2** (*Our vacation plans are elastic*) flexible, fluid, adaptable, adjustable.

**elated** *adj* (*They were elated at their victory*) overjoyed, jubilant, jumping for joy, joyful, delighted, gleeful, ecstatic, euphoric, on cloud nine, in seventh heaven.

**elation** *n* (*their elation at their victory*) jubilation, joy, joyfulness, delight, glee, ecstasy.

**elbow** *vb* (*elbow him out of the way to get to the front of the crowd*) push, jostle, shoulder, knock, bump.

**elderly** *adj* (*the elderly couple next door*) old, advanced in years.

**elderly:—the elderly** *npl* (*be kind to the elderly*) elderly people, older people, senior citizens, pensioners, retired people.

**elect** *vb* **1** (*elect a team captain*) choose, select, pick, opt for, appoint, decide on. **2** (*elect a president*) vote for, choose.

**election** *n* (*vote in an election for a new leader*) ballot, poll.

**electrify** *vb* (*He electrified the audience with his performance*) excite, thrill, rouse, stir, move, fire.

**elegance** *n* (*admire the elegance of the model*) stylishness, style, grace, gracefulness, fashion.

**elegant** *adj* (*the elegant women at the wedding reception*) stylish, graceful, fashionable, tasteful, artistic.

**elegy** *n* (*an elegy for his friend's death*) funeral poem, funeral song, lament, dirge, requiem.

**element** *n* **1** (*the main elements of the project*) component, ingredient, constituent, factor, feature, detail. **2**-(*the natural element of the lion*)-environment, habitat, milieu, sphere.

**elementary** *adj* **1** (*He said that the problem was elementary*) easy, simple, uncomplicated, straightforward. **2** (*students taking a course in elementary mathematics*) basic, fundamental, rudimentary, primary.

**elements** *npl* (*climbers braving the elements*) weather, climate, atmospheric conditions.

**elicit** *vb* (*try to elicit the information from them*) draw out, extract, obtain, get.

**eligible** *adj* (*not eligible for the post/ not eligible to take part in the race*)-qualified, suitable, acceptable, authorized.

**eliminate** *vb* **1** (*She was eliminated from the team*) drop, leave out, exclude, omit, reject. **2** (*a gunman hired to eliminate the members of the other gang*) get rid of, dispose of, destroy, put an end to, kill.

**elocution** *n* (*take lessons in elocution*) speech, diction, enunciation, articulation, voice production, delivery.

**eloquent** *adj* (*an eloquent speech*) articulate, expressive, fluent, persuasive, forceful.

**elude** *vb* (*try to elude the police*) avoid, dodge, evade, escape from, get away from.

**emaciated** *adj* (*emaciated children in the famine region*) skeletal, gaunt, wasted, scrawny, skinny, scraggy.

**embargo** *n* (*place an embargo on trade with that country*) ban, bar, prohibition, interdict.

**embark** *vb* **1** (*passengers were asked to embark early*) board ship, board a plane, go on board. **2** (*someone embarking on a new career*) set out on, begin, start, commence, enter on, set about.

**embarrassed** *adj* (*feel embarrassed when she forgot the words of her speech*) awkward, uncomfortable, self-conscious, upset, disconcerted, discomfited, flustered, confused, abashed, ashamed, mortified.

**embarrassment** *n* (*overcome with embarrassment when she forgot the words of her speech*) awkwardness, discomfort, self-consciousness, discomfiture, confusion, shame, mortification.

**embezzle** *vb* (*embezzle money from his company*) steal, rob, thieve, pilfer, filch, appropriate, misappropriate.

**emblem** *n* (*the emblem of the society*) crest, badge, symbol, sign, device.

**embrace** *vb* (*He embraced his daughter as she got on the train*) hug, cuddle, clasp, cling to, squeeze.

**emerge** *vb* **1** (*They stood around the pool as the swimmers emerged*) come out, come into view, appear, surface, become visible. **2** (*waiting for the facts to emerge*) come out, become known, come to the fore.

**emergency** *n* (*emergencies such as fires*) crisis, danger, accident, extremity.

**emigrate** *vb* (*people emigrating to find work*) move overseas, move abroad, migrate, relocate.

**eminent** *adj* (*an eminent writer*) famous, well-known, distinguished, renowned, notable, noteworthy, great, important, prominent.

**emit** *vb* **1** (*chimneys emitting smoke*) give out, pour out, issue, send forth, discharge, issue. **2** (*emit a scream for help*) utter, express, voice.

**emotion** *n* (*in a voice in which there was no emotion*) feeling, sentiment, passion.

**emotional** *adj* **1** (*an emotional person*) passionate, ardent, demonstrative, excitable. **2** (*an emotional moment*) moving, touching, affecting, poignant, emotive.

**emphasis** *n* **1** (*As far as the interviews were concerned the emphasis was on qualifications*) stress, priority, importance, weight, urgency. **2** (*put the emphasis on the first syllable*) stress, accent, accentuation.

**emphasize** *vb* **1** (*emphasize the importance of working hard*) stress, accentuate, underline, highlight, spotlight, point up. **2** (*emphasize the first syllable*) stress, put the stress on, accentuate.

**emphatic** *adj* (*He issued an emphatic denial*) definite, decided, firm, positive, absolute.

**employ** *vb* **1** (*He wishes to employ three more people in his office*) engage, hire, take on, sign on. **2**-(*His work employs all his time*) take up, occupy, fill, use up. **3**-(*employ modern methods in their factory*) use, make use of, apply.

**employment** *n* (*He is looking for employment in the computing industry*) work, occupation, job.

**empty** *adj* **1** (*an empty house*) vacant, unoccupied, uninhabited, unfilled. **2** (*an empty page*) blank, unused, clean. **3** (*empty threats*) meaningless, futile, ineffective, idle, insubstantial.

**enchant** *vb* (*The children were enchanted by the ballet*) captivate, fascinate, entrance, bewitch, charm, delight.

**enclosure** *n* (*the enclosure for the animals at the dog show*) compound, ring, arena, paddock, fold.

**encounter** *vb* **1** (*She encountered an old friend in the mall*) meet, run into, run across, come upon, (*inf*) bump into. **2** (*encounter problems*) meet, be faced with, face, confront.

**encourage** *vb* **1** (*encourage those who had given up hope*) inspire, hearten, stimulate, motivate, incite, prompt.**2** (*a plan to encourage exports*) boost, promote, help, assist, aid.

**end** *n* **1** (*the far end of the lake*) edge, border, boundary, extremity, tip. **2** (*the end of the movie*) ending, conclusion, close, finish, culmination, denouement. **3** (*the end of the train*) rear, back. **4** (*their end in mind*) aim, objective, intention, purpose. **5** (*meet a peaceful end*) death, demise.

**end** *vb* **1** (*when his membership of the club ends*) come to an end, finish, come to a stop, stop, cease, conclude. **2** (*The incident ended their friendship*) bring to an end, bring to a close, finish, stop, discontinue, wind up.

**endanger** *vb* (*things which endanger the species*) put in danger, expose to danger, put at risk, risk, jeopardize.

**endearing** *adj* (*one of her endearing features*) charming, attractive, loveable, adorable, engaging, sweet.

**endeavor** *vb* (*endeavor to do better*) attempt, try, exert oneself, make an effort, strive.

**ending** *n* (*a happy ending to the novel*) end, finish, close, conclusion.

**endless** *adj* **1** (*endless patience*) unending, without end, unlimited, infinite, everlasting, boundless. **2**-(*an endless chain*) continuous, unbroken, uninterrupted.

**endorse** *vb* (*endorse their course of action*) approve, support, back, champion, uphold, subscribe to.

**endow** *vb* (*She was endowed with good looks*) give, provide, supply, gift, confer.

**endure** *vb* **1** (*unable to endure the traffic noise any longer*) put up with, stand, bear, tolerate, abide. **2**-(*hope that their love would endure*) last, continue, remain, live on, persist.

**enemy** *n* (*the army of the enemy/ regard his former friend as an enemy*) foe, opponent, adversary, rival.

**energetic** *adj* (*not feeling energetic enough to go for a walk*) active, lively, sprightly, vigorous, animated, enthusiastic.

**energy** *n* (*lacking in energy after her illness*) strength, stamina, vigor, power, force, liveliness, vitality, animation.

**enforce** *vb* **1** (*enforce the law*) apply, carry out, administer, implement, impose. **2** (*enforce silence on the group*) force, compel, insist on.

**engage** *vb* **1** (*engage a new nanny*) employ, hire, appoint, take on. **2**-(*engage in a game of chess/be engaged in a bitter argument*) take part in, join in, participate in, enter into. **3** (*an attempt to engage their attention*) attract, catch, draw, gain, capture.

**engaged** *adj* **1** (*The manager is engaged*) busy, occupied, unavailable, (*inf*) tied up. **2** (*The bathroom is-engaged*) occupied, in use. **3**-(*engaged couples*) going to be married, betrothed, affianced.

**engaging** *n* (*an engaging smile*) charming,

attractive, appealing, winning, pleasing, sweet.

**engineer** *vb* (*engineer a secret meeting between them*) bring about, cause, contrive, devise, (*inf*) wangle.

**engrave** *vb* **1** (*engrave their initials on the tree*) carve, etch, inscribe, cut. **2** (*Her words are engraved on his heart*) fix, set, imprint, stamp.

**engross** *vb* (*The book engrossed me*) occupy, absorb, preoccupy, engage, rivet.

**engulf** *vb* (*a town engulfed by a tidal wave*) flood, inundate, swamp, swallow, submerge.

**enjoy** *vb* (*enjoy a trip to the coast*) like, love, be entertained by, take pleasure in, delight in.

**enjoy:—enjoy oneself** *vb* have a good time, have fun, (*inf*) have a-ball (*The children are enjoying themselves at the funfair*).

**enjoyable** *adj* (*an enjoyable occasion*) entertaining, amusing, delightful, pleasant, nice.

**enlarge** *vb* (*enlarge the yard*) expand, extend, add to, amplify.

**enormous** *adj* (*an enormous creature/an enormous load*) huge, immense, massive, vast, colossal, gigantic, mammoth.

**enough** *adj* (*We have enough food*) sufficient, adequate, ample, abundant.

**enroll** *vb* **1** (*enroll for a French course*) register, sign up, enter, volunteer. **2**-(*We enrolled several new recruits in the society*) register, sign up, take on, admit, accept.

**ensue** *vb* (*the argument and the fight that ensued*) follow, come after, result, arise.

**ensure** *vb* (*You must try to ensure that he will be present*) make sure, make certain, guarantee, certify.

**enter** *vb* **1** (*enter the hall*) come into, go into, pass into, move into. **2** (*a bullet entered his chest*) go into, pierce, penetrate. **3** (*enter a competition*) go in for, take part in, participate in. **4** (*enter one's name on the form*) put down, register, record, mark down, note.

**enterprise** *n* **1** (*The festival is an annual enterprise*) project, undertaking, operation, venture. **2** (*The wool firm is a private enterprise*) business, industry, firm, establishment. **3** (*young people showing some enterprise*) resourcefulness, initiative, drive, imagination, spirit, enthusiasm, boldness, (*inf*) get-up-and-go.

**enterprising** *adj* (*an enterprising member of staff*) resourceful, go-ahead, imaginative, spirited, enthusiastic.

**entertain** *vb* (*He entertained the children with conjuring tricks*) amuse, divert, please, delight, interest.

**entertainment** *n* **1** (*several forms of entertainment for leisure hours*) amusement, fun, recreation, diversion, distraction. **2** (*sing*

for the entertainment of the children) amusement, enjoyment, diversion, pleasure, delight, interest. **3** (*the entertainment at the club that evening*) show, performance.

**enthralling** *adj* (*The acrobats gave an enthralling performance*) fascinating, gripping, riveting, spellbinding, enchanting, captivating, entrancing.

**enthusiastic** *adj* (*enthusiastic members of the flying club*) eager, keen, ardent, zealous, passionate, wholehearted, devoted, earnest, fanatical.

**entice** *vb* (*try to entice customers into his store*) lure, tempt, attract, coax, decoy.

**entire** *adj* **1** (*his entire collection of records*) whole, total, complete, full. **2** (*not an entire success*) total, absolute, unqualified, thorough, outright.

**entirely** *adv* (*not entirely true*) absolutely, completely, totally, wholly, altogether.

**entitle** *vb* **1** (*Your pass entitles you to go to three matches*) allow, permit, enable, qualify, give the right to. **2**-(*His novel is entitled "Lost Dreams"*) call, name.

**entrance** *n* **1** (*the entrance to the office block*) way in, entry, doorway, gateway, lobby, porch, foyer. **2** (*gain entrance to the building*) entry, access, admission, admittance. **3** (*the entrance of the principal*) entry, arrival, appearance.

**entrance** *vb* (*We were entranced by-their graceful dancing*) hold spellbound, fascinate, captivate, enchant, enthrall.

**entrant** *n* (*count the number of entrants for the competition*) competitor, contestant, participant, candidate, applicant.

**entreat** *vb* (*She entreated us to go with her*) beg, implore, beseech, plead with, appeal to.

**entrenched** *adj* (*entrenched political ideas*) deep-rooted, well-established, fixed, set, firm, unshakeable, dyed-inthe wool.

**entry** *n* **1** (*the entry to the apartment building*) entrance, doorway, gateway, lobby, porch, foyer. **2** (*gain entry to the office building*) entrance, access, admission, admittance. **3** (*the entry of the ballet dancers*) entrance, arrival, appearance. **4** (*an entry in her diary*) statement, item, record, note, listing.

**envelop** *vb* (*mountain tops enveloped in mist*) cover, blanket, surround, engulf, swathe.

**enviable** *adj* (*He has an enviable collection of CDs*) desirable, tempting, impressive, excellent.

**envious** *adj* (*She was envious when she saw her friend's new car*) jealous, covetous, green, begrudging, resentful.

**environment** *n* (*Children need a loving environment/the ideal environment for tigers*) surroundings, habitat, background, situation, conditions, circumstances, atmosphere, milieu.

**envy** n (*her envy of her neighbor's house*) enviousness, covetousness, jealousy, resentment.

**envy** vb (*She envies her friend her new car*) be envious of, be jealous of, covet, be covetous, begrudge, grudge, resent.

**ephemeral** adj (*the ephemeral life of the mayfly*) short-lived, fleeting, transitory, brief, passing, temporary.

**episode** n 1 (*the second episode of the TV serial*) part, installment, section. 2 (*an unhappy episode in their lives*) incident, event, occurrence, happening, experience.

**equal** adj 1 (*children of equal ability*) the same, identical, like, comparable. 2 (*an equal contest*) even, evenly matched, level. 3 (*not feeling equal to the task*) up to, fit for, ready for, capable of.

**equal** vb 1 (*six plus six equals twelve*) be equal to, come to, amount to, add up to, make, total. 2 (*The runner equaled the record for the race*) match, be level with, reach.

**equate** vb (*They equate money with happiness*) associate, bracket, link, connect.

**equip** vb 1 (*equip the children for their skiing trip*) fit out, rig out, dress. 2 (*equip the hall with gymnastic apparatus*) fit out, furnish, supply, stock.

**equipment** n (*the equipment needed to do the job*) tools, gear, apparatus, materials, things, paraphernalia.

**equivalent** adj (*ask the store to exchange the item for something of equivalent value*) equal, the same, identical, similar, like, comparable, corresponding, matching.

**equivalent** n (*the equivalent of our senators in their country*) counterpart, opposite number, equal.

**era** n (*furniture of the Colonial era*) age, period, time, days, eon, epoch.

**eradicate** vb (*try to eradicate the weed from his yard/A government tries to eradicate tax avoidance*) get rid of, do away with, root out, wipe out, eliminate, extirpate.

**erase** vb (*erase the incorrect passage from the report*) remove, rub out, wipe out, delete, cancel, expunge.

**erect** adj (*Human beings stand erect*) upright, vertical, straight.

**erect** vb 1 (*erect a tent*) put up, set up, set upright, pitch, assemble. 2-(*erect an apartment building*) build, construct, put up, raise.

**erode** vb (*cliffs eroded by the sea*) wear away, wear down, eat away, corrode.

**err** vb 1 (*They erred when they accused him of theft*) be in error, be wrong, be incorrect, make a mistake, be mistaken, get it wrong, miscalculate, (*inf*) slip up. 2 (*pastors who urge the members of their congregation not to err*) do wrong, sin, behave badly, misbehave, transgress.

**errand** n task, job, chore, assignment, mission.

**erratic** adj 1 (*worried about her erratic behavior*) inconsistent, irregular, variable, unstable, unpredictable, unreliable, capricious. 2 (*a driver steering an erratic course*) wandering, meandering, wavering.

**erroneous** adj (*an erroneous statement*) wrong, incorrect, inaccurate, untrue, false, mistaken.

**error** n 1 (*an error in their calculation of the building costs*) mistake, inaccuracy, miscalculation, blunder, fault, oversight, (*inf*) slip-up. 2 (*see the error of his ways*) wrongdoing, sin, evil, misbehavior, misconduct.

**erupt** vb 1 (*A flow of lava erupted from the volcano*) to be discharged, gush, pour out, issue, belch. 2-(*violence erupted between the two gangs*) break out, flare up, blow up, burst forth.

**eruption** n 1 (*an eruption of violence*) outburst, outbreak, flare-up. 2 (*an eruption on her face*) rash, inflammation, outbreak.

**escalate** vb 1 (*The violence has escalated/The war escalated*) increase, intensify, heighten, accelerate, be stepped up, mushroom. 2 (*prices have escalated*) go up, mount, climb, soar.

**escapade** n (*The children were punished for their escapades*) adventure, prank, stunt, trick, (*inf*) lark.

**escape** vb 1 (*The prisoners escaped from the jail*) get away, run away, abscond, bolt, break free, make one's getaway. 2 (*succeed in escaping punishment*) avoid, evade, dodge, elude, steer clear of, sidestep. 3 (*gas escaping*) leak, seep out, discharge, spurt, gush.

**escort** n (*require an escort for the dance*) partner, companion, attendant, (*inf*) date.

**especially** adv 1 (*The products sell well, especially in the summer*) particularly, above all, chiefly, mainly, principally. 2 (*designed especially for her*) specially, specifically, expressly, particularly, exclusively.

**espionage** n (*a novel about espionage*) spying, intelligence, undercover work.

**essay** n (*asked to write an essay on a favorite author*) composition, dissertation, paper, article, thesis, discourse.

**essence** n 1 (*the essence of good speech*) essential part, main ingredient, nature, kernel, quintessence. 2 (*vanilla essence*) extract, concentrate, distillate.

**essential** adj 1 (*essential equipment/It is essential to arrive early*) necessary, vital, indispensable, crucial, important. 2 (*the essential theme of the novel*) basic, fundamental, inherent, principal.

**establish** vb 1 (*establish a computing firm*) set up, form, found, institute, create, inaugurate. 2 (*try to establish his innocence*) prove, show, demonstrate, verify, certify.

**estate** n 1 (*He owns a house in town and a country estate*) property, land property, land, landholding. 2 (*His estate at his death amounted to nearly a million dollars*) assets, resources, effects, possessions, belongings, wealth.

**esteem** n (*hold the writer in great esteem*) regard, respect, admiration, honor, reverence, appreciation.

**estimate** vb (*estimate the cost of repairs*) work out, calculate, assess, gauge, reckon, guess, (*inf*) guesstimate.

**estimation** n 1 (*In our estimation he is the best player*) opinion, view, judgment, consideration, way of thinking, feeling. 2 (*When she lied she went down in our estimation*) good opinion, regard, respect, admiration, approval, favor.

**estuary** n (*boats in the estuary*) river mouth, inlet, cove, bay.

**eternal** adj 1 (*life eternal*) everlasting, endless, without end, perpetual, immortal, infinite. 2 (*We are tired of their eternal quarreling*) endless, incessant, ceaseless, nonstop, constant, continuous, continual, interminable, unremitting.

**ethical** adj (*not an ethical thing to do*) moral, honorable, virtuous, good, decent, honest.

**ethnic** adj (*ethnic restaurants/ethnic customs*) racial, cultural, national.

**etiquette** n (*wedding etiquette*) rules of conduct, accepted behavior, protocol, custom, convention.

**eulogy** n (*a eulogy about their team's performance*) praise, accolade, acclamation, applause, tribute, paean, panegyric.

**evacuate** vb 1 (*people asked to evacuate areas likely to be bombed by the enemy*) leave, vacate, quit, abandon, retreat from, (*inf*) pull out. 2 (*The police evacuated everyone from the area*) move out, clear.

**evade** vb 1 (*try to evade her responsibilities*) avoid, escape from, dodge, shirk, sidestep, (*inf*) duck. 2 (*succeed in evading the enemy*) avoid, escape from, elude, shake off, give the slip to, keep out of the way of, steer clear of.

**even** adj 1 (*even ground*) level, flat, smooth, uniform. 2 (*The temperature of the room must remain even*) constant, uniform, steady, stable, unchanging. 3 (*We gave the children even amounts of money*) equal, the same, identical, like, similar, comparable. 4 (*The score was even at half time*) level, equal, square, tied, drawn. 5 (*people of an even disposition*) calm, placid, serene, composed, unexcitable, unperturbable.

**event** n 1 (*The sad and happy events in their*

lives) happening, occurrence, occasion, episode, incident, experience. 2 (the track events in the Olympic Games) contest, competition, match.

**eventually** adv (She took her driver's test several times and eventually passed) in the end, finally, at last, ultimately.

**everlasting** adj 1 (everlasting life) eternal, endless, without end, perpetual, abiding, immortal, infinite. 2 (their everlasting complaints) endless, nonstop, incessant, ceaseless, continuous, continual.

**evict** adj (get evicted from their house for not paying the rent/get evicted from the club for being under age) throw out, put out, turn out, eject, remove, oust, (inf) chuck out, kick out.

**evidence** n 1 (They will have to produce evidence of his guilt) proof, confirmation, verification, corroboration. 2 (There was evidence of a struggle at the scene of the murder) sign, indication, mark.

**evident** adj (It was evident that he was unwell/an evident improvement) obvious, clear, apparent, plain, noticeable, conspicuous, perceptible, visible.

**evil** adj (appalled at his evil deeds) wicked, bad, wrong, sinful, immoral, villainous.

**exacerbate** vb (His remarks exacerbated the situation) make worse, worsen, aggravate, intensify, add fuel to the fire.

**exact** adj 1 (an exact description) precise, accurate, close, faithful, true. 2 (the exact time) precise, accurate, right.

**exacting** adj (an exacting task) demanding, difficult, hard, arduous, tough, laborious, taxing, onerous.

**exactly** adv 1 (His estimate was exactly right) precisely, absolutely, just, quite, (inf) bang. 2 (repeat the information exactly) word for word, verbatim, literally, to the letter, closely, faithfully.

**exaggerate** vb 1 (exaggerate the length of time the journey took) overstate, overemphasize, overstress, overestimate. 2 (It's not that expensive—you're exaggerating) overstate, embroider, embellish, overdraw, add color, over-elaborate, make a mountain out of a molehill, (inf) lay it on with a trowel, (inf) lay it on thick.

**examine** vb 1 (It is necessary to examine the facts) look at, study, inspect, survey, analyze, review, observe, check out, weigh up. 2-(examine a patient) look at, check over, give a check-up, assess.

**example** n 1 (buy an example of the artist's early work) sample, specimen, instance, illustration. 2-(follow his brother's example) model, pattern, standard. 3 (punish some pupils as an example to-the others) warning, caution, lesson.

**exasperate** vb (She was exasperated by their

objections) annoy, irritate, anger, infuriate, incense, enrage.

**excavate** vb 1 (excavate a trench) dig, dig out, hollow out, scoop out. 2 (excavate an ancient Roman settlement) unearth, dig up, uncover, disinter.

**exceed** vb 1 (His talent as a musician-exceeds that of his brother) be-greater than, be more than, be-superior to, surpass, outstrip, outshine, overshadow, top, cap. 2-(exceed the speed limit) go beyond, go over, do more than, overstep. 3 (at a price not exceeding $5000) be greater than, be more than, go beyond, top.

**exceedingly** adv (She was exceedingly beautiful) extremely, exceptionally, extraordinarily, tremendously, enormously, vastly, greatly, highly, hugely.

**excellent** adj (an excellent player) very good, first-rate, first-class, great, fine, distinguished, superb, outstanding, marvelous, brilliant, (inf) Al, (inf) top-notch.

**exception** n 1 (the whole school will go with the exception of the first class) exclusion, omission. 2 (Their case is an exception) special case, anomaly, deviation, irregularity, oddity, freak.

**exceptional** adj 1 (exceptional weather for the time of year) unusual, uncommon, abnormal, out of the-ordinary, extraordinary, atypical, rare. 2 (people of exceptional talent) excellent, extraordinary, remarkable, outstanding, phenomenal.

**excerpt** n (read an excerpt from one of Shakespeare's plays) extract, passage, quotation, quote, piece, section.

**excessive** n 1 (an excessive amount of water) too much, extravagant, immoderate, undue, inordinate. 2 (The prices seem excessive) exorbitant, outrageous, unreasonable.

**exchange** vb (The children agreed to exchange toys) swap, trade, barter.

**excite** vb 1 (the thought of the party excited the children) thrill, stimulate, rouse, animate, (inf) turn on. 2 (excite feelings of anger in the crowd) cause, bring about, rouse, arouse, incite, provoke, kindle, stir up.

**exclamation** n (He gave an exclamation of surprise) cry, call, shout, yell, shriek.

**exclude** vb 1 (She was excluded from their talks) leave out, keep out, debar, bar, ban. 2 (They cannot exclude the possibility of murder) rule out, set aside, preclude, eliminate.

**exclusive** adj 1 (an exclusive club) select, private, fashionable, chic. 2-(gave them her exclusive attention) complete, undivided, full, absolute, entire, total. 3 (the price exclusive of drinks) excluding, not including, omitting, not counting, excepting.

**excruciating** adj (an excruciating pain in

her stomach) agonizing, acute, severe, intense, extreme.

**excursion** n (go on an excursion to the coast) trip, expedition, jaunt, outing, journey.

**excuse** vb 1 (impossible to excuse their crime) forgive, pardon, condone, justify, defend. 2 (ask to be excused from the gymnastics class) let off, exempt, release.

**excuse** n 1 (their excuse for not arriving on time) defense, justification, reason, grounds, vindication. 2 (His supposed illness was just an excuse for staying off school) pretext, cover-up, pretense.

**execute** vb 1 (Murderers used to be executed) put to death, kill, hang. 2 (execute a plan), carry out, perform, accomplish, fulfill, put into effect, implement.

**exercise** vb 1 (The women were exercising in order to keep fit) do exercises, work out, train. 2 (try to exercise a little patience) use, employ, apply, exert.

**exercise** n 1 (do exercises every morning to keep fit) physical training, workout, drill. 2 (Some exercise is necessary to keep healthy) activity, physical exertion, physical effort. 3-(pupils given an English exercise) task, piece of work, problem.

**exert** vb 1 (They could finish the job in time if they exerted themselves) make an effort, spare no effort, put oneself out, try hard, do one's best, strive, struggle, strain, labor. 2 (It was necessary to exercise some pressure) employ, use, apply, wield.

**exhaust** vb 1 (The long walk exhausted her) tire, tire out, wear out, fatigue, weary, (inf) poop. 2 (We have exhausted our supplies of food) use up, consume, finish, deplete, expend.

**exhaustive** adj (The police made an exhaustive search) intensive, comprehensive, extensive, thorough.

**exhibit** vb 1 (The firm exhibited their latest works) put on show, show, put on display, display, put on view, demonstrate, present. 2 (exhibit patience/exhibit signs of improvement) show, indicate, reveal, demonstrate, express.

**exhibition** n 1 (a book exhibition) show, display, demonstration, presentation, fair, exposition. 2 (an exhibition of bad temper) display,-show, expression, indication, demonstration.

**exile** vb (exiled from their native land) banish, expatriate, deport, expel, outlaw.

**exile** n 1 (sent into exile) banishment, expatriation, deportation. 2-(exiles from their native land) expatriate, deportee, outlaw, refugee, displaced person.

**exist** vb 1 (children believing that fairies exist) be, have being, have existence, live, be living. 2 (difficult to exist on such a low income) live, stay alive, survive.

**exit** n (the exit from the theater) way out, egress.

**expand** vb 1 (substances that expand when heated) grow larger, get larger, increase in size, swell, distend. 2 (expand the business) make larger, make bigger, increase, amplify, add to, extend.

**expanse** n (an expanse of blue water) stretch, area, extent, tract, sweep.

**expect** vb 1 (I expect that they will arrive soon) believe, think, assume, suppose, imagine, presume, surmise. 2 (I am expecting a parcel from them) await, wait for, look for, anticipate, hope for.

**expedite** vb (try to expedite the process) speed up, hasten, hurry, accelerate, step up.

**expedition** n 1 (an expedition to the center of the jungle) journey, exploration, safari, undertaking, quest. 2 (a shopping expedition) trip, outing, excursion, jaunt. 3 (the members of the expedition to climb Everest) group, team, party, company.

**expel** vb 1 (expel him from school/ expel him from the club) throw out, oust, drum out, bar, ban, blackball. 2 (expel them from their native land) banish, exile, drive out, cast out, expatriate, deport.

**expense** n 1 (victory in the war at the expense of many lives) cost, sacrifice. 2 (go to a great deal of expense to buy her a present) outlay, cost, spending.

**expensive** adj (expensive clothes) costly, high-priced, dear, overpriced, exorbitant, extortionate, (inf) steep.

**experience** n 1 (a terrifying experience) event, incident, occurrence, happening, affair, episode. 2 (a job requiring experience as well as a university degree) practical knowledge, skill, practice, training, (inf) know-how, (inf) hands-on experience.

**experiment** n (medical experiments to find new drugs) test, trial, investigation, research, pilot study.

**expert** n (an expert on local history) authority, specialist, professional, pundit, (inf) buff.

**expert** adj (an expert chess player) knowledgeable, specialist, experienced, professional, skillful, proficient, adept, (inf) crack.

**expire** vb 1 (Her membership of the club has expired) run out, be no longer valid, end, come to an end, finish, stop, cease, lapse. 2 (people expiring from lack of food) die, pass away, breathe one's last, decease.

**explain** vb 1 (explain how to work the machine) give an explanation of, describe, define, make clear, spell out, throw light on. 2 (called upon to explain their actions) give an explanation of, account for, give a reason for, justify, defend, vindicate.

**explanation** n 1 (a clear explanation as to how the machine works) description, definition, clarification, interpretation. 2

(unable to accept their explanation for their absence) account, reason, grounds, excuse, justification, defense, vindication

**explode** vb 1 (The bomb exploded) blow up, go off, detonate, burst. 2 (The gas boiler exploded) blow up, burst open, fly into pieces, erupt. 3 (explode his theory) disprove, discredit, refute, invalidate, debunk.

**exploit** n (a book about the exploits of the pioneers) deed, feat, adventure, stunt.

**exploit** vb 1 (exploit the resources which they have) make use of, use, utilize, put to good use, turn to one's advantage, profit by, make capital out of. 2 (a factory-owner who exploited the workers/a man who exploited his friends) make use of, take advantage of, abuse, impose upon.

**explore** vb 1 (explore areas of jungle) travel in, survey, reconnoiter. 2 (explore every possibility) examine, look into, investigate, inquire into, consider, research.

**explosion** n 1 (There was a loud explosion and we discovered the boiler had blown up) bang, blast, boom, rumble, crash, crack, report. 2 (an explosion in the population figures) increase, escalation, mushrooming, rocketing.

**expose** vb 1 (expose her skin to the sun) bare, lay bare, uncover. 2 (newspapers exposing the details of the scandal) reveal, disclose, divulge, make known, uncover, unveil. 3 (expose the baby to harsh weather) lay open to, leave unprotected by, put at risk from.

**express** vb 1 (express their gratitude in a short speech) voice, state, put into words, articulate, utter, make known, communicate. 2 (express their appreciation with a gift of money) show, demonstrate, indicate, convey. 3 (express juice from the oranges) press, squeeze, force out, extract.

**expression** n 1 (We could tell from her expression that she was angry) face, countenance, look, appearance, air. 2 (find the right expression to say what she means) word, words, phrase, term, wording, language, turn of phrase, phraseology. 3 (play the violin piece with expression) feeling, emotion, passion, intensity, vividness.

**extant** adj (a species of bird that is still extant) still existing, in existence, living, alive, existent, surviving, remaining.

**extend** vb 1 (extend the territory which he rules over) expand, increase, enlarge, lengthen. 2 (extend the ladder to its full length) stretch out, draw out, lengthen, elongate. 3 (extend the period of his employment) increase, prolong, lengthen, stretch out, protract. 4 (The lake extends for many miles) continue, stretch, stretch

out, carry on, run on. 5 (extend a warm welcome to the guests) offer, give, proffer, hold out.

**extensive** adj 1 (a house with extensive grounds) large, large-scale, sizeable, substantial, vast, immense. 2 (have extensive knowledge of the Bible) comprehensive, thorough, wideranging, wide, broad. 3 (The storm caused extensive damage to the crops) great, widespread, whole sale, universal.

**extent** n 1 (the extent of her knowledge/the extent of the damage) scope, range, coverage, degree. 2 (the extent of the land around the house) area, expanse, length, stretch.

**exterior** adj (the exterior surface) outside, outer, outermost, outward, external, surface.

**extinct** adj 1 (a species of bird now extinct) died out, wiped out, gone, defunct. 2 (an extinct volcano) inactive, extinguished, burnt out.

**extinguish** vb (extinguish the candles) put out, blow out, quench, snuff out.

**extra** adj 1 (They need extra help to finish the job) more, additional, added, further, supplementary, auxiliary, subsidiary. 2 (We have extra food in our picnic—would you like some?) surplus, spare, left over, superfluous, excess, reserve.

**extract** vb (extract a tooth) pull out, draw out, take out, remove.

**extract** n (read extracts from her novel on the radio) excerpt, passage, selection, quotation, citation.

**extraordinary** adj 1 (have an extraordinary memory) exceptional, unusual, uncommon, rare, striking, remarkable. phenomenal. 2 (It was extraordinary that she survived) amazing, astonishing, remarkable, astounding, surprising, strange.

**extravagant** adj 1 (an extravagant way of life/ It was extravagant to buy such an expensive dress) spendthrift, thriftless, improvident, profligate, wasteful. 2 (He tried to flatter her by paying her extravagant compliments) exaggerated, excessive, outrageous, absurd.

**extreme** adj 1 (in the extreme north of the country) farthest, furthest, outermost, most remote. 2 (in extreme danger) very great, greatest, maximum, utmost, severe. 3 (people who hold extreme political views) immoderate, fanatical, exaggerated, intemperate.

**extremely** adv (She is extremely beautiful) very, exceedingly, exceptionally, extraordinarily, markedly, uncommonly.

**eye** n 1 (have sharp eyes) eyesight, sight, vision. 2 (The police are keeping an eye on her/She is under the eagle eye of the principal) watch, observation, notice, surveillance
.

# F

**fabric** n 1 (*curtains made of a brightly colored fabric*) cloth, material, textile, stuff. 2 (*the fabric of the building/the fabric of society*) framework, frame, structure, constitution.

**fabulous** adj 1 (*stories about fabulous creatures such as dragons*) mythical, imaginary, fictitious, fictional, legendary. 2 (*an emperor of fabulous wealth*) incredible, unbelievable, unimaginable, inconceivable, astonishing. 3 (*They had a fabulous time on vacation*) marvelous, wonderful, superb, great, (*inf*) super.

**face** n 1 (*She had a beautiful face*) countenance, features. 2 (*She came rushing out with an angry face*) expression, look, air. 3 (*the faces of a cube*) front, side, surface. 4 (*She was afraid of losing face in the firm*) prestige, status, standing, dignity. 5 (*She had the face to call us liars*) impudence, impertinence, audacity, effrontery, cheek, (*inf*) nerve.

**face** vb 1 (*an apartment building facing the sea*) look on to, overlook, be opposite to, front on to. 2 (*They are facing many difficulties*) meet, encounter, confront.

**facetious** adj (*please don't make facetious remarks—it is a serious situation*) flippant, frivolous, light-hearted, joking, jocular, funny, amusing.

**fact** n 1 (*difficult to separate fact from fiction*) reality, actuality, truth. 2 (*wish to have all the facts of the case*) detail, particular, factor, piece of information, piece of data, circumstance.

**factor** n (*consider all the factors connected with the situation*) element, point, detail, feature, item, circumstance.

**fade** vb 1 (*The curtains had faded in the sunlight*) lose color, become bleached, become pale, become washed out, dull, dim. 2 (*fresh flowers that had faded*) wilt, wither,-droop, die. 3 (*Hope had faded/Memories of the occasion had faded*) dim, grow less, die away,-dwindle, grow faint, vanish, die.

**fail** vb 1 (*Their attempt to climb the mountain failed*) be unsuccessful, fall through, be in vain, come to nothing, come to grief, (*inf*) flop. 2 (*They failed the exam*) not pass, (*inf*) flunk. 3 (*The engine failed*) break down, stop working, cut out, (*inf*) conk out. 4 (*He fail-ed to-keep us informed*) omit, neglect, forget. 5 (*Her health is-failing*) decline, deteriorate, diminish, dwindle, wane. 6-(*His business has failed*) collapse, crash, go under, go bankrupt, go to the-wall, fold, (*inf*) go bust, (*inf*) flop.

**failing** n (*Untidiness is his main failing*) fault, shortcoming, weakness, flaw, imperfection, defect, foible.

**failure** n (*Our attempt was a complete failure*) non-success, disaster, fiasco, (*inf*) flop.

**faint** adj 1 (*faint traces of paint on the table*) indistinct, unclear, dim, faded, obscure. 2 (*hear a faint sound of laughter*) indistinct, soft, low, muted, feeble. 3 (*a faint smell of violets*) slight, indistinct, delicate. 4 (*have a faint chance of winning the match*) slight, small, remote, vague. 5 (*feel faint*) dizzy, giddy, light-headed.

**faint** vb (*She fainted in the heat*) pass out, collapse, black out, lose consciousness, swoon, (*inf*) conk out.

**fair** adj 1 (*She had fair hair*) blond, yellow, flaxen, pale, light brown. 2 (*the accused was given a fair trial*) just, impartial, unprejudiced, unbiased, objective. 3 (*a fair judge*) fair-minded, just, impartial, unprejudiced, unbiased, open-minded, honest. 4 (*the weather was fair for the picnic*) fine, dry, bright. 5 (*The standard of his work is just fair*) satisfactory, all right, middling, so-so, average, adequate.

**fairly** adv (*She was fairly good at playing the piano*) quite, rather, somewhat, reasonably, passably, tolerably, (*inf*) pretty.

**faith** n 1 (*they have faith in their doctor*) trust, confidence, belief, reliance. 2 (*they are of the Christian faith*) religion, creed, belief, persuasion.

**faithful** adj 1 (*the leader's faithful followers*) loyal, constant, true, devoted, dependable, reliable, trustworthy, staunch. 2 (*a faithful account of the event/a faithful copy of the picture*) accurate, true, exact, precise, close.

**fake** adj 1 (*fake ten dollar bills*) counterfeit, forged, fraudulent, false, imitation, (*inf*) phony. 2 (*wearing a string of fake pearls*) imitation, artificial, synthetic, simulated, mock, sham, ersatz.

**fall** vb 1 (*The leaves fall in autumn*) drop, descend. 2 (*The child fell as she left the bus*) fall down, trip over, stumble, topple over, go head over heels. 3 (*The level of the water in the river was falling in the drought*) sink, subside, abate. 4 (*The price of houses has fallen*) decrease, decline, go down, grow less, plummet, slump. 5 (*a memorial to the soldiers who fell in battle*) die, be killed, be slain, perish, be a fatality, be a casualty. 6 (*Her birthday falls on a Monday this year*) be, take place, occur, happen.

**false** adj 1 (*They gave a false account of their movements to the police*) untrue, wrong, incorrect, inaccurate, erroneous. 2 (*He gave a false name*) assumed, made-up, invented, fictitious, (*inf*) phony. 3-(*false friends*) disloyal, unfaithful, faithless, treacherous, untrustworthy.

**falsehood** n (*accuse him of telling falsehoods*) lie, untruth, fib, story.

**falter** vb 1 (*The young boxer faltered when he saw the size of his opponent*) hesitate, waver, flinch, stumble. 2 (*The speaker was nervous and faltered over his speech*) stumble, stutter, stammer.

**fame** n (*His fame as an artist has spread/seek fame in Hollywood*) renown, eminence, distinction, notability, greatness, glory, honor.

**familiar** adj 1 (*The old man was a familiar sight in the village store*) well-known, common, customary, accustomed, regular, commonplace, everyday. 2 (*workers who were familiar with the computing system*) acquainted with, conversant with, versed in, experienced in, with knowledge of.

**family** n 1 (*people of noble family*) ancestry, parentage, descent, extraction, blood, line. 2 (*The poor old woman has no family*) relatives, relations, people, one's own flesh and blood, next of kin. 3 (*The couple have no family*) children, offspring, progeny, (*inf*) kids.

**fan** n (*a football fan/a fan of the pop star*) admirer, follower, enthusiast, devotee, fanatic, addict, aficionado, (*inf*) buff, (*inf*) freak.

**fancy** n 1 (*the fancy of the poet*) imagination, creativity. 2 (*The person from Mars was just a fancy on the child's part*) figment of the imagination, hallucination, illusion, delusion, fantasy. 3 (*have a fancy for some chocolate*) desire, urge, notion, wish, want, hankering, longing, yearning, (*inf*) yen.

**fancy** vb 1 (*He fancied he saw a ghostly figure*) imagine, think, believe. 2 (*He said that he fancied a drink*) would like, wish, want, desire, hanker after, long for, yearn for, (*inf*) have a yen for.

**fancy** adj (*fancy patterns/fancy decorations*) ornate, elaborate, ornamental, decorated, adorned, embellished, showy, (*inf*) jazzy.

**fantastic** adj 1 (*He had fantastic notions about seeing aliens from Mars*) fanciful, imaginary, wild, strange. 2 (*fantastic figures and shapes in his painting*) strange, weird, bizarre, outlandish, fanciful, whimsical. 3 (*He earns a fantastic amount of money*) huge, enormous, tremendous. 4 (*He thought the concert was-fantastic*) marvelous, wonderful, sensational, superb, excellent.

**fantasy** n 1 (*a children's book which is full of fantasy*) fancy, imagination, creativity, originality, vision. 2 (*She is always having fantasies about winning a lot of money*) flight of fancy, dream, daydream, pipe dream, reverie, illusion.

**far** *adv* 1 (*it is not far to the next village*) a long way, a great distance. 2 (*It is far too soon to know*) by a long way, to a great extent, very much.

**far** *adj* (*the far places of the world*) far-away, far-off, distant, remote, farflung.

**fare** *n* (*Train fares have gone up*) ticket, charge, cost, price.

**far-fetched** *adj* (*They found his story rather far-fetched*) unlikely, improbable, implausible, incredible, unbelievable, unconvincing.

**farm** *vb* (*farm land in the north*) cultivate, till, work.

**fascinate** *vb* (*The children were fascinated by the mime artist*) captivate, enchant, enthrall, entrance, hold spellbound, charm, absorb, engross.

**fashion** *n* 1 (*the fashions of the nineteenth century*) style, trend, taste, craze, vogue. 2 (*She has a job in fashion*) clothes, the clothes industry, couture. 3 (*She arranged things in an organized fashion*) way, manner, method, style, system.

**fashionable** *adj* (*fashionable clothes/ furniture that is no longer fashionable*) in fashion, stylish, up-to-date, in vogue, modern, contemporary, (*inf*) trendy.

**fast** *adj* 1 (*at a fast pace*) quick, rapid, swift, brisk, speedy, hurried. 2 (*fast colors*) fixed, indelible, permanent, colorfast.

**fast** *adv* 1 (*walk fast*) quickly, rapidly, swiftly, briskly, speedily, hurriedly, like the wind. 2 (*a truck stuck fast in the mud*) firmly, tightly, securely, immovably. 3 (*children who were fast asleep*) sound, deeply.

**fast** *vb* (*people who fast during certain religious holidays/fasting in aid of a famine charity*) go without food, eat-nothing, go hungry, starve oneself, deny oneself food.

**fasten** *vb* 1 (*She fastened a brooch to her dress*) attach, fix, clip, pin. 2-(*fasten the dog to the gatepost*) attach, tie, bind, tether. 3 (*The links of the chain are fastened to each other*) join, connect, couple, unite, link.

**fat** *adj* 1 (*fat people trying to lose weight*) plump, obese, stout, overweight, portly, chubby, flabby. 2-(*fat reference books*) thick, big, substantial. 3 (*people told to avoid fat substances for the sake of their health*) fatty, greasy, oily.

**fat** *n* 1 (*require some form of fat to make a cake*) animal fat, vegetable fat, lard, butter, margarine, cooking oil, olive oil. 2 (*She was embarrassed by her fat*) fatness, plumpness, obesity, stoutness, portliness, chubbiness, flab.

**fatal** *adj* (*a fatal blow/a fatal illness*) mortal, deadly, lethal, killing, terminal.

**fatality** *n* (*There were several fatalities in the freeway crash*) death, dead, casualty, mortality.

**fate** *n* (*She wondered what fate had in store for him*) destiny, providence, chance, luck, fortune, the stars, nemesis.

**fateful** *adj* (*a fateful meeting*) critical, crucial, decisive, momentous, important.

**father** *n* 1 (*Her father left her a lot of money*) male parent, (*inf*) dad, (*inf*) daddy, (*inf*) pa, (*inf*) old man. 2-(*the father of modern medicine*) founder, originator, initiator, creator, architect.

**fatigue** *n* (*He was suffering from fatigue after climbing the mountain*) tiredness, weariness, exhaustion.

**fatty** *adj* (*fatty foods*) fat, greasy, oily.

**fault** *n* 1 (*discover a fault in the material*) flaw, defect, imperfection. 2 (*one of the main faults in her character*) flaw, defect, failing, shortcoming, weakness, weak point, deficiency. 3 (*The accident was her fault*) blame, responsibility.

**faulty** *adj* 1 (*a faulty lock*) broken, damaged, defective, unsound. 2 (*take the faulty goods back to the store*) flawed, defective, imperfect.

**favor** *n* 1 (*He did her a favor by giving her a lift*) good turn, good deed, service, kindness. 2 (*He looked on-the new scheme with favor*) approval, approbation, goodwill, friendliness.

**favorable** *adj* 1 (*in less favorable circumstances/ favorable winds*) advantageous, beneficial, helpful, promising, auspicious. 2 (*She hoped to make a favorable impression on her friend's parents*) good, pleasing, agreeable. 3 (*He received a favorable report from his teacher*) good, approving, praising, commendatory, enthusiastic.

**favorite** *adj* (*the child's favorite toy*) best-loved, dearest, favored, chosen, preferred.

**favorite** *n* (*The youngest child is her grandfather's favorite*) pet, darling, idol.

**fear** *n* (*filled with fear at the sight of the strange man*) fright, terror, alarm, panic, apprehensiveness, dread, horror, nervousness.

**fear** *vb* 1 (*They fear their grandfather*) be afraid of, be scared of, be apprehensive of, dread. 2-(*We fear for their safety*) worry, be anxious, feel concerned. 3 (*We fear that they could be right*) be afraid, suspect, have a suspicion.

**fearful** *adj* 1 (*They were fearful of disturbing the guard dogs*) afraid, frightened, terrified, alarmed, apprehensive. 2 (*The smashed cars were a-fearful sight*) terrible, frightful, appalling, ghastly, horrific, horrible, shocking. 3 (*The house was in a fearful mess*) terrible, frightful, appalling, very great.

**fearless** *adj* (*fearless soldiers fighting the enemy/ fearless explorers*) brave, courageous, gallant, valiant, intrepid, bold, heroic.

**feasible** *adj* (*It was not feasible to leave earlier*) possible, practicable, workable, reasonable, realistic, within reason.

**feat** *n* (*read about the daring feats of the knights of old*) deed, act, action, exploit, achievement.

**feather** *n* (*the bird's feathers*) plumage, plumes, down.

**feature** *n* (*the feature of the burglary that confused the police*) aspect, characteristic, side, detail, quality, peculiarity.

**features** *npl* (*She had very regular features*) face, countenance.

**fee** *n* (*the fee for membership of the club*) charge, price, cost, payment, subscription.

**feeble** *adj* 1 (*people who have grown feeble with age*) weak, weakly, frail, infirm, delicate, failing, helpless, debilitated. 2 (*They made a feeble attempt to get there on time*) ineffective, ineffectual, weak, futile, inadequate.

**feed** *vb* (*not make enough money to feed the family*) give food to, nourish, provide for, cater for.

**feel** *vb* 1 (*feel faint at her father's words*) experience, undergo, know, be conscious of, be aware of, notice. 2 (*feel the silky cloth*) touch, stroke, caress, finger, handle, fondle. 3 (*He tried to feel his way to the house in the dark*) grope, fumble. 4 (*The weather feels warmer today*) seem, appear. 5 (*feel the temperature of the water before bathing the baby*) test, try out. 6-(*We feel that we ought to go*) believe, think, consider, be of the opinion, judge.

**feeling** *n* 1 (*Blind people are able to identify objects by feeling*) feel, touch, sense of touch. 2 (*He could not describe his feelings when he lost his job*) emotion, sentiment, sensation. 3 (*There was a feeling of unhappiness about the place*) feel, atmosphere, mood, impression, air, aura. 4 (*My feeling is that we should go*) thoughts, opinion, view, way of thinking, instinct. 5 (*I had a feeling that he would win*) idea, suspicion, funny feeling, hunch.

**feign** *vb* 1 (*feign illness*) pretend, fake, simulate, sham, affect, give the appearance of. 2 (*We thought that he was sleeping but he was only feigning*) pretend, put on an act, put it on, fake, sham, act, play-act.

**fellow** *n* (*a suspicious-looking fellow over there*) man, boy, individual, (*inf*) guy, (*inf*) character.

**fellowship** *n* (*Now that she has retired she misses the fellowship of-her coworkers*) companionship, company, friendship, comradeship.

**female** *n* (*a club just for females*) woman, lady, girl.

**feminine** *adj* 1 (*a very feminine young woman/ feminine clothes*) womanly, ladylike, soft, delicate. **2**-(*a rather feminine man*) effeminate, womanish, unmanly.

**fence** *n* (*build a fence round the yard*) barrier, barricade, railing, paling, picket fence, hedge, wall.

**fence** *vb* **1** (*fence the yard*) enclose, surround, encircle. **2** (*fence in the cows*) shut in, confine, pen.

**fend** *vb* (*He tried to fend off his attacker's blows with his arm/a speaker trying to fend off questions*) ward off, turn aside, deflect, avert, keep off.

**ferment** *vb* **1** (*beer fermenting in vats*) foam, froth, bubble, effervesce. **2** (*He set out to ferment trouble in the crowd*) cause, incite, excite, provoke, stir up, foment.

**ferocious** *adj* **1** (*ferocious animals*) fierce, savage, wild. **2** (*He was injured in a ferocious attack*) fierce, savage, brutal, vicious, violent, murderous, barbaric.

**fertile** *adj* **1** (*fertile soil*) fruitful, productive, rich, fecund. **2** (*a fertile imagination*) inventive, creative, resourceful, ingenious.

**fertilizer** *n* (*put fertilizer on the plot*) plant food, manure, compost.

**fervent** *adj* (*his fervent enthusiasm for football/ a fervent supporter of animal rights*) passionate, ardent, zealous, devout, vehement, eager, earnest.

**festival** *n* (*the village's annual festival*) fete, carnival, gala day.

**fetch** *vb* **1** (*fetch the milk from the store*) get, go for, bring, carry, collect, transport. **2** (*an antique table that fetched thousands of dollars at the auction*) sell for, go for, realize.

**feud** *n* (*There had been a bitter feud between the families for generations*) vendetta, quarrel, dispute, conflict.

**fiasco** *n* (*The picnic was a fiasco because of the weather*) disaster, catastrophe, failure, (*inf*) flop.

**fickle** *adj* (*so fickle that she is always changing boyfriends/fickle weather*) capricious, changeable, variable, unpredictable, unstable, unreliable.

**fictitious** *adj* **1** (*not a real person but a fictitious character*) fictional, made up, invented, imaginary, unreal, mythical. **2** (*He gave a fictitious address to the police*) false, invented, bogus, fake, sham.

**fiddle** *vb* **1** (*fiddling with his pencil instead of writing his essay*) play, fidget, toy, twiddle. **2** (*fiddle with the accounts*) falsify, forge, (*inf*) cook.

**fidelity** *n* (*a leader who looked for fidelity in his followers*) faithfulness, loyalty, devotion, allegiance, constancy, trustworthiness.

**fidget** *vb* (*children fidgeting with boredom*) to be restless, wriggle, squirm. **2** (*pupils fidgeting with their pencils*) fiddle, play, toy, twiddle.

**field** *n* **1** (*look at the cows in the field*) pasture, meadow, paddock. **2** (*working in the field of computing*) area, sphere, line, specialty. **3**-(*the football field*) ground, pitch, arena, stadium.

**fierce** *adj* **1** (*a fierce animal*) ferocious, savage, wild. **2** (*a fierce attack*) ferocious, savage, brutal, vicious, violent, murderous. **3** (*her fierce love of liberty*) passionate, ardent, intense, fervent. **4** (*a fierce wind*) strong, violent, stormy, blustery. **5** (*face fierce competition in the race*) keen, intense, strong, competitive.

**fight** *vb* **1** (*enemy armies fighting*) do battle, wage war, take up arms, meet in combat. **2** (*armies fighting a battle*) wage, carry on, be engaged in. **3** (*two men fighting in the street*) exchange blows, hit each other, punch each other, brawl. **4** (*The two sisters are always fighting with each other*) quarrel, argue, bicker, squabble, disagree, (*inf*) fall out, feud. **5**-(*decide to fight the plans for a new road*) contest, take a stand against, oppose, object to, protest against.

**fight** *n* **1** (*Our army lost the fight*) battle, encounter, engagement. **2**-(*The champion lost the fight*) boxing match. **3** (*two men in a-fight outside the bar*) brawl, fisticuffs, (*inf*) scrap. **4** (*She has had a fight with her sister*) quarrel, argument, disagreement, difference of opinion, squabble, dispute, feud.

**figure** *n* **1** (*write down the figures from 1 to 10*) number, numeral, digit. **2** (*What figure did you have in mind as a salary?*) amount, sum. **3** (*fail to recognize the figures disappearing into the mist*) shape, form, outline, silhouette. **4** (*have rather a plump figure*) body, shape, build, physique. **5** (*a bronze figure of the saint*) likeness, image, statue, carving. **6** (*the figures in the text*) diagram, illustration, drawing, chart.

**figure** *vb* **1** (*figure out the cost of the vacation*) calculate, count, work out, reckon, add up. **2** (*try to figure out why he did it*) work out, make out, understand, comprehend, fathom. **3** (*His mother figures in his novel*) appear, feature, play a part, be mentioned.

**fill** *vb* **1** (*fill the supermarket shelves*) load, stock, supply. **2** (*food that will fill the children*) make full, satisfy, stuff. **3** (*The perfume of roses filled the air*) pervade, permeate, spread through. **4** (*They filled the hole with sand*) stop up, block up, plug. **5** (*fill in the form*) fill up, answer.

**film** *n* **1** (*a film of oil on the road*) layer, coat, coating, covering, sheet. **2** (*see it through a film of tears*) haze, mist, blur. **3** (*a Walt Disney film*) movie, motion picture.

**film** *vb* (*film the wedding ceremony*) shoot, make a movie of, televise.

**filter** *vb* (*filter the coffee*) strain, sieve, sift.

**filth** *n* **1** (*an old basement covered in filth*) dirt, grime, muck, mud, squalor, (*inf*) crud. **2** (*complaining about the filth in some magazines*) pornography, obscenity, smut, bawdiness.

**filthy** *adj* **1** (*filthy houses/filthy hands*) dirty, grimy, grubby, mucky, mud- dy, squalid, unwashed, unclean. **2**-(*filthy literature*) pornographic, obscene, indecent, smutty, bawdy, (*inf*) blue.

**final** *adj* **1** (*the final minutes of the football match*) last, closing, concluding, finishing, terminal. **2** (*The decision of the judges is final*) conclusive, decisive, unalterable, indisputable, definitive, absolute.

**finalize** *vb* (*finalize our arrangements*) complete, conclude, settle, put the finishing touches to.

**finance** *n* **1** (*look for a job relating to finance*) money matters, money management, economics. **2** (*Our finances are low at this time of year*) money, cash, capital, funds, assets, resources.

**finance** *vb* (*look for someone to finance*) pay for, fund, provide capital for, provide backing for, subsidize.

**find** *vb* **1** (*We found a wallet in the street*) come across, stumble on, discover. **2** (*She lost her purse and never found it*) get back, recover, retrieve. **3** (*doctors trying to find a cure for cancer*) discover, come upon, bring to light, uncover, unearth, hit upon. **4** (*He is trying to find a new job*) get, obtain, acquire, procure. **5** (*She found that the food did not agree with her*) discover, realize, become aware, learn.

**fine** *adj* **1** (*hope for a fine day for their picnic*) dry, fair, clear, sunny. **2** (*ornaments made of fine china*) delicate, fragile, dainty. **3** (*summer dresses made of fine material*) light, lightweight, thin, delicate, filmy, flimsy. **4** (*a beach with fine-sand*) powdery, fine-grained. **5**-(*There is only a fine distinction between the two schemes*) tiny, minute, subtle. **6** (*The musician gave a fine performance*) splendid, excellent, first-class, first-rate, outstanding. **7** (*go to a wedding party wearing fine clothes*) elegant, stylish, expensive. **8** (*He was ill but he is fine now*) all right, well. **9** (*If you want to leave early that is fine with us*) all right, acceptable, suitable, (*inf*) OK.

**fine** *n* (*a fine for speeding*) penalty, forfeit.

**finger** *vb* (*children told not to finger the fruit before buying it*) touch, handle, feel, fiddle with.

**finish** *vb* **1** (*workmen who did not finish the job in time*) complete, accomplish, carry out, get done, fulfill. **2** (*when the concert finished/when the work finished*) end, come to an end, conclude, cease, stop, terminate. **3** (*We finished the bread at breakfast*) use,

use up, consume, exhaust, (*inf*) polish off. **4** (*They finish work at five o'clock*) stop, cease, end, discontinue, halt.

**fire** *n* **1** (*modern homes that do not have a fire*) fireplace, hearth, grate. **2** (*Fortunately no one was hurt in the fire*) blaze, flames, conflagration, inferno. **3** (*make a fire to burn the garbage*) bonfire. **4** (*Her playing of the piece was without fire*) passion, ardor, inspiration.

**fire** *vb* **1** (*He fired the gun*) shoot, let off, discharge. **2** (*They were found guilty of firing the farm buildings*) set fire to, set on fire, set alight, ignite. **3** (*His performance fired them with enthusiasm*) inspire, rouse, arouse, stir up, stimulate. **4**-(*He was fired for always being late*) sack, dismiss, (*inf*) axe.

**firm** *adj* **1** (*The ice was not firm enough to skate on*) hard, hardened, solid, set, rigid. **2** (*The poles for the fence must be firm in the ground*) fixed, secure, fast, stable, set, tight. **3** (*We have no firm plans/make a firm arrangement*) fixed, settled, agreed, definite, decided, established. **4** (*They were quite firm about refusing the invitation*) determined, resolute, resolved, decided, adamant, unwavering, obstinate, stubborn. **5**-(*They have become firm friends*) devoted, faithful, loyal, dependable.

**firm** *n* (*he started his own publishing firm*) business, company, organization, establishment, concern.

**first** *adj* **1** (*the first stages of the manufacturing process*) early, earliest, opening, introductory. **2** (*the first airplane*) earliest, original. **3**-(*the first people to arrive*) earliest, soonest.

**first** *n* (*We knew from the first that he was not suitable*) beginning, start, outset, commencement, (*inf*) the word go.

**fit** *adj* **1** (*Is the water fit to drink?*) suitable, good enough, satisfactory, appropriate. **2** (*She was not fit for the job*) suitable, good enough, satisfactory, able, capable, competent, adequate, trained, qualified. **3** (*The baseball player was injured but he is fit now*) well, healthy, in good health, strong, in good condition, in good shape.

**fit** *vb* **1** (*The shoes do not fit*) be the right size, be the correct size. **2** (*fit the parts of the doll's house together*) assemble, put together, join, connect. **3** (*fit the tiles to the floor*) lay, fix, put in place, put in position, position. **4** (*clothes that do not fit the occasion*) suit, be suitable for, be appropriate for, be apt for. **5** (*His account of the accident does not fit with hers*) agree, be in agreement, match, accord, concur, tally.

**fit** *n* **1** (*She had a coughing fit*) bout, attack, spell. **2** (*an epileptic fit*) convulsion, seizure, spasm, paroxysm.

**fitting** *adj* **1** (*The criminal should receive a fitting punishment*) suitable, appropriate, due, apt. **2** (*It was not fitting for her to wear those clothes to a funeral*) proper, right, seemly, decent, decorous, suitable, appropriate.

**fix** *vb* **1** (*fix the bookshelves to the study wall*) attach, fasten, secure, stick, screw, nail. **2** (*fix a date for the party*) set, decide on, settle, arrange, agree on, name. **3** (*He is trying to fix the car*) repair, mend, sort, put right, put to rights.

**fizzy** *adj* (*fizzy drinks*) sparkling, bubbly, effervescent.

**flabbergasted** *adj* (*He was flabbergasted at how much the new car was going to cost*) astounded, amazed, dumbfounded, stunned, staggered, nonplussed.

**flag** *n* (*decorate the streets with flags for the inauguration*) banner, pennant, streamer, standard.

**flag** *vb* **1** (*Their interest in the subject matter is flagging*) fade, fail, decrease, decline, diminish. **2** (*The speeding driver was flagged down by the police*) wave down, signal to stop.

**flair** *n* (*have a flair for languages*) talent, gift, ability, aptitude, bent, genius.

**flake** *n* (*flakes of paint*) *n* chip, shaving, sliver, fragment, bit.

**flame** *n* (*burn with a bright flame*) fire, glow, gleam, brightness.

**flame** *vb* (*The dry wood flamed up*) burn, blaze, burst into flames, catch fire.

**flap** *vb* **1** (*The flags were flapping in the wind*) flutter, wave, swing. **2**-(*birds with wings flapping*) beat, flail, vibrate, thresh.

**flare** *vb* **1** (*The fire suddenly flared up*) blaze, flame. **2** (*Trouble flared up when the army left*) break out, burst out, recur. **3** (*She flares up whenever anyone disagrees with her*) lose one's temper, go into a rage, get angry, fly off the handle.

**flash** *n* **1** (*a flash of light*) blaze, burst, flare, gleam, beam, streak. **2**-(*She was there in a flash*) instant, moment, second, trice, twinkling of an eye.

**flashy** *adj* (*wear flashy clothes*) showy, gaudy, ostentatious, flamboyant, loud, garish, tawdry, (*inf*) jazzy, (*inf*) tacky.

**flat** *adj* **1** (*flat surfaces*) level, horizontal, even, smooth. **2** (*lying in a flat position*) spread out, stretched out, prone, supine, prostrate. **3** (*a flat tire*) deflated, collapsed, burst, punctured. **4** (*The party was rather flat after she had left*) boring, dull, tedious, unexciting, lifeless, uninspired.

**flatten** *vb* **1** (*flatten the surface to make the new road*) make flat, level, even out, smooth out, plane. **2** (*flatten the old buildings to make way for new houses*) pull down, knock down, tear down, demolish, raze

to the ground. **3** (*gales which flattened the crops*) crush, squash, compress.

**flatter** *vb* **1** (*He flatters her whenever he wants to borrow her car*) pay compliments to, compliment, praise, sing the praises of, humor, (*inf*) sweet-talk. **2** (*The dress flatters her*) suit, become, show to advantage.

**flavor** *n* **1** (*people who dislike the flavor of garlic*) taste, savor. **2** (*a sauce in need of flavor*) flavoring, seasoning, spiciness, piquancy. **3**-(*a book that captured the flavor of the times*) spirit, character, feel, feeling, tone, nature, essence, ambience.

**flaw** *n* **1** (*a flaw in the dress material*) defect, imperfection, fault. **2** (*a flaw in the china*) defect, imperfection, fault, crack, chip.

**flee** *vb* (*The villagers fled as the enemy army approached*) run away, run off, escape, take flight, make off, abscond, retreat.

**fleeting** *adj* (*a fleeting feeling of regret*) brief, short-lived, momentary, transient, transitory, ephemeral.

**flesh** *n* **1** (*the flesh and bones of the animals*) meat, brawn, muscle. **2**--(*prefer the pleasures of the flesh to those of the spirit*) body, human body, physical nature.

**flexible** *adj* **1** (*flexible materials*) pliable, pliant, elastic, springy, bendable. **2** (*Our vacation plans are flexible at the moment*) adaptable, adjustable, variable, changeable, open to change.

**flight** *n* **1** (*the flight of the refugees from the war zone*) fleeing, running away, escape, absconding, retreat. **2** (*write a book on the history of flight*) flying, aviation. **3**-(*The flight to Australia from New York is very long*) plane journey, plane trip.

**flimsy** *adj* **1** (*a summer dress made of a flimsy material*) thin, lightweight, light, delicate, sheer. **2** (*a flimsy hut to shelter the refugees*) insubstantial, frail, rickety, ramshackle, makeshift. **3** (*a flimsy excuse for being absent*) feeble, weak, poor, thin, inadequate, unconvincing.

**flinch** *vb* **1** (*The boy flinched as his father raised his fist*) draw back, recoil, shrink, quail, wince. **2** (*soldiers who do not flinch from their duty*) shrink from, shy away from, shirk, dodge, duck.

**fling** *vb* (*fling the garbage into the tip*) throw, toss, hurl, cast, pitch, lob, heave, (*inf*) chuck.

**flippant** *adj* (*She gave a flippant reply to his serious question*) frivolous, shallow, glib, offhand, carefree.

**float** *vb* **1** (*things which can float on water*) stay afloat, be buoyant. **2**-(*marker buoys floating along*) bob, drift. **3** (*balloons floating in the air*) drift, hover, hang.

**flog** *vb* (*people who think that wrongdoers should be flogged*) whip, lash, flay, birch, scourge, beat, thrash, cane.

**flood** n 1 (*property damaged in the flood*) deluge, torrent, spate, inundation. 2 (*After the article in the newspaper there was a flood of correspondence*) abundance, overabundance, profusion.

**flood** vb 1 (*houses damaged by rivers flooding*) overflow, break its banks. 2 (*water which flooded the town*) pour over, inundate, submerge, immerse.

**floor** n (*a house on three floors*) storey, level.

**flop** vb 1 (*His head flopped to one side and he fell asleep*) droop, sag, dangle. 2 (*She flopped into a chair after a hard day's work*) slump, drop, collapse, fall. 3 (*His first play flopped*) fail, be unsuccessful, be a disaster, (*inf*) bomb.

**flourish** vb 1 (*plants which flourish in a dry climate*) thrive, bloom, grow, do well, develop. 2 (*The company is flourishing now*) be in good condition, thrive, be successful, succeed, make progress. 3 (*He flourished the trophy which he had won*) brandish, wave, wield, swing, shake, twirl, hold aloft.

**flow** vb 1 (*rivers flowing*) run, glide, course, stream, ripple, surge. 2 (*a serious wound with blood flowing from it*) gush, well, spurt, spill, ooze.

**flower** n (*put the flowers in a vase*) bloom, blossom.

**flowery** adj 1 (*curtains with a flowery pattern*) floral, flower-covered. 2 (*dislike the flowery language of his writing*) high-flown, ornate, elaborate, bombastic.

**fluent** adj 1 (*a fluent speaker*) eloquent, articulate, smooth-spoken. 2 (*We admired his fluent French*) smooth, flowing, effortless, unhesitating.

**flurry** n 1 (*a sudden flurry of snow*) shower, gust, squall. 2 (*in a flurry of excitement waiting for the visitors to arrive*) fluster, bustle, whirl, fuss, flap.

**flush** vb 1 (*flush the toilet*) rinse out, wash out, cleanse. 2 (*She flushed with embarrassment*) blush, redden, go red, turn red, crimson, color.

**fluster** vb (*The guests flustered her by arriving early*) agitate, unsettle, upset, ruffle, panic, confuse, disconcert, (*inf*) rattle.

**flutter** vb 1 (*birds fluttering their wings*) flap, beat, quiver, vibrate. 2 (*streamers fluttering in the wind*) flap, wave, fly, ripple.

**fly** vb 1 (*We decided to fly to New York rather than go by train*) go by air, go by plane, 2 (*He was flying the plane*) pilot, control, operate. 3 (*watch the birds flying overhead*) hover, flutter, soar. 4 (*flags flying to celebrate the victory*) wave, flap, flutter. 5 (*She flew to the window when she heard the car*) rush, race, run, dash, dart. 6 (*They decided to fly as the enemy army approached*) flee, run away, take flight, make one's escape, escape, retreat.

**foam** n 1 (*the foam on the beer*) froth, head. 2 (*the foam on the soapy water*) froth, bubbles, lather, suds, spume.

**foe** n (*They easily defeated their foes*) enemy, opponent, adversary, rival, antagonist.

**fog** n (*The fog was making it difficult for drivers to see*) mist, haze, smog.

**foil** vb (*The police foiled the thief's attempt to rob the bank*) thwart, frustrate, stop.

**foist** vb (*He tried to foist some of his work on to the junior employees*) force, unload, thrust, impose.

**fold** vb 1 (*fold the sheets*) double over, overlap, crease. 2 (*The firm lost money and folded*) fail, collapse, shut down, go bankrupt, (*inf*) go bust.

**folder** n (*The documents for the meeting were in a folder*) file, binder, cover.

**follow** vb 1 (*She followed her brother into the house*) walk behind, go behind, go after. 2 (*We asked the taxi to follow the car with the thieves in it*) go after, pursue, chase, (*inf*) tail. 3 (*He followed his father as king*) come after, succeed, replace, take the place of. 4 (*They were told to follow the instructions*) obey, observe, keep to, comply with, heed, take notice of. 5 (*The students could not follow what the professor was saying*) understand, comprehend, grasp, fathom. 6 (*He follows the local team*) be a follower of, be a fan of, be an admirer of, be a supporter of.

**fond** adj (*He is very fond of his grandchildren/ She is fond of spicy food*) having love for, having a liking for, keen on, attached to, having a soft spot for.

**food** n 1 (*children with not enough food to survive on*) sustenance, nourishment, provisions. 2 (*The hostess served delicious food*) refreshment, fare, diet, (*inf*) grub.

**foolish** adj 1 (*It was a foolish idea/They thought it was a foolish thing to do*) silly, absurd, senseless, unintelligent, unwise, ill-considered. 2 (*He is a foolish fellow*) stupid, silly, unintelligent, brainless, dense, ignorant, dull-witted, (*inf*) dumb.

**foot** n 1 (*the foot of the pillar*) base, bottom. 2 (*We met at the foot of the road*) bottom, end.

**forbid** vb (*They were forbidden to go on the farmer's land*) prohibit, ban, bar, debar, preclude.

**force** n 1 (*It required a great deal of force to open the door*) strength, power, might, energy, effort, exertion, pressure, vigor. 2 (*They were accused of using force to get him to confess*) pressure, compulsion, coercion, duress, constraint, violence. 3 (*recognize the force of his arguments*) persuasiveness, effectiveness, strength, power, cogency.

**force** vb 1 (*You cannot force them to go with you*) use force on, make, compel, coerce,

bring pressure to bear on, pressure. 2 (*We lost the key and had to force the drawer*) break open, burst open.

**forecast** vb (*We could have forecast that they would win*) predict, foretell, prophesy, foresee, speculate.

**foreign** adj (*customs that were foreign to them*) alien, unfamiliar, strange, unknown, unfamiliar, exotic.

**foresee** vb (*We could not have foreseen those problems*) anticipate, envisage, predict, foretell, forecast, prophesy.

**forfeit** vb (*She had to forfeit her allowance to pay for the damage*) give up, hand over, relinquish, surrender.

**forge** vb (*He forged his father's signature on the check*) falsify, fake, counterfeit, imitate, copy.

**forget** vb 1 (*I forget their address*) be unable to remember, be unable to recall. 2 (*He tried to forget the terrible event*) put out of one's mind, ignore, disregard. 3 (*She forgot her husband's birthday*) overlook, neglect, disregard. 4 (*She forgot her gloves*) leave behind, omit to take.

**forgive** vb (*Their mother forgave them for being late*) excuse, pardon, let off.

**form** n 1 (*describe the form of the crystals*) shape, formation, structure. 2 (*the human form*) body, figure, shape, build, frame, physique, anatomy 3 (*a form of entertainment*) kind, type, sort, variety. 4 (*fill in a form to apply for the job*) document, paper, application.

**form** vb 1 (*form clay into animal shapes*) shape, mold, fashion, model, make. 2 (*They formed a committee to raise money for charity*) set up, establish, found, institute. 3 (*begin to form plans to solve the problem*) put together, draw up, think up, devise, frame. 4 (*icicles began to form in the cold weather*) take shape, develop, appear, materialize.

**forthcoming** adj 1 (*forthcoming events in the town*) future, coming, approaching, imminent. 2 (*The children were not very forthcoming about where they had been*) communicative, talkative, informative, open.

**forthright** adj (*a very forthright person who told them the truth*) direct, frank, candid, blunt, plain-speaking.

**fortunate** adj 1 (*He was fortunate to survive the accident*) in luck. 2 (*They are in a fortunate position to have been offered jobs*) favorable, lucky, advantageous.

**fortune** n 1 (*It was only by good fortune that he found the book*) chance, luck, accident. 2 (*He amassed a great fortune*) wealth, riches, assets, possessions.

**forward** adj 1 (*the forward part of the army*) front, foremost, leading 2 (*They were annoyed at her forward behavior*) bold, brash, brazen, impudent, impertinent, (*inf*) pushy.

**foul** *adj* **1** (*The rotting meat was a foul sight*) disgusting, revolting, repulsive, nauseating, nasty, dirty. **2** (*The air was foul/foul water*) polluted, contaminated, impure, dirty. **3** (*foul weather*) rainy, stormy, wild, rainy, wet, nasty, disagreeable. **4**-(*foul language*) profane, blasphemous, vulgar, crude, coarse, rude, filthy. **5** (*What a foul thing to do*) horrible, nasty, hateful, disgraceful, low, wicked, evil.

**found** *vb* (*found a new company*) set up, establish, institute, start, create.

**fracture** *n* (*fractures in the outer wall*) break, crack, split.

**fragile** *adj* (*china that is very fragile*) delicate, fine, breakable, brittle, frail.

**fragment** *n* (*fragments of glass*) piece, bit, chip, sliver, splinter, particle.

**frail** *adj* **1** (*frail old ladies*) delicate, infirm, weak, slight. **2** (*frail model airplanes*) fragile, breakable, flimsy, insubstantial.

**frame** *n* **1** (*ships built on a frame of steel*) framework, foundation, shell, skeleton. **2** (*a photograph frame*) mounting, mount. **3** (*wrestlers with huge frames*) body, physique, figure,

**frank** *adj* (*He answered in a frank manner*) direct, candid, forthright, plain, open, outspoken, blunt.

**fraud** *n* **1** (*He was accused of fraud*) swindling, sharp practice, dishonesty, crookedness, deceit, deception. **2** (*The magician's act was a fraud*) swindle, hoax, deception, (*inf*) con, (*inf*) ripoff. **3** (*The bill was a fraud*) fake, counterfeit, sham, (*inf*) phony.

**frayed** *adj* (*frayed shirt cuffs*) ragged, tattered, worn.

**freak** *adj* (*a freak storm*) abnormal, unusual, atypical, exceptional, odd, strange, bizarre.

**free** *adj* **1** (*We got free tickets for the concert*) free of charge, for noth- ing, without charge, at no cost, complimentary, gratis. **2** (*They were free of any worries*) without, devoid of, unaffected by, clear of. **3** (*We were free to go anywhere we wanted*) allowed, permitted, able. **4**-(*They asked us to the party but we were not free*) available, unoccupied, not busy, at leisure. **5** (*We looked for a free table in the diner*) unoccupied, empty, vacant, spare. **6** (*nations that wanted to be free*) independent, self-governing, emancipated, autonomous.

**freedom** *n* **1** (*prisoners longing for-their freedom*) liberty, release. **2**-(*nations seeking freedom*) independence, self-government, sovereignty.

**freezing** *adj* **1** (*freezing weather*) icy, frosty, chilly, arctic, wintry. **2** (*We were freezing waiting for the bus*) chilled through, chilled to the marrow, numb with cold.

**frequent** *adj* **1** (*They have frequent storms in that area*) many, numerous, repeated, recurrent, persistent. **2** (*a frequent visitor*) regular, habitual, common, usual, constant.

**fresh** *adj* **1** (*serve fresh fruit for dessert*)-raw, unpreserved, unprocessed. **2** (*a supply of fresh water*) pure, unpolluted, uncontaminated, clean. **3** (*They are hoping for some fresh ideas*) new, modern, original. **4** (*We felt fresh after our vacation*) energetic, invigorated, lively, refreshed, revived.

**friend** *n* (*The children invited their friends to a party*) companion, (*inf*) pal, (*inf*) chum, (*inf*) buddy.

**friendly** *adj* (*friendly neighbors*) amiable, affable, sociable, hospitable, approachable, good-natured, kindly.

**frighten** *vb* (*The children were frightened when they heard the noise*) scare, alarm, startle, terrify.

**front** *n* **1** (*the front of the line*) head, top, beginning. **2** (*They painted the front of the building red*) frontage, façade, face.

**froth** *n* **1** (*froth on the soapy water*) bubbles, lather, suds, spume. **2**-(*froth on the beer*) bubbles, effervescence, head.

**frown** *vb* **1** (*She frowned in anger*) scowl, glower, glare. **2** (*They frowned upon casual clothes at the club*) disapprove of, take a dim view of,-dislike.

**fulfill** *vb* **1** (*He failed to fulfill the tasks given to him*) carry out, perform, discharge, accomplish, complete, execute. **2** (*He was the only person who fulfilled the job requirements*) satisfy, meet, answer, obey.

**full** *adj* **1** (*Their glasses were full*) filled,-brimming, brimful. **2** (*All the hotel rooms are full*) occupied, taken, in use. **3** (*The supermarket was full on Saturdays*) crowded, packed, crammed, chock-full. **4** (*She gave us a full list of the names of-people present*) complete, whole,-entire, comprehensive, detailed, thorough.

**fumble** *vb* **1** (*fumble for his keys in the dark*) grope, feel for. **2** (*the quarterback fumbled*) miss, mishandle.

**fumes** *npl* (*the fumes from the car's exhaust pipe*) gases, smoke, vapor, smell.

**fun** *n* (*The children had fun at the party*) entertainment, amusement, enjoyment, pleasure, a good time.

**function** *n* **1** (*his function in the firm*) role, job, duty, task, responsibility. **2** (*the function of the machine*) use, purpose. **3** (*invited to the firm's annual function*) party, reception, gathering, social occasion, social event.

**fundamental** *adj* (*learn fundamental cooking skills*) basic, rudimentary, elementary, essential, primary.

**funny** *adj* **1** (*They laughed at his funny stories*) amusing, comic, comical, humorous, hilarious, laughable, riotous. **2** (*There was something funny about the way he was behaving*) odd, peculiar, strange, weird, bizarre, suspicious.

**furious** *adj* (*They were furious at being treated rudely*) enraged, infuriated, indignant, angry, wrathful.

**furnish** *vb* **1** (*furnish the room with modern furniture*) equip, fit out, fit up. **2** (*furnish the committee with the required information*) provide, supply, equip, present.

**furniture** *n* (*buy antique furniture for the house*) furnishings, appointments, effects.

**further** *adj* (*require further supplies*) additional, more, extra.

**furtive** *adj* (*The police were suspicious of his furtive behavior*) secretive, stealthy, sneaky, surreptitious, sly.

**fury** *n* (*her parent's fury at the damage caused during the party*) anger, rage, wrath, ire.

**future** *n* **1** (*hope for better things in the future*) time to come, time ahead, time hereafter. **2** (*There is little future for that industry*) prospects, expectations, outlook, likely success.

**future** *adj* (*an advertisement for future events*) coming, approaching, to come.

# G

**gadget** *n* (*a kitchen with a lot of laborsaving gadgets*) appliance, device, piece of apparatus, implement.

**gag** *n* (*The comedian told a series of old gags*) joke, jest, quip, witticism, wisecrack.

**gain** *vb* (*They tried to gain an advantage over the opposition*) get, obtain, acquire, procure, secure, achieve.

**gain** *n* (*their gains from the sale of the company*) profit, return, yield, proceeds, earnings, reward, benefit, (*inf*) pickings.

**gale** *n* (*ships damaged at sea in a gale*) storm, hurricane, squall, tempest, tornado, cyclone.

**gallant** *adj* (*gallant soldiers who died in battle*) brave, courageous, valiant, heroic, plucky, fearless, intrepid, stout-hearted.

**gallop** *vb* **1** (*horses galloping around the field*) canter, prance, frisk. **2** (*The children always gallop home for dinner*) rush, run, dash, race, sprint, hurry.

**gamble** *vb* **1** (*He loves to gamble and loses a lot of money*) bet, place a bet, wager, lay a wager. **2**-(*He gambled when he invested in the company*) take a risk, take a chance, speculate, venture.

**game** *n* **1** (*the children's games*) amusement, entertainment, diversion, sport, pastime, hobby. **2** (*We are all going to the game tomorrow*) match, competition, contest, tournament, athletics event, sports meeting.

**gang** n 1 (*A gang of people had gathered to listen to the speaker*) group, band, crowd, mob, horde. 2 (*The boys formed a gang*) club, clique, circle, set. 3 (*a gang of workmen*) squad, team, troop.

**gangster** n (*the gangsters held up the bank*) mobster.

**gap** n 1 (*crawl through a gap in the wall*) opening, hole, aperture, space, chink. 2 (*The police are trying to fill in a few gaps in the account of the accident*) omission, blank, void, lacuna.

**gape** vb 1 (*They gaped at the sheer size of the huge man*) stare, goggle, gaze. 2 (*The caves gaped before them*) open wide, yawn.

**garden** n (*He grows vegetables in his garden*) yard, plot.

**garish** adj (*The dancers were wearing garish clothes*) flashy, loud, gaudy, bold, flamboyant.

**garland** n (*wearing garlands of flowers round their necks*) wreath, festoon.

**garment** n (*wearing a strange black garment*) piece of clothing, item of clothing, article of clothing.

**garments** npl (*wearing mourning garments*) clothes, clothing, dress, attire, apparel, outfit, garb.

**gash** n (*He gashed his hand when carving the meat*) cut, slash, lacerate, wound, nick.

**gasp** vb (*He was gasping as he reached the top of the mountain*) pant, puff, blow, choke, wheeze.

**gate** n (*the gate at the end of the driveway to the house*) gateway, barrier, entrance.

**gather** vb 1 (*A crowd gathered to hear the speaker*) collect, come together, assemble, congregate, meet. 2 (*gather food for the fire*) collect, get together, accumulate, heap up, store, stockpile, hoard. 3-(*gather blackberries*) pick, pluck, harvest, collect. 4 (*We gather that she is ill*) understand, believe, be led to believe, hear, learn.

**gathering** n (*be invited to the firm's annual gathering*) party, function, get-together, social.

**gaudy** adj garish, bold, over-bright, loud, glaring, flashy, showy, lurid.

**gauge** vb 1 (*He was asked to gauge the length of the yard*) measure, calculate, determine, estimate. 2 (*It is difficult to gauge the extent of his interest in the project*) assess, estimate, judge, guess.

**gaunt** adj (*He looked gaunt after his-long illness*) haggard, drawn, emaciated, skinny, bony, scrawny, scraggy, skeletal, cadaverous.

**gay** adj 1 (*a gay club*) homosexual, lesbian. 2 (*people feeling gay on vacation*) merry, jolly, light-hearted, glad, happy, cheerful, in good spirits. 3 (*girls wearing summer dresses in gay colors*) bright, brightly colored, vivid, brilliant, flamboyant.

**gaze** vb (*tourists gazing at the beauty of the sunset*) stare, eye, contemplate, look fixedly.

**gear** n (*the mountaineers and all their gear*) equipment, apparatus, kit, implements, tackle, things, possessions, belongings, (*inf*) stuff, paraphernalia.

**gem** n (*an engagement ring with sparkling gems*) jewel, precious stone, stone.

**general** adj 1 (*The general feeling is that he is guilty*) common, widespread, broad, wide, accepted, prevalent, universal. 2 (*The general rule is that people have to have three years' experience before getting a job there*) usual, customary, common, normal, standard, ordinary, typical. 3 (*He gave them a general idea of his plans for the business*) broad, non-detailed, vague, indefinite, inexact, rough.

**generous** adj 1 (*he was a generous contributor to the charity*) kind, liberal, magnanimous, benevolent, lavish, openhanded. 2 (*there was a generous supply of food and drinks at the party*) abundant, liberal, plentiful, ample, copious, rich.

**genius** n 1 (*He is a genius at math*) mastermind, prodigy, intellectual, expert. 2 (*people of genius*) brilliance, brains, intellect, intelligence. 3 (*have a genius for making delicious low-cost meals*) gift, talent, flair, bent, knack, aptitude, ability, forte.

**gentle** adj 1 (*She remembered with love her gentle mother*) kind, kindly, lenient, tenderhearted, sweettempered, mild, soft, peaceful. 2-(*her gentle touch*) soft, light, smooth, soothing. 3 (*a gentle breeze*) mild, light, soft, moderate, temperate. 4 (*children learning to ski on gentle slopes*) gradual, slight. 5 (*The dog was a very gentle animal*) tame, placid, docile. 6 (*She tried to give him a gentle hint about-his bad manners*) indirect, subtle.

**genuine** adj 1 (*His excuse for being absent turned out to be genuine*) real, true, authentic, sound, legitimate, valid, (*inf*) kosher, (*inf*) the real McCoy. 2 (*They doubted if his feelings were genuine*) real, sincere, honest, truthful, true, unaffected.

**gesture** n (*He made a gesture to indicate that he agreed*) signal, sign, motion.

**get** vb 1 (*She wondered where she could get a book on antiques*) obtain, acquire, get hold of, come by, procure, buy, purchase. 2 (*He went upstairs to get a book for his mother*) fetch, bring, carry, go for, retrieve. 3 (*They get a high salary*) earn, be paid, bring in, make, clear, take home. 4 (*She got flu last winter*) catch, become infected by, contract. 5 (*The children were getting tired*) become, grow. 6 (*When do you expect to get there?*) arrive at, reach.

7 (*I didn't get what he was talking about*) understand, comprehend, follow, grasp. 8 (*We eventually got her to agree*) persuade, coax, induce, talk (*someone*) into.

**ghastly** adj 1 (*There has been a ghastly road accident*) terrible, horrible, dreadful, frightful, shocking, grim, horrifying. 2 (*She looked ghastly when she went to hospital*) white, white as a sheet, pale, pallid, wan, colorless, drawn, ashen. 3-(*He is an absolutely ghastly man*) dreadful, nasty, unpleasant, disagreeable, hateful, loathsome, foul, contemptible.

**ghost** n (*She imagined that she saw a ghost in the graveyard*) apparition, specter, phantom, spirit, wraith, (*inf*) spook.

**gibberish** n (*They accused him of talking gibberish*) nonsense, twaddle, drivel, balderdash, (*inf*) poppycock, (*inf*) piffle.

**gibe** n (*She was upset at the gibes of her classmates*) sneer, jeer, taunt, mocking, scorn.

**giddy** adj 1 (*feel giddy at the top of the ladder*) dizzy, light-headed, faint, (*inf*) woozy. 2 (*giddy girls who had no interest in having a career*) silly, flighty, frivolous, irresponsible, thoughtless, unstable.

**gift** n 1 (*birthday gifts*) present. 2-(*He was thanked for his gift to the charity*) present, donation, contribution, offering. 3 (*The pupil has a gift for foreign languages*) talent, flair, aptitude, knack, ability, expertise, genius.

**gigantic** adj (*They caught sight of a gigantic mountain through the mist*) huge, enormous, colossal, immense, vast, mammoth, gargantuan.

**giggle** vb (*pupils giggling at the back of the class*) titter, snigger, snicker, laugh.

**girl** n 1 (*She lived in the village as a girl*) young woman, (*inf*) lass. 2-(*The couple have a boy and a girl*) daughter. 3 (*He went to the pictures with his girl*) girlfriend, sweetheart, fiancée.

**gist** n (*Some of his lecture was a bit difficult for the audience but most of them got the gist of it*) drift, substance, essence, sense.

**give** vb 1 (*She lifted the book and gave it to him*) hand, hand over, pass. 2 (*The old lady gave a very large sum of money to the local hospital*) donate, contribute, present, bestow, make over. 3 (*The charity worker was giving out soup and bread to homeless people*) hand out, distribute, allot, allocate, dole out. 4 (*They were given some bad advice*) provide, supply, furnish, offer. 5 (*She gives the impression of being very efficient*) show, display, demonstrate, manifest, indicate. 6-(*The chair gave and the child fell to the floor*) give way, collapse, break, come apart, fall apart.

**giver** n (*the giver of the money to the hospital*) donor, contributor.

**glad** adj 1 (We were very glad to see-our visitors) happy, pleased, delighted. 2 (hear the glad news) happy, delightful, joyful, welcome, cheerful.

**glamorous** adj 1 (glamorous movie stars) beautiful, lovely, attractive, elegant, smart, dazzling, alluring. 2-(She has a glamorous career in advertising) exciting, fascinating, dazzling, high-profile.

**glance** vb 1 (He only glanced at the stranger) take a quick look at, look briefly at, glimpse, peep. 2 (glance through the newspapers at breakfast) skim through, leaf through, flick through, flip through, thumb through, scan. 3 (The bullet glanced off the tree) bounce, rebound, ricochet. 4 (The car glanced the wall as he drove it into the garage) graze, brush, touch, skim.

**glare** n 1 (He was unaware of her angry glares) scowl, frown. 2 (the glare from the headlamps of oncoming cars) flare, blaze, dazzle.

**glass** n (a glass of cold water) tumbler, beaker, goblet.

**gleam** n 1 (a gleam of light) beam, glow, ray, shimmer, sparkle. 2 (the gleam of the polished tables) glow, shine, gloss, sheen, luster. 3 (There is still a gleam of hope) glimmer, ray, trace, suggestion, hint, flicker.

**glib** adj (She was persuaded into buying the goods by a glib salesman) smooth, plausible, smooth-talking, fluent, suave.

**glide** vb (They watched the yachts gliding by) sail, slide, slip, skim, float, drift.

**glimpse** n (She thought that she glimpsed a stranger through the trees) catch sight of, spot, make out, notice, espy.

**glitter** vb (The diamonds glittered in-the candlelight) sparkle, flash, twinkle, flicker, blink, wink, shimmer, gleam, glint.

**gloat** vb (She was gloating over her rival's misfortunes) relish, delight in, take pleasure in, revel in, rejoice in, glory in, crow about.

**global** adj 1 (the possibility of global war) world, worldwide, universal, international. 2 (The company tried to impose a global pay settlement on all its employees) general, universal, across-the-board, comprehensive.

**gloomy** adj 1 (a gloomy November day) dark, overcast, cloudy, dull, dismal, dreary. 2 (an old house full of gloomy rooms) dark, somber, dingy, dismal, dreary, depressing. 3-(He is in a gloomy mood today) in low spirits, depressed, sad, unhappy, miserable, dejected, downcast, downhearted, glum, melancholy.

**glorious** adj 1 (It was a glorious day) bright, beautiful, lovely, sunny. 2-(The procession was a glorious sight) splendid, magnificent, wonderful, marvelous. 3 (celebrate a glorious victory) famous, celebrated, renowned, noble, distinguished.

**glossy** adj (the glossy surfaces of the polished tables) gleaming, shining, shiny, bright, sparkling, shimmering, polished, burnished.

**glow** vb (The lights glowed) gleam, shine, glimmer.

**glow** n 1 (the glow from the table lights) gleam, brightness, glimmer, luminosity. 2 (the glow from the fire) warmth, heat, redness. 3 (She felt a warm glow when she thought of her friends) warmth, happiness, contentment, satisfaction.

**glower** vb (She glowered at her rival) scowl, frown, look daggers at.

**glue** vb (glue the broken pieces together) stick, gum, paste, cement.

**glum** adj (in a glum mood) gloomy, depressed, sad, unhappy, miserable, dejected, downcast, downhearted, melancholy.

**glut** n (a glut of apples on the market) surplus, excess, surfeit, superfluity, overabundance, oversupply.

**gnaw** vb (The dog was gnawing on a bone) chew, munch, crunch, bite, nibble.

**go** vb 1 (go carefully on the icy roads) move, proceed, walk, travel. 2 (It is time to go) go away, leave, depart, withdraw, set off, set out. 3 (The pain has gone) stop, cease, vanish, disappear, fade, be no more. 4 (The machine has stopped going) work, be in working order, function, operate, run. 5-(His beard has gone white) become, grow, turn, get, come to be. 6 (This road goes to the next town) extend, stretch, reach, lead to. 7 (Time went slowly while they were waiting for the train) pass, elapse, slip by. 8 (How did the party go?) turn out, work out, progress, fare. 9 (curtains and carpets that don't go) go together, match, blend, harmonize.

**goal** n (Making a lot of money was his one goal in life/He read out a statement of the goals of the organization) aim, objective, end, purpose, object, target, ambition.

**gobble** vb (children told not to gobble their food) wolf, bolt, gulp, guzzle.

**god** n (the gods of ancient Greece) deity, divinity, divine being, idol.

**God** n (the biblical story about God and Moses) God Almighty, the Almighty, God the Father, Our Maker.

**golden** adj 1 (girls with golden hair) gold-colored, blond, yellow, fair, flaxen. 2 (a golden opportunity) splendid, superb, excellent, favorable, fortunate, advantageous, profitable.

**good** adj 1 (The children were told to be good) well-behaved, well-mannered, obedient, manageable. 2 (She is such a good person who never treats anyone badly) honorable, virtuous, righteous, upright, honest, decent, moral, ethical. 3-(She is noted for her good deeds) helpful, kind, thoughtful, virtuous, admirable, creditable. 4 (He is not a very good driver) competent, capable, able, skillful, adept, proficient, expert, first-class, (inf) A1. 5-(The car does not have very good brakes) efficient, reliable, dependable, trustworthy. 6 (athletes in good condition) fine, healthy, sound, strong, robust, vigorous. 7-(The party was very good) enjoyable, agreeable, entertaining, pleasant, lovely, nice. 8 (We had good weather on vacation) fine, sunny, pleasant.

**gossip** n 1 (I heard that he had been in prison but it turned out to be just gossip) rumor, tattle, tittle-tattle, scandal, hearsay, (inf) mudslinging. 2 (She was having a good gossip with her neighbor) chat, têta à tête, conversation.

**govern** vb (the party that is governing the country) rule, manage, lead, be in power over, be in charge of, preside over, control.

**government** n (He is a member of the government) administration, congress, ministry, council, (inf) the powers that be.

**grab** vb 1 (He was told to grab the end of the rope) catch hold of, take hold of, grasp, clutch, grip. 2 (He grabbed the money and ran) seize, snatch.

**grace** n 1 (admire the grace of the dancers) gracefulness, elegance. 2-(He did not to have the grace to-apologize) manners, courtesy, decency, decorum. 3 (He was at one time the leader's favorite but he fell from grace) favor, goodwill. 4-(pray for God's grace) kindness, forgiveness, mercy, pardon, clemency. 5 (say grace before dinner) blessing, benediction, thanksgiving.

**graceful** adj 1 (They admired the gymnasts' graceful movements) smooth, flowing, supple, agile, easy, elegant. 2 (He gave a graceful speech of thanks) elegant, polished, suave, refined.

**gracious** adj 1 (Our host was very gracious) kind, kindly, benevolent, friendly, amiable, pleasant, cordial, courteous, polite, civil. 2 (their gracious lifestyle) elegant, tasteful, comfortable, luxurious. 3 (believe in a gracious God) merciful, compassionate, lenient, gentle.

**grade** n 1 (What grade are you in?) level, stage, position, rank, standard. 2 (grades of eggs) category, class, classification.

**gradual** adj (There has been a gradual improvement) slow, steady, gentle, moderate, step-by-step, systematic.

**grain** n 1 (have grains of sand in her shoes) particle, granule, bit, piece, fragment, speck. 2 (the farmer grows grain) cereal crop. 3 (We found that there was not a grain of truth in his statement) particle, scrap, iota, trace, hint, suggestion. 4 (*the grain of the wood*) texture, surface.

**grand** *adj* 1 (*the grand houses of the-rich*) great, impressive, magnificent, splendid, imposing, majestic, stately, palatial. 2 (*a grand occasion*) important, great, splendid, magnificent, (*inf*) posh.

**grant** *vb* 1 (*The president granted the journalist an interview*) agree to, consent to, give one's assent to, allow, permit. 2 (*I grant that you may be right*) acknowledge, admit, concede, allow.

**grant** *n* (*get a grant for the research*) allowance, award, subsidy, bursary.

**grapple** *vb* 1 (*The policeman grappled with the burglar*) struggle, wrestle, fight, tussle, clash. 2 (*He is still grappling with the problem of how to get there*) struggle, tackle, handle, deal with, cope with, attend to.

**grasp** *vb* 1 (*He grasped the handrail to prevent himself from falling*) grip, clutch, grab, take hold of, hold on to, clench. 2 (*He seemed unable to grasp the situation*) understand, follow, comprehend, take in, get the drift of.

**grateful** *adj* 1 (*They were grateful to him for his help*) thankful, filled with gratitude, indebted, obliged, appreciative. 2 (*We received a grateful letter for our contribution*) appreciative, thankful.

**grave** *n* (*the grave of the unknown soldier*) burial place, tomb, sepulchre.

**grave** *adj* 1 (*He was in a grave mood when he came back from the hospital*) solemn, serious, earnest, sober, somber, grim, severe, unsmiling. 2 (*There were grave matters to discuss at the meeting*) serious, important, significant, weighty, pressing, urgent, vital, crucial.

**graveyard** *n* (*The funeral procession arrived at the graveyard*) cemetery, burial ground, churchyard.

**graze** *vb* 1 (*He grazed his knee*) scrape, skin, scratch, wound, bruise, abrade. 2 F(*The car grazed the garage wall*) brush, touch, glance off, shave, skim.

**greasy** *adj* 1 (*dislike greasy foods*) fatty, fat, oily. 2 (*The car skidded on the greasy roads*) slippery, slimy.

**great** *adj* 1 (*a great stretch of water*) large, big, extensive, vast, immense, huge. 2 (*The invalid was in great pain*) extreme, severe, intense, acute. 3 (*They have traveled to all the great cities of the world*) major, main, chief, principal, leading. 4 (*the great people of the country*) important, prominent, leading, top, eminent, distinguished, notable, famous. 5 (*He was a great tennis player*) expert, skillful, adept, proficient, masterly, (*inf*) ace, (*inf*) crack. 6 (*They had a great time at the party*) enjoyable, splendid, wonderful, marvelous, (*inf*) fabulous.

**greedy** *adj* 1 (*greedy children who ate all the cakes before some people arrived*) gluttonous. 2 (*people greedy for information*) avid, eager, hungry, desirous of, craving. 3 (*a greedy miser hoarding gold*) grasping, avaricious, acquisitive, miserly, tight-fisted, stingy.

**greet** *vb* 1 (*He greeted his neighbor as he walked down the street*) say 'hello' to, address, hail. 2 (*The hostess greeted her guests*) receive, welcome, meet.

**grief** *n* (*her grief at the death of her husband*) sorrow, sadness, misery, distress, heartbreak, dejection, mourning.

**grievance** *n* (*Management refused to listen to the workers' grievances*) complaint, protest, charge, grumble, (*inf*) gripe.

**grieve** *vb* 1 (*The widow is still grieving*) mourn, be in mourning, lament, be sorrowful, sorrow, be sad, be distressed, fret. 2 (*She was grieved by her son's behavior*) hurt, upset, distress, sadden, wound.

**grim** *adj* 1 (*She held on with grim determination*) determined, resolute, obstinate, unwavering, relentless. 2 (*The teacher was wearing a grim expression*) stern, severe, fierce, forbidding, formidable, somber. 3-(*The murdered corpse was a grim sight*) horrible, dreadful, terrible, frightful, shocking, ghastly, gruesome.

**grime** *n* (*trying to clean the grime from the old house*) dirt, filth, dust, (*inf*) muck, (*inf*) grunge, (*inf*) crud.

**grin** *vb* smile, smile broadly, smile from ear to ear.

**grind** *vb* 1 (*grind coffee beans*) crush, pound, pulverize, powder, mill. 2 (*grind knives*) sharpen, whet, file, polish. 3 (*She had a habit of grinding her teeth*) gnash, grate, rasp.

**grip** *vb* 1 (*She gripped the handrail of the ship*) grasp, clutch, clasp, clench, grab, take hold of, seize. 2-(*The audience was gripped by the exciting play*) absorb, rivet, engross, fascinate, enthrall, hold spellbound.

**grit** *n* 1 (*put grit on icy roads*) gravel, pebbles, dirt, sand, dust. 2 (*He did not have the grit to tell her himself-that he was breaking off the engagement*) courage, bravery, pluck, nerve, backbone.

**groan** *vb* 1 (*The accident victim groaned in pain*) moan, whimper, wail, cry. 2 (*The workers were groaning about their low wages*) grumble, complain, moan, (*inf*) grouse, (*inf*) gripe.

**grope** *vb* 1 (*They had to grope their way in the pitch dark*) fumble, feel. 2 (*She groped for her keys in her purse*) fumble, feel for, fish for, scrabble for.

**ground** *n* 1 (*The ground is very wet after all the rain*) earth, soil, dirt, land, loam. 2 (*She became ill and fell to the ground*) earth, floor, (*inf*) deck. 3 (*They would like*

a new sports ground) stadium, pitch, field, arena, park.

**grounds** *npl* 1 (*They have grounds for concern about their missing son*) reason, cause, basis, foundation, justification. 2 (*The house was set in beautiful grounds*) land, surroundings, property, estate, lawns, gardens, park. 3 (*coffee grounds*) dregs, lees, deposit, sediment.

**group** *n* 1 (*We divided the books into groups*) category, class, set, lot, batch. 2 (*She has joined a cookery group*) society, association, club, circle. 3 (*A group of people gathered to watch the fight*) band, gathering, cluster, crowd, flock, bunch.

**grow** *vb* 1 (*The farmers grow wheat*) cultivate, produce, raise, farm. 2-(*The plants will not grow in this very dry soil*) shoot up, spring up, sprout, germinate, thrive, flourish. 3 (*The boy is growing rapidly*) become taller, get bigger, grow larger, stretch, lengthen, expand, fill out. 4 (*The situation is growing serious*) become, come to be, get, get to be, turn, turn out to be.

**grudge** *vb* (*She grudges them their success*) begrudge, resent, be jealous of, envy, mind.

**grumble** *vb* (*The passengers were grumbling about the train being late*) complain, protest, object, moan, (*inf*) grouse, (*inf*) gripe, (*inf*) beef.

**guarantee** *vb* 1 (*He guaranteed that he would attend the meeting*) promise, pledge, give one's word, give an assurance, vow, swear. 2-(*This ticket guarantees you a seat at the match*) ensure, secure. 3 (*He guaranteed his daughter's car loan*) act as guarantor, provide security for, provide surety for, underwrite, vouch for.

**guard** *n* 1 (*prison guards*) warder, jailer, keeper. 2 (*the castle guards*) sentry, sentinel, custodian, watchman, lookout, garrison. 3 (*put a new guard on the machine*) safety guard, safety device, shield.

**guard** *vb* 1 (*the people who were guarding the jewels*) stand guard over, watch over, protect, safeguard, defend, shield, look after, preserve. 2 (*the people guarding the prisoners*) keep under guard, keep watch over, keep under surveillance, mind, supervise. 3 (*Tourists are asked to guard against thieves*) beware of, be on the alert for, be on the lookout for, keep an eye out for.

**guess** *vb* 1 (*We were asked to guess the weight of the cake*) estimate, predict, (*inf*) guesstimate. 2 (*We guessed that they would take the shortest route*) surmise, conjecture, suppose, assume, reckon.

**guest** *n* (*The hostess welcomed her guests*) visitor, company, caller.

**guide** *vb* 1 (*He guided them down the mountain*) lead, conduct, show, usher, direct, show the way to, escort. 2 (*They asked for someone to guide them in their choice of career*) advise, give advice to, counsel, direct.

**guide** *n* 1 (*They hired a guide to show them round the city sights*) escort, leader, advisor. 2 (*buy a guide to Rome*) guidebook, handbook, directory, manual. 3 (*The lights acted as a guide to shipping*) landmark, marker, signal, beacon. 4 (*The pupils were given an essay as a guide*) model, pattern, standard, example, yardstick.

**guilt** *n* 1 (*It was impossible to prove his guilt*) guiltiness, blame, blameworthiness, culpability, fault, responsibility. 2 (*feelings of guilt at their treatment of her*) guiltiness, guilty conscience, remorse, penitence, shame.

**guilty** *adj* 1 (*He was tried and found guilty*) to blame, blameworthy, culpable, at fault, responsible. 2 (*they felt guilty about not inviting her*) conscience-stricken, remorseful, repentant, penitent, ashamed, shamefaced, sheepish.

**gulf** *n* 1 (*They were asked to find the Gulf of Mexico on the map*) bay, cove, inlet. 2 (*They had a quarrel and there is now a gulf between the two families*) chasm, rift, split, division, divide.

**gullible** *adj* (*The old lady was not gullible enough to be taken in by his story*) naive, ingenuous, foolish, credulous.

**gulp** *vb* 1 (*The children were told not to gulp their food*) bolt, wolf, gobble, devour. 2 (*She tried to gulp back her tears*) fight back, choke back, suppress, stifle, smother.

**gush** *vb* 1 (*Water gushed from the burst pipe*) pour, steam, rush, spout, spurt, flood, cascade. 2 (*She embarrassed the little girls by gushing about their prettiness*) enthuse, be effusive, babble, fuss.

**gust** *n* (*a gust of wind*) puff, rush, flurry, blast, squall.

**gutter** *n* (*flood water running down the gutter*) drain, sewer, sluice, ditch.

# H

**habit** *n* 1 (*It was their habit to eat late in the evening*) custom, practice, routine, convention. 2 (*smoking and other harmful habits*) addiction, dependence, compulsion, obsession.

**habitat** *n* (*the animal's usual habitat*) environment, background, home.

**habitual** *n* 1 (*They went home by their habitual route*) usual, customary, accustomed, regular, routine. 2 (*He is a habitual smoker*) addicted, confirmed, hardened.

**hack** *vb* (*They hacked down the trees*) chop down, cut down, fell, hew.

**hackneyed** *adj* (*The writer is too apt to use hackneyed phrases*) overused, stale, stereotyped, unoriginal, run-of-the-mill, stock.

**haggard** *adj* (*She looked haggard with tiredness*) drawn, gaunt, hollowcheeked.

**haggle** *vb* (*haggle over the price of a shawl in the market*) bargain.

**hail** *vb* (*She hailed her friend in the street*) greet, salute, wave to, say 'hello' to.

**hair** *n* 1 (*She has beautiful hair*) locks, tresses. 2 (*the animal's hair*) fur, coat.

**half-hearted** *adj* (*They made a halfhearted attempt at saving the business*) lukewarm, unenthusiastic, apathetic, indifferent.

**hall** *n* 1 (*The guests left their coats in the hall*) entrance hall, hallway, lobby, vestibule. 2 (*The crowds surged into the hall*) concert hall, auditorium, theater.

**hallucination** *n* (*She thought that she had seen a ghost but it was only a hallucination*) illusion, figment of the imagination, vision, fantasy, apparition.

**halt** *vb* 1 (*The traffic has to halt at the end of the road*) come to a halt, stop, come to a stop, pull up, draw up. 2 (*Work halted when the heating system broke down*) stop, finish, end, break off, discontinue. 3 (*The strike halted progress on the export order*) stop, put a stop to, put an end to, arrest, interrupt, obstruct, impede.

**halve** *vb* (*halve the orange for the two children*) cut in half, divide in two.

**hamper** *vb* (*The bad weather hampered progress on the building*) hinder, impede, obstruct, hold up.

**hand** *n* 1 (*the hand of a clock*) pointer, indicator, needle. 2 (*They had to fire some of the hands*) worker, employee, helper.

**hand** *vb* (*hand the prize to the winner*) hand over, give, pass, transfer, transmit.

**handbook** *n* (*read the instructions in the handbook*) manual, directions, instructions, guide, guidebook.

**handicap** *vb* (*Her lack of qualifications was a handicap to her in her career*) disadvantage, impediment, obstruction, hindrance, block.

**handle** *vb* (*the handle of the tool/the handle of the pan*) shaft, grip, hilt.

**handle** *vb* 1 (*They were asked not to handle the goods before they bought them*) touch, finger, feel, pick up, lift. 2 (*He cannot handle the more difficult pupils*) cope with, deal with, manage, control.

**handsome** *n* 1 (*Her husband is a very handsome man*) attractive, goodlooking. 2 (*The antique table was a handsome piece of furniture*) attractive, fine, elegant, tasteful. 3 (*Her parents gave them a handsome gift as a wedding present*) generous, magnanimous, lavish, sizeable.

**handy** *adj* 1 (*Do you have the book handy?*) to

hand, available, within reach, accessible, nearby. 2 (*That is a handy kitchen utensil*) useful, helpful, convenient, practical. 3 (*It is useful to have someone handy to do repairs around the house*) good with one's hands, practical, capable.

**hang** *vb* 1 (*There were cobwebs hanging from the ceiling in the shed*) hang down, be suspended, dangle, swing. 2 (*She hung the picture from the hook*) suspend, put up. 3 (*She employed him to hang wallpaper*) put up, stick on. 4 (*They hang murderers in some states*) send to the gallows, put a noose on, send to the gibbet, execute, (*inf*) string up.

**hanker** *vb* (*She hankers after a little house in the country*) desire, long for, yearn for, crave, covet, fancy, (*inf*) have a yen for.

**haphazard** *adj* (*The books were arranged in a haphazard way*) random, unsystematic, unmethodical, disorganized, slapdash, careless.

**happen** *vb* 1 (*The accident happened on icy roads*) occur, take place, come about. 2 (*We happened to meet her in the supermarket*) chance. 3 (*Whatever happened to them?*) become of, befall. 4 (*They happened upon some valuable old books*) find, come upon, chance upon, stumble upon.

**happening** *n* (*There has been a series of sad happenings in her life*) event, incident, occurrence, experience.

**happy** *adj* 1 (*The children were happy playing in the sunshine*) cheerful, merry, lighthearted, joyful, carefree. 2 (*They were happy to see their grandparents*) pleased, glad, delighted. 3 (*By a happy chance we found the lost necklace*) fortunate, lucky.

**harass** *vb* (*The children were bored and were harassing their mother*) pester, disturb, bother, annoy, badger, torment, (*inf*) hassle.

**harbor** *n* (*The ships were tied up in the harbor*) quay, jetty, pier, wharf, dock.

**harbor** *vb* 1 (*She was accused of harboring an escaped prisoner*) shelter, give protection to, give asylum to. 2 (*They still harbor resentment against their mother for abandoning them*) have, hold, retain, maintain, cling to, entertain.

**hard** *adj* 1 (*The ground was hard*) solid, solidified, stony, rocky. 2 (*a hard substance*) solid, rigid, stiff, inflexible, tough. 3 (*The work was very hard*) arduous, strenuous, heavy, laborious, tiring, demanding, taxing, exacting. 4 (*The problem was a hard one*) difficult, complicated, complex, involved, intricate. 5 (*They are hard workers*) industrious, diligent, energetic, keen. 6 (*Their father was a hard man*) harsh, stern, severe, ruthless. 7 (*He was wounded by a hard blow to the head*) strong, forceful, powerful, violent. **8** (*She had a hard life*) difficult, uncomfortable, harsh, grim, unpleasant, distressing.

**hardship** *n* (*The refugees are suffering hardship*) adversity, deprivation, want, need, distress.

**harm** *n vb* **1** (*The kidnappers did not harm the child*) hurt, injure, wound, abuse, maltreat. **2** (*The incident harmed his reputation*) damage, mar, spoil.

**harm** *n* **1** (*No harm came to the child*) injury, hurt, pain, suffering, abuse. **2** (*Some harm was done to his reputation*) damage, detriment, loss.

**harmful** *adj* (*The drug is not thought to have any harmful effects*) hurtful, injurious, disadvantageous, detrimental, deleterious.

**harmless** *adj* **1** (*a weed-killer that is thought to be harmless to pets*) safe, innocuous, nontoxic. **2** (*He was just a harmless old man*) innocuous, inoffensive, blameless, innocent.

**harmony** *n* (*The different nationali- ties lived in harmony in the country*) peace, peacefulness, agreement, accord, concord, friendship.

**harsh** *adj* **1** (*The harsh noise grated on their ears*) grating, jarring, rasping, strident, discordant. **2** (*The colors of the walls were a bit harsh*) gaudy, garish, loud, bold. **3** (*It had been a harsh winter*) hard, severe, cold. **4** (*She had been brought up under harsh conditions*) severe, grim, rough, austere. **5** (*He was a harsh ruler*) cruel, brutal, merciless, ruthless, tyrannical. **6** (*The school rules used to be very harsh*) severe, stern, stringent, inflexible.

**haste** *n* (*Haste is required to get the order delivered on time*) speed, swiftness, rapidity, fastness.

**hasty** *adj* **1** (*You should avoid making hasty decisions*) hurried, rushed, impetuous, impulsive. **2**-(*She gave a hasty look at her notes before she spoke*) quick, rapid, swift, brief, fleeting, cursory, superficial. **3** (*She has a hasty temper*) hot, fiery, quick, irritable.

**hat** *n* (*He wore a hat to protect his head from the sun*) cap.

**hate** *vb* **1** (*He hates his rival/She hates football*) loathe, detest, dislike, abhor, have an aversion to. **2**-(*I would hate to upset her*) be reluctant, be loath, be unwilling.

**hateful** *adj* (*She thinks that he is a-hateful person*) loathsome, detestable, abhorrent, revolting, offensive, horrible, nasty.

**hatred** *n* (*He is full of hatred towards his rivals*) hate, loathing, abhorrence, dislike, aversion, ill-will.

**haughty** *adj* (*She looks at everyone in a very haughty way*) arrogant, proud, disdainful, condescending, snobbish.

**haul** *vb* (*They hauled the dead body from the river*) pull, tug, drag, draw, heave.

**have** *vb* **1** (*They have two cats*) own, possess, keep. **2** (*The house has five rooms*) contain, comprise, include. **3** (*She had a lot of trouble with her eldest son*) experience, undergo, go through, endure. **4** (*She will not have such behavior in her house*) permit, allow, tolerate, stand.

**hay** *n* (*They gave hay to the horses*) fodder, straw.

**hazard** *n* (*one of the hazards of being a soldier*) danger, risk, peril, menace.

**hazy** *adj* **1** (*It was rather a hazy day*) misty, foggy. **2** (*Her memory of the event is a bit hazy*) unclear, vague, blurred, fuzzy, muddled.

**head** *n* **1** (*He has a good head for business*) mind, brain, intellect. **2**-(*He was the head of the whole organization*) chief, leader, director, manager, principal, boss. **3**-(*She is at the head of the company*) top, control, command, charge, leadership. **4** (*at the head of the hill*) top, summit, crest, brow, apex. **5** (*She sat at the head of the table*) top, front.

**head** *vb* **1** (*He was heading the expedition*) be in charge of, lead, be in control of, direct. **2** (*They headed for town*) make for, set out for, go to.

**heal** *vb* **1** (*The ointment will heal the wound*) cure, make better, remedy, treat. **2** (*The wound began to heal*) get better, mend, improve.

**health** *n* (*The children are full of health*) healthiness, fitness, strength, vigor.

**healthy** *adj* **1** (*healthy young men playing football*) well, fit, robust, strong, vigorous. **2** (*They live in a-healthy climate*) health-giving, invigorating, bracing. **3** (*They eat a healthy diet*) health-giving, healthful, nutritious, nourishing, wholesome.

**heap** *n* (*heaps of leaves in the yard*) pile, mound, stack, mass, stockpile.

**heap** *vb* (*The children heaped up the leaves in the yard*) pile, stack, stockpile, accumulate.

**hear** *vb* **1** (*I could not hear what she said*) catch, take in. **2** (*We heard that they had gone abroad*) find out, discover, gather, learn.

**heart** *n* **1** (*He loves her with all his heart*) love, passion, affection, emotion. **2** (*She thinks he has no heart*) tenderness, compassion, sympathy, humanity, kindness. **3** (*The discussion did not get to the heart of the matter*) center, core, nucleus, hub, crux.

**hearten** *vb* (*The team were heartened by their success*) cheer, cheer up, uplift, encourage, elate, buoy up.

**hearty** *adj* **1** (*They were given a hearty welcome*) enthusiastic, eager, warm, friendly. **2** (*He has a hearty dislike of deceit*) wholehearted, great, complete, thorough. **3**

(*They ate a hearty breakfast*) substantial, solid, filling, ample.

**heat** *n* (*The heat melted the ice*) hotness, warmth.

**heave** *vb* **1** (*He hurt his back heaving heavy weights*) lift, raise, haul, pull, tug. **2** (*They heaved a sigh of relief*) utter, give, let out.

**heaven** *n* **1** (*Bible stories about heaven*) paradise. **2** (*She thought that lying on a beach in the sun was heaven*) bliss, ecstasy, rapture, supreme happiness.

**heavy** *adj* **1** (*He had to carry heavy weights in his job*) weighty, hefty, substantial, burdensome. **2** (*It proved a heavy task*) hard, difficult, arduous, laborious, demanding, exacting. **3** (*He received a heavy blow to the head*) hard, strong, powerful, forceful, violent. **4** (*He was a heavy man*) large, bulky, hefty, stout, overweight, fat, obese. **5** (*a heavy mist*) dense, thick, solid. **6** (*with heavy heart*) depressed, gloomy, downcast, despondent.

**hectic** *adj* (*They had a hectic day at the office*) busy, frantic, bustling, frenzied.

**hedge** *vb* **1** (*The trees hedged in the garden*) surround, enclose, encircle, fence in. **2** (*She simply hedged when they asked her a direct question*) prevaricate, equivocate, hem and haw, beat about the bush.

**heed** *n* (*They pay no heed to what anyone says*) attention, notice, note, consideration.

**hefty** *adj* (*He is a hefty young man*) heavy, bulky, stout, brawny, muscular, powerfully built.

**height** *n* **1** (*measure the height*) tallness, altitude. **2** (*He died at the height of his career*) culmination, peak, zenith.

**heir/heiress** *ns* (*He was heir to his father's estate*) inheritor, beneficiary, legatee.

**help** *vb* **1** (*She did it to help her parents*) assist, aid, support, lend a hand to. **2** (*They gave her something to help the pain*) ease, soothe, relieve, alleviate, cure.

**help** *n* **1** (*The old lady is in need of some help*) assistance, aid, support. **2** (*There was no help for the condition*) ease, relief, alleviation, cure.

**helpful** *adj* **1** (*He made some helpful suggestions*) useful, of use, beneficial, advantageous, valuable. **2** (*Their neighbors are very helpful people*) supportive, obliging, cooperative, caring, charitable, friendly.

**hereditary** *adj* **1** (*The disease is hereditary*) inherited, genetic, congenital. **2** (*hereditary property*) inherited, bequeathed.

**hero** *n* **1** (*He was the hero of the battle*) victor, champion, celebrity. **2** (*The movie star is the girl's hero*) idol, ideal. **3** (*the hero in the play*) male lead.

**heroic** *adj* (*It was a heroic act to try and save his friend's life*) brave, courageous, valiant, gallant, intrepid, fearless, bold.

**hesitate** *vb* **1** (*She hesitated before making such*

an important decision) pause, delay, hang back, wait, vacillate, waver, shilly-shally. 2 (They hesitate to interfere in their daughter's life) be reluctant, be unwilling, be disinclined, shrink from. 3 (He hesitates a bit when he gets nervous) stammer, stutter, stumble, falter.

**hide** vb 1 (The thieves hid the jewels) conceal, secrete. 2 (The escaped prisoners were hiding in the cellar) take cover, lie low, conceal oneself, go to ground. 3 (clouds hiding the sun) obscure, block, eclipse, obstruct. 4 (She tried to hide her motives) conceal, keep secret, suppress, hush up.

**hide** n (the animal's hide) skin, pelt, coat, fur.

**hideous** adj 1 (The new curtains are hideous) ugly, unsightly, gruesome, grim, repulsive, revolting. 2 (It was a hideous crime) horrible, horrific, shocking, outrageous, dreadful, appalling.

**high** adj 1 (a street with high buildings) tall, lofty, towering. 2 (He has a high rank in the organization) top, leading, prominent, important, powerful. 3 (They have a high opinion of his work) favorable, good, approving, admiring. 4 (She has a very high voice) high-pitched, shrill, sharp, piercing. 5 (The ship was in difficulties in the high winds) strong, intense, forceful, violent.

**highbrow** adj (Her taste in books is rather highbrow) intellectual, scholarly, educated, bookish.

**highlight** n (The trip to the theater was one of the highlights of our trip) high spot, feature, peak, climax.

**hijack** vb (The thieves hijacked the truck) seize, take over, commandeer, expropriate.

**hike** vb (They hiked over the hills) tramp, march, walk, ramble, trek, trudge.

**hilarious** adj (The comedian's jokes were hilarious) uproarious, hysterical, side-splitting, funny, amusing, humorous, comic, entertaining.

**hill** n 1 (The hills behind the town) heights, highland, rising ground, mountain, peak. 2 (The cars went slowly up the steep hill) slope, rise, incline, gradient.

**hinder** vb (The bad weather hindered their efforts to get the bridge built) hamper, impede, hold up, obstruct, delay, curb, block.

**hindrance** n (Their long tight skirts were a hindrance to them when they tried to hurry) impediment, obstacle, obstruction, handicap, drawback.

**hint** n 1 (She gave no hint that she was planning to leave) inkling, clue, suggestion, indication, mention. 2 (He writes a column in the newspaper giving gardening hints) tip, suggestion, pointer. 3 (There was just a hint of ginger in the sauce) trace, touch, dash, suggestion, soupçon.

**hire** vb (The firm is hiring more staff) engage, take on, sign on, appoint, employ.

**hiss** vb 1 (Steam was hissing from the pipe) whistle, wheeze. 2 (The audience hissed at the comedian's bad jokes) boo, jeer.

**historic** n (It was a historic battle/It was a historic event when the country gained its independence) famous, notable, celebrated, memorable, important, significant, outstanding.

**hit** vb 1 (The bully hit the little boy) strike, slap, smack, punch, bang, thump. 2 (The car was out of control and hit the truck) bang into, crash into, knock into, smash into.

**hitch** n (Our travel arrangements were going well but then there was a sudden hitch) snag, hindrance, holdup, obstacle, difficulty, stumblingblock, glitch.

**hoard** vb (They hoarded food in the summer in case of bad weather in the winter/misers hoarding gold) store, stock up, save, accumulate, pile up, gather, collect.

**hoarse** adj (She had a cold and her voice was hoarse) harsh, gruff, husky, croaking, grating, rasping, raucous.

**hoax** n (The bomb threat was a hoax) practical joke, joke, prank, trick, (inf) spoof.

**hobble** vb (Her feet were sore and she had to hobble down to the store) limp, shuffle, totter.

**hobby** n (They work so hard that they have little time for hobbies) pastime, diversion, amusement, sport.

**hold** vb 1 (They held their bags tightly) hold on to, clutch, grip, grasp, cling to. 2 (They held each other close) embrace, cuddle, hug, clasp. 3 (The bank holds all their private documents) have, keep, retain, own, possess. 4 (He holds a position of responsibility) hold down, have, be in, occupy, fill. 5 (One suitcase will not hold all these clothes) contain, take, carry, include. 6 (The bridge will not hold his weight) bear, carry, support, sustain. 7 (police are holding him to help with their inquiries) detain, hold in custody, confine, keep, imprison. 8 (It is difficult to hold the interest of the children) keep, retain, occupy, engage. 9 (I wonder if the warm weather will hold) last, continue, go on, remain, stay. 10 (The old rule does not hold anymore) be valid, be in force, apply. 11 (They hold him responsible for the accident) consider, think, regard, view. 12 (The club holds meetings every month) have, conduct, run.

**hole** n 1 (There was a hole in the hedge/The material was full of holes) opening, aperture, gap, breach, break, crack, rent, slit, perforation, orifice. 2 (There was a huge hole in the ground after the explosion) crater, cavity, chasm, hollow, depression, dip. 3 (the animal's hole) lair, burrow, earth.

**holiday** n (Christmas is the holiday I like best) festival, public holiday, feast day, anniversary.

**hollow** adj 1 (a hollow space) hollowed out, empty, vacant. 2 (She has hollow cheeks) sunken, concave. 3 (We heard a hollow sound) dull, low, muffled, deep.

**hollow** vb (They hollowed out a tree trunk to make a canoe) scoop out, gouge out, excavate.

**holy** adj 1 (The saint's grave was a holy place) blessed, consecrated, sacred, hallowed. 2 (They are holy people) god-fearing, religious, pious, devout.

**home** n 1 (I know where he works but not where his home is) house, residence, abode, domicile, dwelling. 2 (the home of the chimpanzee) habitat, environment, abode. 3 (The old lady is in a home) retirement home.

**honest** adj 1 (honest people who do not steal other people's goods) honorable, upright, good, decent, righteous, moral, virtuous, trustworthy, law-abiding. 2 (She gave honest replies to the questions) true, truthful, sincere, genuine, direct, frank, candid. 3 (He gave an honest judgement) fair, just, impartial, objective, unbiased.

**honor** n 1 (He was a man of honor and handed in the money which he had found) honesty, integrity, uprightness, decency, principle, righteousness, morals, virtue. 2 (His honor was at stake) reputation, good name. 3 (He did not care about the honor of winning) glory, prestige, fame, renown, distinction.

**honorable** adj 1 (honorable people who tell the truth) honest, upright, good, decent, righteous, moral, virtuous, trustworthy, admirable. 2 (It was an honorable victory for the army) famous, renowned, prestigious, notable, distinguished.

**hook** n 1 (a hook used for cutting wheat) scythe, sickle. 2 (hooks for the children's coats) peg. 3 (the hook of the dress) fastener, catch.

**hook** vb 1 (They hooked a fish) catch, take. 2 (hook the trailer on to the car) fasten, secure.

**hooked** adj 1 (She has a hooked nose) hook-shaped, aquiline, curved, bent. 2 (He is hooked on cigarettes) addicted, dependent, obsessed by.

**hooligan** n (The police are looking for the hooligans who damaged the cars) ruffian, thug, vandal, (inf) hood, hoodlum.

**hoop** n (hoops of steel) ring, band, circle, circlet.

**hop** vb (The frogs were hopping everywhere) jump, leap, bound, spring, skip.

**hope** n 1 (We were full of hope for a victory) hopefulness, optimism, confidence, expectation, faith. 2 (Is there any hope of success?) likelihood, prospect.

**hope** vb (We are hoping for victory) have hopes of, be hopeful of, expect, anticipate, look forward to, have confidence in.

**hopeful** adj 1 (We are hopeful of winning) expectant, optimistic, confident. 2 (The news is hopeful) optimistic, promising, encouraging, favorable.

**horde** n (hordes of Christmas shoppers) crowd, swarm, mob, throng, multitude, host.

**horizontal** adj (both the horizontal and vertical supports of the frame/an invalid lying horizontal) flat, level, prone, supine.

**horrible** adj 1 (It was a horrible sight) dreadful, awful, horrid, terrible, frightful, shocking, appalling, grim, hideous, ghastly, gruesome, disgusting, revolting. 2 (She was a horrible old woman) disagreeable, nasty, unpleasant, mean, obnoxious.

**horrify** vb (We were horrified at her behavior) shock, appall, outrage, scandalize, disgust.

**horror** n (They looked at the dead body with horror) terror, fear, alarm, shock.

**horse** n (She rode a brown horse) mount, hack, pony, steed, stallion, mare, racehorse.

**hospitable** adj (The people we stayed with were most hospitable) generous, kind, cordial, sociable, friendly.

**hostage** n (They kept the child hostage) captive, prisoner, pawn, surety.

**hostile** adj 1 (The crowd grew hostile) belligerent, aggressive, antagonistic, angry, unfriendly. 2 (They were quite hostile to the idea) opposed, averse, antagonistic.

**hot** adj 1 (There was no hot food left in the restaurant/hot food straight from the oven) warm, piping hot, boiling, sizzling, scalding. 2 (It was a very hot day) boiling, sweltering, scorching, sultry, torrid. 3 (The sauce was too hot for their taste) spicy, peppery, pungent, sharp. 4 (She had a hot temper) fiery, fierce, furious, violent.

**hotel** n (book in at the local hotel) inn, tavern, guesthouse, boardinghouse, motel.

**house** n 1 (The house they live in is very old) abode, residence, dwelling, home. 2 (They own a publishing house) firm, company, business, establishment, concern.

**house** vb (The apartments house about thirty people) accommodate, lodge, have room for.

**hover** vb 1 (children's kites hovering in the air) hang, flutter, fly, drift, float. 2 (She was hovering behind them hoping to hear what they were talking about) linger, hang about, wait.

**howl** vb 1 (hear the dogs howling) bay, yowl, yelp. 2 (children howling for their mothers) cry, weep, scream, bawl, wail.

**huddle** vb 1 (The children huddled together to keep warm) cuddle up, snuggle, nestle, curl up. 2 (The sheep huddled in the corner of the field) crowd, cluster, squeeze, pack.

**hue** n (ribbons of many hues) color, shade, tone, tint.

**hug** vb (The children hugged their mother) embrace, cuddle, hold close.

**huge** adj (a story about huge monsters) enormous, massive, vast, immense, colossal, gigantic.

**hum** vb 1 (machines humming in the factory) drone, vibrate, throb, whir, buzz. 2 (She was humming a happy tune) croon, murmur, mumble, sing.

**human** n (animals and humans/fairies and humans) human being, mortal.

**humane** adj (It is humane to kill animals when they are in pain) kind, compassionate, sympathetic, merciful, charitable.

**humble** adj 1 (He has achieved much fame but is very humble) modest, unassuming, self-effacing, unpretentious. 2 (a humble background) common, ordinary, low-born, lowly, poor, unimportant. 3 (She hates his humble attitude to his employer) servile, subservient, submissive, obsequious, sycophantic.

**humid** adj (a humid atmosphere) damp, moist, muggy, sticky, steamy, clammy.

**humiliate** vb (She humiliated her husband by criticizing him in public) mortify, make ashamed, humble, disgrace, embarrass.

**humility** n (He showed humility even when he won) humbleness, modesty, self-effacement.

**humorous** adj (He told a very humorous story) funny, amusing, comic, hilarious, facetious, entertaining.

**humor** n 1 (He could not see the humor in the situation) funny side, comedy, farce, absurdity. 2 (his own particular brand of humor) comedy, jokes, jests, wit. 3 (He is not in a very good humor) mood, temper, temperament, frame of mind, disposition.

**hunch** n 1 (He has a hunch on his back) hump, swelling, bump, bulge. 2 (The police have a hunch that he is guilty) feeling, intuition, sixth sense, inkling, suspicion.

**hunger** n 1 (The children died of hunger) starvation, famine. 2 (He has a hunger for knowledge) desire, longing, yearning, craving, thirst.

**hungry** adj 1 (hungry children with nothing to eat) starving, famished, ravenous. 2 (They are hungry for knowledge) eager, anxious, avid, craving, longing for.

**hunk** n (a hunk of cheese) lump, block, chunk, wedge, mass.

**hunt** vb 1 (They are hunting stags) chase, pursue, stalk, track. 2 (She was hunting for her glasses) look for, search for, seek, rummage for, scrabble for.

**hurdle** n 1 (The runner failed to clear the first hurdle) fence, rail, railing, barrier. 2 (There were several hurdles in the way of progress) obstacle, obstruction, impediment, barrier, stumbling block.

**hurl** vb (The crowd hurled stones at the police) throw, fling, cast, pitch, toss.

**hurricane** n (lives lost in the hurricane) tornado, cyclone, typhoon, storm, tempest.

**hurry** vb (You must hurry if you want to catch the train) hurry up, hasten, make haste, speed up, run, dash, (inf) get a move on.

**hurt** vb 1 (His leg was hurt in the accident) injure, wound, bruise, maim. 2 (Her leg hurts) be sore, be painful, ache, throb. 3 (She was hurt by his unkind remarks) upset, wound, grieve, sadden, offend.

**hurtle** vb (The runner hurtled towards the finishing post) race, dash, sprint, rush.

**hush** vb 1 (Try to hush the children) quiet, silence, (inf) shut up. 2 (The crowd suddenly hushed) fall silent, quiet down, (inf) shut up. 3 (They tried to hush up the scandal but the press found out) conceal, suppress, cover up.

**hut** n (a hut in the woods) shed, lean-to, shack, cabin.

**hygienic** adj (Hospitals must be hygienic) sanitary, clean, sterile, germfree.

**hymn** n (sing hymns in church) psalm, religious song.

**hypnotic** adj (hypnotic effects) mesmerizing, mesmeric.

**hypocritical** adj (It is hypocritical of him to go to church as he is a very evil person) insincere, false, deceitful, dishonest, dissembling.

**hypothetical** adj (Let us take a hypothetical case) supposed, assumed, theoretical, imagined.

**hysterical** adj 1 (She became hysterical at the news of his death) frantic, frenzied, in a frenzy, out of control, berserk, beside oneself, distracted, overwrought, demented, crazed. 2 (She told us a hysterical story about her travels) hilarious, uproarious, sidesplitting, comical, funny, amusing.

# I

**idea** n 1 (The idea of death terrifies him) concept, notion. 2 (We asked for their ideas on the subject) thought, view, opinion, feeling. 3 (I had an idea that he was dead) thought, impression, belief, suspicion. 4 (Their idea is to sail round the world) plan, aim, intention, objective. 5 (We need some idea of the cost) estimation, approximation, guess.

**ideal** adj (The conditions were ideal) perfect, faultless, excellent.

**identify** vb 1 (She was able to identify her

*attacker*) recognize, name, distinguish, pinpoint. **2** (*They were able to identify the cause of the problem*) establish, find out, ascertain, diagnose. **3** (*She identifies her mother with security*) associate, connect. **4** (*She identifies with homeless people*) empathize, relate.

**identical** *adj* **1** (*The twins wear identical clothes*) like, similar, matching. **2** (*That is the identical dress that her sister wore last week*) same.

**idiot** *n* (*He was an idiot to behave in that way*) fool, dolt, ass, dunce.

**idiotic** *adj* (*It was an idiotic thing to do*) stupid, foolish, senseless.

**idle** *adj* **1** (*He was an idle fellow who did not want to work*) lazy, indolent, slothful. **2** (*The workers are idle through no fault of their own*) unemployed, jobless.

**idol** *n* **1** (*The worshipers were praying to idols*) god, icon, image, effigy. **2** (*He is a pop idol to the teenagers*) hero/heroine, favorite, darling.

**idolize** *vb* (*The children idolize their grandfather*) adore, love, worship.

**ignite** *vb* **1** (*ignite the fire*) set alight, set fire to, kindle. **2** (*The dry material ignited easily*) catch fire, burn, burst into flames.

**ignorant** *adj* **1** (*They had never gone to school and were quite ignorant*) uneducated, illiterate. **2** (*They were ignorant of the legal facts*) unaware, unconscious, uninformed.

**ignore** *vb* **1** (*The child was told to ignore their insulting remarks*) disregard, take no notice of. **2** (*The pupils were told to ignore the last question in the exam paper*) disregard, omit, (*inf*) skip.

**ill** *adj* **1** (*She has been ill and off work for some time*) unwell, sick, poorly, indisposed, unhealthy, (*inf*) under the weather. **2** (*The medicine has no ill effects*) harmful, detrimental. **3** (*There is ill feeling between the two families*) hostile, antagonistic, unfriendly.

**illegal** *adj* (*They were imprisoned for their illegal deeds*) unlawful, illicit, criminal.

**illegible** *adj* (*Her handwriting was illegible*) unreadable, indecipherable, unintelligible.

**illiterate** *adj* (*people who never went to school and so are illiterate*) uneducated, unschooled, ignorant.

**illness** *n* (*She is suffering from a mysterious illness*) complaint, ailment, disease, disorder, affliction, (*inf*) bug.

**illogical** *vb* (*His behavior was illogical*) irrational, unreasonable, unsound.

**illusion** *n* **1** (*The magician did not really do that—it was just an illusion*) deception. **2** (*The supposed ghost was just an illusion*) hallucination, dream, fantasy **3** (*She was under the illusion the he was unmarried*) delusion, misapprehension, misconception.

**illustrate** *vb* **1** (*She illustrated the children's book*) decorate, ornament. **2** (*He illustrated his theory with examples*) demonstrate, exemplify.

**illustration** *n* **1** (*the colored illustrations in the book*) picture, drawing, sketch, diagram. **2** (*the illustrations which he used to prove his point*) example, case, instance.

**image** *adj* **1** (*There were images of famous saints in the churchyard*) likeness, effigy, statue, figure, representation. **2** (*You can see your image in the mirror*) reflection, likeness.

**imaginary** *adj* (*The child has an imaginary friend*) fictitious, invented, made up, legendary, mythical, unreal, fanciful.

**imagination** *n* **1** (*The poem shows imagination*) creativity, vision, inspiration, fancifulness. **2** (*She thought she saw her father but it was only her imagination*) illusion, fancy, hallucination, dream, figment of the imagination.

**imagine** *vb* **1** (*Can you imagine what life will be like in fifty years?*) picture, visualize, envisage, conceive. **2** (*He imagined that the meeting would last an hour*) presume, assume, suppose, think, believe.

**imitate** *vb* **1** (*She imitated the style used by the writer*) copy, emulate, follow. **2** (*The cruel children imitated the boy with the limp*) mimic, impersonate, mock, parody.

**imitation** *n* (*The portrait is not genuine but an imitation*) copy, reproduction, counterfeit, forgery, fake.

**immature** *adj* **1** (*It was immature of the young man to behave like that*) childish, juvenile, infantile. **2** (*The fruit was picked when it was immature*) unripe, green.

**immediate** *adj* **1** (*There was an immediate reaction to his speech*) instant, instantaneous, prompt, swift, sudden. **2** (*He turned to his immediate neighbor in the hall*) next, near, nearest, adjacent. **3** (*We have no immediate plans to go*) existing, current.

**immediately** *adv* **1** (*He plans to leave immediately*) right away, straight away, at once, without delay. **2** (*They were sitting immediately behind us*) directly, right.

**immense** *adj* **1** (*an immense figure of a man*) huge, enormous, vast, colossal, gigantic, giant. **2** (*There has been an immense improvement*) huge, immense, vast.

**immerse** *vb* **1** (*She immersed the dress in the soapy water*) submerge, plunge, dip, lower. **2** (*They immersed themselves in their work before the exam*) absorb, engross, occupy, preoccupy.

**immoral** *adj* (*Everyone disapproved of his immoral acts*) bad, wrong, evil, wicked, sinful, unethical.

**immortal** *adj* (*Human beings are not immortal*) everlasting, endless, eternal, undying.

**impact** *n* **1** (*Both cars were damaged in the impact*) collision, crash, bump, smash, clash. **2** (*His speech had a powerful impact on the crowd*) effect, influence, impression. **3** (*His nose took the full impact of the blow*) force, shock, impetus, brunt.

**impartial** *adj* (*We had to make sure that the judge was impartial*) unbiased, unprejudiced, disinterested, objective, detached.

**impatient** *adj* **1** (*The children were impatient to get out to play*) eager, anxious, keen, avid. **2** (*The show was late starting and the audience was growing impatient*) restless, restive, agitated, edgy, fidgety.

**impeccable** *adj* (*His performance was impeccable*) faultless, flawless, perfect, exemplary.

**impede** *vb* (*The weather impeded their progress*) hinder, obstruct, hamper, block, check, delay, deter.

**impediment** *n* **1** (*The weather was an impediment to their plans*) hindrance, obstruction, obstacle, handicap, block, check, bar, barrier. **2** (*She has an impediment and has to speak slowly*) stammer, stutter.

**imperative** *adj* (*It is imperative that we leave now*) essential, necessary, urgent, vital, important, crucial.

**imperceptible** *adj* (*The difference between the two vases was imperceptible*) undetectable, unnoticeable, slight, small, minute.

**impersonal** *adj* (*The nurse had a very impersonal manner*) cold, cool, aloof, distant, stiff, formal, detached.

**impersonate** *vb* (*The pupil began to impersonate the teacher*) imitate, copy, mimic, mock, ape.

**impertinent** *adj* (*It was impertinent to speak to the old lady like that*) insolent, impudent, cheeky, rude, impolite, ill-mannered.

**imperturbable** *adj* (*She is imperturbable even in an emergency*) calm, cool, composed, unruffled.

**impetuous** *adj* (*He is given to impetuous actions*) hasty, impulsive, spontaneous, rash, foolhardy.

**implement** *n* (*The garden implements have been stolen/buy new kitchen implements*) tool, utensil, appliance, instrument, device, gadget.

**implore** *vb* (*She implored him to help*) beg, plead with, appeal to, entreat, beseech.

**imply** *vb* (*He implied that she was not telling the truth*) insinuate, hint, suggest, indicate.

**important** *adj* **1** (*It is important to arrive on time*) necessary, essential, vital, crucial, urgent. **2** (*The two countries are having important talks*) significant, critical, crucial, serious, momentous, of great import. **3** (*She noted the important points in the lecture*) chief, main, principal, salient, significant. **4** (*All the important people in the town were invited to the reception*) prominent, notable, foremost, leading, distinguished, eminent, influential.

**impose** vb **1** (*The judge imposed a heavy fine on him*) exact, charge, levy, inflict, enforce. **2** (*She tries to impose her views on all her colleagues*) force, foist, inflict, thrust. **3** (*They felt she was imposing on their mother's generosity*) take advantage, exploit, abuse.

**impossible** adj **1** (*It was obviously an impossible task*) unimaginable, inconceivable, impracticable, impractical, hopeless. **2** (*Life became impossible for them in the damp conditions*) unbearable, intolerable.

**impostor, imposter** ns (*They thought that he was a doctor but he was an impostor*) fake, fraud, charlatan, swindler, cheat, (*inf*) conman.

**impotent** adj (*The small army was impotent in the face of the enemy*) powerless, helpless, weak, feeble.

**impoverished** adj (*impoverished people with no homes*) poor, povertystricken, penniless, impecunious, destitute, indigent.

**impracticable** adj (*The task was totally impracticable*) impossible, out of the question.

**impractical** adj **1** (*The proposed solution was totally impractical*) impossible, non-viable, hopeless, ineffective, useless. **2** (*They are impractical people*) unrealistic, idealistic.

**impress** vb **1** (*The crowd was impressed by his speech*) make an impression on, affect, influence, sway, move, stir. **2** (*You must impress on them the need for silence*) stress, emphasize, inculcate.

**impression** n **1** (*His speech made a powerful impression on his audience*) effect, influence, impact. **2** (*We had the impression that he disliked us*) feeling, idea, notion, sensation, suspicion, hunch. **3** (*He does impressions of the President*) impersonation, imitation, mimicry, parody, takeoff.

**impressive** adj **1** (*It was an impressive building*) imposing, grand, splendid, magnificent. **2** (*He made an impressive speech*) moving, stirring, powerful.

**imprison** vb (*The criminals were imprisoned*) put in prison, jail, lock up, take into custody, incarcerate, confine, detain.

**impromptu** adj (*He made an impromptu speech at the wedding reception*) unrehearsed, unprepared, spontaneous, improvised, extempore, off-the-cuff, ad lib.

**improve** vb **1** (*They tried to improve conditions for the poor*) better, make better. **2** (*The standard of her work has improved*) get better, advance, progress, move on.

**improvise** vb **1** (*They had to improvise a shelter when they lost their tent*) put together, devise, rig up, concoct. **2** (*He has not prepared a speech and so he will have to improvise*) make do, extemporize, ad-lib.

**impudent** adj (*The girl was impudent enough*

to swear at the teacher*) impertinent, insolent, cheeky, bold, forward, brazen, presumptuous.

**impulsive** adj (*He was given to impulsive decisions*) impetuous, impromptu, spontaneous, hasty, rash, thoughtless.

**in** adj **1** (*Short skirts are in*) fashionable, stylish, (*inf*) trendy. **2** (*She is in with the boss*) in favor, favored.

**inadequate** adj **1** (*Their supplies of fuel are inadequate*) insufficient, deficient, scanty, meager. **2** (*She feels that she is an inadequate mother*) incompetent, inefficient, inept.

**inadvertent** adj (*There were a few inadvertent omissions from the list of guests*) accidental, unintentional.

**inane** adj (*It was an inane thing to do*) foolish, stupid, idiotic, absurd, ridiculous.

**inanimate** adj (*inanimate objects*) lifeless, without life.

**inapt** adj (*her inapt remarks*) inappropriate, unsuitable, inapposite.

**inaugurate** vb (*They are inaugurating a new club*) launch, initiate, begin, commence, found, establish.

**inborn** adj (*his inborn pessimism*) inherent, innate, inbred, inherited.

**incense** vb (*He was incensed at the children's behavior*) enrage, annoy, anger, infuriate, exasperate.

**incentive** n (*They gave the workers more money as an incentive*) inducement, incitement, encouragement, motivation, spur.

**inception** n (*She has been a member of the club since its inception*) start, beginning, launch, opening.

**incessant** adj (*They were tired of their neighbor's incessant noise*) neverending, unending, endless, unceasing, continuous, continual, unremitting.

**incident** n (*There were various sad incidents in her life*) event, happening, occurrence, episode, occasion.

**incite** vb **1** (*The speaker tried to incite the crowd to rebellion*) egg on, urge, goad, spur on, excite, rouse, stimulate. **2** (*They incited a rebellion*) provoke, instigate, stir up.

**inclination** n **1** (*He has an inclination to put on weight*) tendency, propensity, predisposition, habit. **2** (*flat ground with a slight inclination*) slope, gradient, rise. **3** (*with a slight inclination of his head*) bow, bending, nod.

**incline** vb **1** (*The land inclines towards the shore*) slope, slant, tilt, bend. **2** (*He inclines towards the left in politics*) tend, lean, veer.

**incline, be inclined to** vbs (*They are inclined to tell lies*) be apt to, have a tendency to, have a habit of, be liable to, be likely to.

**include** vb **1** (*The menu includes all their favorite dishes*) contain, take in, incorporate,

comprise. **2** (*Remember to include their names on the list*) put in, add, insert, enter.

**inclusive** adj **1** (*The hotel quoted an inclusive price*) all-inclusive. **2** (*the total bill inclusive of service charge*) including.

**incognito** adj/adv (*He traveled incognito*) in disguise, disguised.

**incoherent** adj (*She was badly shaken and gave a very incoherent account of the accident*) confused, muddled, jumbled, disjointed, garbled.

**income** n (*his income after tax*) salary, wages, pay, earnings, profits.

**incompatible** adj **1** (*Their two statements are incompatible*) conflicting, contradictory, inconsistent. **2** (*It was obvious before they married that they were incompatible*) unsuited, mismatched.

**incongruous** adj (*The modern steel furniture looked incongruous with the old style of decoration*) out of keeping, unsuitable, unsuited, inappropriate, discordant, strange, odd.

**increase** vb **1** (*Demand for the product has increased*) grow, go up, rise, multiply, mushroom, escalate. **2** (*They have increased the number of college places*) add to, augment, enlarge, extend, expand, raise, (*inf*) step up.

**incredible** adj **1** (*His story seemed quite incredible*) unbelievable, far-fetched, unconvincing, unlikely. **2** (*The gymnast's performance was quite incredible*) extraordinary, marvelous, amazing.

**incriminate** vb (*He was found guilty of the crime and tried to incriminate his friend*) accuse, charge, blame, implicate, involve.

**indecent** adj (*The comedian told indecent jokes*) vulgar, crude, coarse, rude, bawdy, smutty, dirty, blue.

**indefinite** adj **1** (*He gave us rather an indefinite answer*) vague, unclear, confused, ambiguous. **2** (*She was rather indefinite about whether to go or not*) undecided, indecisive, uncertain, irresolute. **3** (*The date for the meeting is indefinite as yet*) undecided, unsettled, uncertain. **4** (*an indefinite shape in the mist*) indistinct, blurred, vague, dim.

**independent** adj **1** (*It is an independent state*) self-governing, autonomous, free. **2** (*The children are grown up and independent*) self-supporting, self-sufficient. **3** (*The firms are independent of each other*) unattached, unconnected, unrelated, separate.

**indicate** vb **1** (*His ragged clothes indicated his poverty*) show, demonstrate, point to, be a sign of, suggest, mean. **2** (*He indicated which direction he was turning*) show, point out, make known.

**indication** n **1** (*Her paleness is an indication of her illness*) sign, symptom, mark, signal.

**2** (*He frowned as an indication of his anger*) demonstration, display, show.

**indifferent** *adj* **1** (*He seemed indifferent about the result of his trial*)-apathetic, unconcerned, detached, unemotional. **2** (*He gave an indifferent performance*) mediocre, run-of-the-mill, commonplace, uninspired, undistinguished.

**indignant** *adj* (*They were indignant at being ignored*) angry, annoyed, irate, furious.

**indispensable** *adj* (*employees who were considered indispensable*) essential, necessary, crucial, imperative.

**indisposed** *adj* ill, unwell, sick, poorly, (*inf*) under the weather.

**indistinct** *adj* **1** (*indistinct noises*) muffled, low. **2** (*The picture was rather indistinct*) blurred, fuzzy, hazy, misty.

**individual** *adj* **1** (*the individual petals of the flower*) single, separate, particular, specific. **2** (*The writer has a very individual style*) characteristic, distinctive, peculiar, original, idiosyncratic.

**indolent** *vb* (*He was too indolent to look for a job*) lazy, idle, slothful.

**induce** *vb* **1** (*The salesman tried to induce them to buy a new car*) persuade, prevail upon, get, press. **2** (*The drug induced a skin reaction*) produce, cause, give rise to, bring about.

**indulgent** *adj* (*The children's grandparents are too indulgent*) permissive, easygoing, doting.

**industrial** *adj* (*an industrial area of the country*) manufacturing.

**industrious** *adj* (*industrious students*) hardworking, diligent, conscientious, assiduous.

**inert** *adj* (*people lying inert after the previous night's party*) inactive, motionless, still.

**inevitable** *adj* (*A guilty verdict seemed inevitable*) unavoidable, inescapable, irrevocable.

**infallible** *adj* (*She claims that it is an infallible cure*) unfailing, foolproof, reliable, sure, certain.

**infamous** *adj* **1** (*He is an infamous criminal*) notorious, villainous, wicked. **2** (*It was an infamous crime*) notorious, scandalous, disgraceful, shocking, outrageous.

**infant** *n* (*She was very ill as an infant*) baby, young child.

**infatuation** *n* (*his infatuation with one of his female colleagues*) love, fancy, obsession, fixation, (*inf*) crush.

**infect** *vb* **1** (*waste material that infected the town's water supply*) contaminate, pollute, taint. **2** (*The wound was infected*) poison, make septic. **3** (*He infected others with his enthusiasm*) influence, affect.

**infectious** *adj* (*an infectious disease*), communicable, transmittable, catching.

**infer** *vb* (*From the evidence the jury inferred that he was guilty*) deduce, reason, conclude, gather.

**inferior** *adj* **1** (*She occupies an inferior position in the firm*) subordinate, lower, lesser, junior, minor, low, humble. **2** (*The firm produces inferior goods*) imperfect, faulty, defective, substandard, shoddy. **3** (*They do not employ inferior workers*) incompetent, second-rate.

**infest** *vb* (*houses infested with rats*) overrun, pervade, invade, plague.

**infidelity** *n* **1** (*accused of infidelity to their king*) disloyalty, unfaithfulness, treachery, perfidy. **2** (*his wife's infidelity*) unfaithfulness, adultery.

**infinite** *adj* **1** (*Space is infinite*) boundless, unbounded, limitless, unlimited, endless. **2** (*She has infinite patience*) unlimited, endless, unending, inexhaustible.

**infirm** *adj* (*The old people are becoming infirm*) frail, failing, feeble, weak.

**inflamed** *adj* **1** (*a badly inflamed arm*) red, reddened, sore, infected, festering, septic. **2** (*inflamed passions*) aroused, roused, excited.

**inflammable** *adj* (*nightgowns made of inflammable material*) flammable, combustible.

**inflammation** *n* (*He was given some ointment to cure the inflammation*) redness, sore, swelling.

**inflate** *vb* **1** (*He had to stop and inflate his bicycle tires*) blow up, pump up. **2** (*a decision that might inflate prices*) increase, raise, boost, escalate.

**inflexible** *adj* **1** (*inflexible substances*) rigid, stiff, hard. **2** (*an inflexible work schedule*) fixed, rigid, unalterable. **3** (*their inflexible attitudes*) stubborn, obstinate, adamant, firm, unaccommodating, unbending.

**inflict** *vb* (*inflict distress on his parents*) administer, deal out, mete out, impose, give.

**influence** *vb* **1** (*Her state of health influenced her decision*) affect, have an effect on, have an impact on, sway, control, determine. **2** (*They would like to influence the jury*) sway, bias, prejudice, bribe.

**influence** *n* **1** (*She had a great deal of influence on her colleagues*) effect, impact, sway, control, power. **2** (*He was under the influence of alcohol*) effect.

**influential** *adj* (*He is an influential figure in the government*) powerful, important, leading.

**inform** *vb* **1** (*We had to inform her that he was dead*) tell, advise, notify, communicate to, impart to. **2** (*He informed on his friends to the police*) betray, (*inf*) blow the whistle on, (*inf*) snitch.

**informal** *adj* **1** (*wear informal clothes at weekends*) casual, comfortable. **2** (*an informal party*) casual, unceremonious, unofficial, simple, relaxed.

**information** *n* **1** (*collect information on all of the countries of the world*) data, facts, statistics. **2** (*When will we receive information about the next meeting?*) news, word, communication, advice, instruction.

**infringe** *vb* **1** (*infringe the rules*) break, disobey, violate, contravene, disregard. **2** (*He infringed on his neighbor's land*) encroach, intrude, trespass.

**infuriate** *vb* (*They were infuriated at being overcharged in the restaurant*) enrage, incense, annoy, anger, exasperate.

**ingenious** *adj* (*They thought up an ingenious plan*) clever, shrewd, cunning, inventive, resourceful.

**ingenuous** *adj* (*She was too ingenuous to try to deceive them*) open, sincere, honest, frank, artless, simple, guileless.

**inhabit** *vb* (*They inhabit a remote area of the country*) live in, dwell in, reside in, occupy.

**inherent** *adj* **1** (*There is an inherent tendency to heart disease in the family*) inborn, inbred, hereditary, congenital. **2** (*It was an inherent part of the design of the building*) intrinsic, innate, essential, basic, fundamental.

**inherit** *vb* **1** (*She inherited a great deal of money from her grandmother*) be left, be bequeathed. **2** (*He inherited the title on his father's death*) succeed to, accede to, assume.

**inheritance** *n* (*He has already spent his inheritance from his father*) legacy, bequest, estate.

**inhibited** *adj* (*She feels inhibited in the presence of her parents*) shy, reticent, reserved, self-conscious, subdued.

**initial** *adj* (*He was involved right from the initial stages of the company*) first, beginning, commencing, opening, early, introductory.

**initiate** *vb* **1** (*They asked him to initiate the proceedings*) begin, start off, commence, open, institute, launch. **2** (*The boys initiated a new member into their gang*) admit, introduce, induct, install, enroll.

**initiative** *n* **1** (*He took the initiative and made the opening speech*) first move, first step, lead, start, beginning. **2** (*There will be promotion prospects for workers with initiative*) enterprise, resourcefulness, inventiveness, drive.

**injection** *n* (*He was given an injection against tetanus*) inoculation, vaccination, shot.

**injure** *vb* **1** (*He injured his leg in the accident*) hurt, damage, wound. **2** (*His behavior has injured his reputation*) damage, ruin, spoil, mar.

**inkling** *n* (*The workers had no inkling that the firm was going to shut down*) hint, clue, indication, suspicion.

**inlet** *n* (*They tied the boat up in a sandy inlet*) cove, bay.

**inn** n (They had a meal at the local inn) pub, tavern.

**inner** adj (the inner layer) inside, interior.

**innocent** adj 1 (The accused was found innocent) not guilty, guiltless, blameless. 2 (innocent young girls) simple, naive, artless, trusting, inexperienced, gullible, virtuous, pure. 3 (It was just innocent fun) harmless, safe, inoffensive.

**innocuous** adj (The substance was found to be innocuous) harmless, safe, non-toxic, non-poisonous.

**innovation** n (The new owner introduced some innovations) new measure, change, alteration.

**innuendo** n (She made an innuendo about his lack of honesty) insinuation, suggestion, hint.

**innumerable** adj (He has been late on innumerable occasions) numerous, countless, many.

**inordinate** n (They caused an inordinate amount of trouble) excessive, undue, unreasonable, uncalled-for.

**inquire** vb 1 (The police are inquiring into the cause of the fire) make inquiries, investigate, look into, probe, query. 2 (We inquired about her mother's health) ask, make inquiries.

**inquiry** n 1 (The police are conducting a murder inquiry) investigation, inquest, interrogation, examination. 2 (She is employed to answer customers' inquiries) query, question.

**inquisitive** adj (She is inquisitive about other people's business) curious, prying, snooping, (inf) nosy.

**insane** adj 1 (The murderer has been declared insane) deranged, demented, unhinged, out of one's mind. 2 (It was insane to take such risks) mad, crazy, idiotic, foolish, stupid, absurd.

**insatiable** adj (He has an insatiable appetite/insatiable for knowledge) hungry, greedy, voracious.

**inscription** n 1 (the inscription on the gravestone) writing, engraving, epitaph. 2 (the inscription in the front of the book) dedication, message.

**insert** vb 1 (She inserted the letter in the envelope) put in, push in, thrust in, slip in. 2 (He decided to insert a few more lines into his report) put in, introduce, enter, interpolate.

**inside** adv (She decided to stay inside in the cold weather) indoors.

**insignificant** adj (concentrate on the main points in the report and ignore the insignificant details) unimportant, minor, trivial, trifling, negligible.

**insinuate** vb 1 (She insinuated that she did not trust him) hint, suggest, imply, indicate. 2 (She succeeded in insinuating herself into the old lady's affections) worm one's way, work one's way, ingratiate oneself.

**insipid** adj (She is a very insipid person) colorless, dull, drab, vapid, uninteresting.

**insist** vb 1 (At first they refused to go but their parents insisted) stand firm, be firm, stand one's ground, be determined, not take no for an answer. 2 (She insisted that they go immediately) demand, command, urge. 3 (He insists that he is innocent) maintain, assert, declare, swear.

**insolent** adj (The pupil was accused of being insolent) impertinent, impudent, cheeky, rude.

**inspect** vb (The police inspected the stolen car) examine, check, scrutinize, study.

**inspiration** n 1 (His wife acts as an inspiration to the artist) stimulus, stimulation, encouragement, motivation, spur. 2 (His poetry lacks inspiration) creativity, originality, inventiveness, imagination. 3 (They were completely puzzled but then he had a sudden inspiration) bright idea.

**install** vb 1 (They have installed a new bathroom) put in, insert, fix, establish. 2 (They installed themselves in comfortable chairs) settle.

**installment** n (They published the novel in installments) part, portion, section.

**instance** n (That was just one instance of his impertinence) case, example, illustration.

**instant** adj (She demanded an instant reply) instantaneous, immediate, onthe-spot, rapid, prompt.

**instant** n (He was gone in an instant) moment, minute, second, trice, (inf) jiffy.

**instinct** n 1 (Some birds migrate by instinct) intuition, sixth sense. 2 (She has an instinct for doing the right thing) ability, knack, aptitude, gift, talent.

**institution** n 1 (He has been living in an institution since he was very young) home, hospital, detention center. 2 (It was one of the village's institutions) custom, tradition, practice.

**instruct** vb 1 (He instructs the students in gymnastics) teach, train, coach, educate. 2 (She instructed the bank to close her account) tell, order, command, direct, bid.

**instructor** n (a sports instructor) teacher, coach, trainer, tutor.

**instrument** n 1 (instruments used by dentists) implement, tool, appliance, apparatus, utensil, gadget. 2 (She plays several instruments) musical instrument.

**insult** n (His insults were quite unjustified) slur, abuse, affront, slight, gibe.

**insult** vb (She was deeply insulted by his accusations) affront, give offense to, abuse, slight, hurt.

**intact** adj (They were pleased to find all their furniture intact after they moved house) whole, in one piece, sound, unbroken, complete, undamaged.

**integrate** vb (They integrated the various parts into a whole) combine, unite, join, amalgamate, merge, fuse.

**integrity** n (No person of integrity would have gotten involved in the scheme) honor, honesty, uprightness, righteousness, decency.

**intellect** n (people of limited intellect) brain, mind, intelligence.

**intellectual** adj (They are an intellectual family) academic, well-educated, well-read, scholarly, bookish, clever.

**intelligent** adj (the more intelligent pupils) clever, bright, sharp, quick, smart, (inf) brainy.

**intend** vb (She intends to leave soon) aim, mean, plan.

**intense** adj 1 (She could not stand the intense heat) severe, acute, fierce, extreme, strong, powerful. 2 (She has an intense desire to travel) deep, profound, passionate, fervent, burning, eager, ardent.

**intent** adj 1 (They were intent on getting there on time) set on, bent on, determined to. 2 (The child wore an intent expression as he worked) absorbed, engrossed, atten-tive, concentrating.

**intention** n (It is his intention to go to university) aim, purpose, intent, goal, objective, design.

**intentional** adj (It was not an accident that he hurt her—it was intentional) deliberate, meant, purposeful, planned, calculated.

**interest** n 1 (He showed no interest in the project) concern, heed, regard, notice, attention, curiosity. 2 (Stampcollecting is one of his interests) hobby, pastime, diversion. 3 (This is a matter of interest to us all) concern, importance, import, consequence.

**interested** adj 1 (The children were not interested) attentive, absorbed, curious. 2 (the interested parties) concerned, involved. 3 (No interested person is allowed to be a judge in the competition) involved, biased, prejudiced, partial, partisan.

**interesting** adj (It was an interesting book) absorbing, engrossing, fascinating, riveting, gripping, amusing, entertaining.

**interfere** vb 1 (He is always interfering in other people's business) meddle with, pry into, intrude into, (inf) poke one's nose into, (inf) put one's oar in. 2 (He lets his sports training interfere with his school work) hinder, impede, hamper, obstruct, get in the way of.

**interior** n 1 (They are painting the interior of the building) inside. 2 (They traveled to the interior of the country) center, middle, heart.

**interlude** n (during the interlude at the theater) interval, intermission, lull, pause.

**intermediate** adj (The team is in an intermediate position in the league) middle, midway, halfway.

**interminable** adj 1 (The journey seemed interminable) endless, never-ending, everlasting 2 (She was tired of his interminable questions) endless, everlasting, ceaseless, incessant, continuous, continual, constant, persistent.

**intermittent** adj (Their telephone has an intermittent fault) occasional, irregular, sporadic, fitful, recurrent.

**internal** adj 1 (They knocked down an internal wall) interior, inside, inner, inward. 2 (the country's internal affairs) home, domestic,.

**international** adj (international issues) global, universal, worldwide.

**interpret** vb 1 (The pupils need someone to interpret the difficult text) explain, clarify, expound, elucidate. 2 (They interpreted her silence as agreement) take, construe, read, understand. 3 (She is employed to interpret for foreign businessmen) translate.

**interrogate** vb (The police are interrogating the suspect) question, ask questions, examine, cross-examine, quiz, give the third degree to, (inf) grill.

**interrupt** vb 1 (people in the audience kept interrupting the politician's speech) cut in on, break in on, butt in on, intrude on, disturb. 2 (They interrupted the meeting to make an important announcement) discontinue, break off, suspend, leave off, delay.

**intersection** n (There was a bad road accident at the intersection) junction, interchange, crossroads.

**interval** n 1 (There was quite an interval between the two meetings) gap, wait, space, period. 2 (during the interval in the theater) intermission, interlude, pause, lull.

**intervene** n 1 (The quarrel between the children was so bad that their parents had to intervene) intercede, mediate, step in, interfere. 2 (A period of several years intervened before they met again) occur, pass, happen, take place, ensue.

**interview** n 1 (The candidates for the job had to attend an interview) meeting, discussion, dialogue, evaluation. 2 (The president was giving an interview to the press) audience, press conference, dialogue, question and answer session.

**intimate** adj 1 (They were intimate friends) close, dear, near, loving, friendly, amicable. 2 (the intimate details of her life as noted in her diary) personal, private, confidential, secret.

**intimidate** vb (They felt intimidated by the three huge men) frighten, scare, alarm, terrify, terrorize, threaten.

**intolerable** adj (an intolerable level of pain) unbearable, unendurable, insufferable, insupportable.

**intolerant** adj (intolerant members of the community who objected to the activities of young people) bigoted, narrow-minded, biased, prejudiced, provincial, parochial.

**intoxicated** adj (They were so intoxicated that they could not walk straight) drunk, tipsy, under the influence, (inf) tight.

**intrepid** adj (intrepid explorers who went into the heart of the jungle) fearless, bold, daring, brave, courageous.

**intricate** adj 1 (an intricate pattern) elaborate, fancy, ornate. 2 (intricate problems) complex, complicated, involved, difficult.

**intriguing** adj (an intriguing story) fascinating, riveting, absorbing, interesting, captivating.

**introduce** vb 1 (She introduced the speaker) present, announce. 2 (She introduced her friends to each other) present, make known. 3 (They introduced new business methods) bring in, initiate, launch, institute, establish, start.

**introduction** n (the introduction to the book) preface, foreword, front matter, prologue.

**introverted** adj (Her sister is very outgoing but she is introverted) inwardlooking, introspective, withdrawn.

**intrude** vb (Although they had been invited to the party they felt as though they were intruding) interrupt, barge in, interfere, butt in.

**intruder** n (The police arrested the intruder) burglar, housebreaker, thief.

**intuition** n (She seemed to know by intuition where her child was) instinct, sixth sense.

**inundate** vb 1 (The river burst its banks and inundated the town) flood, overflow, swamp, deluge, engulf. 2 (They were inundated with complaints) overwhelm, swamp, bog down.

**invade** vb (The enemy army invaded the city) overrun, storm, take over, attack, raid.

**invalid** adj (The doctor visited their invalid mother) ill, sick, ailing, unwell, infirm.

**invaluable** adj (We thanked them for their invaluable help) useful, helpful, precious, inestimable.

**invariable** adj (an invariable temperature/Her style of dress was quite invariable) unchanging, constant, unvarying, fixed, regular, uniform.

**invasion** n (the enemy's invasion of the city) attack, assault, raid, onslaught.

**invent** n 1 (the person who invented television) originate, create, discover, design, devise, think up. 2 (He invented an excuse for-not being present) make up, concoct, fabricate, hatch, (inf) cook up.

**investigate** vb (investigate a murder case) research, examine, explore, inquire into, study.

**invincible** adj 1 (Their army seemed invincible) unbeatable, unconquerable. 2 (The obstacles to progress seem invincible) insuperable, insurmountable, overwhelming.

**invisible** adj 1 (The high hedge made the house invisible to passersby) unseen, unnoticed, out of sight, hidden, concealed. 2 (an invisible repair) inconspicuous, unnoticeable, imperceptible.

**invite** vb 1 (We invited them to dinner) ask, send an invitation to. 2 (The company is inviting applications for sales assistants) ask, request, seek, call for.

**involuntary** adj (Blinking is usually an involuntary reaction) reflex, automatic, instinctive, unthinking, mechanical.

**involve** vb 1 (His new job involves working with computers) entail, include, necessitate, require. 2 (They hoped to involve all the children in the scheme) include, take in, incorporate, concern, interest. 3 (He tried to involve his friends in his plans for the robbery) implicate, associate, mix up. 4 (find a hobby that involves them) interest, absorb, occupy, grip, engross.

**involved** adj (Her excuse seemed very involved) complicated, complex, intricate, elaborate, confused, muddled.

**irate** adj (They tried to calm the irate old man) angry, furious, indignant, infuriated.

**iron** vb (They had to iron their creased shirts) press, smooth.

**iron, iron out** vbs (They had talks to try to iron out their problems) sort out, clear up, straighten out, settle, solve.

**ironic** adj (He has a tendency to make ironic remarks) satirical, mock-ing, scoffing, scornful, sneering, sarcastic.

**irritable** adj (He gets irritable when he is tired) bad-tempered, ill-tempered, cross, touchy, crabby, grumpy, cantankerous.

**irritate** vb 1 (His constant stream of jokes irritates her) annoy, get on one's nerves, try one's patience, try one's nerves, exasperate, infuriate. 2 (The material irritated her skin) inflame, redden, chafe, cause discomfort to.

**isolated** adj 1 (They live in an isolated place) remote, out-of-the-way, outlying, secluded, desolate, inaccessible. 2 (She felt isolated living far away from her family and friends) lonely, solitary, alone, forsaken 3-(The doctors do not think it is an epidemic but just an isolated example of the disease) single, solitary, abnormal, unusual, atypical.

**issue** vb 1 (Smoke issued from the factory chimney) pour forth, discharge. 2 (A steady stream of people issued from the building) come out, emerge, leave, appear from. 3-(New stamps have been issued to mark the occasion/They issued a press release) put out, distribute, circulate, release, disseminate.

**issue** n 1 (*They argue over political issues*) matter, subject, topic, affair, problem. 2 (*They plan to buy the next issue of the magazine*) edition, number, installment. 3 (*They have been having talks about peace but the issue is still in doubt*) result, outcome, decision, conclusion.

**itch** n 1 (*She has an itch in her head*) tingling, prickling, irritation. 2 (*She has an itch to travel*) desire, longing, yearning, craving, hankering, (*inf*) yen.

**item** n 1 (*make a list of items for sale*) object, article, thing. 2 (*There are several items to be discussed at the meeting*) point, matter, issue, thing.

**itinerant** adj (*an itinerant salesman*) traveling, peripatetic.

**itinerary** n (*Our itinerary takes us through Belgium*) route, journey, travels.

# J

**jab** vb (*She jabbed him in the ribs to wake him*) prod, poke, nudge, dig.

**jagged** adj (*the jagged edge of the bread knife*) rough, uneven, pointed, notched, serrated.

**jail** n (*The prisoners have escaped from jail*) prison.

**jail** vb (*The judge jailed him for life*) imprison, send to prison, lock up, put away, confine, incarcerate.

**jam** vb 1 (*They tried to jam too many people into the hall*) crowd, pack, cram, squeeze, crush. 2 (*roads jammed by the sheer volume of traffic*) block, obstruct, congest, clog. 3 (*They jammed a piece of paper under the door to keep it open*) wedge, stick, force, push, stuff.

**jam** n (*bread, butter, and jam*) preserve, jelly.

**jar** vb 1 (*The knife jarred against the metal surface of the box*) grate, rasp, scratch, squeak. 2 (*He jarred his shoulder in the car crash*) jolt, jerk, shake.

**jealous** adj 1 (*She was jealous because her sister won the race*) envious, grudging, resentful, covetous, green with envy. 2 (*He had a jealous wife*) suspicious, distrustful, mistrustful, possessive.

**jeer** vb (*When the politician tried to speak the crowd jeered*) mock, scoff, ridicule, taunt, sneer.

**jerk** vb 1 (*His leg was jerking uncontrollably*) twitch, shake, tremble. 2 (*She jerked the child out of his seat*) pull, yank, tug, wrench. 3 (*The old bus jerked along the country roads*) jolt, bump, lurch, jar.

**jewel** n (*She kept her jewels in a safe*) gem, precious stone.

**jewelry** n (*She wore silver jewelry on her black dress*) jewels, gems, trinkets, ornament.

**jittery** adj (*He was jittery before the exam*) nervous, jumpy, uneasy, anxious.

**job** n 1 (*He took days to finish a simple job*) task, piece of work, chore, assignment, undertaking. 2 (*What is her job?*) occupation, profession, employment, career, trade. 3 (*It was his job to look after the garden*) task, chore, responsibility, concern, function, role.

**jog** vb 1 (*They jogged round the park*) go jogging, run, trot, lope. 2 (*We tried to jog her memory but she had forgotten all about the incident*) prompt, stir, stimulate, refresh.

**join** vb 1 (*We had to join the two pieces of string*) fasten, attach, put together, link, connect, tie. 2 (*We joined in the search party to look for the dog*) take part in, participate in, contribute to. 3 (*We were asked to join the tennis club*) become a member of, take up membership of, enroll in, sign up for. 4 (*The two clubs have joined together*) join forces, amalgamate, merge, combine, ally. 5 (*Their yard joins ours*) adjoin, abut on, border, border on, meet.

**joint** n (*the joints in the water pipes*) join, junction, coupling, seam.

**joint** adj (*The organization of the party was a joint effort*) common, shared, mutual, combined, collective, cooperative, united.

**joke** n 1 (*Her uncle tells very funny jokes*) jest, gag, witticism. 2 (*We took his bike for a joke*) practical joke, prank, hoax, piece of fun, trick, (*inf*) lark.

**joke** vb 1 (*She was hurt by his remark but he was only joking*) tease, fool, pull (someone's) leg. 2 (*He can be rather annoying as he jokes all the time*) tell jokes, crack jokes, jest.

**jolly** adj (*The party was a very jolly occasion*) merry, happy, gay, joyful, cheerful, light-hearted.

**jolt** vb 1 (*The old car jolted along the bumpy roads*) jerk, lurch, bump, bounce. 2 (*The little boy kept getting jolted in the crowd*) bump, jostle, push, shove, nudge. 3 (*His unexpected failure in the exam jolted him*) upset, disturb, perturb, shake, disconcert, stun.

**jostle** vb (*people in the crowd jostling each other to the front*) push, shove, elbow, nudge, bump, knock, jolt.

**jot** vb (*jot down the names of the pupils*) note, make a note of, take down, write down, mark down, list.

**journalist** n (*The local artist was interviewed by a journalist after the exhibition*) reporter, member of the press.

**journey** n (*They were tired after their long train journey*) trip, excursion, expedition, travels.

**joy** n (*their joy at the birth of their daughter*) delight, pleasure, happiness, gladness, rapture.

**joyful** adj (*It was a joyful occasion*) happy, cheerful, merry, gay, jolly, light-hearted.

**judge** vb 1 (*A senior member of the legal profession judged the case*) try, pronounce a verdict. 2 (*The local mayor judged the pets' competition*) adjudicate, arbitrate, evaluate, assess. 3 (*He is too ready to judge others*) pass judgment on, criticize, find fault with. 4 (*We judge that the meat would take an hour to cook*) estimate, guess, surmise, reckon, suppose, consider, think, believe.

**judgment** n 1 (*The judge will give his judgment tomorrow*) verdict, ruling, decision, finding, conclusion. 2 (*He is not a good businessman as he is lacking in judgment*) good sense, sense, shrewdness, wisdom, judiciousness, acumen.

**juicy** adj (*juicy fruit*) succulent, moist, ripe.

**jump** vb 1 (*The dog escaped by jumping over the fence*) leap over, vault, clear, hurdle. 2 (*The game involved the children jumping*) leap, spring, bound, bounce. 3 (*The sudden noise made everyone jump*) start, flinch, jerk.

**junction** n (*The cars collided at the junction*) intersection, interchange, crossroads.

**jungle** n (*wild animals in the jungle*) forest, tropical forest, undergrowth.

**junior** adj 1 (*the junior members of the family*) younger. 2 (*the junior posts in the company*) subordinate, lower, lesser, minor.

**just** adj (*We felt it was a just decision*) fair, honest, impartial, unprejudiced, unbiased, objective.

**just** adv 1 (*He's just a boy*) only, merely. 2 (*I just met them*) now, a moment ago, recently. 3 (*we just caught the bus*) only just, barely, scarcely, (*inf*) by the skin of our teeth. 4 (*The house was just right for them*) exactly, absolutely, precisely, entirely.

**justice** n (*He expects justice from the American courts*) justness, fairness, impartiality, lack of bias, objectivity.

**justify** vb 1 (*He was asked to justify his absence*) account for, give reasons for, give grounds for, explain, defend, excuse. 2 (*His behavior justified our concern for his health*) support, warrant, bear out, confirm.

**jut** vb (*The cliff juts out over the road*) stick out, project, protrude, overhang.

**juvenile** adj 1 (*the juvenile section of the musical competition*) junior, young, youthful. 2 (*We were amazed at their juvenile attitude to losing the game*) childish, immature, infantile.

# K

**keen** *adj* **1** (*The keen pupils asked for extra practice*) enthusiastic, eager, willing, avid, zealous, conscientious. **2** (*people who are keen on football*) fond of, devoted to, having a liking for, being a fan of. **3** (*people who are keen to get more education*) eager, anxious, avid. **4** (*a keen edge on the sword*) sharp, sharp-edged. **5** (*a keen sense of smell*) sharp, acute, sensitive. **6** (*admire her keen mind*) sharp, astute, shrewd, quick, clever, bright, intelligent. **7** (*a keen frost*) intense, extreme, severe.

**keep** *vb* **1** (*She kept the ring which he had given her*) hold on to, retain, (*inf*) hang on to. **2** (*The child keeps all his old magazines*) save up, store, accumulate, hoard, collect. **3** (*The firm tried to keep going*) continue, carry on, persist, persevere. **4** (*The local store keeps a wide range of goods*) stock, sell, carry. **5** (*He does not earn enough to keep a wife and children*) provide, support, maintain, feed. **6** (*Everyone should keep to the rules*) obey, comply with, observe, abide by, carry out. **7** (*Try to keep the news of his accident from his mother*) keep back, keep secret, hide, conceal, withhold, suppress. **8** (*He is late—something must have kept him*) keep back, delay, hold back, detain, hinder.

**keep** *n* (*She pays for her own keep*) board, food, maintenance, support.

**keepsake** *n* (*be given a keepsake of her vacation*) memento, souvenir, reminder, remembrance.

**keg** *n* (*kegs of beer*) barrel, cask, vat, tun.

**kernel** *n* **1** (*hazelnut kernels*) nut, stone, seed. **2** (*try to get to the kernel of the problem*) nub, core, center, heart, (*inf*) nitty-gritty.

**key** *n* **1** (*musical keys*) tone, pitch, timbre. **2** (*find the key to the problem*) clue, guide, pointer, answer, solution, explanation.

**kick** *vb* **1** (*kick the ball*) boot, punt. **2** (*kick the man lying on the ground*) boot, take one's boot to, take one's feet to. **3** (*try to kick the smoking habit*) give up, stop, abandon, quit.

**kidnap** *vb* (*The president's son has been kidnapped*) abduct, snatch, seize, hold to ransom, take hostage.

**kill** *vb* **1** (*He was killed by a member of a rival gang*) take (someone's) life, slay, murder, put to death, execute, assassinate, (*inf*) bump off. **2** (*The news of his death killed all our hopes*) destroy, put an end to, ruin, extinguish, scotch.

**kind** *adj* (*Kind people helped him/They appreciated his kind action*) kindhearted, kindly, generous, charitable, benevolent, helpful, considerate, obliging, thoughtful, friendly, amiable, courteous.

**kind** *n* (*a kind of dog/a kind of car*) type, sort, variety, class, category, brand, make, species.

**king** *n* (*He was crowned king of Denmark*) monarch, ruler, sovereign.

**kingdom** *n* (*The ruler's kingdom extended to the sea*) realm, domain, land, country, territory.

**kink** *n* **1** (*There were some kinks in the rope*) twist, bend, coil, loop, tangle. **2** (*the kinks in her character*) quirk, eccentricity, idiosyncrasy.

**kiosk** *n* (*buy a newspaper from a kiosk*) stall, stand, booth.

**kit** *n* (*He forgot his football kit*) equipment, gear, tackle, stuff, things, paraphernalia.

**klutz** *n* (*Jerry is a terrible klutz*) clumsy person.

**knack** *n* (*He has the knack of getting people to tell him things*) talent, gift, aptitude, flair, ability, skill, expertise.

**kneel** *vb* (*He knelt to pick out some weeds*) get down on one's knees, bend, stoop, crouch.

**knife** *vb* (*He was knifed to death*) stab, pierce, run through, impale.

**knob** *n* **1** (*turn the knob of the door*) handle. **2** (*turn the knob of the radio*) switch. **3** (*trees with knobs on the bark*) bump, bulge, lump, swelling, knot, nodule. **4** (*a knob of butter*) lump, piece, bit.

**knock** *vb* **1** (*They knocked at the door*) tap, rap, bang. **2** (*The child knocked into the table and hurt his head*) bang, bump, collide with, crash into. **3** (*He knocked the boy on the head and he fell over*) strike, hit, slap, smack, box, thump, (*inf*) wallop.

**know** *vb* **1** (*We don't really know the other people in the street*) be acquainted with, have dealings with, socialize with. **2** (*We knew what they were saying about us*) realize, be aware of, be conscious of, notice, recognize. **3** (*He does not know any Spanish*) have knowledge of, understand, comprehend. **4** (*She has known great misfortune*) experience, go through, be familiar with. **5** (*He does not know one of the twins from the other*) distinguish, differentiate, tell.

**knowledge** *n* **1** (*He showed his knowledge by doing well in the exam*) learning, education, scholarship, erudition. **2** (*admire the taxi driver's knowledge of the area*) familiarity, acquaintanceship. **3** (*He has little knowledge of the subject*) understanding, grasp, comprehension, expertise, skill, knowhow.

**knowledgeable** *adj* (*She is very knowledgeable about local history*) informed, well-informed, educated, learned.

**kudos** *n* (*the kudos of being a famous writer*) prestige, fame, honor, glory, praise.

# L

**label** *n* (*put a label on the luggage/the label on the article*) tag, tab, sticker, ticket.

**laborious** *adj* (*undertake a laborious task*) hard, difficult, arduous, strenuous, tiring.

**labor** *n* **1** (*They did not receive much money for their labor*) work, toil, effort, exertion, drudgery. **2** (*employ local labor in the new factory*) workers, employees, workforce.

**labored** *adj* **1** (*the labored breathing of the invalid*) heavy, strained, forced, difficult. **2** (*He has a labored style of writing*) stilted, strained, stiff, unnatural.

**laborer** *n* (*laborers on the building site*) workman, worker.

**labyrinth** *n* **1** (*a labyrinth in the theme park*) maze. **2** (*a labyrinth of cellars under the house/try to make their way through the labyrinth of rules and regulations*) maze, network, tangle, jungle.

**lace** *n* (*lose a lace from her shoe*) shoelace, cord, string.

**lacerate** *vb* (*He lacerated his hand on the cut glass*) cut, tear, gash, slash, rip.

**lack** *n* (*There is a lack of fresh water in the area*) shortage, dearth, insufficiency, scarcity, paucity, want.

**lack** *vb* (*She lacks training for the job*) be lacking, be without, have need of, be short of, be deficient in.

**laconic** *adj* (*She gave a laconic reply*) brief, concise, terse, succinct.

**lad** *n* (*They hired a lad to deliver the newspapers*) boy, youth, young man.

**ladder** *n* (*stand on a ladder to paint the ceiling*) stepladder, steps.

**laden** *adj* (*people laden with shopping*) loaded, burdened, weighed down, encumbered.

**lag** *vb* (*He lagged behind the rest of the runners in the race*) fall behind, linger, dawdle, dally.

**lair** *n* (*the fox's lair*) den.

**lake** *n* (*The children paddled in the lake*) reservoir.

**lame** *adj* **1** (*He has been lame since the accident*) limping, crippled. **2**-(*He gave a lame excuse for being late*) weak, feeble, flimsy, inadequate.

**lamp** *n* (*The lamps were still burning*) light.

**land** *n* **1** (*He went to live in a foreign land*) country, nation, state. **2**-(*The land there will not grow much*) soil, earth, ground. **3** (*a large house with a great deal of land round it*) ground, estate, property. **4** (*prefer traveling on land to traveling by sea*) dry land, terra firma.

**land** vb **1** (*the plane landed*) touch down, come down, alight. **2** (*They met us as we landed at the dock*) dock, disembark.

**landscape** n (*a country with a flat landscape*) countryside.

**lane** n **1** (*take a walk down a country lane*) path, track. **2** (*freeway lanes*) track, course.

**language** n **1** (*the Spanish language*) tongue, speech, mother tongue. **2** (*Children acquire language at different rates*) speech, speaking, talking, words, vocabulary, communication.

**lap** n **1** (*The cat was sitting in its owner's lap*) knee, knees. **2** (*We are on our last lap of the journey*) round, section, stage, leg. **3** (*The runners ran several laps of the track*) circuit, course.

**lap** vb **1** (*The cats lapped up the milk*) drink, lick up. **2** (*The water lapped against the rocks*) wash, beat.

**lapse** n (*We saw him again after a lapse of time*) interval, break, gap, pause, passage.

**large** adj **1** (*They have a large backyard/They are putting up large buildings*) big, sizeable, substantial, tall, high, huge, immense, enormous. **2** (*He is a very large man*) big, burly, heavy, strapping, hulking, hefty, fat. **3** (*We have large supplies of fuel*) big, ample, abundant, copious, liberal, plentiful.

**lash** vb **1** (*The master lashed the slave with a whip*) whip, flog, flail, birch, trash, beat. **2** (*They lashed the boat to the side of the ship*) tie, bind, fasten, tether, strap.

**last** adj **1** (*The last words of the speaker*) final, closing, concluding. **2** (*The last runners arrived exhausted*) hindmost, rearmost, final.

**last** vb **1** (*How long is the meeting likely to last?*) continue, go on, carry on, remain, persist. **2** (*The climbers cannot last on the mountains in these blizzard conditions*) survive, live, endure. **3** (*people said that their marriage would not last*) survive, be permanent, hold out, last long. **4** (*buy shoes that will last*) wear well, last long, be durable.

**late** adj **1** (*Don't wait for her. She is always late*) unpunctual, overdue, behind schedule, slow. **2** (*She still misses her late husband*) dead, deceased.

**lather** n (*The soap made a lot of lather*) suds, soapsuds, bubbles.

**latter** adj (*The latter is the more expensive*) last-named, second, the second of two.

**laugh** vb **1** (*The children laughed heartily at the antics of the clown*) chuckle, chortle, (*inf*) split one's sides, (*inf*) be rolling in the aisles. **2** (*The children laughed at the old-fashioned clothes which the little girl was wearing*) jeer, mock, ridicule, sneer, make fun of, poke fun at.

**launch** vb **1** (*They launched the ship*) float, set afloat. **2** (*They launched a missile*) fire, discharge, send forth. **3** (*We launch our new business tomorrow*) begin, start, embark upon, set up, establish.

**laundry** n (*She does the laundry on Mondays*) washing, wash.

**lavatory** n (*The lavatories are at the back of the plane*) bathroom.

**lavish** adj (*a lavish supply of food*) generous, liberal, abundant, copious, plentiful.

**law** n **1** (*It was a new law issued by Congress*) rule, regulation, statute, act, decree, edict. **2** (*All players must obey the laws of the game*) rule, regulation, instruction, guideline.

**lawful** adj **1** (*They are looking for the lawful owner of the car*) legal, legitimate, rightful. **2** (*It is not lawful to take someone else's property*) legal, permitted, permissible, allowed, authorized.

**lawyer** n (*He hired a lawyer to sue his neighbor for damage to his property*) attorney, legal adviser.

**lay** vb **1** (*We were asked to lay our books on the table*) put down, set down, place, deposit. **2** (*lay the blame on his friend*) place, put, attribute, assign.

**layer** n (*a layer of ice on the road*) coat, sheet, skin, film.

**lazy** adj (*He is very lazy and does not want to work*) idle, indolent, slothful, inactive.

**lead** vb **1** (*They need a strong man to lead the country*) be in charge of, direct, govern, be in command of, manage, head. **2** (*The horse was leading but fell just before the finish*) be in the lead, be in front, be first, be winning. **3** (*He was asked to lead the visitors to their seats*) conduct, guide, direct, escort, usher. **4** (*We hope that they will lead a happy life*) have, live, pass, experience.

**lead** n **1** (*the runners in the lead*) first place, leading position, forefront, vanguard. **2** (*She has the lead in the new play*) leading part, leading role, starring role, principal part.

**leader** n **1** (*the leader of the team of climbers*) head, captain. **2** (*the leader of the country*) head, ruler, commander, chief. **3** (*a leader in the field of fashion/a leader in medical research*) frontrunner, trendsetter, pioneer, trailblazer.

**leading** adj **1** (*They played a leading role in the peace talks*) chief, principal, foremost, important. **2** (*He was one of the leading artists of his day*) foremost, chief, most important, celebrated, eminent, outstanding.

**leaf** vb (*He leafed through the book to see if it was what he was looking for*) flick, skim, browse, glance.

**leaflet** n (*an advertising leaflet*) pamphlet, booklet, brochure, circular, handbill.

**league** n (*clubs forming a football league*) alliance, federation, association, union, group, society.

**leak** vb **1** (*Water was leaking from the hole in the pipe*) escape, ooze, drip, seep, discharge, issue. **2** (*A member of the department leaked information to the press*) reveal, divulge, disclose, make known, pass on.

**lean** vb **1** (*lean the ladder against the wall*) rest, prop, support. **2** (*The ship leaned to one side*) incline, bend, slant, tilt, slope.

**lean** adj **1** (*He was tall and lean*) thin, slender, slim, spare, skinny **2** (*lean meat*) non-fat, low-fat.

**leaning** n (*He has a leaning towards scientific subjects*) tendency, inclination, bent, propensity.

**leap** vb **1** (*The dog leapt over the fence*) jump, spring, bound, vault. **2** (*The children were leaping around excitedly before the party*) jump, bound, bounce, skip, hop, dance. **3** (*House prices have leapt*) soar, rocket, mount, shoot up.

**learn** vb **1** (*They had to learn a new method*) grasp, master, take in, pick up. **2** (*We go to school to learn*) be educated. **3** (*How did you learn that they had gone?*) find out, discover, gather, hear.

**learned** adj (*the learned men of the community*) erudite, educated, well-educated, well-read, scholarly, clever, intellectual.

**learner** n (*drivers who were learners*) trainee, pupil, apprentice.

**lease** vb (*The property was leased to new tenants*) rent out.

**leash** n (*a dog's leash*) lead, tether, chain, cord.

**leather** n (*jackets made of leather*) skin, hide.

**leave** vb **1** (*The guests left hurriedly*) depart, go away, take one's leave, set off. **2** (*He left his job and emigrated*) give up, quit, move from. **3** (*He left his wife and children*) abandon, desert, forsake, turn one's back on. **4** (*He left his gloves in the bus*) leave behind, forget, mislay. **5** (*They were asked to leave their boots by the front door*) place, put, deposit. **6** (*She plans to leave all her money to her nephew*) bequeath, will.

**leave** n **1** (*The soldiers are taking some leave*) vacation, time off. **2** (*They were given leave to take some time off*) permission, consent, authorization. **3** (*They took their leave at midnight*) departure, leave-taking, farewell, goodbye.

**lecture** n (*The students attended a lecture on local history*) talk, speech, address.

**leg** n **1** (*She broke her leg*) lower limb. **2** (*The legs of the tripod for the telescope*) support, upright. **3** (*on the second leg of their journey*) stage, round, stretch, lap, part, portion.

**legacy** n (*He received a legacy in his aunt's will*) bequest, inheritance.

**legal** *adj* (*His action was not quite legal*) lawful, legitimate, law-abiding, permissible.

**legend** *n* (*legends about giants*) myth, saga, epic, folk-tale.

**legendary** *adj* **1** (*giants and other legendary figures*) mythical, fictitious, fictional, fabled. **2** (*legendary Hollywood actors*) famous, renowned, celebrated, illustrious.

**legible** *adj* (*writing that was scarcely legible*) readable, decipherable, clear.

**leisure** *n* (*hobbies he pursued in periods of leisure*) free time, spare time.

**lend** *vb* **1** (*She lent him a book on gardening*) loan, give (*someone*) a loan of, let (*someone*) borrow. **2**-(*The flowers lend a freshness to the room*) add, give, impart, supply.

**length** *n* **1** (*What length is the room?*) distance. **2** (*The audience were bored by the sheer length of the speech*) lengthiness, extensiveness, long-windedness.

**lengthen** *vb* **1** (*They lengthened the skirts*) make longer, elongate, let down **2** (*It will lengthen the time the job takes*) make longer, draw out, prolong, extend, protract. **3** (*It is early spring and the days are lengthening*) become longer, draw out.

**lengthy** *adj* **1** (*He gave a lengthy speech/The meeting was a lengthy affair*) long, long-lasting, prolonged, protracted, too long.

**lenient** *adj* **1** (*a lenient judge*) merciful, clement, forgiving, compassionate, tolerant, gentle. **2** (*The accused was given a lenient sentence*) mild, moderate.

**lessen** *vb* **1** (*They hoped that the storm would lessen*) grow less, get less, abate, subside, ease off, let up, dwindle, decrease. **2** (*He was given pills to lessen the pain*) reduce, decrease, ease, relieve, soothe, assuage.

**lesson** *n* **1** (*The children are having a French lesson*) class. **2** (*The Bible story is meant to teach a lesson*) moral, message, example, warning.

**let** *vb* (*They let the children play in the back yard*) allow, permit, give permission to, authorize.

**lethal** *adj* (*The blow to his head proved lethal*) fatal, deadly, mortal, terminal, destructive.

**lethargic** *adj* (*They felt lethargic after a heavy lunch*) sluggish, inactive, listless, sleepy, lazy, languid.

**letter** *n* **1** (*the letters of the alphabet*) character, symbol. **2** (*We sent a letter of thanks*) message, note, epistle.

**level** *adj* **1** (*We need a level surface to build it on*) even, flat, smooth, flush, horizontal. **2** (*The scores were level at half time*) equal, even, neck and neck. **3** (*We need to keep the room at a level temperature*) even, uniform, regular, consistent, stable, constant.

**level** *n* **1** (*At eye-level*) height, altitude. **2** (*The elevator will take you to the second level*) floor, story. **3** (*The two gymnasts are at about the same level of competence*) stage, standard, grade.

**liable** *adj* **1** (*The hotel is not liable for customers' lost belongings*) responsible, accountable, answerable, at fault. **2** (*people who climb high buildings are liable to get injured*) in danger of, at risk of, subject to, vulnerable. **3** (*She is liable to burst into tears if you criticize her*) likely, apt, inclined, prone.

**liberal** *adj* **1** (*a liberal supply of food*) abundant, copious, ample, plentiful, generous, lavish. **2** (*Her parents have very liberal ideas*) tolerant, broadminded, unprejudiced, enlightened.

**liberty** *n* **1** (*a country that values its liberty*) freedom, independence. **2**-(*The prisoners were suddenly given their liberty*) freedom, release, discharge, emancipation.

**license** *n* (*He showed the police his driver's license*) permit, certificate, document, documentation.

**license** *vb* (*He is licensed to carry a gun*) authorize, permit, allow.

**lid** *vb* (*He removed the lid from the jar*) cover, top, cork, stopper.

**lie** *n* (*It was obvious that he was telling a lie*) untruth, falsehood, fib, white lie.

**lie** *vb* **1** (*The jury felt that the witness was lying*) tell a lie, tell a falsehood, fib, dissemble. **2** (*The doctor asked him to lie on the sofa*) recline, stretch out, be supine, be prone, be prostrate, be horizontal. **3** (*The village lies at the foot of a hill*) be situated, be located, be. **4**-(*The volcano lies dormant*) be, continue, remain.

**life** *n* **1** (*when life began on earth*) existence, being. **2** (*They worked hard all their lives*) lifetime, life span, existence. **3** (*The children were full of life*) liveliness, animation, vitality, vivacity. **4** (*He was the life of the party*) spirit, vital spark, moving force. **5** (*They published a life of Winston Churchill*) biography, autobiography.

**lifeless** *adj* **1** (*A lifeless figure lay on the shore*) dead, deceased. **2** (*He seems to prefer lifeless objects to people*) inanimate, without life. **3**-(*lifeless stretches of the world*) infertile, barren, sterile, bare, desolate. **4** (*The actor gave rather a lifeless performance*) spiritless, colorless, uninspired, flat, lackluster.

**lift** *vb* **1** (*They lifted the sacks on to the truck*) hoist, pick up, raise, carry. **2** (*They lifted the ban*) raise, remove, withdraw, revoke, relax, end. **3** (*The mist soon lifted*) rise, disperse, disappear.

**light** *n* **1** (*By the light of the candles*) illumination, brightness, brilliance, shining. **2** (*They carried a light to the window*) lamp, flashlight. **3** (*They struck a light*) flame, spark. **4** (*We would prefer to arrive in the light*) daylight, daytime, day. **5** (*He began to see things in a different light*) aspect, angle, slant, approach, viewpoint, point of view.

**light** *adj* **1** (*a light, airy room*) bright, well-lit **2** (*wearing light clothes*) light-colored, pale, pastel. **3** (*She had very light hair*) light-colored, fair, blond, pale. **4** (*The suitcases are quite light*) easy to carry, portable. **5** (*A suit of a light material*) lightweight, thin, flimsy, delicate. **6** (*The child is very light for her age*) slight, small, thin. **7**-(*He is able to do only light tasks*) easy, simple, effortless, undemanding, unexacting. **8** (*She woke up with a light heart*) happy, merry, carefree, cheerful. **9** (*They were told that it was not a light-matter*) frivolous, unimportant, insignificant, trivial, trifling. **10** (*There was a light wind blowing*) gentle, soft, slight.

**light** *vb* **1** (*They light the fire in the evenings*) ignite, kindle, set fire to, set alight. **2** (*The fireworks lit up the sky*) illuminate, brighten, lighten.

**lighten** *vb* **1** (*The sky lightened*) grow light, grow bright, grow brighter, brighten. **2** (*We had to lighten the donkey's load*) make lighter, lessen, reduce.

**lightweight** *adj* **1** (*wearing a lightweight suit in the heat*) light, thin, flimsy. **2** (*He is rather a lightweight writer*) insignificant, unimportant, trivial.

**like** *prep* **1** (*It was like her to lose her temper*) typical, characteristic, in keeping with. **2** (*She writes rather like Jane Austen*) in the manner of, in the same way as, resembling.

**like** *adj* (*They have like tastes*) similar, identical, corresponding, compatible.

**like** *vb* **1** (*They seemed to like each other right away*) have a liking for, be fond of, be attracted to, be keen on, love, admire, appreciate, approve of. **2** (*She does not like pop music*) enjoy, delight in, relish, be partial to, have a preference for. **3** (*We would like to go to the party but we have another engagement*) wish, want, desire, prefer.

**likelihood** *n* (*There is no likelihood of our arriving on time*) possibility, probability, chance, prospect.

**likely** *adj* **1** (*It is likely that she will fail*) probable, to be expected, possible. **2** (*It is likely to be wet there at that time of year*) liable, apt, inclined. **3** (*They gave a likely enough reason for being absent*) plausible, feasible, reasonable, credible. **4** (*She found a likely place to build a house*) suitable, appropriate, fitting, acceptable, reasonable.

**likeness** *n* (*There is a distinct likeness between the two faces*) similarity, resemblance, sameness.

**limb** *n* **1** (*He injured his limbs in the-accident*)

arm, leg, extremity. **2**-(*They cut a limb from the tree because it was keeping out the light from the house*) branch, bough.

**limelight** *n* (*She was a movie actress who enjoyed the limelight*) public eye, public notice.

**limit** *n* **1** (*They were fishing outside the agreed limits*) boundary, border, extremity, cut-off point. **2** (*They tried to impose some kind of limit on their expenditure*) limitation, ceiling, maximum, restriction, restraint. **3** (*The climb up the mountain pushed their powers of endurance to the limit*) utmost, maximum, extremity, end.

**limit** *vb* **1** (*They tried to limit their expenditure*) restrict, restrain, curb, hold in check. **2** (*She felt that having children would limit her freedom*) restrict, restrain, curb, impede, hinder, hamper.

**limp** *vb* (*He still limps after the accident to his leg*) be lame, hobble.

**limp** *adj* **1** (*a salad consisting of tomatoes and a few limp lettuce leaves*) drooping, floppy, wilting, sagging. **2** (*They felt limp in the heat*) drooping, wilting, lethargic, exhausted.

**line** *n* **1** (*The pupils were asked to draw a line*) stroke. **2** (*There was dirty line around the bathtub*) band, strip, stripe, seam. **3** (*The old woman had a face full of lines*) wrinkle, furrow, crease, groove. **3**-(*A line of police kept back the crowd*) row, column, chain, cordon, procession, file. **4** (*She is hanging the washing on a line in the back yard*) clothesline, rope, string, cable, wire. **5** (*The police are taking a tough line against the wrongdoers*) course of action, policy, approach, position, procedure.

**line** *vb* **1** (*Age had lined her face*) wrinkle, furrow, crease. **2** (*Beech trees lined the avenue*) border, edge. **3** (*The children were asked to line up outside their classroom*) form a line, stand in line, wait in-line.

**linger** *n* **1** (*The smell of fried fish lingered in the hall*) stay, remain, persist, hang around. **2** (*Some of the students lingered to ask the professor questions*) stay behind, wait behind, hang around, loiter, delay, stay, remain.

**link** *n* **1** (*A link has been established between smoking and certain illnesses*) connection, association, relationship, tie-up, tie-in. **2** (*They have strong family links*) bond, attachment, tie, **3** (*the links of the chain*) loop, ring, coupling.

**link** *vb* **1** (*She has lost the piece that links the two parts together*) join, connect, fasten together, attach, couple. **2** (*The police are linking the murder with a previous one*) connect, associate, relate, bracket together.

**lip** *n* (*the lip of the cup*) edge, rim, brim, border, brink.

**liquid** *adj* (*a liquid substance*) fluid, flowing, runny, watery.

**liquidize** *vb* (*She liquidized the mixture*) liquefy, crush, purée, put in the blender.

**liquor** *n* (*He drinks only fruit juice, not liquor*) spirits, alcohol, alcoholic drink, strong drink.

**list** *n* (*make a list of the titles of the books*) record, catalog, register, inventory, table.

**list** *vb* **1** (*please list the articles which you bought*) make a list of, note down, write down, itemize, enumerate, enter, record, register. **2** (*The ship listed in the storm*) lean, tilt, tip, heel over.

**listen** *vb* (*They listened carefully to what the teacher was saying*) pay attention to, take heed, heed, take notice of, hear.

**listless** *adj* (*The tourists were feeling listless in the heat*) lethargic, sluggish, weak, exhausted, inactive.

**litter** *n* **1** (*with litter lying all over the park*) garbage, debris, refuse, waste, junk, trash. **2** (*a litter of pups*) family.

**little** *adj* **1** (*a little man/a little object*) small, slight, short, tiny, minute, diminutive, mini, infinitesimal, microscopic. **2** (*a little book*) small, concise, compact. **3** (*You will gain little advantage from doing that*) hardly any, scant, slight, negligible. **4** (*They had a little argument about which of them should pay the bill*) small, minor, petty, trivial, trifling, unimportant, insignificant. **5** (*They have nasty little minds*) mean, narrow, small, shallow.

**little** *n* **1** (*He will take a little of the milk*) touch, trace, bit, dash, spot. **2** (*You will see him in a little*) short time, little while, minute, moment.

**live** *adj* (*live animals/live bodies*) alive, living, breathing, existing, animate.

**live** *vb* **1** (*in the days when dinosaurs lived*) be alive, exist, have life, be. **2** (*The casualty was not expected to live*) survive, last, endure. **3** (*old customs that live on*) survive, stay, remain, continue, abide. **4** (*They live on fruit and vegetables*) eat, feed on. **5** (*They live by begging*) make a living, subsist, support oneself, maintain oneself. **6** (*They live in an apartment*) dwell, inhabit, reside, lodge, occupy.

**lively** *adj* **1** (*They are very lively children*) active, energetic, spirited, sprightly, perky. **2** (*They had a lively discussion on local politics*) animated, spirited, stimulating, enthusiastic.

**livid** *adj* **1** (*Their father was livid when he saw the damage they had done to the car*) furious, enraged, infuriated, fuming. **2** (*He had a livid mark on his forehead*) bruised, discolored, blackand- blue, purplish, bluish. **3** (*the livid faces of the dead*) ashen, pale, pallid, ghastly.

**load** *n* **1** (*The donkey had a heavy load*) burden, weight. **2** (*the truck's load*) cargo, freight, contents.

**load** *vb* **1** (*They helped to load the truck*) fill, fill up, pack, stack. **2** (*He loaded the gun*) prime, charge, fill.

**loaf** *vb* (*loafing around the house instead of working*) laze, idle, lounge.

**loan** *vb* (*They loaned him money*) lend, give on loan.

**loathe** *vb* (*They used to be friends but now they loathe each other*) hate, detest, abhor, have an aversion to.

**local** *adj* (*They attend the local school*) nearby, near, neighborhood.

**locality** *n* (*There are several hotels in the locality*) area, district, region, neighborhood, vicinity.

**locate** *vb* **1** (*They plan to locate the hotel near the beach*) place, position, situate, site, build, establish. **2** (*We finally located the cause of the trouble with the engine*) find, discover, detect, identify, pinpoint.

**lock** *vb* **1** (*They locked the door*) bolt, bar, fasten, secure. **2** (*The guards locked the prisoners up*) shut up, confine, imprison.

**logical** *adj* **1** (*His argument was not at all logical*) reasoned, rational, sound, coherent. **2** (*It seemed the logical thing to do*) rational, reasonable, sensible, intelligent.

**loiter** *vb* **1** (*There were gangs of youths loitering on the street corners*) hang around, hang about, wait, skulk, lounge, loaf, idle. **2**-(*They loitered along the road to school*) dawdle, dally, saunter, dillydally.

**lone** *adj* (*The sailors saw a lone yachtsman*) solitary, single, sole, unaccompanied, by oneself.

**lonely** *adj* **1** (*She lived by herself and sometime felt lonely*) friendless, lonesome, forlorn, neglected, desolate, isolated, unhappy, sad. **2** (*a lonely landscape*) desolate, isolated, remote, out-of-the-way, deserted.

**long** *adj* (*a piece of wood three yards long*) in length, lengthways, lengthwise. **2** (*It was a long journey*) lengthy, extended, slow, prolonged. **3** (*He gave a long speech*) lengthy, prolonged, protracted, long-drawnout, wordy, long-winded.

**long** *vb* (*They longed for a long cool drink*) yearn for, wish for, desire, crave, pine for, hanker after.

**longing** *n* (*They had a longing for some sunshine*) yearning, wish, desire, craving.

**long-winded** *adj* (*a long-winded speech*) wordy, verbose, rambling, lengthy, long-drawn-out, prolonged, protracted.

**look** *vb* **1** (*We looked and saw a beautiful painting*) take a look, observe, view, contemplate, gaze, stare, examine, study. **2** (*She looks ill*) appear, seem. **3** (*The dining room of the hotel looks south*) face, overlook.

**loom** *vb* **1** (*A dark figure loomed out of the shadows*) appear, emerge, materialize. **2** (*The exams are looming*) be imminent, be close, be ominously close.

**loop** n (*loops of ribbon*) coil, hoop, circle, curl.

**loose** adj 1 (*They wore loose clothes*) loose-fitting, slack, wide, baggy. **2**-(*The table leg is loose*) not secure, insecure, movable, wobbly, unsteady, shaky. **3** (*The rope was loose*) slack, untied, unfastened. **4**-(*The pigs were loose in the village street*) at large, at liberty, free, unconfined.

**loose** vb (*She loosed the dogs when she saw the strange man in the back yard*) let loose, set free, release, unleash, untie.

**loosen** vb 1 (*He loosened his belt*) slacken, let out, undo, unfasten, unhook. **2** (*He loosened his grip on the rail*) relax, slacken, weaken.

**loot** n (*The police found the burglar's loot*) booty, haul, plunder, spoils.

**loot** vb (*Gangs looted the stores after the fire in the city center*) plunder, pillage, ransack, rob, burglarize.

**lose** vb 1 (*We lost our keys*) mislay, misplace, forget. **2** (*They lost their way in the dark*) stray from, wander from. **3** (*She lost a lot of blood*) be deprived of. **4** (*They lost several opportunities*) miss, pass, neglect, waste. **5** (*Our team lost*) be defeated, suffer defeat, be conquered.

**loss** n (*The firm made a loss in that financial year*) deficit, non-profit.

**lost** adj 1 (*They eventually found the lost gloves*) missing, misplaced, mislaid, forgotten. **2** (*lost opportunities*) missed, passed, neglected, wasted.

**lot** n 1 (*A lot of people were present*) a great many, many, a good deal, a great deal, numerous, an abundance, plenty, masses. **2** (*She weeps a lot*) a good deal, much, many times. **3** (*The furniture was sold at auction as one lot*) collection, set, batch, quantity.

**lotion** n (*a lotion to soothe his sunburned skin*) cream, salve, ointment.

**lottery** n (*He hoped to win a lot of money in the lottery*) draw, sweepstakes, drawing of lots.

**loud** adj 1 (*The children were frightened by the loud noise*) noisy, blaring, booming, deafening, ear-splitting. **2** (*She disliked the loud colors in the restaurant*) garish, gaudy, flamboyant, flashy, vulgar. **3** (*She disapproved of their loud behavior*) noisy, rowdy, boisterous, rough.

**loutish** adj (*Because of their loutish behavior he was asked to leave the bar*) boorish, oafish, churlish.

**love** n 1 (*He showed his love by sending her red roses*) affection, fondness, care, concern, attachment, devotion, adoration, passion. **2** (*The child has a great love of chocolates*) liking, weakness, partiality, relish.

**love** vb 1 (*It was obvious that she loved him*) be in love with, care for, be fond of, adore, (*inf*) have a crush on. **2** (*She loves fresh peaches*) like, have a weakness for, be partial to, enjoy.

**lovely** adj 1 (*She is a lovely girl*) beautiful, pretty, attractive, good-looking, charming, enchanting. **2**-(*We had a lovely time at the party*) delightful, pleasant, nice, marvelous, wonderful.

**low** adj 1 (*a low table*) short. **2** (*a low position in the firm*) inferior, humble, subordinate, junior. **3** (*She spoke in a low voice*) soft, quiet, whispered, hushed. **4** (*She was feeling low after her defeat*) in low spirits, down, down-hearted, dejected, depressed, despondent. **5** (*They have a low opinion of him*) unfavorable, poor, bad, adverse, negative, hostile. **6** (*Our supplies of food are low*) sparse, meager, scarce, scant, scanty, paltry, inadequate. **7** (*It was a low thing to do*) nasty, mean, foul, vile, base, dishonorable, despicable, wicked, evil.

**lower** vb 1 (*They lowered the flag*) let down, take down, haul down. **2** (*They have lowered the prices*) reduce, decrease, bring down, cut, slash. **3** (*She was asked to lower her voice/ They lowered the volume of the radio*) soften, hush, turn down.

**loyal** adj (*They have been loyal friends to me*) faithful, true, trusted, trustworthy, trusty, reliable, dependable, devoted, constant.

**loyalty** n (*They showed their loyalty to the king*) faith, faithfulness, fidelity, allegiance, trustworthiness, reliability, dependability, devotion, constancy.

**lucid** adj 1 (*Her explanation was extremely lucid*) clear, crystal clear, plain, intelligible, graphic. **2** (*an old man who was scarcely lucid*) sane, in one's right mind, rational, compos mentis, (*inf*) all there.

**luck** n 1 (*She found the perfect apartment just by luck*) chance, fortune, destiny, fate, accident, serendipity. **2** (*We wished them luck*) good luck, good fortune, success, prosperity.

**lucky** adj 1 (*She seemed a very lucky person who always got what she wanted*) fortunate, favored, advantaged. **2** (*She didn't know the answer—it was just a lucky guess*) fortunate, providential, opportune, timely, auspicious.

**lucrative** adj (*His business is very lucrative*) profitable, profit-making, moneymaking, remunerative.

**ludicrous** adj (*It was a really ludicrous suggestion*) absurd, ridiculous, laughable, foolish, silly, crazy, preposterous.

**luggage** n (*They carried her luggage to the train*) bags, baggage, suitcases, things, belongings.

**lull** vb 1 (*They lulled the child to sleep*) soothe, hush, quiet. **2** (*Their fears were lulled*) soothe, quiet, silence, calm, allay, ease.

**lull** n (*They left while there was a lull in the storm*) pause, respite, interval, break, letup.

**lumber** n (*The lumber was stacked in the yard*) logs, timber, trees, wood.

**lumber** vb 1 (*He lumbered towards us*) clump, shuffle, trudge. **2** (*I got lumbered with the worst job*) burden, hamper, impose on.

**luminous** adj (*a clock with a luminous dial*) lighted, lit, shining, phosphorescent.

**lump** n 1 (*She bought a lump of cheese*) chunk, hunk, wedge, piece, mass. **2** (*He got a lump on the head when he fell*) bump, swelling, bulge, knob, bruise.

**lunatic** adj (*It was a lunatic thing to do*) insane, mad, foolish, stupid, idiotic, senseless, absurd, ludicrous.

**lunge** vb 1 (*She lunged at her attacker with a knife*) stab, jab, thrust, poke. **2** (*He lunged towards the door when he saw his attacker*) charge, dive, spring, leap, bound.

**lurch** vb (*drunk men lurching home*) stagger, sway, reel, roll, weave, stumble, totter.

**lure** vb (*The evil men lured the children into their car*) entice, attract, induce, inveigle, decoy, tempt, cajole.

**lurid** adj 1 (*She hated the lurid colors on the walls of the restaurant*) gaudy, garish, flamboyant, loud. **2**-(*The newspaper published the lurid details of the murder*) gory, gruesome, macabre, sensational, melodramatic, explicit.

**lurk** vb (*She saw a figure lurking in the shadows*) skulk, lie in wait, crouch, slink, prowl.

**luscious** adj (*luscious peaches*) juicy, delicious, succulent, mouth-watering.

**lust** n (*They needed to satisfy their lust for power*) greed, craving, desire, yearning, hunger.

**luxurious** adj (*They live in luxurious surroundings*) opulent, affluent, sumptuous, splendid, magnificent, wealthy, expensive, rich, costly, lavish, deluxe.

**luxury** n (*After they won the lottery they lived in luxury*) opulence, affluence, splendor, magnificence, wealth, ease.

**lynch** vb (*The townspeople lynched the man who had murdered the child*) put to death, execute, hang, kill, murder.

**lyrics** npl (*He wrote the lyrics of the pop songs*) words, libretto, book, text.

# M

**machine** n apparatus, appliance, instrument, device, mechanism.

**machinery** n 1 (*the machinery in the factory*) apparatus, equipment, gear, plant. **2** (*the machinery of government*) workings, organization, system, agency.

**mad** adj 1 (*mothers who were mad with*

their children) annoyed, angry, furious, enraged. **2** (He is always engaging in mad schemes) insane, crazy, idiotic, foolish, absurd, foolhardy, rash. **3** (They are mad about jazz) passionate, enthusiastic, keen, fervent, fanatical. **4**-(She went mad with grief) insane, demented, deranged, of unsound mind, crazed, crazy, unbalanced, unhinged.

**magazine** n (She was looking for a fashion magazine) periodical, journal, paper.

**magic** adj **1** (people who believe in magic) witchcraft, sorcery, wizardry, enchantment, the occult, voodoo. **2** (the magic performed by the entertainer) conjuring tricks, illusion, sleight of hand.

**magician** n **1** (rather a frightening story about a magician) sorcerer, witch, wizard, warlock, enchanter. **2** (They hired a magician for the children's party) conjurer, illusionist.

**magnificent** adj **1** (a magnificent royal procession/a magnificent feast) splendid, grand, impressive, superb, glorious. **2** (It was a magnificent game of tennis) excellent, skillful, fine, impressive, outstanding.

**magnitude** vb **1** (try to estimate the magnitude of the explosion) extent, size, dimensions, volume, bulk. **2** (We were surprised at the magnitude of the flu epidemic) size, extent, vastness, extensiveness. **3** (fail to appreciate the magnitude of the problem) scale, importance, significance.

**maid** n (the hotel maids) domestic worker, domestic, servant.

**mail** n **1** (The mailman delivered the morning mail) letters. **2** (She sent the package by mail) postal service. **3** (The knights of old wore mail) chain, coat of mail, armor.

**main** adj (the main points in the discussion/the main cities in the world) chief, principal, leading, foremost, major, important.

**mainly** adv (They mainly lived on fruit and vegetables) for the most part, mostly, on the whole, largely.

**maintain** vb **1** (He has always maintained that he is innocent) declare, insist, assert, state, proclaim, claim. **2** (He has a family to maintain) keep, support, provide for, take care of, look after. **3** (He maintained a steady speed throughout the journey) keep, keep up, continue, sustain.

**major** adj **1** (play a major part in the victory) important, leading, principal, great, crucial. **2** (the major part of his fortune) larger, greater, bigger, main. **3** one of our major artists) leading, chief, foremost, greatest, main, outstanding, notable, eminent.

**majority** n (the majority of the people) most, bulk, mass, main body.

**make** vb **1** (make furniture at his woodwork class) build, construct, assemble, fabricate, form, fashion. **2** (try not to make

a noise) create, produce, bring about. **3** (He made a bow to the audience) perform, execute, carry out, effect. **4** (They made him apologize) force, compel. **5** (The bride's father made a speech) give, deliver, utter. **6** (He made a fortune before he was thirty-five) earn, gain, acquire, obtain, get. **7** (She will make a wonderful mother) become, grow into, turn into. **8** (We made an appointment to see him) arrange, fix, agree on, settle on, decide on. **9** (6 and 2 make 8) add up to, amount to, come to, total. **10** (He made the v into a y by mistake) alter, change, turn, transform. **11**-(He hoped to make his destination by nightfall) reach, arrive at, get to, achieve. **12** (We could not make out what he was saying) understand, follow, work out, hear. **13** (He made up an excuse for not being present) invent, think up, concoct, fabricate.

**make** n (various makes of car) brand, kind, variety, sort, type.

**make-believe** n (She said that she saw a fairy but it was only make-believe) fantasy, pretense, imagination.

**make-believe** adj (the child's makebelieve friend) fantasy, made-up, pretended, feigned, imaginary, fictitious, unreal.

**make-up** n (She put on her make-up in the bathroom) cosmetics.

**male** adj (male creatures) masculine, manly, virile.

**male** n (two males and a female) man, boy, gentleman.

**malicious** adj (She received an anonymous malicious letter) spiteful, vindictive, vicious, venomous, nasty, bitter, evil.

**malignant** adj **1** (The doctor discovered that she had a malignant growth) cancerous. **2** (a malignant disease/a malignant influence) dangerous, destructive, fatal, deadly, harmful.

**maltreat** vb (Her parents were accused of maltreating her) abuse, ill-treat, harm, injure, molest.

**mammoth** adj (They faced a mammoth task/a mammoth serving of ice cream) huge, enormous, gigantic, vast, colossal, massive.

**man** n **1** (three men and a woman) male, gentleman, (inf) guy. **2** (man and animals) mankind, humankind, the human race, humans.

**manage** vb **1** (He manages the whole firm) run, be in charge of, be head of, control, preside over, administer. **2** (We don't know how they managed to survive/manage the work) succeed in, contrive, achieve, accomplish, effect. **3** (It is going to be a large dinner party. Will you manage?) cope, get by. **4**-(She really cannot manage such a lively horse) handle, cope with, deal with, control.

**manager** vb (the workers and the departmental

manager) head, superintendent, supervisor, boss, chief, administrator.

**mandatory** adj (Taking part in the conference was not mandatory) compulsory, obligatory, imperative, essential.

**maneuver** vb (He maneuvered the piece of metal into position) guide, steer, ease, move, negotiate, manipulate.

**maneuver** n **1** (army maneuvers) movement, operation, exercise. **2**-(It was a clever maneuver to try and obtain promotion) move, tactic, trick, stratagem, scheme, ploy, ruse.

**manhandle** vb **1** (The men had to manhandle the piano upstairs) maneuver, haul, heave, push. **2**-(The police were accused of manhandling the protesters) knock about, maul, mistreat, illtreat, abuse, (inf) beat up.

**mania** n **1** (Sometimes he suffers from depression and sometimes from mania) frenzy, hysteria, wildness, derangement, madness, insanity. **2** (They have a mania for attending auction sales) fixation, obsession, compulsion, fascination, passion, enthusiasm, fad.

**manipulate** vb **1** (manipulate the controls of the aircraft) handle, operate, use, manage, maneuver. **2** (A clever lawyer can manipulate a jury) influence, control, guide, exploit.

**mankind** n (the history of mankind) man, humankind, the human race, Homo sapiens.

**manly** adj **1** (a manly figure) masculine, virile. **2** (showing manly characteristics) manful, brave, courageous, gallant.

**manner** n **1** (She does the work in an efficient manner) way, means, fashion, style, method, system. **2**-(They dislike their employer's manner) attitude, behavior, conduct, bearing, look.

**manners** npl (The children should be taught better manners) polite behavior, politeness, courtesy, social graces, etiquette.

**mannish** adj (rather a mannish voice) masculine, unfeminine, unwomanly, (inf) butch.

**mansion** n (The rich family live in a huge mansion) manor house, stately home.

**manual** adj (a manual gear change) by hand, hand-operated. **2** (manual rather than intellectual skills are needed) physical.

**manual** n (an instruction manual with the washing machine) handbook, instructions, guide, guidebook.

**manufacture** vb (a factory manufacturing computer parts) make, produce, build, construct, turn out.

**manure** n (farmers spreading manure on the ground) dung, fertilizer.

**many** adj (many people did not turn up) numerous, a large number, innumerable, map 57 means

countless, (*inf*) a lot of, (*inf*) lots of, (*inf*) oodles of.

**map** *n* (*a map of the city center*) chart, plan, diagram, guide.

**march** *vb* 1 (*The soldiers marched along*) walk, stride, tramp, parade, file. 2 (*Time marches on*) progress, advance, go on, continue.

**margin** *n* 1 (*They won by a narrow margin*) amount, difference. 2 (*We have so little money that there is little margin for error*) scope, room, allowance, latitude, leeway. 3 (*the margin of the lake*) edge, side, border, verge, boundary.

**marginal** *adj* (*There has been only a marginal improvement*) slight, minimal, small, tiny, minor, insignificant.

**mark** *n* 1 (*the dirty marks on the tablecloth*) stain, spot, speck, smear, streak, blotch, smudge. 2 (*a mark of respect*) sign, symbol, indication, token. 3 (*His war experiences had left their mark on him*) impression, effect, impact, influence, imprint.

**mark** *vb* 1 (*The hot teacups marked the table*) stain, smear, streak, blotch, smudge. 2 (*mark the battle sites on the map*) indicate, label, flag, tag. 3 (*teachers marking exam papers*) correct, assess, evaluate, appraise. 4 (*They marked his birthday with a huge party*) celebrate, commemorate, observe. 5 (*You should mark what the principal says*) pay attention to, take heed of, heed, note, take notice of, mind.

**market** *n* (*tourists buying souvenirs in the market*) marketplace, bazaar. 2 (*There is no market for such expensive goods in this part of the city*) demand, call, need.

**maroon** *vb* (*He was marooned on a desert island*) abandon, forsake, desert, strand.

**marriage** *n* 1 (*the marriage of their daughter to the son of their best friends*) wedding. 2 (*Their marriage lasted twenty years*) matrimony, union.

**marry** *vb* 1 (*The couple will marry later in the year*) be married, wed, be wed, become man and wife, (*inf*) tie the knot, (*inf*) get hitched. 2 (*They decided to marry their skills and set up business together*) join, unite, combine, merge.

**marsh** *n* (*plants that grow in marshes*) marshland, bog, swamp, mire, quagmire.

**martial** *adj* 1 (*the martial arts*) warlike, militant, combative, belligerent, pugnacious. 2 (*martial law*) military, army.

**martyr** *n* (*early martyrs killed because of their Christian faith*) victim, sufferer.

**marvel** *n* (*The pyramids are one of the marvels of the world*) wonder, sensation, phenomenon, miracle.

**marvel** *vb* (*We marveled at the exploits of the acrobats*) be amazed, be astonished, stare, gape, wonder-at.

**marvelous** *adj* 1 (*admire the marvelous exploits of the acrobats*) amazing, astonishing, astounding, sensational, breathtaking, spectacular, remarkable, extraordinary. 2-(*We had a marvelous evening at the theater*) splendid, wonderful, glorious, excellent, enjoyable.

**masculine** *adj* 1 (*That tends to be a masculine habit*) male, manlike. 2-(*She says she likes really masculine men*) manly, virile, (*inf*) macho.

**mash** *vb* (*mash the potatoes*) pulp, purée, crush, pound.

**mask** *vb* (*We planted trees at the bottom of the field to mask the view of the factory*) screen, camouflage, hide, conceal, cover up, blot out.

**mass** *n* 1 (*a mass of wood*) block, lump, hunk, chunk, piece. 2 (*measure the mass of the body*) size, dimension, bulk, capacity. 3 (*A mass of people attended the meeting*) many, crowd, throng, mob, crowd, host.

**massacre** *vb* (*The world was shocked at the massacre of civilians*) slaughter, carnage, mass murder, butchery, pogrom.

**massage** *vb* (*She massaged their stiff limbs*) knead, rub, pummel.

**masses** *npl* (*The leader did not care what the masses thought*) the people, the common people, the public, the populace, the mob.

**massive** *adj* (*They built a massive wall round their estate*) huge, enormous, immense, vast, colossal, gigantic, mammoth.

**master** *n* 1 (*In earlier times a master would have many servants*) lord, owner, employer. 2 (*He likes to think that he is master in the household*) chief, head, boss. 3 (*He is master of the ship*) captain, skipper. 4 (*Several golf masters took part in the tournament*) expert, professional, virtuoso, genius, (*inf*) ace.

**master** *vb* 1 (*unable to master his horse/He must try to master his emotions*) control, subdue, check, curb, quell. 2 (*She seems unable to master the techniques of driving*) learn, grasp, understand, (*inf*) get the hang of.

**match** *n* 1 (*Take bets on who will win the football match*) contest, competition, game, tournament, trial, bout. 2 (*She was no match for the stronger player*) equal, equivalent, counterpart, rival. 3 (*Their parents tried to arrange a match*) marriage, union.

**mate** *n* 1 (*the mate of this glove*) fellow, pair, match. 2 (*Her friends think she is looking for a mate*) spouse, partner, husband/wife.

**material** *n* 1 (*dresses made of a silky material*) cloth, fabric, stuff, textile. 2 (*organic material*) matter, substance, stuff. 3 (*research material for his novel*) information, facts, details, data.

**materialize** *vb* 1 (*We had very elaborate plans but they did not materialize*) happen, come into being, come about, occur. 2 (*Suddenly figures materialized out of the fog*) appear, come into view, become visible, emerge.

**maternal** *adj* (*maternal feelings*) motherly.

**matrimony** *adj* (*She feels she is not ready for matrimony*) marriage, wedlock.

**matted** *adj* (*The child's hair was dirty and matted*) tangled, knotted, tousled, unkempt.

**matter** *n* 1 (*There are important matters to discuss*) topic, issue, subject. 2 (*It was no laughing matter*) affair, business, situation, circumstance. 3-(*waste matter*) material, substance, stuff. 4 (*What is the matter with the car?*) problem, trouble, difficulty. 5 (*matter oozing from the wound*) pus, discharge.

**matter** *vb* (*Will it matter if we arrive a bit late?*) be of importance, be important, make any difference, count, be relevant.

**mature** *adj* 1 (*mature human beings*) adult, grown-up, grown, fully grown. 2 (*mature fruit/mature cheese*) ripe, ripened, ready, mellow.

**maul** *vb* 1 (*The zoo keeper was mauled by a lion*) tear to pieces, lacerate, mutilate, mangle.

**maximum** *adj* (*the maximum number*) highest, greatest, utmost.

**maybe** *adv* perhaps, possibly.

**maze** *n* (*get lost in the maze of corridors in the hospital*) labyrinth, network, mesh, confusion.

**meadow** *n* (*cows grazing in the meadow*) field, pasture, grassland, prairie.

**meager** *adj* (*unable to feed themselves on their meager supply of money*) sparse, scarce, scanty, paltry, inadequate, insufficient, (*inf*) measly.

**mean** *vb* 1 (*What did his words mean?*) signify, indicate, convey, denote, stand for, suggest, imply. 2 (*We did not mean to hurt her*) intend, plan, set out, aim, propose. 3 (*I am afraid that this will mean war*) lead to, involve, result in, give rise to.

**mean** *adj* 1 (*It was a mean thing to take the child's sweets*) nasty, disagreeable, unkind, spiteful, foul, vile, contemptible, hateful, cruel. 2-(*He's too mean to buy anyone a Christmas present*) miserly, niggardly, parsimonious, penny-pinching, grasping, greedy.

**meaning** *n* 1 (*He does not know the meaning of the word*) sense, significance, drift, gist, implication. 2-(*His life seems to have no meaning any more*) point, value, worth. 3 (*She gave him a look full of meaning*) significance, eloquence.

**means** *n* 1 (*We have no means of getting there*) way, method, manner, course. 2 (*His father is a man of means*) wealth, riches, money, property, substance. 3 (*They do not have the means to buy the car) money, capital, finance, funds, resources.

**measure** n **1** (use a linear measure) standard, scale, system. **2** (They had to take drastic measures to stop the truancy in the school) action, act, course of action, step, means.

**measure** vb (measure the length of the room) calculate, estimate, compute.

**measurement** n (take the measurements of the room) size, dimensions, proportions, extent, capacity.

**mechanism** n (the mechanism that drives the machine) machinery, workings, apparatus, device.

**meddle** vb (His neighbors tried to meddle in his affairs) interfere, intrude, pry, butt in.

**media** npl (The politician blamed his unpopularity on the media) the press, journalists, radio and television.

**medicine** n (The doctor gave the patient some medicine) medication, drug, medicament.

**mediocre** adj (She used to be at the top of the class but her work this-semester has been mediocre) average, ordinary, indifferent, middling, passable, adequate, uninspired.

**meditate** vb (take time to meditate on the gravity of the matter) think about, contemplate, reflect on, consider, deliberate on.

**medium** adj (of medium height) average, middling.

**meek** adj (meek people being bullied by the others) docile, gentle, humble, patient, long-suffering.

**meet** vb **1** (I met an old friend by chance in the main street) encounter, come across, run into, bump into. **2** (The committee meet on Thursday afternoons) gather, assemble, congregate. **3** (They met the demands of the job) satisfy, fulfill, comply with. **4** (meet one's responsibilities) carry out, perform, execute. **5** (He met death bravely) face, encounter, confront. **6** (where the two roads meet) join, connect, unite, adjoin.

**meeting** n **1** (A politician addressed the meeting) gathering, assembly, conference. **2** (a happy meeting between the two old friends) encounter.

**melancholy** adj (in a melancholy mood) depressed, dejected, gloomy, (inf) blue.

**melancholy** n depression, gloom, blues, low spirits.

**mellow** adj **1** (mellow fruit) ripe, mature, juicy, luscious. **2** (She spoke in mellow tones) sweet, tuneful, melodious, dulcet. **3** (in a mellow mood after a good dinner) cheerful, happy, genial, jovial.

**melodious** adj (melodious sounds) tuneful, musical, harmonious, dulcet.

**melodramatic** adj (Her reaction to the news was rather melodramatic) theatrical, overdone, extravagant.

**melt** vb **1** (The sun had melted the snow) thaw, soften. **2** (solids melting rapidly) dissolve, thaw, defrost, soften.

**memento** n (He gave her a memento of their vacation) souvenir, keepsake, token, remembrance.

**memorable** adj (a memorable occasion) unforgettable, momentous, significant, notable,.

**memory** n **1** (Her memory of the event is rather hazy) recollection, recall. **2** (They built a statue in memory of the soldiers killed in the war) remembrance, commemoration, honor.

**menacing** adj (He gave them a menacing look) threatening, ominous, frightening, sinister.

**mend** vb **1** (He mended the broken table) repair, fix, renovate, restore. **2** (She mended the children's socks) darn, sew, patch.

**mention** vb **1** (She mentioned your name as someone who might be interested in the job) refer to, allude to, touch on. **2** (She did mention that she was thinking of leaving) remark, comment, observe.

**mercenary** adj (She is very mercenary and wants to marry a rich man) grasping, greedy, avaricious, (inf) gold-digging.

**merciful** adj (a merciful judge) lenient, compassionate, forgiving, sympathetic, humane.

**mercy** n (The judge showed mercy to the man who had stolen money to feed his children) leniency, clemency, pity, compassion, forgiveness.

**merge** vb **1** (The two firms have merged and staff have been made redundant) amalgamate, combine, unite, join forces. **2** (The colors in the picture seemed to merge) blend, fuse, mingle.

**merit** n **1** (He put forward the merits of the scheme) advantage, asset, plus, good point. **2** (She received a certificate of merit) distinction, credit. **3** (The artist's work is thought to have little merit) worth, value.

**merry** adj (merry children) cheerful, gay, happy, light-hearted, joyful.

**mess** n **1** (their mother asked them to clear up the mess in the kitchen) clutter, litter, shambles, disorder, untidiness.

**message** n (They were out and so we left a message for them) note, memo, word, information, news, communication.

**method** n (teaching methods) system, technique, procedure, routine.

**microscopic** adj (microscopic insects) tiny, minute, minuscule.

**middle** n (The children formed a circle and the little girl was in the middle/right in the middle of the city) center, heart.

**might** n (unable to overcome the might of the enemy) power, force, strength.

**mighty** n **1** (a mighty blow) powerful, strong, forceful, hefty. **2** (mighty mountains) huge, massive, vast, enormous, colossal.

**migrate** vb (birds migrating to the south in the summer/people migrating to find work) move, relocate.

**mild** adj **1** (mild climate/mild weather) moderate, warm, soft, balmy. **2** (She is usually of a mild disposition but she really lost her temper at the children) gentle, tender, soft-hearted, warmhearted, compassionate, lenient, calm. **3** (a mild sauce) subtle, bland, non-spicy.

**militant** adj (in a militant mood) belligerent, aggressive, pugnacious, combative, warlike.

**mimic** vb (The pupil was caught mimicking the teacher) impersonate, give an impersonation of, imitate, copy, parody.

**mind** vb **1** (I am sure that they won't mind if you use the phone) object, care, bother, be upset, complain, disapprove. **2** (You should mind your own business) attend to, pay attention to, concentrate on. **3** (Tell him to mind the low ceiling—he might bump his head) be careful of, watch out for, look out for, beware of.

**mind** n **1** (She failed her exams although she has a good mind) brain, intellect, powers of reasoning. **2** (It brought thoughts of her father to mind) memory, recollection, remembrance.

**mingle** vb **1** (the colors mingled) mix, blend. **2** (She was too shy to mingle with the other guests at the party) mix, socialize, circulate.

**miniature** adj (a miniature railroad) small-scale, mini, diminutive, minute, tiny.

**minimum** adj (the minimum price) lowest, smallest, least, bottom.

**minute** adj **1** (insects which are minute creatures) tiny, diminutive, microscopic, minuscule. **2** (There is just a minute difference between the two) tiny, insignificant, infinitesimal, negligible.

**miracle** n (miracles described in the Bible) wonder, marvel.

**miraculous** adj (She made a miraculous recovery from the accident) amazing, remarkable, extraordinary, incredible.

**mirage** n (The travelers thought they saw an oasis in the desert but it was a mirage) hallucination, illusion, vision.

**mirror** n (She looked in the mirror to apply her make-up) glass.

**mirth** n (There was a lot of mirth at the party) laughter, merriment, hilarity, revelry.

**misadventure** n (He had the misadventure to break his leg) bad luck, accident, misfortune, mischance.

**misbehave** vb (The children misbehaved when their mother was away) behave badly, be naughty, be disobedient, (inf) act up.

**miscellaneous** *adj* (*a miscellaneous collection of old clothes for the rummage sale*) assorted, mixed, varied, motley.

**mischief** *n* (*children who are bored and getting up to mischief*) naughtiness, bad behavior, misbehavior, misconduct, wrongdoing, trouble.

**mischievous** *adj* (*mischievous children*) naughty, badly behaved, disobedient, rascally, roguish.

**miser** *n* (*The old miser would not give any money to charity*) scrooge, skinflint, niggard, (*inf*) cheapskate.

**miserly** *adj* (*They were too miserly to give any money to charity*) mean, niggardly, parsimonious, tight-fisted, Scrooge-like, (*inf*) stingy.

**misery** *n* (*the misery of being homeless and hungry*) wretchedness, hardship, suffering, unhappiness, distress, sorrow.

**misfortune** *n* 1 (*He endured many misfortunes before becoming a successful businessman*) trouble, setback, adversity, calamity, disaster. 2-(*By misfortune we missed the last train*) bad luck, ill luck, accident.

**misgiving** *n* (*We had misgivings about lending them the car*) qualm, doubt, reservation, suspicion.

**mislead** *vb* (*She deliberately tried to mislead her parents*) misinform, deceive, hoodwink.

**misplace** *n* (*Grandpa has misplaced his glasses again*) lose, mislay.

**miss** *vb* 1 (*He missed a great opportunity*) pass up, let go, 2 (*The children are missing their mother*) long for, pine for. 3 (*He missed the shot*) bungle, botch, muff. 4 (*We tried to-miss heavy traffic by leaving early*) avoid, evade, escape, dodge. 5-(*Try not to miss anything out when you give an account of the accident*) leave out, omit, forget, overlook.

**missile** *n* (*The army invested in guided missiles*) projectile, rocket.

**mist** *n* (*There was a morning mist but it soon lifted*) haze, fog.

**mistake** *n* 1 (*His homework was full of mistakes*) error, inaccuracy, fault, blunder, (*inf*) slip-up, (*inf*) howler.

**misty** *adj* 1 (*a misty morning*) hazy, foggy. 2 (*only a misty idea of what we are supposed to be doing*) vague, hazy, nebulous. 3 (*My eyesight is a bit misty just now*) blurred, fuzzy.

**mix** *vb* 1 (*mix the ingredients for the cake*) blend, combine, put together. 2 (*She never mixes with the rest of the people on the block*) socialize, associate with, have dealings with. 3 (*The demands of her job and looking after children just don't mix*) be compatible. 4 (*She mixed up the-two parcels and sent us the wrong one*) muddle, jumble, confuse. 5-(*I-think that he is mixed up in the crime*) involve, implicate.

**mixed** *adj* (*a mixed lot of old clothes for the rummage sale*) miscellaneous, assorted, varied, motley.

**mixture** *n* 1 (*pour the cake mixture into a pan*) mix, blend, compound, concoction. 2 (*There was quite a mixture of people on the jury*) miscellany, assortment, variety, mix, collection.

**moan** *vb* 1 (*The injured woman moaned in pain*) groan. 2 (*She was always moaning about how poor she was although she spent a lot of money on clothes*) complain, grumble, whine, (*inf*) grouse, (*inf*) gripe, (*inf*) beef.

**mob** *n* (*an angry mob of protesters*) crowd, horde, throng, multitude.

**mobile** *adj* (*a mobile phone/a mobile shop*) movable, transportable, traveling.

**mock** *vb* (*The children mocked the new girl because she was wearing very thick glasses*) ridicule, jeer at, sneer at, laugh at, tease, mimic.

**model** *n* 1 (*a model of an old airplane*) replica, copy, imitation. 2-(*What model of car would you like?*) design, style, variety, type. 3-(*The architects showed us the model of the new apartment building*) prototype, design, pattern. 4-(*She wants to be a model*) fashion model. 5 (*The art teacher used one of the pupils as a model*) artist's model, subject, sitter.

**moderate** *adj* 1 (*moderate winds*) mild, gentle, light. 2 (*We had moderate success*) reasonable, acceptable, tolerable, adequate, middling, average. 3 (*The prisoners' demands seemed moderate*) reasonable, within reason, fair. 4 (*a moderate lifestyle*) restrained, controlled, sober, steady.

**modern** *adj* 1 (*politicians in modern times*) present-day, present, contemporary, current. 2 (*Her ideas on education are very modern/modern styles of clothes*) up to date, new, advanced, progressive, fashionable, (*inf*) trendy.

**modest** *adj* 1 (*He had accomplished a great deal in life but was very modest*) unassuming, self-effacing, humble. 2 (*They are rich but live in a modest house*) humble, plain, simple, inexpensive. 3-(*Their demands seemed very modest*) small, slight, limited, reasonable, moderate. 4 (*She was asked to wear modest clothes for the occasion*) demure, decent, decorous.

**modify** *vb* (*They may have to modify the design of the new plane slightly*) alter, change, adjust, vary.

**moist** *adj* 1 (*moist weather*) wet, damp, dank, rainy, humid, clammy. 2 (*soil moist after the rain*) wet, damp. 3 (*a moist fruit-cake*) juicy, soft.

**moisture** *n* (*moisture running down the walls of the damp house*) water, liquid, wetness, wet, dampness.

**mold** *n* 1 (*cheese covered in mold/ old wood with a layer of mold*) fungus, mildew. 2 (*put the jelly in a mold to set/hot metal left to set in a mold*) shape, cast.

**moldy** *adj* (*food having gone moldy in the cupboard*) mildewed, musty.

**mole** *n* (*a small mole on her back*) blemish, blotch, discoloration.

**molest** *vb* (*he was accused of molesting female colleagues*) paw.

**moment** *n* 1 (*The peculiar noise lasted only a moment*) short time, instant, second, flash, (*inf*) jiffy. 2-(*It was a moment of great importance when the leaders first met*)-time, occasion, point in time. 3-(*discuss matters of great moment*) importance, significance, note, seriousness.

**momentous** *adj* (*a momentous event in history*) crucial, important, significant, serious.

**monarch** *n* (*French monarchs*) ruler, sovereign, king/queen.

**money** *n* (*They have enough money to buy a new car*) cash, capital, finance, (*inf*) wherewithal.

**monitor** *vb* (*doctors monitoring the patient's condition*) watch, observe, check, keep an eye on.

**monotonous** *adj* 1 (*people who have to do monotonous jobs*) without variety, repetitious, routine, humdrum, boring, dull, tedious. 2-(*He has a very monotonous voice*) flat, droning.

**monstrous** *adj* 1 (*They serve monstrous helpings of food/monstrous trucks speeding down the freeways*) huge, immense, vast, colossal. 2 (*Firing the workers was a monstrous thing to do*) shocking, outrageous, disgraceful, scandalous, terrible, dreadful, foul, vile, despicable.

**monument** *n* (*a monument to soldiers who died in the war*) memorial, statue, shrine.

**mood** *n* 1 (*They were in a happy mood*) humor, temper, state of mind, disposition. 2 (*She is in a mood*) bad mood, bad temper, sulk.

**moody** *adj* (*Teenagers are often accused of being moody*) temperamental, unpredictable, irritable, short-tempered, bad-tempered, touchy, sulky.

**moor** *vb* (*moor the boat in the harbor*) secure, tie up, fasten, anchor.

**mope** *vb* (*Since her boyfriend went away she has been moping around the house*) be miserable, be unhappy, brood, fret, sulk, idle, languish.

**moral** *adj* (*They are far too moral to break the law*) upright, honorable, virtuous, righteous, law-abiding, pure.

**morale** *n* (*The team's morale was low after their third defeat in a row*) spirit, confidence, self-confidence, heart.

**morsel** *n* (*a morsel of cheese*) mouthful, bite, piece, bit, crumb, little.

**mortal** adj **1** (a mortal blow) deadly, fatal, lethal, destructive. **2** (All of us are mortal) human, earthly.

**mostly** adv (The people in the group were mostly quite young) for the most part, mainly, in the main, on the whole, largely, chiefly.

**mother** n (her mother and father) female parent, (inf) mom, (inf) mommy.

**motherly** adj (The school matron is a very motherly person) maternal, kind, loving, warm.

**motion** adj (sickness caused by the motion of the boat) movement, moving.

**motivate** vb (trying to motivate the children into reading novels) stimulate, inspire, stir, persuade.

**motive** n (She seems to have had no motive for the murder) reason, cause, grounds, basis.

**mottled** adj (skin with rather a mottled appearance) blotchy, speckled, flecked, spotted, marbled.

**motto** n ('Service with a smile' is the store's motto) slogan, saying, watchword.

**mound** n (mounds of leaves in the back yard) heap, pile, stack, bank.

**mount** vb **1** (mount the stairs to the platform) climb, ascend, go up. **2**-(mount the bicycle) get on, climb on. **3** (He mounted the picture on a piece of cardboard) fix, attach. **4** (mount a book exhibition) put on, set up, stage, organize, arrange. **5** (If you save a little each week your savings will soon mount up) grow, increase, accumulate, pile up. **6** (House prices are mounting) rise, go up, increase, soar, escalate.

**mountain** n **1** (A climber was injured on the mountain) peak, hill. **2** (They received mountains of mail complaining about the program) pile, mound, heap, stack.

**mourn** vb (She is still mourning after the death of her husband last year) grieve, sorrow, be sad.

**mournful** adj (wearing a mournful expression) sad, sorrowful, dejected, gloomy.

**mouth** n **1** (the mouth of the river) outlet, estuary. **2** (the mouth of the cave) opening, entry, entrance.

**move** vb **1** (They moved slowly round the room) walk, go, proceed, progress. **2** (We moved the furniture from one room to another) carry, transport, transfer, convey, shift. **3** (He is moving because he has a new job) move house, relocate, leave, go away. **4**-(She was moved by the sight of the orphan children) affect, touch, upset, disturb. **5** (The sight moved her to tears/They finally felt moved to act) rouse, stir, influence, induce, prompt. **6** (At the meeting she moved that the chairman resign) propose, put forward, suggest.

**move** n (It is difficult to predict what our opponent's next move will be) act, action, step, deed.

**moving** adj **1** (the moving parts of the machinery) movable, mobile. **2**-(the moving force behind the scheme) driving, stimulating, dynamic. **3** (a moving story about two orphans) touching, affecting, emotional, emotive.

**mow** vb (mow the grass) cut, clip, trim.

**mud** n dirt, slime, sludge, (inf) muck.

**muddle** vb **1** (She accidentally muddled the books in the library) confuse, mix up, jumble up, disorganize, mess up. **2** (New faces tend to muddle the old woman) confuse, bewilder, perplex, puzzle.

**muffle** vb **1** (You must muffle yourself up against the cold) wrap up, cover up. **2** (try to muffle the loud noise) stifle, suppress, deaden, quiet.

**mug** n (a mug of cocoa) beaker, cup.

**mug** vb (They mugged an old man to get his wallet) attack, assault, rob, (inf) beat up.

**muggy** adj (muggy weather) close, stuffy, sultry, oppressive, humid, clammy.

**multiple** adj (She received multiple fractures in the accident) many, several, numerous, various.

**multiply** vb **1** (mice multiplying rapidly) reproduce, breed. **2** (Their troubles seem to be multiplying) increase, grow, spread, accumulate.

**multitude** n (They were surprised at the multitude of people who turned up for the meeting) crowd, horde, mob.

**mumble** vb (mumbling a few words) mutter, whisper, murmur.

**munch** vb (munching an apple) chew, bite, gnaw.

**mundane** adj (a meeting supposedly designed to discuss important church issues but ending up discussing mundane matters) commonplace, common, ordinary, everyday, routine, normal, typical.

**murder** n (charged with murder) killing, slaying, homicide, slaughter.

**murder** vb (convicted of murdering his father) kill, slay, put to death, (inf) do in, (inf) bump off.

**murky** adj **1** (murky water) muddy, dirty, cloudy, opaque. **2** (a murky time of day) dark, dim, gloomy.

**murmur** vb (She murmured that she wanted to leave) whisper, mutter, mumble.

**muscle** n (He strained the muscle while highjumping) tendon, sinew, ligament.

**muscular** adj (muscular young men involved in body building) brawny, strapping, hefty, burly.

**muse** vb (He mused over the situation) think about, consider, contemplate, meditate on, reflect on.

**mushroom** vb (fast-food restaurants mushrooming everywhere) spring up, shoot up, sprout, boom, thrive.

**music** n (people enjoying the music) melody, tune, air, rhythm.

**musical** adj (a musical sound) tuneful, melodic, melodious, sweet-sounding, dulcet.

**muss** vb (Climbing through the hedge had mussed her hair) disarrange, tousle, dishevel, make untidy.

**muster** vb (The general mustered the troops/ He had to muster all his energy to climb the stairs) gather, summon, rally.

**musty** adj (a musty smell in the old house) moldy, stale, fusty, stuffy, airless, damp.

**mute** adj (animals making a mute appeal for help) silent, speechless, unspoken, dumb, wordless.

**muted** adj (muted colors) soft, subtle, subdued, discreet, understated.

**mutilate** vb (soldiers horribly mutilated in the war) cripple, maim, mangle, disfigure, dismember.

**mutinous** adj (a mutinous crew on board ship) rebellious, revolutionary, insubordinate, disobedient, unruly.

**mutiny** n (mutiny on board ship) rebellion, revolt, insurrection, revolution, riot.

**mutter** vb (She muttered that she did not want to go) mumble, murmur, whisper, complain.

**mutual** adj (They have mutual friends) common, shared, joint.

**mysterious** adj **1** (There were mysterious noises coming from the room where they were getting ready for the party) peculiar, strange, odd, weird, curious, puzzling. **2** (They were being very mysterious about where they were going) secretive, reticent, evasive.

**mythical** adj **1** (The dragon is a mythical creature) legendary, mythological, fabulous, imaginary, fictitious. **2**-(She is always talking about her rich uncle but we think that he is a-mythical figure) imaginary, fantasy, make-believe, invented, made up, (inf) pretend.

# N

**nag** vb **1** (She is always nagging her husband) scold, carp at, find fault with, bully. **2** (children nagging their mother to buy them sweets) pester, badger, harass, (inf) hassle.

**nail** n (the joiner's wood and nails) pin, tack.

**naive** adj (She was so naive that she believed every word he said) gullible, trusting, innocent.

**naked** adj **1** (She could not answer the door as she was naked after her shower) nude, in the nude, undressed, unclothed, bare, stark naked. **2** (a naked flame) unprotected, uncovered, exposed. **3** (the naked truth) undisguised, unadorned, stark, plain, simple.

**name** n **1** (We don't know the name of the book)

title. **2** (*He made his name in the theater*) reputation, fame, renown, distinction.

**nap** n catnap, sleep, doze, (*inf*) snooze, (*inf*) forty winks.

**narrate** vb (*The old man narrated the story of his life*) tell, relate, recount, describe.

**narrow** adj **1** (*They have very narrow wrists*) slender, slim, thin. **2**-(*They stock only a narrow range-of goods*) limited, restricted, small.

**narrow-minded** adj (*She was too narrow-minded to listen to other people's points of view*) intolerant, prejudiced, bigoted, biased.

**nasty** n **1** (*The rotting meat was a nasty sight*) unpleasant, disagreeable, horrible, foul. **2** (*a nasty old woman*) disagreeable, bad-tempered, spiteful, mean.

**nation** n (*an organization consisting of the nations of the world*) country, land, state.

**nationalistic** adj (*He is nationalistic and does not like foreigners*) patriotic, chauvinistic.

**native** adj **1** (*the native plants of the region*) indigenous, original, local. **2** (*their native instincts*) natural, inborn.

**natural** adj **1** (*a store selling natural produce*) organic, pure. **2** (*natural behavior*) unaffected, simple, genuine, spontaneous, normal. **3** (*their natural instincts*) inborn, native, instinctive. **4** (*The illness took its natural course*) usual, normal, regular, ordinary, common.

**nature** n **1** (*The children are interested in nature*) environment, Mother Nature, creation. **2** (*He has a warm nature*) temperament, disposition, character, personality.

**naughty** adj (*The children were being naughty*) badly behaved, bad, mischievous, misbehaving, disobedient.

**nauseate** vb (*The sight of the rotting meat nauseated her*) sicken, make sick, turn one's stomach, disgust, revolt.

**navigate** vb (*He navigated the ship through the narrow straits*) steer, pilot, direct, guide, maneuver, drive.

**near** adj (*The station is very near*) nearby, close, at hand, handy.

**nearly** adv **1** (*We nearly drowned*) almost, all but, as good as, practically. **2** (*They collected nearly $500*) almost, roughly, approximately.

**neat** adj **1** (*children looking neat going to school*) tidy, smart, spruce. **2** (*They made a mess of the neat room*) tidy, orderly.

**necessary** adj (*They took the necessary action in time*) essential, needful, indispensable, required, vital.

**need** n **1** (*There is no need to shout*) necessity, requirement, obligation, call. **2** (*Their needs are very few*) want, wish, demand, requirement. **3** (*The charity helps people in need*) want, poverty, deprivation.

**neglect** vb (*She went to the movies and neglected her work*) pay no attention to, disregard, ignore, overlook, skip, shirk.

**negligent** adj (*He was found negligent for falling asleep on duty*) neglectful, careless, inattentive, sloppy.

**negotiate** vb **1** (*The two sides succeeded in negotiating a settlement*) work out, arrange, agree on. **2**-(*The two sides are negotiating about a financial settlement*) bargain, hold talks, discuss.

**neighborhood** n (*They are moving to a new neighborhood*) district, area, region, locality.

**nerve** n **1** (*Climbing the outside of the tower requires nerve*) courage, bravery, daring, pluck, (*inf*) guts. **2**-(*They had the nerve to ask us to pay more*) impertinence, impudence, cheek, brazenness, effrontery, temerity.

**nervous** adj **1** (*He was feeling nervous about his visit to the doctor*) edgy, on edge, tense, anxious, agitated. **2** (*They are very nervous people*) timid, anxious, edgy, tense, apprehensive.

**network** n **1** (*The pattern consisted of a network of lines*) latticework, mesh. **2** (*When looking for work she contacted her network of old friends*) system, organization.

**neutral** n **1** (*It is essential for referees-to be neutral*) impartial, unbiased,-unprejudiced, open-minded, detached, disinterested. **2** (*She was looking for curtains in neutral colors*) indefinite, colorless, beige, stone.

**never** adv (*She never lies*) not ever, not at all, at no time, under no circumstances.

**new** adj **1** (*They are buying a new car*) brand-new, unused. **2** (*We need some new ideas*) fresh, original, imaginative. **3** (*They have introduced a new system of cataloging books*) different, modern, up-to-date.

**news** npl (*There has been no news of the missing climbers*) information, facts, communication, word, data.

**next** adj **1** (*the next bus/the next president*) following, subsequent, succeeding. **2** (*the next house in the avenue*) neighboring, adjacent, adjoining, closest, nearest.

**nibble** vb (*mice nibbling on a piece of cheese*) bite, gnaw, munch.

**nice** adj **1** (*His father is a nice person*) pleasant, friendly, kind, agreeable, charming. **2** (*We had a nice time at the theater*) pleasant, enjoyable, delightful. **3** (*It was a nice day for the wedding*) fine, sunny, dry. **4** (*There is a nice distinction in meaning between the two words*) fine, subtle, minute, precise.

**night** n (*when night fell*) nighttime, darkness, dark.

**nimble** adj **1** (*The old lady was still very nimble*) agile, lithe, quick-moving, spry. **2** (*The knitters had very nimble fingers*) supple, deft.

**nip** vb **1** (*The dog nipped her ankle*) bite, snap at. **2** (*The little boy cried out when his friend nipped him*) pinch, tweak, squeeze.

**noble** adj **1** (*the king and the noble people of the land*) aristocratic, high-born, titled, blue-blooded. **2**-(*a soldier decorated for his noble deeds*) brave, courageous, gallant, heroic, honorable. **3** (*The tourists admired the city's noble buildings*) impressive, imposing, magnificent, stately, grand.

**nod** vb **1** (*He nodded his head in agreement*) bow, incline, bob. **2**-(*The audience began to nod*) nod off, drop off, fall asleep, doze.

**noise** n (*They were kept awake by the noise of traffic*) sound, loud sound, din, racket, clamor, row, commotion, hubbub, bedlam, pandemonium.

**noisy** adj **1** (*The teacher tried to quiet the noisy children*) rowdy, boisterous, loud. **2** (*noisy music*) loud, blaring, deafening, ear-splitting.

**nondescript** adj (*She was wearing nondescript clothes*) unremarkable, undistinguished, commonplace, ordinary.

**nonsense** n (*They told her that she was talking absolute nonsense*) garbage, drivel, twaddle, gibberish, balderdash.

**normal** adj **1** (*temperatures that were normal for the time of year*) average, usual, common, standard, ordinary, typical. **2** (*He is of more than normal size*) average, standard.

**nosy** adj (*They have nosy neighbors*) inquisitive, prying, curious, interfering, (*inf*) snooping.

**notable** adj **1** (*the notable achievements of the politician*) noteworthy, outstanding, remarkable, memorable, important, significant. **2**-(*All-the notable people in the town were present at the reception*) noted, of note, distinguished, well-known, eminent, prominent.

**notch** n (*make notches in the stick*) nick, dent, cut, indentation.

**note** n **1** (*It is wise to keep a note of how much you spend*) record, account. **2** (*I wrote her a note thanking her*) letter, line, message. **3** (*His advice is worthy of note*) notice, attention, heed, observation, **4** (*people of note in the community*) distinction, eminence, prestige, fame. **5** (*There was a note of sadness in her voice*) tone, sound.

**note** vb **1** (*She noted the details in her diary*) write down, jot down, put down, enter. **2** (*The police noted that he seemed frightened*) notice, observe, perceive, detect.

**notice** n **1** (*Very little escapes the Principal's notice*) attention, observation, heed. **2** (*We have received notice of a meeting to be held next week*) notification, information, news, announcement. **3** (*a notice on the board giving details of the meeting*) poster, handbill, information sheet, bulletin, circular. **4** (*Several workers have received a* month's notice) notice to quit, the sack, (inf) marching orders.

**notice** vb (We could not help noticing the bruise on her face) see, observe, note, detect, spot, perceive, discern.

**noticeable** adj **1** (The scar on her cheek was quite noticeable) visible, obvious, plain, plain to see. **2** (There had been a noticeable improvement in the pupil's work) marked, obvious, evident, conspicuous, distinct.

**notify** vb (They notified the police about the stranger on their land) inform, tell, advise, acquaint.

**notion** n (They have some peculiar notions) idea, belief, opinion, conviction, theory, thought.

**notorious** adj (He is a notorious criminal) infamous, well-known, scandalous.

**nourishing** adj (give the children nourishing food) nutritious, healthy, wholesome, beneficial.

**novel** adj (He had a novel approach to the teaching of history) new, fresh, different, original, unusual.

**novelty** n (We bought some little seaside novelties) knick-knack, trinket, bauble, souvenir, memento.

**novice** n (They are complete novices at the game) beginner, learner, trainee, apprentice, newcomer, recruit.

**nude** adj (They were sunbathing nude) in the nude, naked, stark naked, bare, undressed, unclothed.

**nudge** vb (She nudged him in the ribs to tell him to keep quiet) prod, jab, poke, dig, elbow, push.

**nuisance** n (She regards the cat next door as a nuisance) pest, bother, irritant, problem, trial, bore.

**numb** adj (Her fingers were numb with cold) without feeling, immobilized, frozen, paralyzed.

**number** n **1** (write down all the numbers) figure, numeral, digit. **2** (A large number of people attended) quantity, amount, collection. **3** (This is last week's number of the magazine) issue, edition, copy.

**numerous** adj (He has numerous reasons for leaving) many, very many, innumerable, several.

**nurse** vb (She nursed the sick child) take care of, look after, tend, treat.

**nutritious** adj (get the children to eat nutritious food instead of junk food) nourishing, healthy, health-giving, wholesome, beneficial.

# O

**oath** n (swear an oath to support the Constitution) vow, promise, pledge, word.

**obedient** adj (obedient children/obedient dogs) biddable, well-behaved, welltrained, docile.

**obey** vb **1** (obey the school rules) observe, abide by, comply with, keep to. **2** (soldiers obeying orders) carry out, perform, fulfill, execute. **3** (children taught to obey their parents) be dutiful to, follow the orders of.

**object** n **1** (pick up a wooden object lying on the sidewalk) thing, article, item. **2** (The object of the exercise was to collect money for charity) aim, goal, purpose, point, objective. **3** (the object of their abuse) target, focus, recipient.

**object** vb (We objected to the way they handled the situation) raise objections to, protest against, complain, take exception to, grumble.

**objection** n (There were several objections to the scheme) protest, complaint, grumble.

**objectionable** adj (He is a most objectionable young man/We found her manner objectionable) offensive, obnoxious, unpleasant, disagreeable, nasty.

**objective** adj (Referees have to be objective) impartial, unbiased, unprejudiced, neutral, disinterested, detached.

**objective** n (Our objective was to get there before nightfall) object, aim, goal, target, intention.

**obliged** adj (You are not obliged to say anything at this stage) bound, compelled, forced, required.

**obliging** adj (We have very obliging neighbors) helpful, accommodating, willing, generous, cooperative.

**oblivious** adj (They were oblivious to the danger they were in) unaware, heedless, unheeding, unmindful, unconscious, ignorant.

**obnoxious** adj (he is obnoxious when he is drunk) offensive, objectionable, unpleasant, disagreeable, nasty, horrible, odious.

**obscene** adj (obscene videos) pornographic, indecent, blue, bawdy, smutty, dirty.

**obscure** adj **1** (For some obscure reason they suddenly decided to leave) unclear, hidden, concealed, puzzling, mysterious. **2** (a book by an obscure poet) unheard of, unknown, little known, insignificant.

**obscure** vb **1** (The new apartment building obscures our view of the lake) hide, conceal, screen, block out. **2** (His remarks simply obscured the issue) confuse, muddle, complicate, cloud.

**observant** adj (The observant lad was able to give a description of the car) sharp-eyed, eagle-eyed, attentive, heedful, vigilant.

**observe** vb **1** (He observed a man watching his neighbor's house) see, catch sight of, notice, perceive, witness. **2** (All players must observe the rules of the game) obey, keep, abide by, adhere to, comply with,

follow, heed. **3** (She observed that it was going to rain) remark, comment, state, announce.

**obsession** n (She has an obsession about having a spotlessly clean house) fixation, preoccupation, compulsion, mania.

**obsolete** adj (The factory uses obsolete machinery/The book has a great many obsolete words) outworn, outmoded, antiquated, out-of-date, oldfashioned, archaic.

**obstacle** n (the obstacles in the way of progress) hindrance, impediment, obstruction, barrier, bar, hurdle.

**obstinate** adj (The two sisters had a quarrel and were too obstinate to apologize) stubborn, pig-headed, mulish, headstrong, unyielding.

**obstreperous** adj (The police tried to control the obstreperous crowd) unruly, disorderly, rowdy, boisterous, rough, wild, turbulent, riotous.

**obstruct** vb **1** (fallen trees obstructing the flow of traffic) block, bar, check, halt. **2** (The protesters tried to obstruct progress on the building of the new freeway) hinder, delay, impede, hamper, block, interrupt, hold up.

**obstruction** n (obstructions to progress) obstacle, impediment, hindrance, hurdle, barrier, bar.

**obtain** vb (We tried to obtain a copy of the book) get, get hold of, acquire, come by, procure, gain.

**obvious** adj (It was obvious that she was crying/The bruise on his face was very obvious) clear, clear-cut, plain, noticeable, evident, apparent.

**occasion** n **1** (They met on several occasions) time, point. **2** (The leaving party was a sad occasion) event, incident, occurrence, happening. **3** (She will go abroad if the occasion arises) opportunity, chance, opening. **4** (They met at a festive occasion) function, gathering, party.

**occasional** adj (It will be a fine day with occasional showers) infrequent, irregular, sporadic, rare, odd.

**occupation** n (write down your occupation on the application form) job, employment, profession, business, trade, career.

**occupied** adj **1** (All the hotel rooms are occupied) full, in use, engaged, taken. **2** (The new houses are all occupied already) inhabited. **3** (The manager is occupied just now and cannot speak to you) busy, engaged, (inf) tied up.

**occupy** vb **1** (How many people occupy this apartment?) inhabit, live in, reside in, dwell in. **2** (The enemy army occupied the city) take possession of, seize, invade, capture. **3** (How does she occupy her leisure hours?) fill, use, utilize, take up. **4** (They occupy junior posts) hold, have, fill.

**occur** *vb* **1** (*The police think the murder occurred last night*) take place, happen, come about. **2** (*The same mistakes occur throughout the piece of work*) arise, be found, appear, be present. **3** (*It occurred to me that I had seen her before*) come to, enter one's head, strike.

**occurrence** *n* (*Car theft is a common occurrence these days*) event, incident, happening.

**odd** *adj* **1** (*We thought her behavior was odd*) strange, peculiar, weird, bizarre, outlandish, abnormal, curious. **2** (*She thinks of him at odd moments*) occasional, random, irregular. **3** (*He found an odd sock*) spare, left over, single, unmatched.

**odious** *adj* (*Our new neighbors are odious people*) horrible, nasty, loathsome, detestable, hateful, objectionable, offensive.

**odor** *n* (*the odor of frying onions*) smell, aroma, scent, fragrance, stink, stench.

**offend** *vb* (*He offended her parents by not thanking them for the meal*) hurt, upset, displease, annoy.

**offense** *n* **1** (*They were punished for the offense which they committed*) crime, misdeed, wrong. **2** (*His ungrateful behavior caused offense*) upset, displeasure, annoyance, disapproval.

**offensive** *adj* **1** (*He was forced to apologize for his offensive remarks*) hurtful, upsetting, distressful, abusive. **2** (*He is an offensive person/We noticed an offensive smell*) unpleasant, nasty, horrible, foul, vile, objectionable, odious.

**offer** *vb* **1** (*He offered several suggestions*) put forward, propose, submit, suggest. **2** (*We offered to babysit for them*) volunteer. **3** (*The job offers good career prospects*) give, present, afford, supply, furnish.

**office** *n* **1** (*His office is on the top floor*) place of business, workplace, room. **2** (*He holds the office of company secretary*) post, position, appointment, job.

**official** *adj* **1** (*receive official permission/the official documents*) authorized, formal, licensed, certified, legal. **2** (*We had to wear evening dress to the official function*) formal, ceremonial.

**officious** *adj* (*the officious man at the desk*) interfering, meddlesome, bumptious, self-important.

**offspring** *n* (*a couple with no offspring*) children, family, young.

**oil** *n* **1** (*fry the food in oil, not lard*) cooking oil. **2** (*oil to lubricate the hinges of the gate*) grease, motor oil, lubricant.

**oil** *vb* (*oil the rusty hinges of the gate*) grease, lubricate.

**oily** *adj* (*She dislikes oily food*) greasy, fatty.

**ointment** *n* (*put ointment on his wound*) medication, cream, lotion.

**old** *adj* **1** (*a ward in the hospital full of old people*) elderly, aged, (*inf*) long in the tooth. **2** (*She was wearing old clothes to dig the garden*) worn, shabby. **3** (*tired of his old ideas*) oldfashioned, outdated, out-of-date, outmoded, antiquated. **4** (*the old ruins in the center of the town*) dilapidated, rundown, ramshackle, crumbling. **5** (*He collects old cars*) antique, veteran, vintage. **6** (*in the old days*) past, bygone, earlier. **7** (*an old girlfriend*) former, ex-, previous.

**old-fashioned** *adj* (*old-fashioned clothes/old-fashioned ideas*) outof-date, outdated, unfashionable, outmoded.

**omen** *n* (*They were superstitious and thought that walking under a ladder was a bad omen*) sign, portent, forewarning, prophecy.

**ominous** *adj* (*We heard the ominous sound of gunfire*) threatening, menacing.

**omit** *vb* (*We omitted his name from the invitation list in error*) leave out, exclude, miss out, delete, eliminate.

**onlooker** *n* (*The police tried to move on the onlookers at the accident scene*) observer, witness, eyewitness, spectator, bystander.

**ooze** *vb* (*pus was oozing from the wound*) flow, discharge, seep, exude, leak, drip.

**opaque** *adj* **1** (*opaque glass*) non-transparent, cloudy. **2** (*The waters were opaque with mud*) cloudy, dark, murky, hazy.

**open** *adj* **1** (*The door was open*) ajar, unlocked, unbolted, unfastened. **2** (*open boxes*) uncovered, unsealed. **3** (*find some open spaces for the children to run around in*) unfenced, unenclosed, extensive, broad, spacious. **4** (*maps lying open on the table*) spread out, unfolded. **5** (*She was quite open about her hatred of them*) frank, candid, forthright, honest, blunt, plainspoken. **6** (*There was open hostility between them*) obvious, evident, visible, unconcealed.

**opening** *n* **1** (*an opening in the hedge/an opening in the wall*) gap, space, aperture, hole, breach. **2** (*at the opening of the meeting*) beginning, start, commencement, outset. **3** (*There is an opening in the firm for a receptionist*) vacancy, position, post, place.

**operate** *vb* **1** (*The machine suddenly ceased to operate*) work, function, go, run. **2** (*Can you operate this machine?*) work, use, handle. **3** (*The surgeon had to operate on her leg*) perform surgery on.

**operation** *n* **1** (*She had to have an operation on her leg*) surgery. **2** (*The troops took part in a military operation*) maneuver, campaign, action.

**opinion** *n* (*We were asked to give our opinions on the state of the company*) view, point of view, viewpoint, thought, belief, idea.

**opponent** *n* (*his opponent in the competition*) rival, adversary, opposition, enemy, foe.

**opportunity** *n* **1** (*You should go abroad if the opportunity arises*) chance, occasion. **2** (*It was a good opportunity to spend some time with her family*) chance, occasion, time, moment.

**oppose** *vb* (*Some of the committee opposed the company's plans for expansion*) contest, take a stand against, argue against.

**opposite** *adj* **1** (*rows of houses opposite each other*) facing, face-to-face. **2** (*The two brothers were on opposite sides in the dispute*) opposing, rival, competitive, warring. **3** (*They hold opposite views*) differing, different, contrary, conflicting, contradictory, incompatible.

**oppress** *vb* (*The cruel tyrant oppressed the poor people of the villages*) crush, abuse, maltreat, persecute.

**oppressive** *adj* **1** (*the oppressive regimes of the world*) tyrannical, despotic, repressive, undemocratic, harsh, severe, brutal. **2** (*They were unable to sleep in that oppressive weather*) close, stifling, stuffy, sultry.

**opt** *vb* (*He opted for a red car*) choose, select, pick, settle on, decide on.

**optimistic** *adj* **1** (*We were optimistic about our chances of success*) hopeful, confident. **2** (*He was in an optimistic mood*) hopeful, confident, cheerful, positive.

**option** *adj* (*We had only two options—to accept his offer or resign*) choice, alternative.

**optional** *adj* (*Attendance at the meeting is optional*) voluntary, non-compulsory, discretionary.

**oral** *adj* (*He was asked to give an oral report of the events*) spoken, verbal, by word of mouth.

**orator** *n* (*The crowds gathered to hear the orator*) speaker, public speaker.

**orbit** *n* (*The spacecraft made an orbit of the earth*) revolution, circle.

**ordeal** *n* (*The climb up the mountain in blizzard conditions was a real ordeal*) test, trial, tribulation, suffering, torment, torture, nightmare.

**order** *n* **1** (*Soldiers must obey orders*) command, direction, instruction, decree. **2** (*The teacher restored order in the rowdy class*) calm, peace, control, discipline, good behavior. **3** (*They put the room in-order after the party*) order- liness, neatness, tidiness. **4** (*Is the machine in working order?*) condition, state, shape. **5** (*arrange the words in alphabetical order*) arrangement, grouping, sequence, series, system, categorization. **6** (*place an order for his new novel*) request, booking, reservation.

**order** *vb* **1** (*the general ordered the soldiers to shoot*) command, direct, instruct, bid. **2** (*The store did not have the book and so we ordered it*) place an order for, book, reserve.

**orderly** *adj* **1** (*an orderly piece of-work*) organized, methodical, systematic. **2** (*an*

**orderly** crowd) wellbehaved, disciplined, quiet, peaceful, restrained.

**ordinary** adj 1 (We followed our ordinary procedure) usual, normal, standard, common, customary, regular, routine, typical. 2 (lead ordinary lives/ordinary people) unremarkable, unexceptional, average, run-of-themill, commonplace, humdrum.

**organization** n (He is head of the organization) company, firm, corporation, association, society, club, group.

**organize** vb 1 (organize the books in alphabetical order by the name of the author) arrange, group, sort, classify, categorize. 2 (We organized a Christmas party for the children) arrange, coordinate, set up, put together, run, see to.

**origin** n 1 (discuss the origin of life) source, basis, creation, start, commencement. 2 (the origin of the word) derivation, etymology, root.

**original** adj 1 (the original owners of the house) first, earliest, initial. 2 (The judges are looking for original work) innovative, inventive, creative, new, fresh, novel, unusual.

**ornament** n 1 (There was a row of ornaments on the shelf) knickknack, trinket, bauble. 2 (an outfit entirely without ornament) decoration, adornment.

**ornate** adj 1 (an ornate style of architecture) decorated, elaborate, fancy, fussy, showy. 2 (her ornate writing style) elaborate, flowery, high-flown, pompous, pretentious.

**orthodox** adj (people who question orthodox ideas) conventional, accepted, established, traditional, standard.

**ostentatious** adj (She was wearing a very ostentatious dress) showy, conspicuous, obtrusive, loud, pretentious, over-elaborate.

**other** adj 1 (We shall have to use other methods) different, alternative. 2 (give some other examples) more, additional, further.

**outbreak** n (an outbreak of measles) epidemic, flare-up.

**outcast** n (He was an outcast from his native land) exile, refugee, outlaw.

**outcome** n (The outcome of the talks was that the workers went on strike) result, consequence, upshot, conclusion, effect.

**outcry** n (the outcry when the hospital was threatened with closure) protest, commotion, outburst, uproar, clamor, hullabaloo.

**outer** adj (the outer layer) outside, exterior, external, surface.

**outfit** n (her wedding outfit) clothes, ensemble, costume, clothes.

**outing** n (The children went on an outing to the park) trip, excursion, jaunt, expedition.

**outlaw** n (a book about outlaws who escaped from prison) criminal, fugitive, outcast, bandit.

**outlet** n 1 (water pouring through the outlet) way out, exit, vent, opening. 2 (an outlet for their farm produce) market.

**outline** n 1 (They saw the outline of someone against the wall) silhouette, shadow, profile, shape. 2-(They gave an outline of their plans) summary, synopsis, rough idea.

**outline** vb (We outlined our plans to the committee) sketch out, summarize.

**outlook** n 1 (The upstairs bedroom has a wonderful outlook) view, prospect, aspect. 2 (She is quite ill but the outlook is good) future, prediction, forecast. 3 (He has a depressed outlook on life) view, opinion, attitude.

**outlying** adj (outlying areas of the country) remote, distant, far-flung.

**outrageous** adj 1 (They objected to the drunk man's outrageous behavior) disgraceful, shocking, scandalous, offensive, intolerable. 2-(The invading army committed outrageous acts) terrible, dreadful, abominable, foul, vile. 3 (The prices in that restaurant are outrageous) exorbitant, excessive, preposterous.

**outside** n 1 (They painted the outside of the building white) exterior, surface. 2 (The fruit is dark green on the outside) exterior, surface, skin, shell.

**outskirts** npl (a mall on the outskirts of the town) suburbs, outlying area.

**outstanding** adj 1 (He is an outstanding artist) excellent, exceptional, remarkable, eminent, noted, wellknown. 2 (His bill is still outstanding) unpaid, owing, due.

**outward** adj 1 (the outward layers) outer, outside, external, exterior. 2-(His outward cheerfulness hid his grief) external, superficial, visible, discernible.

**outwit** vb (He tried to cheat in order to win but the other player outwitted him) outsmart, trick, fool, dupe.

**oval** adj (an oval face) egg-shaped, ovoid.

**overcome** vb 1 (Our army succeeded in overcoming the enemy) defeat, conquer, beat, vanquish, overthrow, crush. 2 (He tried to overcome his disability) conquer, master, triumph over.

**overdue** adj (The train is overdue) late, delayed, unpunctual.

**overheads** npl (try to reduce the firm's overheads) expenses, expenditure, outlay, costs.

**overjoyed** adj (They were overjoyed when their baby was born) elated, thrilled, delighted, ecstatic.

**overlook** vb 1 (Her bedroom window overlooks the lake) face, have a view of, look out on. 2 (He said he would overlook the error just this once) disregard, ignore, pay no attention to, let pass, turn a blind eye to, condone. 3 (He overlooked a note at the foot of the contract) miss, fail to notice.

**oversight** n (Omitting your name from the list was an oversight) mistake, error, blunder, slip-up.

**overthrow** vb (overthrow the invading army) overcome, defeat, conquer, vanquish, beat, overwhelm.

**overwhelm** vb 1 (A tidal wave overwhelmed the village) flood, swamp, inundate, deluge, engulf. 2 (They overwhelmed the invading army) overcome, defeat, conquer, vanquish, crush.

**owing** adj (We had to pay the money owing right away) outstanding, unpaid, due.

**own** adj (Each of the girls had her own car) individual, personal, particular, private.

**own** vb 1 (They own two cars) have, possess, keep. 2 (You have to own that he may be right) admit, acknowledge, allow, concede. 3 (The boy finally owned up to his crime) confess, admit, acknowledge, (inf) come clean.

**owner** n 1 (the owner of the car) possessor, keeper, holder. 2 (the owner of the business) proprietor, boss.

# P

**pack** vb 1 (They packed their suitcases) fill, load, stuff, cram. 2 (They packed their old clothes in a trunk) place, put, store, stow. 3 (protesters packed the hall) fill, crowd, throng, mob, cram, jam, press into, squeeze into.

**package** n (The mailman tried to deliver a package) parcel.

**packet** n (a packet of soap powder) carton, pack, package, container.

**padding** n (use cotton padding to pack the jewelry) filling, packing, wadding, lining, stuffing.

**painful** adj (The leg that she injured is still very painful) sore, hurting, aching, throbbing, smarting, agonizing, excruciating.

**paint** vb 1 (They are painting the walls) apply paint to, decorate. 2 (He painted the view from his bedroom window) portray, depict, draw, sketch.

**painting** n (the paintings hanging in the gallery) picture, portrait, sketch, drawing.

**pale** adj 1 (She looks pale after her illness) white, whitish, white-faced, colorless, wan, drained, pallid, pasty, peaked, ashen, as white as a sheet, as white as a ghost. 2 (She always wears pale colors) light, light-colored, muted, subdued, pastel.

**pan** n (the pans on the stove) saucepan, pot, frying pan, wok.

**panic** n (They were filled with panic at the sight of the flames) alarm, agitation, hysteria, fear, fright, terror, trepidation.

**paper** n 1 (I saw it in today's paper) newspaper. 2 (choose a paper for the living room) wallpaper, wall-covering. **3** (*The students have to write a paper on Shakespeare's 'Hamlet'*) essay, report, dissertation, article, treatise, thesis. **4** (*get a photocopy of all the papers for today's meeting*) document, legal paper.

**paralyze** *vb* **1** (*His legs were paralyzed in the accident*) immobilize, make powerless, numb, deaden, cripple, disable. **2** (*The traffic system was paralyzed in the snowstorm*) immobilize, bring to a halt, bring to a stop, bring to a standstill.

**parcel** *n* (*The mailman tried to deliver a parcel*) package.

**pardon** *vb* **1** (*The prisoner was pardoned by the governor*) reprieve, let off, release, absolve, acquit, exonerate. **2** (*He asked her to pardon him for being so ill-tempered*) excuse, forgive, let off, condone.

**part** *n* **1** (*the last part of the book*) section, portion, segment, bit. **2**-(*the parts of the machine*) component, bit, constituent. **3** (*She went to the northern part of the island*) section, area, district, quarter, sector. **4** (*Originally the book was issued in several parts*) section, bit, episode, volume. **5** (*He apologized for the part which he played in the hoax*) role, function, responsibility, job. **6** (*She plays the part of Joan of Arc in the play*) role, character.

**part** *vb* **1** (*They had to part when he went back to his own country*) separate, say goodbye. **2** (*After three years of marriage they have decided to part*) separate, leave each other, split up, break up, divorce, go their separate ways. **3**-(*The police parted the crowd to reach the troublemakers at the front*) divide, separate, break up.

**partial** *adj* **1** (*There was only a partial improvement in his work*) part, in part, incomplete, limited, imperfect. **2** (*The referee was accused of being partial*) biased, prejudiced, partisan, discriminatory, unfair, unjust.

**partial:—be partial to** *adj* (*She is partial to seafood*) like, have a liking for, love, be fond of, have a weakness for.

**particular** *adj* **1** (*You must pay particular attention to what he says*) special, exceptional, unusual. **2** (*In this particular case I think we should be generous*) specific, individual, single. **3** (*She is particular about who cuts her hair*) fussy, fastidious, selective, discriminating, (*inf*) picky, (*inf*) choosy.

**partner** *n* **1** (*They are business partners*) associate, colleague, co-owner. **2** f(*the burglar and his partner in crime*) ally, confederate, accomplice. **3** (*All her friends and their partners were invited to the wedding*) husband/ wife, spouse, boyfriend/ girlfriend.

**party** *n* **1** (*It was he who was host at the party*) social gathering, social function, function, reception, (*inf*) get-together **2**

(*They were part of the hunting party*) group, band, company, contingent. **3** (*a certain party who shall remain nameless*) person, individual.

**pass** *vb* **1** (*The car passed us on a dangerous stretch of road*) go past, outdistance, catch up with. **2**-(*Trucks passed along the road all night*) go, proceed, drive, run, travel. **3** (*Time passed quickly*) go past, advance, roll by, flow by, slip by. **4** (*How does he pass the time now he has retired?*) spend, fill, occupy, take up, use, while away. **5** (*He passed her the papers for the meeting*) hand over, give, reach. **6**-(*The estate passes to his eldest son on his death*) be passed on, be transferred, be signed over to. **7**-(*All the students have passed the exams*) be successful, get through, gain a pass. **8** (*Congress passed the new bill*) vote for, accept, prove, adopt, sanction. **9** (*The judge passed sentence*) pronounce, utter, deliver, declare. **10** (*Eventually the hurricane passed*) run its course, die out, fade, finish. **11** (*They were still friends after everything that had passed between them*) occur, happen, take place.

**past** *adj* **1** (*They were congratulated on their past successes*) former, previous, prior, foregoing. **2** (*He has become very ill in the past few days*) recent, preceding, last. **3** (*the history of past ages*) gone by, bygone, former.

**pastime** *n* (*He is going to have to take up a pastime in his retirement*) hobby, recreation, diversion, distraction, leisure activity, amusement, entertainment.

**path** *n* **1** (*a winding path up the mountain*) pathway, trail, track, way. **2** (*They are studying the moon's path*) course, route, circuit, orbit.

**pathetic** *adj* **1** (*The starving children were a pathetic sight*) pitiful, pitiable, moving, touching, affecting, poignant, distressing, heartbreaking. **2** (*He could not play cricket and made only a few pathetic attempts to hit the ball*) feeble, inadequate, unsatisfactory, poor.

**patient** *adj* (*There is nothing to be done about the delayed flight—we shall have to be patient*) calm, composed, restrained, tolerant, forbearing, resigned, stoical, uncomplaining.

**pause** *n* (*There was a pause in the music while he changed the tape*) interval, lull, break, halt, gap.

**pay** *vb* **1** (*They had to pay a huge amount for that house*) pay out, spend, lay out, part with, (*inf*) shell out, (*inf*) fork out, (*inf*) fork over. **2**-(*He will get paid at the end of the job*) give payment to, remunerate. **3** (*He enjoys the work but it doesn't really pay*) be profitable, make money, be remunerative. **4**-(*He pays his bills right away*) settle,

defray. **5** (*He likes to pay compliments to women*) bestow, offer, extend.

**peaceful** *adj* **1** (*They were at war but conditions between the countries are now peaceful*) peaceable, at peace, friendly, amicable. **2** (*The old man looked peaceful lying asleep in his chair*) at peace, tranquil, serene, calm, composed, placid, undisturbed. **3** (*They longed for a house in a peaceful country setting*) quiet, restful, tranquil, calm, still.

**peculiar** *adj* **1** (*She wears such peculiar hats*) strange, odd, funny, weird, bizarre, eccentric, outlandish, unconventional, offbeat. **2**-(*There was a peculiar smell in the hall*) odd, unusual, strange, curious, abnormal. **3** (*a manner of walking that is peculiar to her*) characteristic, typical, individualistic, special, unique.

**peel** *vb* **1** (*peel the skin from the fruit*) pare, remove. **2** (*peel the fruit*) pare, skin. **3** (*Her skin was peeling after sunbathing*) flake off, scale off.

**peg** *n* (*They fastened the pieces of wood with a peg*) pin, nail, screw, bolt, spike, skewer.

**penetrate** *vb* **1** (*The knife of the attacker did not penetrate the skin*)-pierce, bore, perforate, stab. **2**-(*unable to penetrate the dense jungle*) go through, get through, enter, infiltrate.

**people** *npl* **1** (*an issue that should be decided by the people*) the public, the general public, the common people, the populace, the electorate. **2** (*an area inhabited by a nomadic people*) population, tribe, race, nation. **3** (*A lot of people were expected to attend*) individuals, persons. **4** (*Her people should be looking after her*) relatives, relations, family, folk.

**perfect** *adj* **1** (*Her performance on the piano is perfect*) flawless, faultless, impeccable, consummate, ideal, supreme, excellent, marvelous. **2** (*a perfect set of the encyclopedia*) complete, full, whole, entire. **3** (*The boy is a perfect fool*) absolute, utter, complete, out-and-out, thoroughgoing.

**perform** *vb* (*They performed all the tasks which they were given*) carry out, do, execute, discharge, effect, fulfill.

**perfume** *n* (*a garden full of the perfume of roses*) scent, fragrance, aroma, smell, bouquet.

**peril** *n* (*animals in peril*) danger, risk, jeopardy, menace, threat.

**period** *n* **1** (*during the Tudor period of English history*) time, age, era, epoch. **2** (*Her condition worsened over a period of years*) time, space, interval, spell, stretch, span.

**perish** *vb* **1** (*The food perished in the heat*) go bad, go off, decay, rot, decompose. **2** (*villagers who perished in the earthquake*) die, be killed, lose one's life.

**permanent** *adj* (*The accident left him with a*

**permanent** *limp*) lasting, perpetual, persistent, enduring, abiding, eternal, endless, never-ending, unending.

**permission** *n* (*He took his father's car without permission*) authorization, leave, sanction, consent, assent, agreement, approval.

**permit** *vb* (*Her parents would not permit her to stay out late*) give permission to, allow, let, give leave, authorize, action, consent to, assent to, agree to.

**persecute** *vb* (*people who were persecuted for their religious beliefs*) oppress, abuse, maltreat, torment, torture, victimize.

**persevere** *vb* (*You must persevere in your attempts to get a job*) persist, keep at, keep on, continue, carry on, be resolute, be determined, be insistent.

**persistent** *adj* 1 (*their persistent attempts to buy the land*) determined, relentless, unrelenting, constant, continual, incessant, endless. 2 (*persistent people who will not give up trying*) persevering, determined, resolute, insistent, obstinate, tenacious.

**personal** *adj* 1 (*His reasons for being off work are purely personal*) private, confidential, individual, secret. 2 (*her personal interpretation of the piece of music*) individual, individualistic, idiosyncratic, peculiar.

**personality** *n* 1 (*She has a very pleasant personality*) nature, disposition, temperament, character. 2-(*It is a job for someone with personality*) character, charisma, magnetism, charm. 3 (*There were many TV personalities at the dinner*) celebrity, dignitary, famous name, VIP.

**personnel** *n* (*the person in the firm in charge of personnel*) human resources, staff, employees, workers, workforce.

**persuade** *vb* (*Could you try to persuade her to go?*) influence, induce, talk into, win over, prevail upon, cajole, wheedle.

**pessimistic** *adj* (*He has a pessimistic outlook on life*) gloomy, cynical, defeatist, fatalistic, resigned, distrustful.

**pest** *n* (*He thought the child was a pest*) nuisance, bother, irritant, trouble, worry, problem, inconvenience, trial.

**pet** *n* (*The boy is teased by the other pupils about being the teacher's pet*) favorite, darling, apple of one's eye.

**petty** *adj* (*have no time to discuss the petty details of the case*) trivial, trifling, minor, unimportant, inconsequential, slight.

**phobia** *n* (*She has a phobia about spiders*) aversion, fear, dread, horror, loathing, revulsion, (*inf*) hangup.

**pick** *vb* 1 (*They are picking fruit*) gather, collect, harvest, pull. 2 (*The little girls was asked to pick a toy*) choose, select, pick out, single out, opt for, plump for, decide upon, settle on. 3 (*The burglar*

*picked the lock*) break open, force, pry open.

**picture** *n* 1 (*a picture painted by a famous artist*) painting, drawing, sketch, likeness, portrait, illustration. 2 (*He was paid to take pictures at the wedding*) photograph, photo, snapshot. 3 (*The novel painted a distressing picture of Victorian England*) scene, view, vision, impression, description, portrayal, account, report. 4 (*a horror picture*) movie, motion picture.

**pie** *n* (*a piece of apple pie*) tart, quiche, pastry.

**pill** *n* (*medicine in the form of pills*) tablet, capsule.

**piece** *n* 1 (*put the pieces of the jigsaw together*) bit, part, section, segment, component, unit. 2 (*a quilt made of pieces of cloth*) length, bit, remnant, scrap. 3 (*a piece of pie*) bit, chunk, wedge, hunk, lump. 4 (*Each of his children will get a piece of his estate*) bit, share, slice, portion, percentage. 5-(*The valuable vase smashed to pieces*) bit, fragment, smithereens, shard. 6 (*an impressive piece of antique furniture*) example, sample, specimen, instance, illustration. 7 (*a musical piece*) work, creation, com-position, opus. 8 (*The journalist wrote a piece on the war*) article, item, story, report.

**pierce** *vb* 1 (*Did the knife pierce the skin?*) penetrate, puncture, prick, perforate, stab, pass through, enter. 2 (*pierce the piece of leather to make a leash for the dog*) perforate, bore, drill. 3 (*The cries of the bird pierced the air*) fill, pervade, penetrate.

**pile** *n* 1 (*dead leaves in piles around the park*) heap, mound, stack, collection, stockpile, mountain. 2 (*We have a pile of homework*) great deal, abundance, (*inf*) lots, (*inf*) oodles. 3 (*He made his pile forging money*) fortune, wealth, money.

**pillar** *n* (*the pillars at the front of the temple*) column, post, upright, support, pilaster.

**pin** *vb* 1 (*Can you pin the brooch to my dress?*) fasten, fix, secure, attach. 2 (*The man was pinned under the overturned tractor*) hold, press, pinion, restrain, immobilize.

**pinch** *vb* 1 (*She pinched her friend's arm to wake her up*) nip, tweak, squeeze. 3 (*Her new shoes are pinching her toes*) hurt, crush, squeeze. 4 (*She pinched a flower from the garden*) take, filch, pilfer, purloin, (*inf*) swipe.

**pious** *adj* (*pious members of the parish*) religious, godly, devout, god-fearing, righteous.

**pitch** *vb* 1 (*They pitched their tent in a field*) put up, set up, erect, raise. 2 (*The children began to pitch stones into the lake*) throw, cast, fling, hurl, toss, heave, (*inf*) chuck. 3 (*The ships were pitching in the high winds*) roll, rock, lurch, sway.

**pity** *n* 1 (*They felt pity for the poor orphans*) compassion, sympathy, commiseration, distress, sadness. 2-(*The tyrant showed the prisoners no pity*) mercy, leniency, kindness, clemency. 3 (*It was a pity that their bus was late*) shame, crying shame, misfortune.

**placard** *n* (*placards advertising the show*) poster, notice, sticker.

**place** *n* 1 (*This is the place where she lost the ring/the place where he built the houses*) spot, location, site, setting, position, situation, area, region. 2 (*She won third place in the competition*) position, grade, level, rank. 3 (*It was not his place to sort out the dispute*) responsibility, job, task, function, role. 4 (*The pupil returned to her place*) seat, position.

**plain** *adj* 1 (*It was plain to all of us that she was in pain*) clear, crystal-clear, obvious, evident, apparent, manifest, unmistakable, noticeable, conspicuous. 2 (*We need a plain statement of what happened*) clear, straightforward, simple, intelligible, lucid. 3 (*The style of decoration is very plain*) simple, restrained, bare, austere, stark, basic, unadorned, spartan. 4 (*She is very beautiful now and yet she was rather plain as a child*) unattractive, unprepossessing, ugly.

**plan** *n* 1 (*They have plans to expand the firm/ The prisoners have an escape plan*) scheme, strategy, tactics, system, method, project. 2-(*Their vacation plans have been ruined*) arrangements, schedule, program, procedure, method, system. 3 (*Their plan was to travel overnight*) aim, intention, objective, scheme, proposal. 4 (*The architect's plans for the new building are on show*) drawing, blueprint, representation, model.

**play** *vb* 1 (*Children need time to play*) amuse oneself, enjoy oneself, entertain oneself, have fun. 2 (*The children were playing in the back yard with the dog*) play games, frolic, romp, frisk, gambol, cavort. 3 (*He likes to play football*) take part in, engage in, be involved in, participate in. 4 (*Our team is playing against strong opposition*) compete against, take on, oppose, challenge, vie with, contend with. 5 (*She plays the piano*) perform on. 6 (*The children played tricks on their grandfather*) perform, carry out, do, execute, discharge. 6 (*She played Ophelia in 'Hamlet'*) play the part of, act the part of, perform, portray.

**plead** *vb* (*They pleaded for mercy*) beg, entreat, implore.

**pleasant** *adj* 1 (*It was a very pleasant occasion*) agreeable, enjoyable, pleasing, delightful, nice, good, lovely, entertaining, amusing 2 (*Our neighbors are very pleasant*) agreeable, friendly, amiable, affable, likeable, charming.

**please** vb 1 (*We were going to go to the theater but it is difficult to find a show that will please everyone*) give pleasure to, satisfy, suit, delight, amuse, entertain. 2 (*Whatever advice you give her she will do as she pleases*) wish, want, like, choose, prefer, see fit.

**pleasure** n 1 (*a gift that will bring their mother a great deal of pleasure*) happiness, joy, delight, enjoyment, amusement, entertainment, satisfaction. 2 (*one of the old man's few pleasures*) joy, delight, enjoyment, recreation, diversion.

**plentiful** adj (*plentiful supplies of fuel*) abundant, copious, ample, profuse, generous, liberal, large.

**plot** n 1 (*They uncovered a plot to assassinate the President*) conspiracy, intrigue. 2 (*The novel has a complicated plot*) theme, action, story, subject. 3 (*He grows potatoes on his vegetable plot*) garden, patch.

**plump** adj (*She was plump as a little girl*) chubby, tubby, fat.

**plunder** vb (*They crossed the border and plundered the enemy villages*) rob, raid, loot, pillage, lay waste.

**poetry** n (*He writes poetry as a hobby*) poems, verse, verses.

**point** n 1 (*The spear had a very sharp point*) tip, end, top. 2 (*She reached a point where she could not go on*) stage, position, situation, circumstances, time. 3 (*at some point during the meeting*) time, juncture, stage. 4 (*They discussed the various points in the report*) detail, item, particular, issue, subject, topic. 5 (*The speaker spoke at length but few people got the point of his talk*) meaning, significance, import, substance, gist, drift. 6 (*He took ages to get to the point when he was declaring them redundant*) main point, salient point, crux of the matter, crux, heart of the matter, (*inf*) nitty-gritty. 7 (*What is the point of this discussion?*) aim, purpose, intention, object, objective, goal. 8-(*That is one of the weak points of the argument/He has many good points*) aspect, feature, attribute, quality, characteristic, trait. 9 (*the team that has most points*) mark.

**point:—point out** vb (*We pointed out the benefits*) draw attention to, call attention to, identify, indicate, show, mention, specify.

**pointless** adj 1 (*It was pointless to continue the search after dark*) in vain, useless, futile, to no purpose, senseless, stupid 2 (*They made a few pointless comments*) worthless, meaningless, insignificant, irrelevant.

**poisonous** adj 1 (*an area with poisonous snakes*) venomous. 2 (*poisonous chemical substances*) toxic, deadly, lethal, fatal.

**poke** vb 1 (*The child tried to poke a pencil in the electric socket*) jab, push, thrust, shove, stick. 2 (*He poked his friend in the ribs to get him to stop laughing*) jab, prod, dig, nudge, elbow.

**polish** vb 1 (*She has to polish the furniture*) wax, shine, buff up, burnish. 2 (*She wants to polish up her French before she goes on vacation*) improve, revise, perfect, brush up.

**polite** adj 1 (*Children taught to be polite*) well-mannered, mannerly, courteous, civil, well-bred, wellbehaved. 2 (*the way things are done in polite society*) well-bred, civilized, cultured, refined, genteel.

**pollute** vb (*chemicals that pollute the water*) contaminate, taint, infect, adulterate, poison, befoul, dirty.

**pompous** adj (*They were kept out of the building by a pompous official*) selfimportant, presumptuous, overbearing, egotistic, officious.

**poor** n 1 (*poor people with not enough money to live on*) poverty-stricken, penniless, needy, in need, impoverished, deprived, destitute, hard up, badly off. 2 (*It was a poor attempt*) inadequate, unsatisfactory, inferior.

**popular** adj 1 (*The place is popular with young people*) liked, favored, approved, in demand, in fashion. 2 (*ideas that were popular at the time*) current, accepted, widespread, common, general.

**population** n (*The population of the area is mainly elderly*) people, inhabitants, residents, community.

**portion** n 1 (*Each of his children got an equal portion of his fortune*) part, share, division, piece, bit, quota, percentage. 2 (*The restaurant serves children's portions on request*) serving, helping, quantity. 3 (*They bought four portions of the cake*) piece, bit, slice, section, segment, lump, chunk.

**position** n 1 (*He had been sitting in an uncomfortable position*) posture, attitude, pose. 2 (*try to find the position of the wrecked ship*) location, whereabouts. 3 (*These trees grow well in a shady position*) situation, location, place, spot, area, setting. 4 (*He is in a very fortunate position*) situation, state, circumstances, condition. 5 (*the position of the team in the league tables*) place, level, grade, status, rank, ranking. 6 (*The position of manager is vacant*) situation, post, job, role. 7 (*people of position in society*) rank, status, influence, standing, prestige.

**positive** adj 1 (*She is positive that she saw him*) sure, certain, confident, convinced. 2 (*try to give some positive criticism of the essays*) constructive, helpful, useful. 3 (*He should try to have a more positive attitude to life*) optimistic, hopeful, confident, determined. 4 (*The results of the medical tests were positive*) affirmative. 5 (*He is a positive fool*) absolute, utter, complete, total, out-and-out.

**possess** vb 1 (*They do not possess a car*) own, be the owner of, have. 2-(*He thought that he was possessed by devils*) control, dominate, influence, bewitch.

**possessions** npl (*Our apartment is full of her possessions*) belongings, property, goods, things, personal effects.

**possible** adj 1 (*It is not possible to get there on time*) feasible, practicable, achievable. 2 (*one possible solution*) likely, potential, conceivable, imaginable.

**post** n 1 (*He hammered in posts to make a fence*) stake, pole, upright. 2 (*The post has already been filled*) job, position, appointment, situation.

**postpone** vb (*They have had to postpone the wedding*) put off, put back, defer, delay, put on ice.

**pounce** vb (*The cat pounced on the mouse*) swoop, spring, leap, jump.

**pound** vb 1 (*She pounded the seeds to a powder*) crush, smash, beat, pulverize, grind. 2 (*She pounded her father's chest with her fists*) beat, pummel, strike, hit, hammer. 3 (*Her heart was pounding*) beat heavily, throb, pulse, pulsate, palpitate. 4 (*They pounded along the sidewalk*) tramp, tread heavily.

**pour** vb 1 (*Water began to pour from the burst pipe*) rush, gush, stream, spout, spurt, flow. 2 (*pour cream over the pie*) let flow, splash, spill. 3 (*It was pouring*) come down in torrents.

**poverty** n need, want, deprivation, hardship.

**power** n 1 (*the power of speech*) ability, capability, capacity, faculty. 2-(*The tyrant had her in his power*) control, command, rule, domination, mastery, authority. 3 (*people of power gaining victory over the weak*) powerfulness, strength, force, forcefulness, might, vigor, effectiveness. 4 (*electricity and other kinds of power*) energy.

**powerful** adj 1 (*weight-lifters of powerful build*) strong, sturdy, strapping, tough, mighty. 2 (*the most powerful members of the community*) dominant, controlling, influential, authoritative, strong, forceful, vigorous. 3 (*She drew up a powerful argument against the scheme*) strong, forceful, effective, convincing, persuasive, compelling.

**practical** adj 1 (*They want people with practical experience of the job*) applied, experienced, skilled, handson. 2 (*She is very bright academically but not at all practical*) sensible, down-to-earth, realistic, businesslike. 3 (*wear practical footwear for walking*) sensible, functional, useful, utilitarian.

**practice** vb 1 (*She has to practice her piano performances*) rehearse, go over, run through, work at, prepare, train for, study for, polish up. **2** (*She seems quite unable to practice selfcontrol*) carry out, perform, execute, do. **3** (*They practice medicine*) work in, be engaged in.

**praise** *vb* **1** (*They praised her performance*) applaud, express admiration for, admire, compliment, pay tribute to, sing the praises of. **2**-(*praise God*) worship, glorify, honor, exalt.

**precarious** *adj* **1** (*It was rather a precarious journey through the jungle*) risky, dangerous, hazardous, perilous. **2** (*a precarious way to earn one's living*) risky, unreliable, uncertain, unsure, chancy, unpredictable.

**precious** *adj* **1** (*a necklace full of precious stones*) valuable, costly, expensive. **2** (*family photographs that are very precious to her/her precious memories*) valued, treasured, cherished, prized, beloved, dear.

**precise** *adj* **1** (*We need to know her precise words*) exact, actual, literal. **2** (*at that precise moment*) very, exact, actual, particular. **3** (*He is a very precise person*) exact, careful, accurate, meticulous.

**predict** *vb* (*She claimed to be able to predict the future*) foretell, forecast, foresee, prophesy.

**predominant** *adj* (*Red is the predominant color in the pattern*) chief, main, principal, dominant.

**prefer** *vb* **1** (*She prefers the blue pattern to the yellow*) like better, favor, choose, select, pick, opt for, plump for. **2** (*They could drive but they prefer to go by train*) like better, would rather, would just as soon, favor, choose.

**prejudiced** *adj* (*They have a prejudiced attitude towards people of a-different race/prejudiced employers*) biased, discriminatory, partial, partisan, bigoted, intolerant, unfair, unjust.

**premature** *adj* (*the premature birth of the baby*) too soon, too early.

**premonition** *n* (*She had a premonition that something tragic was going to happen*) feeling, foreboding, presentiment, intuition, hunch.

**prepare** *vb* **1** (*They must prepare their proposal to present it to the committee*) get ready, arrange, assemble, draw up, put together. **2**-(*prepare a meal*) make, cook, put together.

**presence** *n* **1** (*the presence of chemical waste in the drinking water*) existence. **2** (*They are asking for our presence at the meeting*) attendance. **3** (*They felt inadequate in the presence of the great man*) company, vicinity, proximity.

**present** *adj* **1** (*pollutants were present in the water supply*) existing, existent. **2** (*There should be a nurse present*) in attendance, here, there, on hand. **3** (*in the present situation*) current, existing, present-day, contemporary.

**present** *n* **1** (*thinking about the present rather than the future*) now, today, the present moment. **2** (*a present on her birthday/a present for all their hard work*) gift, reward.

**presentable** *adj* (*make yourself presentable before you see the Principal*) tidy, well-groomed, smart, spruce.

**preserve** *vb* **1** (*try to preserve the old village traditions*) keep, keep up, continue, maintain, uphold, conserve. **2** (*a substance to preserve wood*) protect, conserve. **3**-(*They had to preserve the city from enemy attack*) protect, save, safeguard, keep, defend. **4** (*preserve some money for one's old age*) keep, put aside, save, retain.

**press** *vb* **1** (*You should press the door bell again*) push. **2** (*villagers pressing grapes to make wine*) crush, squeeze, compress. **3** (*need an iron to press her skirt*) iron, smooth. **3** (*The mother pressed the tired child against her*) clasp, hold, pull, squeeze, crush, hug. **4** (*They are pressing the committee for a decision*) urge, entreat, implore, pressure, put pressure on.

**pressure** *n* **1** (*They had to exert a great deal of pressure to get the door open*) force, strength, weight. **2** (*She tried to withstand the pressure of her parents to get her to stay at home*) force, compulsion, constraint, duress. **3** (*the pressures of modern living*) strain, stress, tension.

**prestige** *n* (*He does not want to lose his prestige in the community*) status, kudos, standing, importance, reputation, esteem, influence.

**pretend** *vb* (*He was not sleeping at all—he was just pretending*) put on an act, put it on, play-act, sham, fake, dissemble.

**pretense** *n* **1** (*She did not really faint—it was just pretense*) dissembling, sham, faking, make-believe. **2** (*They left on the pretense that they were going to a meeting*) pretext, excuse.

**pretty** *adj* (*She is a very pretty girl*) attractive, good-looking, lovely, nicelooking.

**pretty** *adv* (*She was feeling pretty annoyed*) rather, quite, very.

**prevent** *vb* **1** (*Her parents tried to prevent her marrying him*) stop, halt, restrain, prohibit, bar, hinder, obstruct, impede, hamper. **2** (*try to prevent the spread of the infection*) stop, halt, arrest, check, block, check, hinder, obstruct, impede.

**previous** *adj* **1** (*the previous chairman*) former, preceding, ex-, foregoing. **2** (*We met on a previous occasion*) earlier, prior, former.

**price** *n* (*ask the price of the bookcase*) cost, charge.

**prick** *vb* **1** (*The child pricked the balloon with a pin*) pierce, puncture, stab, gash. **2** (*She pricked her finger on the needle*) jab, jag, stab, wound. **3** (*Their eyes began to prick in the smoke from the fire*) smart, sting, tingle.

**pride** *n* **1** (*They take pride in their work*) satisfaction, gratification, pleasure. **2** (*Her pride was hurt when he left her for another girl*) self-esteem, self-respect, ego. **3** (*He is guilty of the sin of pride*) conceit, vanity, arrogance, egotism, selfimportance, (*inf*) big-headedness.

**prim** *adj* (*He is much too prim to join in the fun*) proper, demure, straitlaced, stuffy, starchy, prudish, (*inf*) goodygoody.

**prime** *adj* **1** (*meat of prime quality*) top, best, first-class, superior, choice, select. **2** (*His prime ambition was to make money*) chief, main, principal. **3** (*The prime cause of the infection was the water*) basic, fundamental.

**prime** *n* (*in the prime of life*) peak, height, zenith, acme.

**principal** *adj* **1** (*the principal members of the organization*) chief, leading, foremost, dominant. **2** (*the principal issues to be discussed*) main, major, key, essential.

**principle** *n* **1** (*the principles of socialism*) idea, theory, philosophy, basis, code. **2** (*He is a man of principle*) morals, ethics, integrity, uprightness, honor.

**prison** *n* (*He was sent to prison for theft*) jail.

**private** *adj* **1** (*a private discussion between committee members*) confidential, secret, privileged, (*inf*) hushhush. **2** (*She wished to be private to think about things*) undisturbed, uninterrupted, alone, solitary. **3** (*She would not disclose-her private thoughts*) personal, intimate, secret. **4** (*He found a private place in the large garden*) secluded, quiet, out-ofthe-way.

**privileged** *adj* (*She comes from a privileged background*) advantaged, favored, elite.

**probable** *adj* (*the probable outcome/It is probable that he will lose*) likely, expected.

**problem** *n* **1** (*an arithmetic problem*) question, puzzle, poser, brain-teaser. **2** (*They have had a few financial problems*) difficulty, trouble, complication, predicament.

**proceed** *vb* **1** (*We were unsure as to how to proceed*) act, take action, move, progress. **2** (*We proceeded up the mountain as fast as we could*) make one's way, carry on, go on, advance, go forward, progress.

**process** *n* **1** (*the manufacturing process*) operation, activity, stages. **2** (*a new process for cleaning carpets*) system, method, technique, procedure.

**process: in the process of (something)** (*They are in the process of moving house*) in the midst of, in the course of.

**procession** *n* (*a procession to celebrate the town's centenary*) parade, march, cavalcade.

**produce** vb **1** (*an agricultural area-that produces a wide variety of crops*) yield, bear, give. **2** (*a cat-that has just produced kittens*) give birth to, bear. **3** (*His article produced an angry response*) cause, give rise to, evoke, generate, start, spark off. **4**-(*The country produces a great many goods for export*) make, manufacture, turn out. **5** (*The police have-produced proof that he is guilty*)-bring forward, present, advance.

**product** n (*a firm specializing in electronic products*) commodity, goods, wares, merchandise.

**profit** n (*They made little profit from the sale*) gain, return, yield, proceeds, income.

**profitable** adj (*The business is no longer profitable*) profit-making, moneymaking, commercial, lucrative.

**program** n **1** (*watch the television program*) production, show, performance, broadcast. **2** (*she has started an exercise program*) plan, course.

**progress** n **1** (*They have been discussing the matter for ages but they have made little progress*) headway, advancement. **2** (*Her work shows no sign of progress*) headway, advancement, improvement.

**project** n (*take part in a project to build a new swimming pool*) plan, undertaking, enterprise, venture, operation.

**prominent** adj **1** (*prominent members of the government*) leading, chief, foremost, eminent, top. **2**-(*The palm trees are a prominent feature of the area*) striking, conspicuous, noticeable, obvious, eye-catching. **3** (*She has prominent cheekbones*) protruding, obvious.

**promise** n **1** (*She made a promise that she would be there*) pledge, vow, bond, assurance, commitment. **2** (*A young skater of promise*) potential, talent, flair. **3**-(*There was a promise of good times to come*) indication, sign, suggestion, hint.

**promote** vb **1** (*They plan to promote him to manager*) upgrade, elevate. **2** (*The company is promoting a new line of perfume*) advertise, publicize, push, (*inf*) plug. **3** (*They need volunteers to promote the cause of animals' rights*) support, champion, further, advance, help, assist, boost.

**prompt** adj (*They will expect a prompt reply*) rapid, swift, quick, fast, speedy, immediate, instant.

**proof** n **1** (*The police had little proof of his guilt*) evidence, confirmation, corroboration. **2** (*The workmen had no proof of their identity*) evidence, verification, authentication, certification.

**proper** adj **1** (*the proper behavior on such an occasion*) right, correct, suitable, fitting, appropriate, acceptable, conventional. **2** (*put the plates in their proper place in the-kitchen*) right, correct, usual, own.

**property** n (*items that were his property*) belongings, possessions, things, goods.

**proportion** n **1** (*an area with a high proportion of agricultural workers*) ratio, distribution. **2** (*He gives a large proportion of his earnings to the church*) part, share, percentage, measure.

**propose** vb **1** (*We are proposing to go by train*) plan, intend, aim, suggest. **2** (*They proposed some alterations to the system*) put forward, submit, recommend, advocate. **3** (*They proposed him as chairman*) put forward, nominate, suggest.

**prosper** vb (*The family began to prosper*) thrive, do well, succeed, flourish, make good.

**prosperous** adj (*prosperous people with a great deal of money to spend*) well-off, wealthy, affluent, rich, successful.

**protect** vb (*They wished to protect the child from danger*) safeguard, guard, keep, preserve, shield, defend.

**protest** n (*They lodged a protest against the closure of the school*) objection, opposition, complaint, disagreement, dissent, outcry.

**proud** adj **1** (*He is rich and now too-proud to talk to his former neighbors*) conceited, vain, arrogant, egotistical, haughty, boastful, supercilious, (*inf*) snooty. **2** (*He was proud of his son's achievement*) gratified, appreciative, pleased, happy.

**prove** vb (*evidence that proved his innocence*) establish, determine, confirm, corroborate.

**provide** vb **1** (*They provided the-money for the trip*) give, supply, donate, contribute. **2** (*a job that provides opportunity for travel*) give, grant, offer, afford, present.

**prowl** vb (*burglars prowling round the house*) roam, skulk, slink, sneak.

**pry** vb (*She likes to pry into her neighbors' affairs*) interfere, meddle, snoop.

**public** adj **1** (*public feeling is against the new road*) popular, general, common. **2** (*make their views public*) known, plain. **3** (*public figures*) well-known, prominent, eminent, influential.

**publicity** n **1** (*She only did it to get publicity in the press*) public attention, public interest. **2** (*The reception was part of the publicity for her book*) promotion, advertisement, advertising, (*inf*) hype.

**pull** vb **1** (*He pulled the nail out of the wall*) pull out, draw out, take out, extract, remove. **2** (*They began to pull the rope*) haul, tug, (*inf*) yank. **3** (*The child was pulling a toy train behind him*) haul, drag, trail, tow, tug. **3** (*The athlete has pulled a muscle*) strain, sprain, wrench.

**punch** vb (*The boy punched him on the nose*) strike, hit, box.

**punctual** adj (*It is important to be punctual at meetings*) on time, prompt, in good time.

**punish** vb **1** (*The boy was punished for damaging the car*) discipline, chastise, smack, slap. **2** (*criminals punished for doing wrong*) discipline, penalize.

**puny** adj (*too puny to fight against such a strong opponent*) weak, weakly, frail, feeble, undersized, stunted, slight, small.

**pure** adj **1** (*breathing in the pure mountain air*) clean, clear, fresh, unpolluted, uncontaminated, untainted, wholesome. **2** (*dishes of pure gold*) unalloyed, unmixed, unadulterated, true, real. **3** (*people who are expected to be of pure-character*) virtuous, honorable, moral, ethical, righteous, blameless, uncorrupted, impeccable, flawless, spotless. **4** (*It was pure folly to do-that*) sheer, utter,-absolute, downright, total, complete, out-and-out. **5** (*The students are studying pure science*) theoretical, abstract.

**purpose** n **1** (*What was the purpose of their inquiries?*) reason, point, motivation, cause, grounds, justification. **2** (*The young man should try to get a purpose in life*) aim, goal,-objective, object, target, aspiration, ambition. **3** (*The search for the missing goods lacked purpose*)-determination, resoluteness, resolve, firmness, perseverance. **4** (*The talks went on all night but to little purpose*) worth, use, usefulness, value, advantage, benefit, avail.

**pursue** vb **1** (*The policeman pursued the bank robber*) go after, run after, follow, chase, give chase to, trail, stalk, shadow, (*inf*) tail. **2** (*The police are pursuing a line of inquiry in the murder case*) follow, proceed with, go on with, continue with. **3** (*She wishes to pursue a career in medicine*) follow, be engaged in, work in. **4** (*They are pursuing their goal of making a fortune*) strive towards, be intent on.

**push** vb **1** (*The little boy pushed his friend into the pool*) shove, thrust, propel, ram, drive. **2** (*She pushed her way to the front of the crowd*) force, shove, thrust, press, elbow, shoulder, jostle. **3** (*push the button to start the machine*) press. **4** (*He said that his parents pushed him into going to college*) force, coerce, press, dragoon, browbeat, prod, goad, urge. **5** (*The company held a reception to push their new product*) promote, advertise, publicize, boost, (*inf*) plug.

**put** vb **1** (*They were asked to put the books on the desk*) place, lay, set down, deposit. **2** (*They tried to put the blame on their friend*) place, lay, attach, attribute, assign. **3** (*She put the value of the anti- que vase at $4000*) assess, evaluate, calculate, reckon, guess, (*inf*) guesstimate. **4** (*You should put the idea to your parents*) put forward,

**propose**, present, submit. **5** (*He put a large sum of money on the horse*) place, bet, wager, gamble.

**puzzle** *vb* (*Her parents were puzzled by the change in her behavior*) perplex, mystify, baffle, bewilder, nonplus, stump.

# Q

**qualified** *adj* **1** (*a qualified doctor/ She is qualified to teach*) trained, certified, equipped. **2** (*They gave the-plan qualified approval*) limited,-conditional, modified, restricted.

**quarrel** *n* (*The sisters have had a quarrel*) disagreement, argument, row, fight, difference of opinion, dispute, wrangle, altercation, misunderstanding.

**question** *n* **1** (*She was unable to answer his questions*) inquiry, query, interrogation. **2** (*We must consider the question of safety*) issue, matter, point, subject, topic.

**quick** *adj* **1** (*You will have to be quick to catch the bus*) fast, swift, rapid, speedy. **2** (*She wants a quick reply to her letter*) prompt, without delay, immediate. **3** (*She took a quick look at the instructions*) hasty, brief, fleeting, cursory.

**quiet** *adj* (*It was very quiet in the church*) hushed, silent, soundless, noiseless. **2** (*He spoke in quiet tones*) soft, low, hushed, whispered, inaudible. **3** (*lead a quiet life in the country*) peaceful, tranquil, calm, serene, placid, untroubled, undisturbed. **4** (*They are both rather quiet people*) reserved, taciturn, uncommunicative, reticent, placid, unexcitable. **5** (*She dresses in quiet colors*) restrained, unobtrusive, muted, subdued, subtle, conservative, sober, dull. **6**-(*They kept the news of their engagement quiet*) secret, confidential, private, (*inf*) hush-hush.

**quit** *vb* **1** (*He quit his job last month*) leave, give up, resign from. **2** (*He quit smoking a year ago*) give up, swear off, abstain from, desist from.

**quite** *adj* **1** (*Has he quite recovered after his accident?*) completely, totally, entirely, fully, wholly. **2** (*She is quite good at tennis but she will not win the match*) fairly, relatively, moderately, somewhat, rather.

# R

**race** *vb* (*runners racing towards the finishing post*) run, sprint, dash, speed, bolt, dart.

**race** *n* (*Humankind is divided into races*) ethnic group, racial division.

**racial** *adj* (*racial discrimination*) ethnic, race-related.

**racism** *n* racial discrimination, racial prejudice.

**rack** *n* (*a spice rack*) frame, framework, stand, shelf, support, holder.

**racket** *n* **1** (*We couldn't sleep because of the racket from the party next door*) din, noise, commotion, row, hubbub, disturbance. **2** (*They think he was involved in a drugs racket*) fraud, criminal scheme.

**radiant** *adj* **1** (*They could not see properly in the radiant light*) brilliant, shining, bright, gleaming, irradiant. **2** (*The winners looked radiant*) joyful, elated, ecstatic, delighted.

**radiate** *vb* **1** (*The fire radiated a fierce heat*) send out, emit, disperse. **2** (*roads radiating out from downtown*) branch out, spread out, diverge.

**radical** *adj* **1** (*There have been radical changes in their business methods*) thorough, complete, total, sweeping, exhaustive, drastic, violent. **2** (*She holds radical political views*) extremist, fundamental.

**rage** *n* **1** (*She went into a rage when they criticized her*) temper, tantrum. **2** (*She was filled with rage at the sight of her rival*) fury, anger, annoyance, exasperation.

**rags** *npl* (*The homeless woman was dressed in rags*) tatters.

**raid** *n* **1** (*enemy raids on the town*) attack, assault, onslaught, invasion, foray, sortie. **2** (*a bank raid*) robbery, break-in.

**railing** *n* (*the railing round the balcony*) rail, paling, barrier, fence.

**rain** *vb* (*It was raining during the match*) pour, drizzle.

**rainy** *adj* (*things to do on a rainy weekend*) wet, damp, showery, drizzly.

**raise** *vb* **1** (*They need a crane to raise the wrecked car*) lift, hoist, heave up, elevate. **2** (*The news raised our hopes*) increase, boost, build up, stimulate. **3** (*They had to raise the temperature in the greenhouse*) put up, increase, augment, intensify. **4** (*The local hotels raise their prices in the summer*) put up, increase, inflate, (*inf*) hike up. **5**-(*They raise turkeys*) breed, rear. **6**-(*He raises cereal crops*) grow, cultivate, produce, farm. **7** (*They have raised several children*) rear, bring up, nurture.

**rake** *vb* **1** (*rake up the leaves in the fall*) scrape up, collect, gather. **2**-(*They raked the soil before planting the seeds*) smooth, level, flatten, even out. **3** (*The burglars raked through her things*) search, hunt, ransack, rummage, rifle.

**rally** *n* **1** (*They held a rally to support the governor's campaign*) meeting, mass meeting, gathering, assembly, convention, demonstration. **2** (*Stock market prices fell but then there was a sudden rally*) recovery, revival, improvement, comeback.

**rally** *vb* **1** (*The crowd rallied to support the governor*) assemble, gather, convene, unite. **2** (*The invalid was seriously ill but she has rallied*) recover, recuperate, revive, get better, improve, pull through, take a turn for the better.

**ram** *vb* **1** (*ram the clothes into the suitcase in a hurry*) force, cram, stuff, thrust. **2** (*His car rammed ours*) hit, strike, run into, collide with, bump.

**ramble** *vb* **1** (*They rambled over the hills for the afternoon*) walk, hike, wander, roam. **2** (*The professor rambled on without the students understanding a word*) babble, drone.

**rampage** *vb* (*children rampaging around their neighbor's back yard*) rush, charge, tear, run riot.

**ramshackle** *adj* (*They bought a ramshackle farm house and are going to rebuild it*) tumbledown, brokendown, run-down, dilapidated, derelict, crumbling.

**random** *adj* (*ask a random selection of the population how they were going to vote*) haphazard, chance, arbitrary, indiscriminate, unsystematic, unmethodical, unplanned, accidental.

**range** *n* **1** (*a range of mountains*) row, line, chain. **2** (*It was not within their range of vision*) scope, field, area, limit, reach. **3** (*The store stocks a wide range of goods*) selection, assortment, variety.

**range** *vb* **1** (*prices range from $10 to $200*) extend, stretch, go, vary. **2** (*The books are ranged according to subject*) arrange, classify, categorize, group, class, organize. **3** (*sheep ranging over the hills*) roam, rove, ramble, wander, stray.

**rank** *n* **1** (*What is the soldier's rank?*) grade, position. **2** (*The salary in the organization is according to rank*) grade, level, position, status. **3** (*The people in the big house were people of rank*) nobility, aristocracy, eminence, power, influence.

**ransack** *vb* **1** (*Raiders ransacked the stores after the explosion*) loot, plunder, rob, rifle, pillage. **2**-(*We ransacked the house to try to find the lost passport*) search, rummage, scour, turn upside down.

**rap** *vb* **1** (*She rapped on the door*) knock, tap, bang, hit, strike. **2** (*The book was rapped by the critics*) criticize, blame, reprimand.

**rapid** *adj* (*They set off at a rapid pace*) swift, fast, quick, speedy, hurried, hasty, brisk, lively.

**rapture** *n* (*their rapture at the birth of their child*) joy, ecstasy, bliss, euphoria, delight.

**rare** *adj* **1** (*The wild flower was a rare specimen*) unusual, uncommon, out of the ordinary, atypical, remarkable. **2** (*He made one of his rare appearances*) infrequent, few and far between, sparse, sporadic.

**rascal** *n* **1** (*The child was a real little-rascal*)

imp, scamp, scalawag. **2**-(*Her husband is a rascal who is always in trouble with the police*) rogue, ne'erdo-well, good-for-nothing, scoundrel, villain.

**rash** *adj* (*Leaving her job to go round the world proved to be a rash decision*) impetuous, reckless, hasty, impulsive, unthinking, incautious, imprudent, foolhardy.

**rash** *n* **1** (*She woke up with a rash on her face*) spots, redness, eruption, hives. **2** (*There has been a rash of car thefts in the area*) spate, outbreak, wave, flood, series, run, plague, epidemic.

**rasping** *adj* (*She has a rasping voice/the rasping noise of a knife on metal*) grating, discordant, jarring, harsh, rough, gruff, croaky.

**rate** *n* **1** (*They walked at a very fast rate*) pace, speed, tempo, velocity. **2** (*the bank's rate of interest*) ratio, proportion, scale, degree. **3**-(*The hotel is charging its winter rates*) price, charge, cost, fee, payment.

**rate** *vb* **1** (*How would you rate the team's performance?*) judge, assess, evaluate, measure, weigh up, rank, class. **2** (*She rates more respect from them*) deserve, merit, be entitled to.

**rather** *adv* **1** (*She would rather go than stay*) for preference, just as soon, from choice. **2** (*She is pretty rather than beautiful*) more. **3** (*She tends to be rather blunt but is really rather kind*) quite, fairly, somewhat, slightly.

**ratify** *vb* (*The two sides still have to ratify the agreement*) confirm, endorse, sign, approve, sanction.

**ratio** *n* (*the ratio of teachers to students in the school*) proportion, percentage, fraction.

**rational** *adj* **1** (*It seemed a rational decision*) sensible, reasonable, logical, sound, intelligent, wise, judicious. **2** (*His mind has been affected but he has a few rational moments*) sane, balanced, lucid, coherent.

**rattle** *vb* **1** (*The windows rattled in the wind*) bang, clatter, clank, jangle. **2** (*She rattled the door knocker*) bang, knock, rap. **3** (*The speaker was obviously rattled by some of the questions from the audience*) agitate, disturb, fluster, upset, shake.

**raucous** *adj* (*the raucous singing of the drunk men*) strident, shrill, grating, jarring, discordant, piercing.

**ravenous** *adj* (*They were ravenous after walking all day*) famished, starving, hungry.

**raw** *adj* **1** (*She prefers to eat raw vegetables*) uncooked, fresh. **2** (*raw sugar*) unrefined, unprocessed, crude, natural. **3** (*She has a raw place on her elbow from when she fell over*) red, sore, inflamed, tender, abraded, grazed. **4** (*They are raw recruits who have joined the army*) inexperienced, untrained, unskilled, callow, green. **5** (*It

was a raw winter's day*) cold, chilly, bitter.

**ray** *n* **1** (*The rays of light showed up the dust on the furniture*) beam, shaft, streak, gleam, flash. **2** (*There did not seem to be a ray of hope left*) glimmer, flicker, trace, indication, suggestion.

**reach** *vb* **1** (*He reached his hand out for the book*) stretch, extend. **2**-(*The child could not reach the door handle*) get hold of, grasp, touch. **3** (*We finally reached our destination*) get to, arrive at. **4** (*He has not reached the required standard*) get to, achieve, attain.

**react** *vb* **1** (*How did he react when he discovered that she had gone?*) behave, act, respond. **2** (*The teenagers are reacting against their parents' beliefs*) rebel against.

**read** *vb* **1** (*She read a book while she waited*) peruse, study, pore over, browse through. **2** (*Can you read his handwriting?*) decipher, make out. **3** (*They read his silence as consent*) interpret, take to mean.

**ready** *adj* **1** (*The meal is ready*) prepared, completed. **2** (*They are ready for battle*) prepared, equipped, organized, all set. **3** (*Her neighbors are always ready to help*) willing, eager, keen, inclined, disposed. **4**-(*She was ready to collapse when she got to the foot of the mountain*) about to, on the point of, in danger of. **5** (*She always has a ready answer*) prompt, quick, rapid, swift, speedy. **6** (*Have you got your ticket ready?*) available, to hand, accessible.

**real** *adj* **1** (*things connected with the real world*) actual, factual. **2** (*The coat was made of real leather*) genuine, authentic. **3** (*She showed signs of real emotion*) genuine, authentic, sincere, unfeigned, honest, truthful. **4** (*He has been a real friend*) true, sincere.

**realistic** *adj* **1** (*The model of the bear was very realistic*) lifelike, true-to-life, naturalistic, authentic. **2** (*He has to try to be realistic about his job prospects*) practical, down-to-earth, matter-offact, sensible, level-headed, unromantic, no-nonsense.

**realize** *vb* **1** (*We began to realize that she was ill*) understand, grasp, take in, become aware, appreciate, recognize. **2** (*I hope that she realizes her dreams*) fulfill, achieve, attain, accomplish.

**really** *adv* **1** (*It was a really beautiful day*) truly, genuinely, undoubtedly, unquestionably, indeed. **2** (*The performer is dressed as a woman but is really a man*) in fact, in actual fact, in truth.

**rear** *n* **1** (*They sat at the rear of the train*) back. **2** (*They were at the rear of the line for the tickets*) back, tail, end.

**rear** *vb* **1** (*She reared three children by herself*) bring up, raise, care for. **2** (*The farmer rears turkeys*) breed, raise, keep.

**reason** *n* **1** (*There seemed no reason for his behavior*) grounds, cause, basis, motive,

justification. **2** (*The old man has lost his reason*) sanity, mind.

**reasonable** *adj* **1** (*It seemed a reasonable thing to do*) logical, rational, practical, sensible, intelligent, wise, sound. **2** (*I thought that he was quite a reasonable person*) fair, just, decent, unbiased. **3** (*The prices in the new restaurant were quite reasonable*) inexpensive, moderate, modest, cheap.

**rebel** *vb* **1** (*The crew are rebelling*) mutiny, riot, revolt, rise up. **2** (*teenagers rebelling against their parents' authority*) defy, disobey, react against.

**rebellion** *n* (*They joined in a rebellion against the government*) revolt, revolution, insurrection, uprising, rising, riot.

**rebellious** *adj* (*the rebellious troops/the rebellious children*) defiant, disobedient, unruly, unmanageable, intractable, mutinous, insurgent.

**rebuke** *vb* (*Her teacher rebuked her for being late*) reprimand, scold, chide, admonish, rap, (*inf*) tell off.

**recall** *vb* **1** (*She was unable to recall his name*) call to mind, remember, recollect, think of. **2** (*The manufacturers have recalled a batch of cars with faulty brakes*) call back, withdraw.

**recede** *vb* **1** (*The flood water began to recede*) go back, retreat, subside, ebb. **2** (*The danger seems to have receded*) grow less, lessen, fade, diminish.

**receive** *vb* **1** (*She said that she mailed the goods but we never received them*) get, be in receipt of. **2** (*She received many benefits from the arrangement*) get, obtain, acquire, meet with. **3** (*She received treatment for cancer*) get, experience, undergo. **4** (*She got ready to receive her dinner guests*) welcome, greet, entertain.

**recent** *adj* (*The doctor tries to keep up with recent medical developments*) new, fresh, latest, modern, up-to-theminute.

**recite** *vb* (*The little girl was asked to recite a poem*) say, repeat, speak, deliver.

**reckless** *adj* (*He later regretted his reckless action*) rash, careless, thoughtless, inattentive, incautious, irresponsible, negligent.

**reclaim** *vb* **1** (*They went to the police station to reclaim their property*) get back, recover, retrieve. **2** (*They reclaimed desert land for farming*) get back, recover, retrieve, regain, restore, save, salvage, rescue.

**recline** *vb* (*The invalid reclined on a sofa*) lie down, lie, stretch out, lean back, be recumbent, rest, repose, lounge.

**recognize** *vb* **1** (*I failed to recognize my cousin after all these years*) know, know again, identify, recall, call to mind, recollect, remember. **2**-(*The authorities are refusing to recognize his claim to the title*) acknowledge, accept, allow, grant, validate. **3** (*He recognized that he had been at fault) realize, be aware, appreciate, admit, acknowledge. 4-(His genius as a composer was not recognized in his lifetime) appreciate, honor, pay homage to, reward.

**recoil** vb (He recoiled when he realized that his fellow thief had a gun) flinch, shrink, draw back, wince.

**recollect** vb (I cannot recollect his name) remember, recall, call to mind, think of.

**recommend** vb 1 (He recommended a cure for a cold) commend, advocate, speak favorably of, approve, vouch for. 2 (They recommend caution in that case) advise, urge.

**reconcile** vb 1 (The couple separated for a time but have now been reconciled) bring together, reunite. 2 (They quarreled but have now reconciled their differences) settle, resolve, put to rights. 3 (We have now reconciled ourselves to our misfortune) resign oneself, accept, make the best of it.

**record** n 1 (He is using local records to write a history of the area) register, documents, information, data, chronicles, annals. 2 (She kept a record of her vacation expenses) account, note, description, report, diary, register. 3 (She played a dance record) album.

**record** vb 1 (All births, marriages and deaths must be recorded) register, enter, note, document, minute, catalog. 2 (The group have recorded their second album) make, cut, tape, videotape.

**recount** vb (They recounted the tale of their adventure) tell, relate, narrate, unfold, repeat.

**recover** vb 1 (She has been seriously ill but she is now recovering) get well, get better, recuperate, improve, rally, pull through. 2 (They recovered some of their stolen property) get back, regain, recoup, retrieve, reclaim, repossess, redeem. 3 (They recovered land from the sea) reclaim, restore, salvage, save.

**recreation** n 1 (His recreations include windsurfing as well as painting) hobby, pastime, diversion, amusement, distraction. 2 (What does he do for recreation?) leisure, relaxation, amusement, entertainment, fun, pleasure, diversion, distraction.

**recruit** vb (The club is hoping to recruit new members) enroll, enlist, sign up, take on.

**recur** vb (His illness has recurred) come back, return, reappear.

**recurrent** adj (a recurrent fault) recurring, repeated, repetitive, periodic, frequent.

**recycle** vb (recycle paper products) reuse, use again, reprocess, salvage.

**red** adj 1 (She was red with embarrassment) flushed, blushing. 2 (Her face goes red in the cold) ruddy, florid.

**reduce** vb 1 (reduce the amount of food they eat) cut, curtail, decrease, lessen,

diminish. 2 (Drivers should reduce speed) decrease, moderate, lessen, lower. 3 (prices have been reduced) cut, lower, mark down, slash, cheapen.

**redundant** adj (a piece of writing full of redundant words) unnecessary, superfluous, surplus.

**refer** vb 1 (He referred to the difficulty of the task in his speech) mention, allude to, touch on, speak of. 2 (She referred the complaint to the manager) pass, hand on, direct, transfer. 3 (If you do not know the meaning of the word you should refer to a dictionary) consult, look up, turn to.

**referee** n (select a referee for the match) umpire, judge, adjudicator, arbiter, arbitrator, (inf) ref.

**reference** n 1 (She made no reference to the previous day's quarrel) mention, allusion. 2 (His comments have no reference to the case being discussed) relation, relevance, connection, bearing, application. 3 (She asked her former teacher for a reference when she applied for a job) character reference, testimonial, commendation.

**refined** adj 1 (refined sugar) processed, purified, treated. 2 (She felt she was too refined to mix with them) polished, cultivated, cultured, civilized, well-bred.

**reflect** vb 1 (Glass reflects light) send back, throw back, diffuse. 2 (His expression reflected his mood) show, indicate, reveal, communicate. 3 (She needed time to reflect on her problems) think about, consider, contemplate, mull over, ponder.

**reflection** n (his reflection in the mirror) image, likeness.

**reform** vb (make efforts to reform the educational system) improve, make better, better, amend, rectify, reorganize, revolutionize.

**refreshing** adj 1 (a refreshing cool drink/a refreshing cool breeze) invigorating, reviving, bracing, exhilarating. 2 (Some of his ideas seemed very refreshing) fresh, new, novel, original, different.

**refuge** n 1 (They sought refuge from their enemies/seek refuge from the storm) asylum, sanctuary, protection, safety, shelter, cover. 2 (The building was a refuge for the homeless) safe house, sanctuary, shelter, retreat, haven.

**refugee** n (refugees from the famine area) fugitive, exile, displaced person, stateless person.

**refuse** vb (She refused their invitation) turn down, reject, decline.

**refuse** n (dispose of household refuse) garbage, waste, debris, litter, trash.

**regard** vb 1 (The policeman was regarding them closely as they tried to get into the car) look at, watch, observe, study, eye. 2 (He regards his job prospects with optimism) look

on, view, consider. 3 (They regard him as rather a fool) consider, judge, rate, assess.

**regard** n 1 (They paid no regard to his advice) heed, notice, attention. 2 (He is held in high regard in the firm) respect, esteem, admiration.

**region** n (the cold regions of the world) area, territory, section, tract, zone, part, place.

**register** vb 1 (The hotel guests were asked to sign the register) list, record, directory. 2 (He used the register of births for his research) record, chronicle, annals. 3 (the register of her voice) range, scale, reach, gamut.

**register** vb 1 (They registered the birth of their son/They had to register their arrival on the list) record, put on record, enter, write down. 2 (The thermostat registered seventy degrees) read, indicate, show, display. 3 (Her face registered her surprise) show, express, display, reveal.

**regret** vb (She regrets that she did it) feel sorry, feel repentant, feel remorse, repent, to be ashamed of.

**regretful** adj (She gave a regretful smile) apologetic, repentant, contrite, remorseful, penitent.

**regular** adj 1 (The mailman did not follow his regular route) usual, customary, accustomed, habitual, normal. 2 (The breathing of the patient is regular) even, steady, rhythmic. 3 (They planted the trees at regular intervals) even, fixed, uniform. 4 (You will have to apply through the regular channels) usual, standard, official, conventional, orthodox.

**regulation** n (traffic regulations) rule, order, law, decree.

**rehearse** vb (The actors were rehearsing the play) practice, try out, go over, run through.

**reject** vb 1 (She has rejected their invitation) refuse, turn down, decline. 2 (She rejected the baby at birth) abandon, forsake, renounce, cast aside.

**rejoice** vb (They rejoiced on hearing that they had won) be joyful, be happy, be glad, be delighted, be overjoyed, celebrate.

**relapse** n (The patient was improving but then suffered a relapse) setback, turn for the worse.

**relate** vb 1 (He related the story of his misfortune) tell, recount, describe, narrate, report. 2 (information not relating to the matter) apply, be relevant, concern, have a bearing on.

**relations** npl 1 (She has no relations in the area) family, kin. 2 (They have business relations) dealings, associations.

**relationship** n 1 (I don't think there is any relationship between the two events) connection, association, link. 2 (Their relationship is over) friendship, partnership, love affair.

**relax** vb **1** (*He relaxes by swimming*) rest, unwind, take it easy, be at leisure, amuse oneself. **2** (*He relaxed his grip on the dog's leash*) loosen, lose, slacken, weaken **3**-(*The police will not relax their efforts to find the criminal*) reduce, lessen, decrease, diminish.

**release** vb **1** (*The police have released the suspect*) free, set free, let out, set loose, liberate. **2** (*They were tied up by the burglars and could not release themselves*) set free, free, untie, undo. **3** (*They have released the details of the crime*) make public, make known, issue, announce, disclose, put out, circulate, publish.

**relentless** adj **1** (*The judge was completely relentless*)• ruthless, unmerciful, merciless, pitiless, unforgiving, harsh, cruel. **2** (*their relentless efforts to persuade him*) persistent, persevering, unremitting, nonstop, unceasing.

**relevant** adj (*the information was not-relevant to the discussion*) applicable, pertinent, apposite, appropriate.

**reliable** adj **1** (*her most reliable friends*) dependable, trustworthy, true, loyal, devoted. **2** (*The evidence was not considered reliable*) dependable, trustworthy, well-founded, sound.

**relieve** vb **1** (*a drug to relieve the pain*) alleviate, soothe, assuage, ease, reduce. **2** (*collect money to-relieve the distress of the famine victims*) help, assist, aid, bring aid to. **3** (*She was to relieve the nurse on duty*) take over from, take the place of, stand in for, substitute for. **4** (*look for something to relieve the monotony of her life*) break up, interrupt, vary, lighten.

**religious** adj **1** (*take part in a religious ceremony/a religious discussion*) church, holy, divine, theological. **2**-(*She comes from a religious family*) churchgoing, pious, devout, Godfearing.

**relinquish** vb (*He relinquished his right to the title*) give up, renounce, surrender.

**reluctant** adj **1** (*a reluctant witness*) unwilling, unenthusiastic, grudging **2** (*She was reluctant to go*)-unwilling, disinclined, loath, averse.

**rely** vb (*She was relying on her parents for help*) depend on, count on, bank on, trust, put one's faith-in.

**remain** vb **1** (*She remained calm in the emergency*) stay, keep, continue. **2** (*Only a few of the original inhabitants remained*) be left, survive, last, endure. **3** (*He has to remain in hospital*) stay, wait.

**remark** n (*She made some critical remarks*) comment, statement, observation.

**remarkable** adj (*It was a remarkable achievement for one so young*) extraordinary, unusual, exceptional, outstanding, impressive.

**remedy** n (*a remedy for the common cold*) cure, treatment.

**remember** vb **1** (*I cannot remember his name*) recall, call to mind, recollect, think of. **2** (*Try to remember to mail the letter*) keep in mind, bear in mind.

**reminisce** vb (*old people reminiscing about their youth*) call to mind, recall, remember, recollect, think back on.

**remorse** n (*She showed remorse for her wrongdoing*) regret, penitence, compunction, contriteness.

**remote** adj **1** (*They live in a remote mountain village*) distant, far-off, outof- the way, isolated. **2** (*She is rather a remote person*) distant, aloof, reserved, unfriendly. **3** (*There is a remote possibility that he will win*) outside, unlikely, slender, slight.

**remove** vb **1** (*They removed their shoes*) take off. **2** (*She was asked to remove her books from the table*) move, shift, take away, carry away. **3** (*They tried to remove him from his post*) get rid of, throw out, dismiss, fire, expel, evict, oust. **4** (*She has had a tooth removed*) take out, pull out, extract.

**renounce** vb **1** (*He renounced his claim to the land*) give up, relinquish, surrender, waive. **2** (*They renounced their religion*) give up, abandon, turn one's back on, forsake.

**renovate** vb (*They are renovating an old farm house*) modernize, restore, recondition, overhaul.

**renown** n (*Her renown as a singer spread*) fame, acclaim, reputation, eminence, prestige.

**rent** vb (*They rented a boat*) charter, lease.

**repair** vb **1** (*The mechanic repaired the car*) mend, fix, put right, overhaul. **2** (*They repaired the torn clothes*) mend, sew, darn, patch.

**repeal** vb (*They have repealed that law*) revoke, annul, declare null and void, nullify, cancel, retract.

**repeat** vb **1** (*He was asked to repeat his statement to the committee*) say again, iterate, restate, recapitulate. **2** (*The boy repeated his father's words*) say again, echo, quote, parrot. **3** (*They have to repeat the task*) redo, do again, duplicate.

**repel** vb **1** (*They succeed in repelling their attackers*) drive back, push back, repulse, fend off, ward off. **2**-(*The sight of the rotting meat repelled them*) revolt, disgust, nauseate, sicken.

**repent** vb (*She committed a sin but she has repented*) feel regret, feel remorse, be sorry, be repentant, be penitent, be contrite.

**repercussion** n (*He could not have foretold the repercussions of his actions*) consequence, effect, result, reverberation.

**repetitive** adj (*His work consists of repetitive tasks*) repeated, unchanging, monotonous.

**replica** n (*The original of the necklace is in a museum—this is a replica*) copy, duplicate, reproduction, imitation, model.

**reply** n **1** (*She gave no reply to his question*) answer, response, retort, rejoinder. **2** (*He received a reply to his letter*) answer, response, acknowledgement.

**report** n **1** (*the firm's annual financial report*) statement, record, register. **2** (*a newspaper report of the accident*) account, article, piece, story, write-up. **3** (*They heard the report of a gun*) bang, explosion, blast, boom, crack.

**report** vb **1** (*They reported that they had been successful*) announce, communicate, tell, relate. **2** (*The soldiers were to report for duty at noon*) present oneself, announce oneself, appear, arrive. **3** (*They reported him to the police*) inform on, accuse, tell on, complain about, (*inf*) rat on.

**repose** n (*enjoy some repose after his hard work*) rest, relaxation, respite, time off, sleep.

**represent** vb **1** (*A closed fist represents violence*) symbolize, stand for, epitomize, personify. **2** (*The queen was represented in the picture as a warrior*) depict, portray, picture, show. **3** (*His lawyer represented him*) appear for, act for, speak for, be the representative of.

**repressive** adj (*a repressive regime*) repressing, tyrannical, despotic, dictatorial, oppressive, harsh, stern.

**reprieve** vb (*The woman was reprieved because she had killed in self-defense*) pardon, let off, spare.

**reprimand** vb (*The pupils were reprimanded for being late*) rebuke, scold, chide, reprove, admonish, reproach, rap, (*inf*) tell off.

**reprisal** n (*When their village was attacked they took reprisals on the attackers*) retaliation, vengeance, revenge, retribution, redress, requital.

**reproach** n (*She was upset by his words of reproach*) criticism, censure, condemnation, reprimand, reproof.

**reproduce** vb **1** (*Can the photocopier reproduce colored documents?*) copy, photocopy, duplicate. **2** (*We were unable to reproduce the lighting effect we produced last week*) repeat, recreate, emulate. **3**-(*Rabbits reproduce quickly*) breed, bear young, procreate, multiply.

**repulsive** adj (*It was a repulsive sight*) revolting, repellent, disgusting, nauseating, offensive, objectionable, loathsome, nasty, horrible, foul.

**reputable** adj (*get a reputable firm to do the work*) respected, respectable, well-thought-of, esteemed, reliable, dependable.

**reputation** n 1 (*The firm has a bad reputation for shoddy work*) name. 2 (*The incident damaged their reputation*) good name, respectability, esteem.

**request** vb (*They requested more help*) ask for, seek, apply for, demand, beg for, plead for, petition.

**require** vb 1 (*They require more money*) need, have need of, be short of, lack, want. 2 (*The job requires concentration*) need, involve, take, call for. 3 (*The police required him to go to the police station*) order, instruct, command.

**rescue** vb (*They rescued the drowning man from the river/They rescued the men from prison*) save, get out, extricate, free, liberate.

**research** n (*They were carrying out medical research into new drugs*) investigation, exploration, inquiry, study, analysis.

**resemble** vb (*She resembles her mother*) look like, be like, bear a semblance to, be similar to, take after, put one in mind of, remind one of.

**resent** vb (*She resents the fact that her sister earns more money than she does*) begrudge, grudge, be bitter, feel aggrieved, envy, be jealous.

**reserve** vb 1 (*We reserved seats for the play*) book, order. 2 (*You should reserve some fuel for the winter*) keep, put aside, conserve, save, store. 3 (*They should reserve judgement until they have heard all the facts*) postpone, delay, defer.

**reserved** adj (*She is very reserved and does not speak to many people*) shy, retiring, diffident, reticent, aloof, distant, unsociable, uncommunicative.

**reside** vb (*He resides in a large house in Boston now*) live in, stay in, occupy, inhabit, dwell in.

**residence** n 1 (*They have an impressive Colonial residence*) house, dwelling place, domicile. 2 (*They take up residence next week*) occupation, occupancy, tenancy.

**resident** n 1 (*the residents of the new apartment building*) occupant, occupier, inhabitant. 2 (*the hotel residents*) guest, visitor.

**resign** vb 1 (*He resigned yesterday*) give notice, leave. 2 (*He resigned from his job yesterday*) leave, quit, give up.

**resist** vb (*The troops resisted the invading army*) fight against, stand up to, withstand, hold out against, defy, oppose, repel.

**resolve** vb 1 (*She resolved to try harder*) decide, make up one's mind, determine, settle. 2 (*They seemed unable to resolve the problem*) solve, sort out, work out, clear up, answer.

**resourceful** adj (*resourceful people who made do with what they had*) ingenious, inventive, creative, imaginative, clever, capable.

**respect** n 1 (*They had great respect for him as a painter*) esteem, high regard, admiration,

reverence, deference. 2 (*With respect to the matter under discussion*) reference, relevance, regard, relation. 3 (*The plan was not perfect in all respects*) aspect, facet, feature, way, sense, particular, point, detail.

**respectable** adj (*Her neighbors do not think that she is very respectable*) of good reputation, upright, honorable, honest, decent, worthy.

**response** n (*They asked several questions but received no response*) answer, reply, acknowledgement, reaction.

**responsible** adj 1 (*They said that he was responsible for the damage*) blameworthy, to blame, guilty, at-fault, accountable, answer-able. 2 (*They need a responsible person to look after the children*) mature, sensible, level-headed, stable, reliable, dependable, trustworthy.

**rest** n 1 (*a period of rest after work*) repose, relaxation, leisure, ease, inactivity, sleep. 2 (*She is going away for a rest*) break, vacation.

**restless** adj 1 (*The children got restless in the afternoon*) fidgety, restive, agitated. 2 (*They passed a restless night*) wakeful, fitful.

**restrain** vb 1 (*They tried to restrain him from jumping off the bus*) prevent, hold back, impede. 2 (*She tried to restrain her laughter*) suppress, curb, check, stifle, contain. 3 (*It was her job to restrain the dogs*) control, keep under control, subdue, curb.

**restrict** vb 1 (*The long tight skirt restricted her freedom of movement*) hinder, hamper, impede, obstruct. 2 (*He was told by the doctor to restrict his consumption of salt*) limit, regulate, control, moderate.

**restricted** adj 1 (*a restricted space*) cramped, confined. 2 (*There is a restricted area around the military camp*) out of bounds, off limits, private.

**result** n (*His illness was a result of overwork*) effect, consequence, upshot, outcome, repercussion.

**retain** vb 1 (*They were asked to retain their train tickets*) keep, hold on to, hang on to. 2 (*The village still retains some of the old traditions*) keep, maintain, continue, preserve.

**retaliate** vb (*They hit the new boy and he retaliated*) take revenge, seek retribution, take reprisals, get even.

**reticent** adj (*He was very outgoing but his wife was very reticent*) reserved, diffident, uncommunicative, taciturn, silent.

**retiring** adj (*Very few people know her as she is very retiring*) shy, diffident, bashful, self-effacing, unassertive.

**retreat** vb 1 (*The army retreated before the enemy*) withdraw, go back, fall back, take flight, flee, beat a retreat. 2 (*The tide retreated*) go back, recede, ebb.

**retrieve** vb (*He tried to retrieve his stolen prop-*

erty) get back, recover, regain, recoup, reclaim.

**return** vb 1 (*Their parents will return tomorrow*) come back, go back, reappear. 2 (*She asked him to return the book which she had lent him*) give back, send back.

**reveal** vb 1 (*She took off her coat and revealed a white dress*) show, display, exhibit, expose, uncover. 2 (*The press revealed the truth about the affair*) disclose, divulge, tell, let out, make known.

**revenge** n (*He wanted revenge for his brother's murder*) vengeance, retribution, retaliation, reprisal.

**reverse** vb 1 (*They reversed their roles for the day*) change, exchange, swap, trade. 2 (*They have reversed their previous decision*) alter, change, overturn, repeal, revoke. 3 (*He reversed the car*) back. 4 (*reverse the coat*) turn round, put back to front.

**revise** vb 1 (*She had to revise the text of the manuscript*) amend, emend, correct, alter, edit, improve. 2 (*We have had to revise our vacation plans*) reconsider, review, alter, change.

**revolt** vb 1 (*The sight of the dried blood revolted her*) disgust, repel, nauseate, sicken, (*inf*) turn one off. 2 (*The citizens are revolting against the tyrant*) rebel, rise up, take up arms, mutiny.

**revolution** n 1 (*There was a revolution against the government*) rebellion, revolt, uprising, insurrection, mutiny, riot. 2 (*There has been a revolution in the computer industry*) complete change, transformation, reformation, innovation. 3 (*one revolution of the wheel*) rotation, round, whirl, spin. 4 (*The satellite made a revolution of the sun*) orbit, circuit, turn.

**revolve** vb 1 (*The wheel revolved slowly*) go round, turn, rotate, spin, whirl. 2 (*The planet revolves round the sun*) orbit, circle. 3 (*His world revolves round his family*) center on, focus on, concentrate on.

**reward** n (*He received a reward for bravery*) award, prize, recompense, gift, decoration, medal.

**rhythm** n (*The tune had a fast rhythm*) beat, pulse, throb, tempo, cadence.

**rich** adj 1 (*rich people who owned several houses*) wealthy, affluent, well off, prosperous, well-to-do, moneyed. 2 (*a house with rich furnishings*) costly, expensive, opulent, luxurious, sumptuous, splendid, magnificent. 3 (*The area has a very rich soil*) fertile, fruitful, productive, fecund. 4 (*curtains of a very rich color*) strong, deep, vivid, intense, brilliant. 5 (*The country has rich supplies of oil*) abundant, copious, ample, plentiful.

**rid:—get rid of** vb (*She should get rid of those old clothes*) dispose of, throw away, throw out, jettison, dump.

**riddle** n (*unable to solve the riddle*) puzzle, conundrum, poser.

**ridiculous** adj 1 (*It was a ridiculous thing to do*) absurd, pointless, senseless, foolish, inane. 2 (*He told us a ridiculous story about his vacation/She always wears ridiculous hats*) absurd, comical, funny, laughable, humorous, ludicrous. 3-(*It is ridiculous that he got away with the crime*) shocking, outrageous, monstrous, preposterous, incredible.

**right** adj 1 (*They all gave the right answer*) correct, accurate. 2 (*He was not the right person for the job*) suitable, appropriate, fitting, desirable. 3 (*He is not in his right mind*) sane, sound, rational, sensible. 4 (*They thought the judge did not make the right decision*) just, fair, impartial, good, honest, virtuous.

**rigid** adj 1 (*It was made of a rigid substance*) stiff, hard, taut, inflexible, unbending. 2 (*The principal was a rigid disciplinarian*) strict, severe, stern, stringent, harsh, inflexible.

**ring** n 1 (*She wore a gold ring*) band, hoop. 2 (*They saw a ring around the moon*) circle, loop. 3-(*He jumped into the boxing ring*) arena, area, enclosure. 4 (*The police have discovered a spy ring*) gang, organization, league, combine, syndicate.

**ring** vb 1 (*church bells ringing*) toll, sound, peal, chime. 2 (*The hall rang with music*) resound, reverberate, echo, resonate. 3 (*He said that he would ring back*) call, phone, telephone.

**riot** n (*There was a riot in the crowd when their leader was arrested*) rebellion, revolt, uprising, insurrection, mutiny, uproar.

**ripe** adj (*ripe fruit in the fruit bowl*) mature, ready to eat, ready, mellow.

**rise** vb 1 (*The balloon will rise into the air*) go up, climb, ascend. 2-(*the mountains rising behind the village*) rear up, tower, soar, loom. 3 (*She always rises early*) get up. 4-(*prices are expected to rise*) go up, increase, mount, escalate, rocket. 5 (*The dough for the bread failed to rise*) puff up, swell, expand. 6 (*The stream rises in the mountains*) originate, begin, start, flow from.

**risk** n 1 (*There is a risk of flooding*)-danger, chance, possibility, likelihood. 2 (*Their actions put lives at risk*) danger, peril, jeopardy.

**rival** n (*her rival in the competition*) opponent, opposition, adversary.

**roar** vb 1 (*The lion roared*) bellow. 2 (*He roared in rage*) bellow, yell, bawl, shout.

**robbery** n (*The criminals committed robbery*) burglary, theft, stealing, larceny.

**robust** adj (*in robust health*) strong, vigorous, tough, rugged, sturdy, stalwart.

**rock** vb 1 (*The boat began to rock in the storm*) roll, lurch, pitch, swing, sway, wobble. 2 (*rock the cradle*) sway, swing.

**rogue** n (*He was a rogue who ended up in prison*) scoundrel, rascal, villain.

**role** n 1 (*her role in the play*) part, character. 2 (*He attended in his role as chairman*) capacity, position, function, post.

**roll** vb 1 (*The wheels began to roll*) turn, go round, rotate, revolve, spin. 2 (*roll up a newspaper to swat a fly*) furl, coil, fold. 3 (*roll the pie crust*) flatten level, smooth, even out. 4 (*as time rolls on*) pass, go by. 5 (*as the ship rolled*) rock, lurch, pitch, toss, swing, sway.

**romantic** adj 1 (*She has a very romantic idea of what it is like to live in a remote village*) unrealistic, impractical, idealistic, starry-eyed. 2 (*romantic words on a greeting card*) loving, amorous, sentimental. 3 (*She seemed to them a romantic figure*) fascinating, glamorous, mysterious, exotic, exciting.

**rope** n (*tie the logs up with a rope*) string, cord, cable, line.

**rotate** vb 1 (*The wheels rotate*) turn, go round, revolve, spin. 2 (*They rotate the jobs*) alternate, take turns.

**rotten** adj 1 (*rotten food*) bad, moldy, decaying, decomposed, putrid, rancid, stinking. 2 (*rotten wood*) decaying, crumbling, disintegrating, corroding. 3 (*What a rotten thing to do!*) nasty, mean, foul, despicable, contemptible.

**rough** adj 1 (*sand down the rough surface of the table*) uneven, bumpy, jagged, rugged, irregular. 2-(*They have a dog with a rough coat*) shaggy, bushy, hairy, coarse, bristly. 3 (*people with rough voices*) gruff, hoarse, harsh, husky. 4-(*rough weather at sea*) stormy, squally, wild,-inclement. 5 (*He goes around with a rough crowd*) rowdy, disorderly, wild, uncouth, coarse, loutish, boorish. 6 (*at a rough estimate*) approximate, inexact, imprecise. 7-(*He made a rough sketch of the house*)-rough-andready, hasty, quick, sketchy, rudimentary.

**round** adj (*a round shape*) circular, ring-shaped, spherical.

**route** n (*They went home by a different route*) way, road, course.

**routine** n (*He hates to have his routine upset*) custom, habit, practice, procedure.

**row** n 1 (*children standing in rows*) line, column, series. 2 (*empty rows of seats in the theater*) line, tier, rank.

**row** n 1 (*The two brothers had a row over money*) argument, disagreement, dispute, squabble, quarrel, fight. 2 (*the row coming from the party*) noise, din, ruckus, uproar, commotion.

**rowdy** adj (*the rowdy drunks*) unruly, disorderly, noisy, boisterous, loud, wild.

**rub** vb 1 (*She rubbed his sore neck*) massage, knead. 2 (*The child began to rub the cat's back*) pat, caress, fondle. 3 (*rub off the dirty mark*) wipe off, remove, erase. 4-(*rub the ointment into the skin*) apply, work in, spread.

**rude** adj 1 (*The children were very-rude*) ill-mannered, bad-mannered, impolite, discourteous, impertinent, impudent, cheeky. 2-(*They told rude jokes*) vulgar, coarse, smutty, dirty, bawdy, blue.-3 (*The peasants had only a-few-rude tools*) crude, primitive,-rough, rudimentary, simple.

**ruffian** n (*The old man was attacked by a gang of ruffians*) rogue, thug, villain, hooligan, scoundrel, hoodlum, bully.

**rugged** adj 1 (*a rugged landscape*) rough, uneven, irregular, bumpy, rocky, jagged. 2 (*rugged men who do hard physical work*) tough, strong, stalwart, robust, sturdy, muscular, brawny.

**ruin** vb 1 (*The storm ruined the crops*) spoil, damage, wreck, wreak havoc on, destroy, lay waste. 2 (*The recession ruined many small businesses*) bring to ruin, bankrupt, make insolvent, impoverish.

**rule** vb 1 (*The emperor ruled over several countries*) govern, preside over, have control over, have authority over, be in command of. 2 (*The judge ruled that the accused be released*) order, command, direct, decide.

**rumor** n (*Rumor has it that he has gone*) gossip, hearsay, the grapevine.

**run** vb 1 (*They had to run to catch the bus*) race, sprint, dash, rush, bolt, charge. 2 (*Do the trains run on Sundays?*) operate, go, travel. 3 (*water running down the walls*) flow, stream, pour, gush. 4 (*The dye from the black pants ran on to the white shirt*) spread, mix with. 5 (*He runs a successful business*) operate, conduct, carry on, manage, administer, control, be in charge of, rule. 6 (*They left the-engine running*) go, operate, function.

**rural** adj (*a house in a rural setting*) country, rustic, pastoral.

**ruse** n (*He gained entrance to the house by a ruse*) trick, stratagem, subterfuge, dodge, ploy, deception, hoax.

**rush** vb (*They rushed to switch off the water*) hurry, hasten, make haste, run, race, dash.

**ruthless** adj (*He was a ruthless tyrant*) merciless, pitiless, relentless, unforgiving, harsh, severe, heartless, cruel.

# S

**sacred** adj 1 (*playing sacred music*) religious, church, spiritual, devotional. 2 (*The temple was a sacred place*) holy, blessed, hallowed, consecrated, godly, divine. **3** (*In Hinduism the cow is a sacred animal*) sacrosanct, protected.

**sad** *adj* **1** (*She felt sad when her friend went away*) unhappy, miserable, wretched, dejected, downcast, in low spirits, depressed, gloomy, melancholy. **2** (*She tried to forget the sad events of her childhood*) unhappy, unfortunate, distressing, tragic. **3** (*He thought that the country was in a sad state*) sorry, wretched, unfortunate, regrettable, deplorable, disgraceful.

**safe** *adj* **1** (*The children are safe indoors*) safe and sound, secure, protected, uninjured, unscathed, free from harm, free from danger, out of harm's way. **2** (*Is the building a safe place for the children to play?*) secure, sound, risk-free. **3** (*She is a safe person to look-after the children*) reliable, dependable, trustworthy. **4** (*a safe driver*) careful, cautious, prudent.

**sail** *vb* (*We sail at dawn*) set sail, embark, put to sea, put off.

**salary** *n* (*He earns a good salary*) wage, pay, earnings, remuneration.

**same** *adj* **1** (*That is the same dress which she wore yesterday*) identical, selfsame, the very. **2** (*We ate the same old food, week after week*) identical, similar, unchanging, unvarying.

**sample** *n* **1** (*The artist showed the advertising agency a sample of her work*) specimen, example, illustration, instance. **2** (*They gave the questionnaire to a sample of the population*) cross-section, sampling, random sample.

**sane** *adj* (*He said that he had not been sane when he committed the murder*) of sound mind, in one's right mind, rational, compos mentis, lucid, (*inf*) all there.

**sarcastic** *adj* (*They were hurt by her sarcastic remarks*) caustic, acerbic, sardonic, sneering, mocking, scoffing, derisive.

**satisfactory** *adj* (*They did not find her work satisfactory*) adequate, good enough, all right, acceptable, passable, up to scratch, up to standard.

**satisfied** *adj* **1** (*They were satisfied with the results/the satisfied customers*) pleased, happy, content. **2**-(*The police were satisfied that he was innocent*) convinced, sure, certain, positive. **3** (*They felt satisfied after one course of the meal*) full.

**satisfy** *vb* **1** (*students who satisfy the college entrance requirements*) fulfill, meet, be sufficient for. **2** (*products that satisfy the demands of the customers*) fulfill, gratify. **3** (*find some cool water to satisfy their thirst*) quench, slake, satiate. **4** (*He was able to satisfy her parents that she was telling the truth*) convince, persuade, assure.

**savage** *adj* **1** (*attacked by a savage animal*) ferocious, fierce, wild. **2**-(*During the attack she received a savage blow to the head*) vicious, brutal. **3** (*He was really savage to his family*) brutal, cruel, vicious, harsh, grim, barbarous, merciless. **4** (*The explorers were attacked by a savage tribe*) primitive, uncivilized, wild.

**save** *vb* **1** (*try to save some money for a vacation*) put aside, set aside, put by, keep, reserve, conserve, stockpile, hoard. **2** (*It will save a lot of inconvenience*) prevent, obviate, rule out. **3** (*He saved his friend from death*) rescue, deliver, snatch, free.

**say** *vb* **1** (*say a few words*) speak, utter, voice, pronounce. **2** (*You should say what you are thinking*) express, tell, put into words, state, communicate, make known, articulate. **3** ('*It's snowing heavily,*' *she said*) state, remark, announce.

**scandalous** *adj* **1** (*a politician who had to resign because of his scandalous behavior*) disgraceful, dishonorable, shocking, outrageous, disreputable, improper. **2** (*scandalous rumors circulating about the family*) slanderous, defamatory. libelous, scurrilous.

**scant** *adj* (*take scant notice of what her mother said*) little, slight, minimal, inadequate, insufficient.

**scar** *n* (*The accident left him with a scar on his face*) blemish, mark, blotch, disfigurement.

**scarce** *adj* (*Copies of the book are scarce now—it was published so long ago*) rare, few, few and far between, in short supply, scant, uncommon, unusual.

**scare** *vb* (*The sight of the man scared the children*) frighten, make afraid, alarm, startle, terrify, terrorize.

**scatter** *vb* **1** (*scatter the birdseed*) spread, disseminate, sow, sprinkle. **2** (*The crowd scattered when the police arrived*) disperse, break up, separate, disband.

**scene** *n* **1** (*They visited the scene of the battle*) site, location, position, spot. **2** (*The photographs were taken against a winter scene*) background, setting, landscape, view, vista, outlook. **3** (*It was a moving scene when child and mother were reunited*) event, incident, happening, situation. **4** (*The child made a scene when she did not get her own way*) fuss, outburst, commotion, to-do, upset, row.

**scenery** *n* (*tourists admiring the scenery*) view, outlook, prospect, vista, landscape.

**scent** *n* **1** (*He bought her an expensive scent for her birthday*) perfume, fragrance. **2** (*the scent of roses in the room*) perfume, fragrance, smell. **3** (*the scent of newly baked bread*) aroma, smell, bouquet, odor. **4** (*dogs following the scent of the rabbits*) trail, track, spoor.

**scheme** *n* **1** (*They have developed a-scheme to outwit the police*) plan, program, project, system, procedure, strategy, design, tactics. **2** (*a modern color scheme*) arrangement, system.

**scoff** *vb* (*They began to scoff at his efforts to bake a cake*) jeer at, mock at, laugh at, ridicule.

**scold** *vb* (*Her parents scolded her for being late*) rebuke, reprimand, chide, upbraid.

**score** *n* **1** (*What was the score at half time?*) result, outcome. **2** (*She noticed a deep score on the table*) scrape, scratch, groove, cut, mark.

**scorn** *n* (*He treated everyone else's ideas with scorn*) contempt, disdain, mockery, derision.

**scowl** *vb* (*He scowled when they disagreed with him*) frown, glower, glare, look daggers.

**scrap** *n* **1** (*use scraps of material to make a patchwork quilt*) remnant, fragment, bit, piece, snippet. **2**-(*feed the dog scraps of food*) piece, bit, morsel, particle. **3** (*He collects scrap metal*) waste, junk. **4**-(*There was not a scrap of sincerity in what she said*) bit, grain, iota, trace, whit.

**scrape** *vb* **1** (*scrape the surface of the table*) scratch. **2** (*The child fell and scraped her knee*) graze, scratch, abrade, cut.

**scratch** *vb* **1** (*try to scratch an itchy spot on her back*) rub, tear at. **2** (*She scratched her hand on a rusty nail*) graze, cut, abrade, skin, lacerate, wound.

**scream** *vb* (*He screamed when the heavy weight fell on him*) shriek, shout, yell, howl, squeal, yelp, wail.

**screen** *n* (*trees to act as a screen from the wind*) shelter, shield, protection, guard.

**scruffy** *adj* (*He was told to tidy up, that he was too scruffy to go to school*) untidy, unkempt, disheveled, messy, slovenly.

**scurry** *vb* (*The children were late and scurried home*) hurry, hasten, rush, run, race, dash, scamper.

**seal** *vb* **1** (*They sealed the parcel before mailing it*) fasten, secure, close up, shut. **2** (*They filled the jars with fruit and sealed them*) make airtight, close, shut, cork. **3**-(*The police sealed off the area*) cordon off, shut off, close off. **4**-(*They have sealed a deal*) settle, secure, clinch.

**search** *vb* **1** (*The police are searching for clues to the crime*) look for, seek, hunt for, ferret out. **2** (*They searched the building for the missing jewels*) look through, hunt through, rifle through, scour.

**seat** *vb* (*We require a table that seats twelve people*) accommodate, hold, have room for.

**secluded** *adj* (*a secluded part of the large garden*) sheltered, private, remote, out-of-the-way.

**secret** *adj* **1** (*They were told to keep the matter secret*) confidential, private, under wraps, (*inf*) hush-hush. **2** (*a desk with a secret drawer*) hidden, concealed.

**secretive** *adj* (*She is very secretive about where she is going*) reticent, uncommunicative, taciturn, silent.

**section** *n* **1** (*He bought the wood paneling in sections*) part, segment, piece, portion, bit. **2** (*a book divided into sections*) part, division, chapter. **3** (*the children's section of the bookstore*) part, department.

**secure** *adj* **1** (*The children feel secure at their grandparents' house*) safe, protected, free from danger, out of harm's way. **2** (*They can no longer look forward to a secure future*) safe, settled, solid, dependable, reliable. **3** (*The stepladder is not very secure*) steady, stable, sturdy, solid.

**see** *vb* **1** (*They could not see the farm house through the mist*) make out, catch sight of, spot, glimpse, look at, discern, perceive, notice, observe, view. **2** (*I see what he means*) understand, grasp, get, comprehend, follow, take in. **3** (*I will go and see where he is*) find out, discover, learn, ascertain. **4** (*We asked her to see that the children went to bed early*) make sure, be sure, ensure, mind, see to it, take care. **5**-(*When she asked if she could go on vacation her parents said that they would have to see*) think, have a think, give it some thought, consider, reflect. **6** (*The two friends see each other once a week*) meet, arrange to meet. **7**-(*He saw his mother to her door*) escort, accompany, usher, guide, lead. **8** (*Did you see the documentary on TV last night?*) watch, look at, view.

**seek** *vb* **1** (*The police are seeking more information*) search for, look for, hunt for. **2** (*After the accident she was advised that she should seek help from a counselor*) request, ask for, solicit.

**seem** *vb* (*They seem rather pleasant people*) appear to be, look to be, give the impression of being.

**seemly** *adj* (*They thought that her behavior was far from seemly*) decent, proper, decorous, fitting, suitable, appropriate, becoming.

**seize** *vb* **1** (*He seized a hanging branch to pull himself out of the water*) grab, grab hold of, take hold of, grasp, grip, clutch at. **2**-(*Kidnappers seized the children*) snatch, kidnap, abduct.

**seldom** *adv* (*We seldom see them*) rarely, hardly ever, infrequently.

**select** *vb* (*The little boy was asked to select a toy as a present*) choose, pick, opt for, decide on, settle on, plump for.

**set selfish** *adj* (*The child is selfish and will not share anything with his friends*) self-centered, self-seeking, egotistic, egocentric.

**sell** *vb* **1** (*They plan to sell their house soon*) put on sale, put up for sale. **2** (*stores selling food*) offer for sale, stock, carry, deal in, market.

**send** *vb* **1** (*send a package by airmail*) dispatch, convey, transport, remit, mail. **2** (*She sent her-parents a message that she was-well*) communicate, convey, transmit.

**sensational** *adj* (*newspapers with a sensational story about a politician*) spectacular, exciting, dramatic, startling, shocking, scandalous.

**sense** *n* **1** (*a sense of smell*) sensation, faculty, feeling. **2** (*They have no sense of honor*) awareness, understanding, appreciation. **3** (*He now has a sense of shame*) feeling. **4** (*The child had the sense to wait for her mother*) common sense, intelligence, judgment, cleverness, wisdom, practicality. **5** (*a word with more than one sense*) meaning, definition.

**sensitive** *adj* **1** (*She has very sensitive skin*) delicate, fine, soft. **2**-(*She is very sensitive to noise*) easily affected by, susceptible to. **3** (*She is a very sensitive person*) responsive, perceptive, sympathetic, understanding. **4** (*She is too sensitive to work in such a competitive firm*) over-sensitive, thinskinned, touchy. **5** (*The two sides were discussing a very sensitive issue*) delicate, difficult, problematic, thorny.

**sentence** *n* **1** (*The judge delivered his sentence*) judgment, verdict, ruling, decision. **2** (*Her attacker is serving a ten-year sentence*) prison sentence, prison term.

**sentimental** *adj* **1** (*The vase is not valuable but she has a sentimental attachment to it*) emotional, nostalgic. **2** (*The group were singing sentimental love songs*) emotional, romantic, mawkish, maudlin, (*inf*) soppy, (*inf*) schmaltzy.

**separate** *adj* **1** (*The two issues are quite separate*) unconnected, unrelated, divorced, distinct, different. **2** (*They have separate apartments*) individual, independent, different.

**series** *n* (*a series of sporting events/a series of misfortunes*) succession, progression, sequence, chain, train, run, cycle, order.

**serious** *adj* **1** (*The principal was looking very serious*) solemn, grave, earnest, unsmiling, somber, sober. **2** (*The accident victim has serious injuries*) bad, grave, critical, acute, dangerous. **3** (*They have several serious matters to discuss*) grave, important, weighty, of consequence, urgent, pressing, crucial, vital. **4** (*make a serious attempt at the championship*) earnest, determined, resolute, honest, sincere.

**serve** *vb* **1** (*He has served his master loyally for many years*) be in the service of, work for, be employed by. **2** (*people who have served the community*) be of service to, be of use to, help, assist, benefit, support.

**3** (*He served three years in the army*) spend, carry out, fulfill, complete. **4** (*a sofa that will also serve as a bed*) function, act as, do duty as. **5**-(*The hostess is just about to serve the first course*) dish up, give out, deal out. **6** (*She is trying to find a salesperson to serve her*) attend to, assist.

**service** *n* **1** (*She retired after forty years' service with the firm*) work, employment. **2** (*We did him a service by telling him the truth about his friends*) good turn, benefit, advantage, help, assistance. **3** (*His car is due for a service*) overhaul, check-up, repair, maintenance. **4**-(*guests at the wedding service*) ceremony, rite, ritual.

**session** *n* (*old friends having a good gossip session*) time, period, spell.

**set** *vb* **1** (*set their suitcases down on the sidewalk*) put, put down, lay down, place, deposit. **2** (*set the jewel in a gold ring*) fix, embed, arrange, mount. **3** (*set the thermostat*) regulate, adjust. **4** (*set the house on fire*) put, cause to be, start. **5** (*The jelly will not set*) solidify, thicken, harden, gel. **6** (*At what time does the sun set?*) go down, sink, subside. **7** (*The runner set a new record for the course*) set up, establish, settle, create, institute. **8**-(*We must set a date for the annual dinner*) fix, establish, settle, agree on, decide on, select. **9** (*His behavior set them talking*) start, cause. **10** (*The teacher set the children an exam*) assign, allot.

**settle** *vb* **1** (*We must settle on a date for the annual dance*) set, decide on, agree on, fix, arrange, choose, select. **2** (*I hope they settle the dispute soon*) clear up, resolve, bring to an end, conclude. **3** (*He wants to settle his financial affairs before he dies*) set to rights, put in order, arrange, clear out, straighten up. **4**-(*enough money to settle their bills*) pay, meet. **5** (*The coffee dregs had settled at the foot of the cup*) sink, subside, fall. **6** (*She was so upset that the doctor had to give her something to settle her*) calm, calm down, quiet, sedate, compose, tranquilize. **7** (*The family emigrated from Ireland to settle in America*) make one's home, take up residence, go to live, move to. **8** (*a part of America settled by Scots*) establish, colonize, occupy, inhabit, populate.

**sever** *vb* **1** (*In the accident he severed his leg at the knee*) cut off, chop off, lop off. **2** (*He had to sever the logs in two*) divide, split. **3** (*The two families quarreled and severed relations with each other*) break off, suspend, end, terminate.

**several** *adj* **1** (*She has invited several people to dinner*) some, a number of, a few. **2** (*Eventually we all went our several ways*) separate, different, respective, individual, particular.

**severe** *adj* **1** (*He wore a very severe expression*)

stern, grim, forbidding, disapproving, somber, serious. 2-(*The tyrant ruled over a severe regime*) harsh, hard, strict, cruel, brutal, savage, merciless. 3 (*She always wore severe clothes*) plain, simple, unadorned, austere. 4 (*We have had a severe winter*) harsh, hard, extreme. 5 (*She suffers from severe pain in her legs*) extreme, intense, fierce, strong, violent, very bad.

**shabby** *adj* 1 (*She wore shabby clothes*) worn, threadbare, scruffy. 2 (*The house is looking rather shabby*) dilapidated, run-down, broken-down, tumbledown, ramshackle, dingy, seedy, squalid, slum-like. 3 (*The way he treated her was shabby*) despicable, dishonorable, mean, shoddy.

**shade** *n* 1 (*They sat in the shade of a tree*) shadow, cover. 2 (*a shade of blue*) color, tint, tone, hue. 3 (*a shade against the light*) screen, shield, cover, blind.

**shadow** *n* 1 (*We sat in the shadow of the tree*) shade, cover. 2 (*the shadow of the children on the wall*) silhouette, outline, shape.

**shady** *adj* 1 (*sit in a shady part of the back yard on a hot day*) shaded, shadowy, sheltered, screened, dark, dim. 2 (*The store is run by rather-a-shady character*) suspicious, suspect, questionable, devious, underhand, dishonest, dishonorable.

**shake** *vb* 1 (*The child shook her piggy bank to hear the coins jingling*) rattle, jolt, jerk. 2 (*The car shook as we drove over the stony roads*) bump, jolt, bounce, rock, roll. 3 (*The child was feverish and was shaking*) shiver, quiver, tremble, quake, shudder. 4 (*Her failure had shaken her confidence for future tournaments*) undermine, lessen, weaken. 5 (*She was obviously shaken by the news of the accident*) disturb, upset, shock, agitate, perturb, disquiet, disconcert.

**shame** *n* 1 (*He seemed to feel no shame at his crime*) guilt, remorse, compunction, discomfiture, humiliation. 2 (*It was a shame that it rained on the picnic*) pity, misfortune, bad luck, ill-luck. 3 (*She felt that he had brought shame to the school by his action*) disgrace, dishonor, scandal, discredit, disrepute, ignominy.

**shape** *n* 1 (*children playing with pieces of cardboard of different shapes*) form, formation, outline. 2-(*Help came in the shape of a passing motorist*) form, guise, appearance. 3 (*put the jelly in shapes*) mold. 4 (*The players must be in good shape for tomorrow's game*) condition, state, fettle, trim.

**share** *n* (*Each of them will receive a share of the profits*) portion, part, quota, percentage, division, allocation.

**sharp** *adj* 1 (*need a sharp knife to carve the meat*) keen, razor-edged. 2 (*The child was injured by a sharp length of metal*) pointed, spiky. 3-(*She felt a sharp pain in her side*) acute, intense, keen, piercing,

stabbing, severe. 4 (*The sauce had rather a sharp taste*) pungent, sour, tart, bitter, biting. 5 (*There is a sharp drop to the sea just there*) steep, sheer, abrupt, precipitous. 6-(*He was sharp enough to realize that they were trying to swindle him*) clever, shrewd, bright, smart, intelligent. 7 (*She sounded rather sharp on the phone*) abrupt, brusque, curt, short.

**sheer** *adj* 1 (*It was sheer stupidity to behave like that*) utter, downright, total, complete, out-and-out. 2 (*It was a sheer drop to the sea*) steep, abrupt, sharp, precipitous.

**sheet** *n* 1 (*sheet of glass*) piece, length, panel. 2 (*a sheet of ice on the roadway*) layer, coat, coating, cover, covering, film, blanket, carpet. 3 (*sheets of water left after the flood*) expanse, stretch.

**shelf** *n* (*build a shelf for the books*) ledge.

**shield** *vb* (*try to shield her eyes from the sun/ shield the children from danger*) protect, screen, guard, safeguard.

**shine** *vb* (*The street lights were shining*) gleam, glow, glint, sparkle, flash, glitter, shimmer.

**shiver** *vb* (*They began to shiver with cold*) shake, quiver, tremble, shudder, quake.

**shock** *vb* 1 (*She was shocked by the state of the slum housing*) appall, horrify, outrage, disturb, amaze, astound, traumatize.

**short** *adj* 1 (*He is too short to reach the branch*) small, tiny, diminutive. 2-(*short vacation/a short relationship*) brief, short-lived, short-term,-fleeting, transitory, transient, ephemeral. 3 (*She was asked to write a short account of the incident*) brief, concise, succinct, terse. 4 (*She was rather short on the phone*) sharp, brusque, abrupt, curt. 5 (*Their supply of money is getting a-bit short*) deficient, insufficient, scarce, scanty, sparse, meager, tight.

**shot** *n* 1 (*hear a shot*) gunfire, report of a gun, bang, blast, explosion. 2-(*take a shot at winning*) try, attempt, effort, (*inf*) go, (*inf*) stab. 3-(*take shots at trying to hit the target*) turn, opportunity. 4 (*tourists taking shots of the cathedral*) photograph, photo, snapshot, film. 5-(*have to have several shots before going on a trip to the tropics*) vaccination, inoculation, injection, (*inf*) jab.

**shout** *vb* (*They shouted to attract his attention/ He shouted out in pain*) cry, call, yell, howl, roar, scream, bellow.

**show** *vb* 1 (*show the new products to the customers*) display, exhibit, present, demonstrate, set forth. 2-(*show them how to use the machine*) demonstrate, point out, explain, teach, instruct. 3 (*He showed his displeasure by leaving the meeting early*) indicate, demonstrate, express, manifest, make known, reveal. 4 (*The effects of his illness are beginning to show*) be visible,

be seen, be obvious, appear. 5 (*The ushers showed the guests to their seats at the wedding service*) escort, accompany, guide, usher, conduct.

**shrewd** *adj* (*a shrewd businessman*) astute, clever, smart, sharp.

**shrill** *adj* (*a shrill voice*) high-pitched, high, sharp, piercing, penetrating, screeching, shrieking.

**shrink** *vb* 1 (*That blouse might shrink in the wash*) get smaller. 2-(*The market for goods like that will shrink*) grow less, become smaller, contract, diminish, fall off, drop off. 3 (*They shrank from him in fear*) draw back, coil, flinch, cringe.

**shut** *vb* (*please shut the door when everyone is here*) close, fasten, secure, lock.

**shy** *adj* (*She is too shy to say much in public*) bashful, diffident, reserved, reticent, retiring, withdrawn, self-effacing, self-conscious, timid.

**sick** *adj* 1 (*She has been sick and is off work*) ill, unwell, indisposed, poorly, ailing, below par, (*inf*) under the weather. 2 (*She felt sick on the sea voyage*) nauseated, queasy, bilious. 3 (*He is sick of his present job*) tired, weary, bored, jaded, (*inf*) fed up. 4 (*That was rather a sick joke*) morbid, macabre, ghoulish, gruesome.

**side** *n* 1 (*flowers growing by the side of the river*) edge, border, verge. 2-(*the upper side of the desk*) surface, part. 3 (*They live on the north side of the town*) part, area, region, district, quarter, section, neighborhood. 4 (*discuss all sides of the problem*) aspect, angle, facet, point of view, viewpoint, standpoint. 5 (*on his side in the dispute*) camp, faction, party, group, wing. 6 (*the side that is playing against them tomorrow*) team, squad.

**sight** *n* 1 (*It was her first sight of the old family house*) view, glimpse. 2-(*The child was told to stay within sight of her parents*) view, range of vision, field of vision. 3 (*Her sight is now poor*) eyesight, vision, eyes, power of sight. 4 (*visitors going on a tour of the town's sights*) spectacle. 5 (*What a sight she was in that hat*) spectacle, eyesore, mess, (*inf*) fright.

**sign** *n* 1 (*Her thinness was a sign of her illness*) indication, symptom, evidence, clue. 2 (*a sign indicating the way to the museum*) signpost, notice, placard. 3 (*He gave them a sign to stay still*) signal, gesture, motion, movement, gesticulation. 4 (*mathematical signs*) symbol. 5-(*They believed that they would be given a sign of forthcoming tragedy*) omen, portent, warning, presage.

**silent** *adj* 1 (*It was very silent on the hills at night*) quiet, hushed, peaceful, tranquil. 2 (*They were completely silent as he told them the news*) speechless, wordless, without speaking, mute, taciturn, mum, uncommunicative. **3** (*She was upset by their silent reproach*) unspoken, wordless, unsaid, unexpressed, tacit, implicit.

**silly** *adj* **1** (*She is a very silly person*) foolish, stupid, irresponsible, giddy, frivolous, immature. **2** (*It was a very silly thing to do*) foolish, stupid, senseless, idiotic, unwise, foolhardy, irresponsible, ridiculous, absurd, (*inf*) dumb.

**simple** *adj* **1** (*It was a very simple task*) easy, uncomplicated, elementary, straightforward, effortless. **2** (*You will have to explain it to them in simple language*) plain, uncomplicated, clear, straightforward, direct, intelligible. **3** (*They are wealthy but lead a very simple life*) ordinary, modest, unpretentious, humble. **4** (*She was a simple peasant girl*) unsophisticated, innocent, naive, ingenuous, inexperienced. **5** (*The boy is a bit simple*)-simple-minded, feeble-minded, backward, retarded.

**sin** *n* (*They will be punished for their sin*) wrong, wrongdoing, evil, evildoing, badness, crime, offense, immorality.

**sincere** *adj* **1** (*Her apology was obviously sincere*) genuine, real, true, honest, wholehearted, heartfelt.

**single** *adj* **1** (*Only a single flower was left blooming*) sole, solitary, one, lone, isolated, by itself. **2** (*He is still single*) unmarried, unwed, unattached, free.

**sink** *vb* **1** (*The ship began to sink*) go under, submerge, founder, capsize. **2** (*He sank to his knees to ask forgiveness*) fall, drop, slump. **3** (*The invalid is thought to be sinking rapidly*) decline, deteriorate, fail, fade.

**sit** *vb* **1** (*The audience were asked to sit*) sit down, take a seat, be seated. **2** (*Their suitcases were sitting on the sidewalk*) be placed, be situated. **3** (*The court sits every day*) be in session, meet, assemble.

**situation** *n* **1** (*a cottage in a picturesque situation*) place, position, location, setting, site. **2** (*The firm is in an unstable financial situation*) circumstances, state, state of affairs, condition, predicament. **3** (*There is a vacant situation in the accounts department*) post, position, job, place.

**size** *n* (*measure the size of the room*) dimensions, measurements, proportions, area, extent.

**skeptical** *adj* (*She was skeptical about her chances of success*) doubtful, dubious, distrustful, mistrustful, unconvinced.

**skillful** *adj* (*He is a very skillful carpenter*) skilled, able, good, competent, adept, accomplished, expert, deft, masterly.

**slack** *adj* **1** (*She has lost a lot of weight and her clothes are now slack*) loose, baggy. **2** (*Since he stopped exercising his muscles have gotten slack*) limp, flabby, flaccid. **3**-(*Business is slack just now*) slow, quiet, inactive, sluggish. **4** (*The pupils have gotten rather slack*

*about their work*) negligent, neglectful, remiss, careless, slapdash, slipshod.

**slap** *vb* (*She slapped his face*) strike, hit, whack, (*inf*) wallop.

**sleep** *n* (*have a short sleep after lunch*) nap, doze, rest, (*inf*) snooze, (*inf*) forty winks.

**sleepy** *adj* **1** (*She had not had much rest and was feeling sleepy*) tired, drowsy, lethargic, sluggish. **2** (*a sleepy little town*) quiet, peaceful, inactive.

**slight** *adj* **1** (*There had been a slight improvement*) small, little, minute, subtle, modest. **2** (*slight matters*) unimportant, minor, insignificant, trifling, trivial. **3** (*She was very slight*) slightly built, slender, slim, small, delicate.

**slip** *vb* **1** (*The old lady slipped on the ice and broke her leg*) slide, skid, slither, lose one's footing. **2**-(*The cup slipped from her grasp*) fall, slide, drop. **3** (*She became upset and slipped from the room*) steal, creep, sneak. **4** (*She just had time to slip on some clothes*) put on, pull on. **5** (*Some people think that educational standards have slipped*) drop, fall, decline, deteriorate, degenerate.

**slope** *n* **1** (*The floors of the building are on a slight slope*) slant, angle, inclination, tilt, dip. **2** (*They had picnic on a grassy slope*) hill, hillock, bank, rise.

**slow** *adj* **1** (*They moved along at a very slow pace*) slow-moving, leisurely, unhurried, dawdling, snail-like. **2** (*Getting planning permission can be a slow process*) slow-moving, drawnout, long-drawn-out, prolonged, protracted, time-consuming. **3** (*pupils who are rather slow*) slow-witted, of below-average intelligence, with learning difficulties, stupid, unintelligent. **4** (*Business is rather slow*) slack, quiet, sluggish.

**sly** *adj* (*It is difficult to know what he is doing— he is very sly*) cunning, crafty, wily, artful, sneaky, devious, underhand, scheming, shifty, furtive.

**small** *adj* **1** (*The child is very small for her age*) little, tiny, slight, short, diminutive, undersized. **2** (*It was just a small mistake*) slight, minor, unimportant, insignificant, trifling, trivial. **3** (*He is rich and powerful but came from small beginnings*) humble, low, lowly, modest, poor, inferior.

**smart** *adj* **1** (*You must try to look smart for your job interview*) well-dressed, elegant, neat, spruce. **2**-(*The child is smart for her age*) clever, bright, intelligent, sharp.

**smash** *vb* **1** (*She smashed several plates when washing up*) break, shatter. **2** (*He smashed his father's car*) crash, wreck, collide. **3** (*Our hopes of success were smashed*) shatter, ruin, wreck.

**smell** *n* **1** (*the smell of roses*) scent, perfume, fragrance. **2** (*The smell of freshly baked bread*) aroma, odor. **3** (*The smell of rotting meat*) stink, stench.

**smooth** *adj* **1** (*smooth surfaces*) even, level, flat, plane. **2** (*The sea was very smooth*) calm, still, flat, tranquil. **3** (*He is responsible for the smooth running of the firm*) trouble-free, steady, regular, effortless. **4** (*young men with smooth faces*) cleanshaven, hairless. **5** (*She was approached in the store by a smooth salesman*) smooth-tongued, suave, glib, urbane, courteous, gracious.

**smother** *vb* **1** (*She was accused of trying to smother the old lady with a pillow*) suffocate, stifle, asphyxiate. **2** (*She tried to smother a giggle*) suppress, stifle, muffle.

**snag** *n* (*He did not see the possible snags in his plans*) drawback, hitch, catch, obstacle, stumbling-block, glitch.

**snap** *vb* **1** (*The branch suddenly snapped*) break, splinter, fracture, crack. **2** (*She snapped her fingers*) click, crack. **3** (*The dog snapped at our ankles*) bite, snarl, growl. **4**-(*She was tired and began to snap at the children*) speak irritably, shout, growl, snarl. **5** (*She was behaving very calmly and then she suddenly snapped*) collapse, break down.

**snatch** *vb* **1** (*She was late and had to snatch a piece of toast from the table and run for the bus*) grab, seize, take hold of. **2** (*The thief snatched my purse at the airport*) rob, steal, make off with. **3** (*They snatched the millionaire's child and demanded a ransom*) kidnap, abduct, seize, grab.

**sneer** *vb* (*sneering at her attempts*) smirk, snicker, snigger, scoff, scorn, mock, jeer.

**snobbish** *adj* (*She has a very snobbish attitude towards people who are badly off*) arrogant, haughty, proud, disdainful, condescending, supercilious, (*inf*) snooty, (*inf*) uppity.

**soak** *vb* **1** (*They got soaked in the storm*) drench, wet through, saturate. **2** (*soak the dress in cold water to remove the stain*) steep, immerse. **3** (*blood soaking through the bandage*) penetrate, permeate.

**sob** *vb* (*She began to sob as her mother left*) weep, cry, wail.

**sociable** *adj* **1** (*Our neighbors are very sociable people*) friendly, affable, social, gregarious, communicative, outgoing.

**soft** *adj* **1** (*The car got stuck in soft mud*) spongy, mushy. **2** (*The ground by the river was very soft*) swampy, spongy, boggy. **3** (*soft substances such as dough*) pliable, pliant, flexible, malleable. **4** (*a dress of a soft material*) smooth, silky, velvety. **5** (*dresses in soft colors*) pale, light, pastel, muted, subdued, restrained. **6** (*The lighting in the room was very soft*) low, dim, faint, muted, subdued. **7** (*She spoke in a soft voice so that the others would not hear*) quiet, hushed, low, faint, whispered. **8** (*parents accused of being too soft with their children*) lenient, indulgent, easygoing, permissive, liberal.

**soil** n 1 (*The soil is very poor in that area*) earth, ground, dirt. 2 (*troops killed on foreign soil*) land, country.

**solemn** adj 1 (*She wore a solemn expression*) grave, serious, unsmiling, somber. 2 (*It was a solemn occasion*) serious, grave, important, formal, grand, stately, dignified, ceremonious. 3 (*a solemn promise*) earnest, sincere, genuine, honest.

**solid** adj 1 (*a solid rather than a liquid substance*) firm, hard, dense, thick. 2 (*jewelry made of solid gold*) pure, unalloyed, complete. 3 (*solid houses made of stone and built to last*) substantial, strong, sturdy.

**solitary** adj 1 (*He leads a solitary life with no family or friends*) lonely, lonesome, friendless, unsociable. 2 (*A solitary tree in the barren landscape*) single, lone, sole, by oneself/itself.

**solution** n 1 (*unable to find the solution to the mathematical problem*) answer, result, resolution. 2 (*a solution of salt and water*) suspension, mixture.

**soothe** vb 1 (*an ointment to soothe the painful sunburn*) ease, alleviate, assuage, lessen, reduce. 2 (*He tried to soothe the crying baby*) quiet, calm, pacify.

**sophisticated** adj 1 (*She regards herself as being a sophisticated city-dweller*) worldly, experienced, cultivated, cultured, urbane, suave, cosmopolitan. 2 (*an office equipped with sophisticated electronic equipment*) advanced, complex, complicated, elaborate.

**sore** adj 1 (*She has a sore patch on her arm*) painful, in pain, aching, tender, raw, smarting, inflamed, bruised. 2 (*people in sore need of somewhere to live*) urgent, pressing, desperate, critical, dire.

**sorry** adj 1 (*He is not at all sorry for his misdeeds*) apologetic, regretful, ashamed, repentant, penitent, remorseful, contrite. 2 (*We were sorry to hear that she was ill*) sad, unhappy, distressed, regretful. 3 (*They felt sorry for the homeless people*) sympathetic, compassionate, full of pity, moved.

**sort** n (*several different sorts of vegetable/a new sort of computer*) kind, variety, type, class, category, make, brand.

**sound** n 1 (*There was not a sound from the children's room*) noise. 2 (*The sound of someone playing the guitar*) noise, music. 3 (*We did not like the sound of their plans for improvement*) impression, idea.

**sour** adj 1 (*a sauce that was rather sour*) tart, acid, bitter, sharp. 2 (*milk that had turned sour*) curdled, bad, rancid, off. 3 (*He is a sour old man*) ill-tempered, disagreeable, irritable, cross.

**space** n 1 (*travel in space*) outer space, infinity. 2 (*large pieces of furniture that take up a great deal of space*) room, expanse, area, scope. 3 (*There was only a narrow space between each house*) gap, interval, opening, break. 4 (*There is a space on the form to explain why you want the job*) blank space, blank, empty space, gap. 5 (*They both died within the space of two years*) time, period, span, interval, duration. 6 (*There are no spaces left on the course*) place, room.

**spare** adj 1 (*take a spare pair of socks*) extra, additional, reserve, supplementary, surplus. 2 (*She works long hours and has little spare time*) free, unoccupied, leisure.

**sparse** adj (*a sparse covering of grass*) scanty, meager, slight.

**spasm** n 1 (*He is in agony with stomach spasms*) contraction, cramp. 2 (*limb spasms*) twitching, convulsion. 3 (*a sudden spasm of coughing*) fit, paroxysm, convulsion, bout, attack.

**speak** vb 1 (*Did he speak the truth?*) say, tell, state, utter, voice, express, pronounce. 2 (*The two sisters quarreled and have not spoken to each other for years*) talk to, converse with, communicate with, chat. 3 (*The professor is to speak for an hour*) talk, lecture, deliver a speech.

**special** adj 1 (*We were asked to take special care of the book*) especial, particular, exceptional, extra special. 2 (*It was a special occasion for the old people*) unusual, exceptional, remarkable, out-of-the-ordinary, notable, outstanding, memorable, significant, important, momentous.

**spectacular** adj (*a spectacular firework display*) striking, remarkable, impressive, magnificent, splendid, sensational, breathtaking, dramatic.

**speech** n 1 (*the power of speech*) talk, communication. 2 (*He was drunk and his speech was slurred*) diction, enunciation, pronunciation. 3 (*He gave a speech thanking everyone*) talk, lecture, address.

**speed** n 1 (*the speed at which they were going*) rate. 2 (*They moved with amazing speed*) rapidity, swiftness, fastness, quickness, haste, hurry.

**spend** vb 1 (*They will have to spend a great deal of money on that house*) pay out, lay out, expend, (*inf*) fork out, (*inf*) shell out. 2 (*They spend hours on the beach*) pass, while away, fill, occupy. 3 (*A great deal of effort was spent on the task*) use, employ, apply, devote.

**spill** vb (*Water was spilling from the bucket as she walked*) flow, pour, overflow, brim over, run over, slop over.

**spirit** n 1 (*His spirit was troubled*) soul, psyche, inner self. 2 (*They were people of determined spirit*) character, temperament, disposition, quality. 2 (*He required spirit to undertake the journey*) courage, bravery, mettle, pluck, determination. 4 (*The children performed the play with spirit*) liveliness, animation, enthusiasm, energy, vivacity, verve.

**spite** n (*She damaged her friend's bike out of spite*) malice, maliciousness, ill-will, hostility, resentment, vindictiveness.

**splendid** adj 1 (*We had a splendid vacation*) excellent, fine, first-class, superb, marvelous, wonderful, great. 2 (*a splendid royal palace*) magnificent, sumptuous, imposing, impressive, glorious, luxurious.

**split** vb 1 (*split the logs for the fire*) break, chop, cut. 2 (*The plate seemed just to split in two*) break, snap, splinter. 3 (*The robbers split the profits from the burglary amongst themselves*) divide, share, apportion, distribute. 4 (*The argument over the local school split the town into two groups*) divide, separate. 5 (*The couple have split up*) separate, part, divorce, break up.

**spoil** vb 1 (*a substance that spoiled the surface of the table*) damage, mar, impair, blemish, deface, ruin, destroy. 2 (*She spoils her daughter*) overindulge, indulge, pamper, cosset, coddle, mollycoddle.

**spot** n 1 (*spots of paint on the clothes*) mark, speck, fleck, dot, smudge, stain, blotch. 2 (*get ointment for the spots on her chin*) pimple, pustule, boil, blemish. 3 (*a pleasant spot for a country cottage*) place, area, location, site, situation, setting.

**spread** vb 1 (*They spread rumors*) circulate, disseminate, transmit, propagate, publicize. 2 (*Feeling against the new road is spreading*) extend, increase, proliferate, escalate, mushroom. 3 (*The farmer spread fertilizer on the fields*) lay, put, apply, cover. 4 (*The bird spread its wings and flew off*) stretch, extend, open out, unfurl.

**squeeze** vb 1 (*squeeze limes to make a cool drink*) squash, crush, compress. 2 (*She squeezed his arm to attract his attention*) pinch, press, grip. 3 (*She squeezed the dress to get the water out*) wring, twist, press. 4 (*They squeezed the water from the wet sweaters*) extract, press, force, express. 5 (*The speaker was so popular that the audience was squeezed into the hall*) crush, squash, pack, crowd, cram, jam, wedge.

**stage** n 1 (*the stages in the production process*) point, step, period, level, phase. 2 (*the first stage of the journey*) lap, leg, phase. 3 (*She was too nervous to go on the stage*) platform, dais, rostrum, podium.

**stand** vb 1 (*The audience was asked to stand*) rise, get to one's feet, get up, be upright, be erect, be vertical. 2 (*The apartment building that used to stand here*) be, be situated, be located. 3 (*stand the bookcase against the wall near the fireplace*) place, put, position, erect, set up. 4

(*They appealed against the judge's ruling but the sentence stood*) remain, stay, hold, hold good, prevail. **5** (*She cannot stand loud noise*) put up with, tolerate, bear, endure, abide.

**start** *vb* **1** (*before the war started*) begin, commence, get underway, come into being. **2** (*start the machine*) turn on, put on, set in motion, activate. **3** (*She started a new society*) begin, commence, set up, establish, found, launch.

**state** *n* **1** (*a system in a state of chaos*) condition, situation, circumstances, position, state of affairs, predicament. **2** (*She was in a tearful state*) condition, mood, humor, frame of mind. **3** (*His mother got into a state when he did not come home*) panic, fluster, (*inf*) flap. **4** (*occasions of state attended by the President*) pomp, ceremony, majesty, grandeur. **5**-(*the various states in the world*) country, nation, land.

**state** *vb* (*state their reasons for going*) express, voice, utter, say, declare, tell, announce.

**stay** *vb* **1** (*They left but we decided to stay*) remain, wait, linger. **2** (*She stayed angry a long time*) remain, continue. **3** (*They stayed at a small hotel*) put up, reside.

**steady** *adj* **1** (*drive at a steady pace*) uniform, even, regular, consistent. **2** (*try to keep the table steady on the moving ship*) stable, immovable, unmoving, motionless. **3** (*her steady love for him*) constant, unchanging, unfaltering, continuous, endless. **4** (*require a steady young person for the job*) sensible, level-headed, calm, reliable.

**step** *n* **1** (*take one step nearer the sea*) stride. **2** (*She listened for her father's steps on the stairs*) footstep, footfall, tread. **3** (*She took a-rash step*) act, course of action, move, deed. **4** (*look- ing for the-next step in his promotion*) stage, level, grade, rank, degree. **5**-(*a broken step on the ladder*) rung, tread.

**stick** *vb* **1** (*The child began to stick the pictures in a book*) glue, paste, gum, attach, fix, pin, tack. **2** (*She stuck a knife in the meat to see if it was cooked*) thrust, push, jab, poke, insert. **3** (*The machine has stuck*) jam, stop, halt, come to a halt.

**stiff** *adj* **1** (*a piece of stiff cardboard*) rigid, hard, unyielding, inflexible. **2** (*Her muscles are stiff after the long climb*) tight, tense, taut. **3** (*The robbers received a stiff sentence*) severe, harsh, hard, heavy, drastic, stringent. **4** (*She was rather stiff when the young couple arrived*) formal, cold, aloof.

**still** *adj* **1** (*It was a still day*) calm, windless. **2** (*They were asked to stay completely still*) motionless, immobile, stationary. **3** (*The house was still*) quiet, peaceful, silent, hushed.

**stop** *vb* **1** (*They tried to stop the fight*) bring to a halt, halt, end, finish, terminate, bring

to a standstill, wind up. **2** (*She could not stop shivering*) refrain from, desist, cease, leave, hinder, impede, obstruct.

**story** *n* **1** (*a story about dragons*) tale, fairy story, myth, legend, fable. **2** (*the story of how he got home*) account, report.

**straight** *adj* **1** (*The picture is not straight*) level, in line. **2** (*a straight line*) non-curving, unbent. **3** (*They would not give a straight answer*) direct, forthright, frank, candid, honest, sincere.

**strange** *adj* **1** (*It was a strange sight*) peculiar, odd, queer, bizarre, weird. **2** (*a market stocking strange fruits*) exotic, foreign, alien, unfamiliar.

**strong** *adj* **1** (*require someone strong to lift the heavy furniture*) powerful, muscular, well-built, burly, sturdy, strapping, robust. **2**-(*strong doors at the castle entrance*) solid, heavy, sturdy. **3**-(*They have a very strong argument against closing the station*) sound, powerful, cogent, compelling. **4** (*There is a strong similarity between the two styles*) marked, noticeable, pronounced, distinct, definite, striking. **5** (*They have strong feelings on the subject of education*) intense, fervent, passionate. **6** (*wearing strong colors*) bright, vivid, deep, intense. **7**-(*strong coffee*) concentrated. **8**-(*take strong measures*) active, firm, severe, drastic, extreme.

**stupid** *adj* **1** (*He is too stupid to follow the instructions*) unintelligent, dumb, dense, dim, dull-witted, foolish. **2** (*It was a stupid thing to do*) foolish, absurd, silly, dumb, idiotic, unwise, unintelligent.

**suggest** *vb* **1** (*suggest a plan of action*) propose, put forward, recommend, advocate. **2** (*What are you suggesting?*) hint at, insinuate, imply.

**suit** *vb* **1** (*find a time for the meeting that suits both of them*) be suitable for, be convenient for. **2** (*a style of dress that does not suit her*) become. **3** (*You must try to suit your speech to the occasion*) fit, tailor, adapt, adjust.

**suitable** *adj* **1** (*The books are not suitable for the course*) suited, right, appropriate, apt, in keeping with. **2** (*come at a suitable time*) convenient, acceptable.

**supply** *n* (*have a supply of fuel for the winter*) store, stock, reserve, pile, mass, heap, hoard, stockpile.

**supply** *vb* (*They supply us with fuel*) give, provide, furnish, equip.

**support** *vb* **1** (*the uprights that support the bridge*) bear, prop up, hold up, shore up, underpin. **2** (*He supported the Democrats in the election*) back, champion, assist, aid, help, be on the side of, vote for. **3** (*support the cause of animal rights*) back, champion, promote, further, favor, defend. **4** (*evidence to support his point of view*) back,

bear out, substantiate, corroborate, confirm. **5** (*She works long hours to support the family*) maintain, provide for, look after, sustain.

**suppose** *vb* (*I suppose he will get there as soon as he can*) assume, presume, think, believe, expect, imagine.

**sure** *adj* **1** (*The police have to be sure that he is guilty*) certain, definite, positive, convinced, confident. **2** (*He felt that the project was a sure winner*) certain, definite, guaranteed, inevitable, (*inf*) in the bag. **3** (*a sure remedy for warts*) certain, unfailing, infallible, reliable, dependable.

**suspicious** *adj* **1** (*We are a bit suspicious of his story*) doubtful, distrustful, mistrustful, skeptical, disbelieving. **2** (*The circumstances of the case are rather suspicious*) odd, strange, queer, questionable, (*inf*) fishy. **3** (*a house now occupied by a suspicious character*) shady, shifty.

**sweater** *n* (*wear a warm sweater*) jersey, pullover, top, sweatshirt.

**sweet** *adj* **1** (*children who love sweet foods*) sugary, syrupy. **2**-(*the sweet smell of roses*) fragrant, perfumed, scented. **3** (*the sweet sound of the flute*) musical, tuneful, dulcet, melodious. **4**-(*What a sweet little girl*) delightful, charming, appealing, attractive. **5** (*She was always very sweet to us*) charming, pleasant, friendly, generous, kind, kindly, amiable.

**sympathy** *n* **1** (*They expressed their sympathy to the widow*) compassion, commiseration, pity, condolence, support, concern, consideration. **2** (*They have some sympathy for the cause of the protesters*) goodwill, approval, favor, support.

**synthetic** *adj* (*objects made of synthetic material*) man-made, manufactured, artificial, fake, mock.

**system** *n* **1** (*the public transportation system*) structure, organization, arrangement, set-up. **2** (*a new system for filing information*) method, process, means, technique.

# T

**table** *n* **1** (*pupils doing their homework at a table*) counter, bench, desk. **2** (*a book containing many tables*) diagram, chart, figure. **3** (*a table of contents at the front of the book*) list, catalog, index.

**tablet** *n* **1** (*take tablets for a headache*) pill, capsule. **2** (*The hotel provided tablets of soap*) bar, cake.

**tackle** *vb* (*He is going to tackle the job alone*) deal with, undertake, attempt, take on, apply oneself to.

**tactful** *adj* (*You will have to be tactful as she is*

*very sensitive*) diplomatic, discreet, delicate, subtle, sensitive.

**tactics** *npl* (*They used dishonest tactics to win*) strategy, maneuvers, scheme, plan, policy.

**tail** *n* **1** (*a fox's tail*) brush, scut. **2** (*We were at the tail of the line*) end, rear, back. **3** (*The police were on his tail*) trail, scent.

**tail** *vb* **1** (*police tailing the crook*) follow, shadow, stalk. **2** (*Business tails off at the end of fall*) dwindle, decrease, drop off, fall away, peter out, die away.

**take** *vb* **1** (*The child took his mother's hand*) take hold of, grasp, seize, grip, grab, clutch, **2** (*The soldiers took several prisoners*) seize, catch, capture, arrest. **3** (*Someone has taken the teacher's pen*) remove, go off with, pick up, move, steal, (*inf*) pinch. **4** (*She took her sister to the pictures*) escort, accompany, conduct, guide. **5** (*The journey takes two hours*) take up, use, need, require, call for. **6** (*The bus will take you right there*) transport, carry, convey. **7** (*He took the books to school with him*) carry, bear, fetch, convey. **8** (*She decided to take the red dress*) choose, pick, select, buy, purchase. **9** (*She took the bad news well*) receive, accept, deal with, cope with. **10** (*She takes Latin at school*) study, learn, be taught. **11** (*I take it that you do not agree*) understand, gather, assume, believe.

**tale** *n* **1** (*a fairy tale*) story, anecdote, legend, fable, narrative. **2** (*We hear tales of his bad behavior*) talk, rumor, gossip.

**talented** *adj* (*They are very talented musicians*) gifted, accomplished, able, capable, expert.

**talk** *vb* **1** (*The children were scolded for talking in class*) speak, express oneself, communicate, chatter, chat, gossip. **2** (*He was talking nonsense*) speak, say, utter, voice. **3** (*people are talking about her wild behavior*) gossip, comment, spread rumors.

**talk** *n* **1** (*The professor gave an interesting talk*) lecture, speech, address. **2** (*She wanted to have a talk with him about her career*) chat, discussion, conversation, tête à tête, (*inf*) confab.

**talkative** *adj* (*so talkative that no one else gets a chance to say anything*) garrulous, loquacious, voluble.

**tall** *adj* **1** (*Many good basketball players are tall*) big. **2** (*a town with many tall buildings*) high, lofty, towering.

**tame** *adj* (*The animal is quite tame*) domesticated, gentle.

**tamper** *vb* (*Someone had tampered with the papers on her desk*) interfere with, meddle with, fiddle with.

**tangled** *adj* **1** (*tangled hair/tangled wool*) entangled, twisted, knotted, matted. **2** (*tangled financial affairs*) confused, muddled, jumbled, complicated, involved.

**tap** *vb* **1** (*tap on the door*) knock, rap, bang. **2** (*Someone tapped me on the shoulder*) touch, pat.

**target** *n* **1** (*The archer failed to hit the target*) mark, bull's-eye. **2** (*The target for the appeal is $50,000*) goal, aim, objective. **3** (*The new girl is the target of all their teasing*) butt, victim, scapegoat.

**task** *n* (*tasks to be done around the house*) job, chore, duty, assignment.

**take (someone) to task** to reprimand or criticize (*someone*) (*The teacher took the student to task for his untidy homework*).

**taste** *n* **1** (*The food had an odd taste*) flavor, tang. **2** (*her taste in-literature*) like, liking, preference, inclination, predilection. **3** (*a house furnished with great taste*) style, elegance, refinement, discrimination.

**tasteless** *adj* **1** (*The soup was tasteless*) flavorless, bland, insipid, watery. **2** (*tasteless Christmas decorations in the stores*) vulgar, tawdry, flashy, garish. **3** (*She made a few tasteless remarks*) unseemly, indelicate, vulgar.

**teach** *vb* **1** (*She teaches the younger children*) educate, give lessons to, instruct, coach, train. **2** (*He teaches history*) give lessons in, give instruction in. **3** (*His father taught him how to ride a bike*) instruct, train, show.

**tease** *vb* **1** (*The cat will scratch you if you tease it*) torment, annoy, bother, provoke. **2** (*She was upset by his remark but he was only teasing*) joke, fool.

**technique** *n* **1** (*The tennis player is trying out a new technique*) method, system, approach. **2** (*We admired the technique of the sculptor*) skill, expertise, artistry, proficiency, knack.

**tedious** *adj* (*The work is tedious*) boring, monotonous, dull, wearisome.

**tell** *vb* **1** (*We told them the news*) inform, make known, impart, communicate, announce, disclose, declare. **2** (*He told the children a story*) recount, relate, narrate. **3** (*The children were told to go home*) instruct, order, command, direct. **4** (*They know her secret but promised not to tell*) tell tales, blab, give the game away, let the cat out of the bag, (*inf*) spill your guts. **5** (*We could not tell which twin was which*) distinguish, differentiate.

**temper** *n* **1** (*She is in a temper*) bad mood, ill humor, rage, fury, tantrum. **2** (*He is of uncertain temper*) temperament, disposition, nature, character, mood. **3** (*She lost her temper*) composure, self-control, coolness, calm, good humor.

**temperamental** *adj* (*She is a good worker but she is very temperamental*) excitable, emotional, volatile, moody.

**temporary** *adj* **1** (*They have got temporary jobs*) short-term, provisional, imperma-

nent. **2** (*His interest in golf was only temporary*) short-lived, brief, fleeting, ephemeral, transient.

**tempt** *vb* (*She was on a diet but was tempted by the sight of the chocolates*) entice, lure, attract, seduce.

**tendency** *n* **1** (*They have a tendency to tell lies*) inclination, leaning, propensity. **2** (*The upward tendency of the temperature graph*) movement, direction, trend, bias.

**tender** *adj* **1** (*The meat was tender*) not tough, juicy, succulent, soft. **2** (*She has a tender area on her head*) sore, painful, aching, irritated, inflamed. **3** (*The old man seems fierce but has a tender heart*) compassionate, soft-hearted, kind, sympathetic, caring, gentle.

**tense** *adj* **1** (*They are feeling tense as they wait for the results of the exam*) strained, under a strain, under pressure, overwrought, distraught, worked up, anxious, uneasy. **2** (*You have to keep the rope tense*) tight, taut, rigid, stretched, strained.

**tentative** *adj* **1** (*The toddler took a few tentative steps*) hesitant, hesitating, faltering, uncertain, cautious. **2** (*She asked if she could make a tentative suggestion*) speculative, exploratory, experimental, trial, untried.

**term** *n* **1** (*a document full of technical terms*) word, expression, phrase, name, title. **2** (*the mayor's term of office*) period, time, spell, interval, duration.

**terrible** *adj* **1** (*refugees who endured terrible hardship*) dreadful, appalling, shocking, horrible, horrific, grim. **2** (*the terrible heat from the fire*) extreme, severe, intolerable. **3** (*There was a terrible smell from the drains*) nasty, foul, vile, offensive, obnoxious. **4** (*He is a terrible dancer*) very bad, poor, incompetent, useless, dreadful, (*inf*) rotten.

**terrify** *vb* (*Walking through the graveyard at night would terrify her*) frighten, scare, alarm, petrify, terrorize.

**terror** *n* **1** (*She was gripped with terror when she heard the noise*) fear, dread, alarm, panic. **2** (*That boy's a little terror*) rascal, rogue, imp, hooligan.

**test** *n* **1** (*The children are having an English test*) exam, examination. **2** (*a hearing test*) examination, check, assessment, appraisal, investigation, exploration. **3** (*the test of a successful movie*) criterion, touchstone, yardstick, standard, measure.

**test** *vb* **1** (*test the child's hearing*) examine, check, assess, appraise, investigate, explore, analyze. **2** (*The children's behavior really tested his patience*) try, tax, strain. **3** (*test the car*) try out, try.

**text** *n* **1** (*The text of his speech was world poverty*) topic, subject, subject matter, theme. **2** (*in the introduction, not in the text of the book*) body, main part. **3** (*He is responsible for the text but not the illustrations of the book*) words, wording.

**thankful** *adj* (*Her parents were thankful that she was safe*) grateful, full of gratitude, appreciative, relieved.

**thaw** *vb* (*The ice began to thaw*) melt, defrost, liquefy.

**theft** *n* (*There have been a series of thefts from stores*) stealing, robbery, thieving, burglary, larceny, pilfering.

**theoretical** *adj* (*He was describing a theoretical situation rather than an actual one*) hypothetical, speculative, assumed.

**thick** *adj* **1** (*Thick snow lay on the roads*) deep. **2** (*She was reading a very thick book*) fat, substantial. **3**-(*She thinks that she has thick legs*) broad, wide, fat, large, solid. **4** (*a thick rope to tie up the logs*) strong, stout, sturdy. **5** (*A thick mist descended*) dense, heavy, solid. **6** (*a voice thick with emotion*) husky, gruff, hoarse, rough, guttural, throaty.

**thief** *n* (*The thief got away with his-watch*) robber, pickpocket, shoplifter, mugger, burglar, housebreaker.

**thin** *adj* **1** (*She is thin and ill-looking*) underweight, skinny, scrawny, emaciated, gaunt, skeletal. **2** (*She is on a diet to try to get thin*) slim, slender, svelte, light. **3** (*a design formed of thin lines*) fine, narrow, delicate. **4** (*a dress made of a very thin material*) light, lightweight, delicate, flimsy, sheer, filmy. **5** (*She is worried about having thin hair*) sparse, scanty, wispy. **6** (*The custard was too thin*) dilute, watery, runny. **7** (*They had hoped for a large crowd but the audience was rather thin*) sparse, scarce, scanty, meager. **8** (*rather a thin voice*) weak, low, feeble, faint. **9** (*It was rather a thin excuse*) flimsy, weak, feeble, poor, unconvincing, inadequate.

**thing** *n* **1** (*There was a huge pile of things on the table*) article, item, object. **2** (*It was a sensible thing to do*) action, act, deed, undertaking. **3** (*It was a dreadful thing to happen*) incident, event, occurrence, happening. **4** (*Calmness is a useful thing to have in a crisis*) quality, characteristic, attribute, trait. **5** (*There are a few things which we should discuss*) fact, point, detail, particular. **6** (*The poor thing had nowhere to go*) wretch, creature. **7** (*She has a thing about spiders*) phobia, fear, aversion, dislike, horror.

**think** *vb* **1** (*You must think before you act*) reflect, deliberate, concentrate, contemplate, ponder, ruminate. **2**-(*The old lady was thinking about the past*) remember, recall, call to mind, reminisce. **3** (*We think that they will arrive tomorrow*) believe, expect, suppose, imagine, assume. **4** (*He is thought to be brilliant*) consider, regard, hold, deem.

**thirst** *adj* **1** (*They nearly died of thirst in the desert*) thirstiness, dehydration. **2** (*They had a great thirst for knowledge*) desire, craving, longing, yearning, avidity, eagerness, keenness.

**thorough** *adj* **1** (*The police conducted a thorough investigation*) exhaustive, in-depth, comprehensive, intensive, extensive. **2** (*He is a slow worker but he is thorough*) meticulous, painstaking, punctilious, assiduous, careful. **3** (*He is a thorough villain*) thoroughgoing, utter, out-and-out, absolute, sheer, complete.

**thought** *n* **1** (*He is now incapable of rational thought*) thinking, powers of reasoning. **2** (*She was deep in thought*) thinking, reflection, contemplation, deliberation, musing. **3** (*I had a sudden thought as to what we should do*) idea, line of thought, notion. **4**-(*We shall give the matter some thought*) consideration, attention, heed, regard. **5** (*We asked her for-her thoughts on the subject*) idea, opinion, view, feeling. **6** (*In giving gifts it is the thought that counts*) thoughtfulness, consideration, care, kindness, compassion.

**thoughtful** *adj* **1** (*He seemed in a thoughtful mood*) reflective, contemplative, meditative, introspective, absorbed. **2** (*She is a thoughtful daughter*) considerate, attentive, caring, solicitous, helpful, kind, kindly.

**threaten** *vb* **1** (*The bully threatened the younger children*) make threats, menace, intimidate, browbeat, bully, pressure. **2** (*pollution threatens the environment*) be a threat to, menace, be a danger to, endanger, put at risk, jeopardize, put in jeopardy, imperil. **3** (*Rain was threatening*) be imminent, loom, be impending.

**thrifty** *adj* (*They have to be thrifty as they do not have much money*) economical, careful, frugal, sparing.

**thrill** *vb* (*The children were thrilled by the display of acrobatics*) excite, stimulate, arouse, stir, electrify, give joy to, (*inf*) get a kick out of.

**thrive** *vb* **1** (*The house plants thrive in that room*) flourish, do well, burgeon. **2** (*The firm is now thriving*) flourish, prosper, do well, boom.

**throb** *vb* (*His pulse throbbed normally/Her heart throbbed*) beat, pulse, palpitate, pound, vibrate, thump.

**throw** *vb* **1** (*He threw a brick through the window*) hurl, fling, toss, cast, lob, sling, (*inf*) chuck. **2**-(*She threw him a warning glance*) cast, send, give, bestow on. **3** (*She threw away all her old clothes*) throw out, discard, dispose of, get rid of, dispense with, (*inf*) dump. **4**-(*The question completely threw him*) baffle, bamboozle, dumbfound, disconcert, astonish.

**thrust** *vb* **1** (*He thrust the present into her hands*) push, shove, ram. **2** (*They thrust the door open*) push, shove, drive, press, propel. **3** (*They thrust their way to the front of the crowd*) push, shove, press, force, shoulder, elbow, jostle.

**thud** *n* (*The box fell with a loud thud*) thump, bang, crash, wham.

**thug** *n* (*The thug attacked the old man*) ruffian, villain, hoodlum, hood, rogue, tough.

**thump** *vb* **1** (*He turned round and thumped his attacker*) strike, hit, punch, wallop, smack, slap, batter. **2** (*Her heart was thumping in terror*) thud, pulse, pulsate, throb, palpitate. **3** (*He thumped on the table*) bang, batter, beat, crash, knock.

**thwart** *vb* (*Their plans for expansion were thwarted*) frustrate, foil, check, block, obstruct, impede, hamper, stop.

**tidy** *adj* **1** (*The room was very tidy*) neat, orderly, in order, in good order, clean, shipshape, spick-and-span, spruce. **2** (*Everyone had to be tidy for the school photograph*) neat, wellgroomed, spruce. **3** (*He is not a tidy person*) neat, orderly, organized, methodical, systematic.

**tie** *vb* **1** (*He tied the string*) knot, make a bow in. **2** (*They tied the parcel with string*) bind. **3** (*They had to tie the dog to the gate*) tie up, tether, fasten, secure, attach, fix. **4** (*The two teams tied for first place*) draw, be equal, be even, be neck and neck.

**tight** *adj* **1** (*She wore a tight skirt instead of a full one*) tight-fitting, close-fitting, figure-hugging, narrow. **2** (*You must keep the rope tight*) taut, rigid, stiff, tense, stretched, strained. **3** (*She kept a tight grip on her mother's hand*) fast, secure. **4** (*We need a jar with a tight lid*) airtight, watertight, sealed, hermetically sealed. **5** (*make sure that the screws are tight*) secure, fast, fixed. **6** (*a tight mass of fibers*) compact, compressed. **7** (*Space was tight in the small house*) cramped, restricted, limited. **8** (*Security was tight at the meeting of the presidents*) strict, rigorous, stringent. **9** (*Money was tight*) scarce, scant, in short supply, limited, inadequate, insufficient.

**time** *n* **1** (*in the time of the cavemen*) period, age, era, epoch. **2** (*He seemed fine the last time I-saw him*) occasion, point, juncture. **3** (*He felt that it was time to leave*) moment, point, stage. **4** (*I worked in Spain for a time*) while, period, spell. **5** (*It was a tune in waltz time*) rhythm, measure, tempo, beat.

**timetable** *n* (*give out copies of the conference timetable*) schedule, program, list, agenda.

**timid** *adj* **1** (*The pupils were too timid to stand up to the bullies*) timorous, fearful, afraid,

**tingle** apprehensive, frightened, scared, cowardly. **2** (*She was too timid to ask the pop star for his autograph*) timorous, shy, bashful, diffident, reticent, retiring.

**tingle** *vb* (*Her fingers were tingling*) prickle, tickle, itch, sting, quiver, tremble.

**tint** *n* **1** (*The artist had several tints to choose from*) color, shade, tone. **2** (*an auburn hair tint*) dye, colorant, coloring.

**tiny** *adj* **1** (*a tiny insect*) minute, diminutive, miniature, microscopic, infinitesimal, minuscule. **2** (*a tiny amount of water*) small, trifling, negligible, minor, insignificant.

**tip** *vb* **1** (*The dog tipped over the garbage can*) upset, overturn, topple, capsize. **2** (*She tipped the water into the bucket*) pour, empty. **3** (*The cupboard tends to tip*) tilt, lean, list, cant. **4** (*He tipped the horse to win*) back, put one's money on, recommend. **5**-(*tip the waiter*) give a tip to, reward.

**tip** *n* **1** (*the tip of the iceberg*) point, peak, top, apex. **2** (*the tips of his fingers*) end, extremity. **3** (*give the waiter a tip*) gratuity, reward, remuneration. **4** (*She gave him a few tips on cooking*) hint, suggestion, advice. **5** (*a racing tip*) recommendation.

**tired** *adj* **1** (*They were tired after their long walk*) weary, fatigued, worn out, exhausted. **2** (*The comic told a series of tired jokes*) stale, hackneyed, outworn, trite, banal. **3** (*They were tired of her endless complaints*) bored, weary.

**tiresome** *adj* (*She finds the work tiresome*) wearisome, tedious, boring, dull, monotonous, unexciting, uninteresting.

**title** *n* **1** (*the title of the book*) name. **2** (*What title does the king's nephew have?*) form of address, name, designation.

**tolerate** *vb* **1** (*We could not tolerate the noise from next door*) put up with, stand, bear, endure. **2** (*people should be able to tolerate views that are different from theirs*) permit, allow, recognize, sanction, brook.

**tone** *n* **1** (*He enjoys the sweet tone of the flute*) sound, pitch, timbre. **2**-(*He spoke in a whispered tone*) voice, intonation, inflection. **3** (*The tone of his letter was threatening*) mood, spirit, manner, tenor, vein, gist. **4** (*She was dressed in tones of blue*) tint, shade, tinge.

**tool** *n* (*The workman forgot one of his tools*) implement, instrument, utensil, gadget, appliance.

**top** *n* **1** (*They reached the top of the mountain*) peak, summit, crest, apex. **2** (*They are at the top of their careers*) height, peak, pinnacle, zenith, acme, culmination, climax. **3** (*replace the top on the bottle*) lid, cap, stopper, cork. **4** (*They were at the top of the line*) head, front. **5** (*The child wore a white summer top*) sweater, sweatshirt, jersey, blouse, shirt, T-shirt.

**topical** *adj* (*The pupils were asked to write about something topical*) newsworthy, in the news, current, contemporary, up-to-date.

**toss** *vb* **1** (*She tossed the book on the sofa*) throw, fling, hurl. **2** (*ships tossing on the waves*) rock, roll, sway, lurch, pitch, heave. **3** (*The horse tossed its head*) throw back, jerk. **4** (*They tossed and turned unable to sleep*) thrash, writhe, tumble.

**total** *adj* **1** (*the total amount of money*) complete, entire, whole, full. **2** (*He's a total fool*) complete, thorough, utter, absolute, downright.

**touch** *vb* **1** (*The two wires should touch*) be in contact, come together, meet. **2** (*She touched his arm*) put her hand on, tap, pat. **3**-(*You shouldn't touch his private things*) handle, pick up, hold, fiddle with, interfere with. **4** (*They were touched by the orphan's sad story*) affect, move, upset, disturb. **5** (*Some firms were not touched by the recession*) affect, have an effect on, concern, have a bearing on.

**tough** *adj* **1** (*objects made of a tough substance*) strong, durable, solid, sturdy, rigid, stiff. **2** (*The meat was tough*) chewy, leathery, gristly, sinewy. **3** (*They had to be tough to survive the weather conditions*) hardy, rugged, robust, sturdy, strong. **4** (*The job was very tough*) difficult, hard, arduous, strenuous, laborious. **5** (*They had a tough life*) hard, harsh, austere, rugged, rough, grim, difficult. **6** (*the tough kids of the district*) rough, rowdy, unruly, disorderly, wild, violent, law-breaking.

**tourist** *n* (*foreign tourists visiting the city*) visitor, traveler, sightseer, vacationer.

**tower** *n* (*a church tower*) spire, steeple, belfry, turret.

**trace** *n* **1** (*We could find no trace of where they had camped*) mark, sign, remains, vestige, indication, evidence. **2** (*There was not a trace of shame in his expression*) bit, hint, suggestion, suspicion, shadow, jot, iota. **3** (*follow the animal's traces*) track, trail, spoor, scent.

**trace** *vb* (*They were unable to trace their lost son/We tried to trace the missing letter*) find, discover, detect, track down, unearth, ferret out.

**track** *n* **1** (*The hunters were following the tracks of the bear*) marks, traces, prints, trail, spoor, scent. **2**-(*They followed the track up the mountain*) path, road, trail. **3** (*The train suddenly left the track*) rail, line. **4** (*The runners had to run ten times round the track*) course, running track, racetrack.

**trade** *n* (*He is in the export trade*) commerce, business.

**tradition** *n* (*keep up the old traditions*) custom, habit, belief, practice, convention, institution.

**traffic** *n* (*The noise of traffic kept him awake*) vehicles, cars.

**tragedy** *n* (*She was sad because of some tragedy in her life*) disaster, calamity, misfortune, adversity.

**tragic** *adj* **1** (*appalled at her tragic story about her childhood*) sad, unhappy, pathetic, moving, distressing, pitiful. **2** (*She was killed in a tragic accident*) disastrous, calamitous, catastrophic, terrible, dreadful, appalling, dire.

**trail** *vb* **1** (*They trailed the fallen trees behind them*) tow, pull, drag, haul, draw. **2** (*They trailed the moose through the forest*) follow, pursue, track, trace, tail, shadow.

**train** *vb* **1** (*She is training the students in cooking techniques*) teach, coach, instruct, educate, give lessons to. **2** (*She is training to be a vet*) study, learn. **3** (*The football players have to train every evening*) work out, do exercises, practice.

**tramp** *n* **1** (*tramps with no place to sleep*) transient, hobo, vagrant, derelict, down-and-outer. **2** (*go for a tramp over the hills*) hike, trek, march, ramble, wander, walk.

**tranquil** *adj* **1** (*a tranquil country scene*) peaceful, restful, quiet, still, serene. **2** (*a very tranquil person*) calm, serene, placid, composed.

**transfer** *vb* (*He transferred the furniture from one house to another*) move, shift, take, carry, convey, transport.

**transform** *vb* (*The new furnishings transformed the room*) change, alter, transfigure, revolutionize.

**transmit** *vb* (*transmit the information electronically*) pass on, transfer, communicate, spread, send, carry.

**transparent** *adj* **1** (*things made of a transparent material*) clear, seethrough. **2** (*They were impressed by his transparent honesty*) obvious, clear, unmistakable, evident, noticeable, apparent.

**travel** *vb* **1** (*They travel a lot in the course of their work*) journey, move around, take a trip. **2** (*the speed at which sound travels*) be transmitted, proceed, progress. **3** (*They travel the country begging*) journey, cross, traverse, roam, wander.

**treacherous** *adj* (*He was betrayed by a treacherous friend*) traitorous, disloyal, faithless, double-dealing, untrustworthy.

**treasure** *n* (*They looked for buried treasure*) riches, valuables, wealth, fortune.

**treat** *vb* **1** (*He treated his children badly*) act towards, behave towards, deal with, cope with, use. **2** (*They treated his remarks as a joke*) regard, consider, view. **3** (*The doctor treated the patient*) attend to, cure, heal, give treatment to, give medication to. **4** (*treat the wood with something to preserve it*) apply to, put on. **6** (*They treated us to dinner*) pay for, entertain, take out.

**7** (*She treats the subject in an original way*) deal with, discuss, consider, write about, speak about.

**tremble** *vb* (*They were trembling with fear*) shake, quiver, quake, shudder.

**tremendous** *adj* **1** (*It made a tremendous difference to their lives*) huge, enormous, great, immense, vast, colossal. **2** (*She is a tremendous cook*) excellent, exceptional, remarkable, wonderful, fabulous.

**trend** *n* **1** (*witness an upward trend in prices*) tendency, drift, swing, course. **2** (*She always follows fashion trends*) fashion, style, fad.

**trial** *n* **1** (*She was a witness at a murder trial*) court case, case, hearing. **2**-(*He is giving the young man a trial as a trainee mechanic*) trial period, probation. **3** (*cars having passed safety trials*) test, try-out, check. **4**-(*facing the trials of life*) trouble, worry, burden, hardship, suffering.

**trick** *n* **1** (*He gained entry to her house by a trick*) deception, hoax, ruse, stratagem, subterfuge. **2** (*The children played tricks on each other*) practical joke, joke, hoax, prank.

**trick** *vb* (*He was tricked into giving her his life's savings*) cheat, deceive, delude, mislead, hoodwink, dupe, swindle, defraud.

**trip** *vb* (*She tripped over her shoe laces*) stumble, lose one's footing, lose one's balance, slip, fall, tumble.

**trip** *n* (*They went on a trip to the coast*) excursion, outing, jaunt, expedition.

**triumphant** *adj* **1** (*He gave a triumphant shout when he won*) exultant, joyful, jubilant. **2** (*the triumphant team*) winning, victorious, successful.

**trivial** *adj* (*They quarreled over something trivial*) unimportant, insignificant, inconsequential, petty, minor, negligible.

**trouble** *n* **1** (*Their teenage children are causing them some trouble*) worry, bother, anxiety, disquiet, unease, inconvenience, difficulty, problems. **2** (*There has been a great deal of trouble in her life*) misfortune, difficulty, hardship, distress, suffering, unhappiness, sadness. **3** (*Our hosts went to a great deal of trouble*) bother, inconvenience, disturbance, fuss, effort. **4** (*There was a bit of trouble in the restaurant last night*) disturbance, disorder, strife, fighting, commotion. **5** (*He has chest trouble*) disorder, disease, illness.

**trust** *vb* **1** (*We do not trust his judgment*) place one's trust in, have confidence in, have faith in, believe in, be convinced by. **2** (*You can trust them to help if they offer*) rely on, bank on, depend on, count on, be sure of. **3** (*We trust that you will be there*) hope, assume, presume, expect, suppose.

**true** *adj* **1** (*What she said is true*) truthful, accurate, right, correct, genuine, reliable. **2** (*They have been true friends since childhood*) real, genuine, loyal, faithful, trustworthy, reliable, dependable. **3** (*The book gives a true account of the war*) accurate, correct, exact, precise, faithful, close.

**trustworthy** *adj* (*He thinks that all his employees are trustworthy*) reliable, dependable, loyal, staunch, faithful, trusty, honest, honorable.

**truth** *n* **1** (*There seemed little truth in what he said*) truthfulness, accuracy, correctness, rightness, validity, veracity. **2** (*Truth is often stranger than fiction*) reality, actuality.

**try** *vb* **1** (*You must try to do well*) attempt, aim, endeavor, make an effort, exert oneself, strive, struggle. **2** (*We tried a new kind of cereal*) try out, test, evaluate. **3**-(*The children are trying her patience*) tax, strain, exhaust. **4** (*He was the judge who tried the case*) hear, judge, adjudicate.

**trying** *adj* **1** (*They had had a trying day*) taxing, demanding, difficult, stressful, hard, tough, arduous. **2**-(*The children were particularly trying that day*) troublesome, tiresome, annoying, irritating, exasperating.

**tuck** *vb* **1** (*She tucked her blouse into her skirt*) push, ease, insert, stuff. **2** (*tuck the child in at night*) cover up, wrap up. **3** (*They tucked into a hearty meal*) eat, devour, wolf down, gobble up.

**tug** *vb* **1** (*She tugged at the rope*) pull, jerk, yank. **2** (*The child tugged a toy cart behind him*) drag, draw, tow, lug.

**tumble** *vb* **1** (*Watch that the child does not tumble*) fall over, fall headlong, topple, stumble, trip. **2**-(*prices have tumbled*) fall, drop, plummet, plunge, slump.

**tune** *n* (*a group playing a folk tune*) melody, air, song.

**turn** *vb* **1** (*The wheel began to turn*) go round, rotate, revolve, spin, whirl, twirl. **2** (*He turned the car in the driveway*) turn round, reverse, make a U-turn. **3** (*He turned the steaks over on the grill*) turn over, flip over, invert, reverse. **4** (*The weather turned stormy*) become, grow, get. **5**-(*Tadpoles turn into frogs*) become, change into. **6** (*The car turned the corner*) go round, round. **7** (*He turned the attic into a bedroom*) convert, change, transform, alter, modify.

**tussle** *n* (*The two boys had a tussle to gain possession of the bag*) struggle, fight, scuffle, skirmish.

**tweak** *vb* (*The boy tweaked his friend's ear*) twist, pinch, nip, pull, jerk.

**twilight** *n* (*They walked home at twilight*) dusk, half-light.

**twinkle** *vb* (*The stars twinkled*) sparkle, glitter, glint, flicker, shimmer.

**twist** *vb* **1** (*The extreme heat had twisted the metal*) bend, warp, distort, buckle. **2** (*He twisted the string round his finger*) wind, coil, curl, twine, twirl, loop. **3** (*The road twists up the mountain*) curve, wind, zigzag, snake, meander. **4**-(*The ropes became twisted*) entangle, tangle, entwine. **5** (*They twisted his words*) distort, garble, misrepresent, falsify. **6** (*She twisted her head round to look at him*) turn, swivel, screw.

**type** *n* **1** (*a type of plant/a type of person*) kind, variety, sort, form, class. **2**-(*in italic type*) print, face, font.

**twitch** *n* **1** (*Her arm gave a twitch*) spasm, jerk, jump, quiver, tremor. **2** (*He has a twitch in his eye*) blink, flutter, tic.

# U

**ugly** *adj* **1** (*an ugly monster/ugly buildings*) hideous, unattractive, unprepossessing, horrible, frightful. **2** (*The war situation grew more ugly*) dangerous, threatening, menacing, ominous, hostile, nasty.

**umpire** *n* (*The umpire in the tournament*) referee, judge, adjudicator, arbitrator, (*inf*) ref.

**unanimous** *adj* (*The committee was unanimous in its decision to close down the club*) agreed, united, likeminded, at one, in harmony, with one voice.

**unaware** *adj* (*They were unaware of what people were saying about them*) unconscious, ignorant, oblivious, heedless, (*inf*) in the dark.

**uncanny** *adj* **1** (*There were uncanny happenings in the graveyard at night*) strange, odd, mysterious, eerie, weird, unnatural, supernatural. **2** (*She bore an uncanny resemblance to her grandmother*) remarkable, striking, extraordinary, astonishing, incredible.

**uncertain** *adj* **1** (*The result of the talks is still uncertain*) unknown, undetermined, unsettled, up in the air. **2** (*We are uncertain about whether to go or stay*) unsure, doubtful, undecided, dubious, unresolved, indecisive, wavering, in two minds. **3** (*The future is uncertain*) unpredictable, risky, chancy.

**uncouth** *adj* (*uncouth table manners*) rough, coarse, uncivilized, unrefined, unpolished, boorish, ill-bred.

**under** *prep* **1** (*She sat under the tree*) below, underneath, beneath. **2** (*prices under $10*) below, less than, lower than. **3** (*army ranks under major*) low, lower than, inferior to, subordinate to, junior to.

**undergo** *vb* (*undergo a terrible experience*) go through, experience, be subjected to, endure.

**underground** adj 1 (an underground shelter) subterranean, sunken. 2-(an underground organization) secret, clandestine, undercover, surreptitious.

**undergrowth** n (The animals emerged from the undergrowth) thicket, brushwood.

**underhand** adj (She got the job by underhand methods) deceitful, devious, crafty, cunning, sneaky, furtive, dishonest.

**underline** vb (The burglary underlined the need for security staff) emphasize, stress, highlight.

**undermine** vb (They tried to undermine the authority of the manager) weaken, impair, damage, destroy.

**understand** vb 1 (We did not understand his instructions) comprehend, grasp, take in, follow, fathom, interpret. 2 (She failed to understand how the homeless people felt) appreciate, sympathize with. 3 (We understand that he has left) gather, hear, be informed, learn, believe.

**understanding** n 1 (They have a very poor understanding of the facts) comprehension, grasp, knowledge, awareness. 2 (His powers of understanding are poor) reasoning, brain power, (inf) gray matter. 3 (The two businessmen did not sign a contract but they had an unofficial understanding) agreement, gentleman's agreement, arrangement, deal, pact. 4-(She treated the difficult situation with great understanding) sensitivity, consideration, insight, compassion, sympathy. 5 (It was our understanding that he was leaving) belief, opinion, feeling.

**undertake** vb (They agreed to undertake the difficult task) take on, assume, tackle, set about, enter upon.

**underwear** n (wear warm underwear in winter) underclothes, underclothing, undergarments, lingerie.

**undo** vb 1 (She undid the hook on her dress) unfasten, unhook, unbutton, untie, loosen, open. 2-(They undid all his good work) destroy, ruin, wreck, upset. 3 (She called to undo the arrangements for the meeting) cancel, annul, revoke, set aside.

**unearth** vb 1 (The police have unearthed new information about the murder) uncover, discover, find, come across, bring to light, expose, turn up. 2 (The dog unearthed an old bone) dig up, excavate, exhume.

**unearthly** adj (They heard an unearthly shriek coming from the cave) eerie, uncanny, supernatural, ghostly, weird.

**uneasy** adj (They felt uneasy when their son did not arrive home) anxious, worried, concerned, troubled, nervous.

**unemployed** adj (He has been unemployed for a year) jobless, out of work.

**unfasten** vb (unfasten the gate/unfasten the knot) undo, open, loose, untie, unlock.

**unfortunate** adj 1 (in unfortunate circumstances) adverse, disadvantageous, unfavorable. 2 (The unfortunate girl lost all her money) unlucky, out of luck, luckless, wretched, unhappy. 3 (It was a most unfortunate remark) regrettable, inappropriate, tactless.

**unhappy** adj (She was unhappy when her dog died) sad, miserable, sorrowful, dejected, gloomy.

**uniform** adj 1 (pieces of cloth of uniform length) same, alike, like, equal, identical. 2 (keep the room at a uniform temperature) constant, unvarying, unchanging, regular, even.

**uninterested** adj (They were completely uninterested in the subject) bored, indifferent, apathetic.

**union** n (a union of youth clubs) association, alliance, league, federation.

**unique** adj 1 (a unique specimen) one and only, single, sole, solitary, exclusive. 2 (The salesman pointed out the unique features of the dishwasher) distinctive, unequalled, unparalleled.

**unit** n 1 (The English course is divided into units) component, part, section, portion, element. 2-(The meter is a unit of length) measurement, measure, quantity.

**unite** vb 1 (The two sides united to fight their common enemy) join, join together, get together, join forces, amalgamate, combine, merge. 2 (They decided to unite the two teams) join, combine, amalgamate, merge, link, fuse.

**universal** adj (poverty is a universal problem) general, widespread, common, global, international, worldwide.

**universe** n (the wonders of the universe) world, cosmos.

**unlikely** adv (It is unlikely that they will arrive on time) improbable, doubtful.

**unlucky** adj 1 (He was unlucky not to win/a most unlucky young man) out of luck, luckless, down on one's luck, unfortunate, hapless. 2-(By an unlucky set of circumstances they failed to arrive on time) unfortunate, adverse, disadvantageous, unfavorable.

**unmarried** adj (She is unmarried and lives with her parents) single, unwed, unattached.

**unpleasant** adj (an unpleasant experience/an unpleasant person) disagreeable, nasty, horrible.

**unreal** adj (a story about an unreal world) imaginary, fictitious, makebelieve, mythical.

**unruly** adj (The teacher could not control the unruly children) rowdy, wild, disorderly, noisy, uncontrollable, unmanageable.

**unsightly** adj (unsightly modern apartment building in a historical area) ugly, unattractive, hideous, horrible.

**unsuccessful** adj (Their attempt to save the firm was unsuccessful) without success, in vain, failed, futile, useless, ineffective.

**untangle** vb (untangle the knots) disentangle, unravel, straighten out.

**untidy** adj 1 (The room where the children were playing was very untidy) in disorder, disordered, disarranged, chaotic, disorganized. 2-(The children were scolded for being untidy) disheveled, unkempt, rumpled, messy.

**untie** vb (untie the gate/untie the string) undo, unfasten, loosen.

**untrue** adj (We felt that his account of the accident was untrue) false, fallacious, erroneous, wrong, inaccurate.

**unusual** adj (His behavior was unusual) uncommon, out of the ordinary, abnormal, odd, different, irregular.

**unwell** adj (She is unwell and is off work) ill, sick, ailing, unhealthy, (inf) under the weather.

**unwilling** adj (They were unwilling to set off so late) reluctant, disinclined, loath, averse.

**upbringing** n (They had a very strict upbringing) rearing, training.

**upheaval** n (Moving house caused a terrible upheaval) disturbance, disruption, disorder, turmoil, chaos, confusion.

**upkeep** n (pay for the upkeep of the house) maintenance, running, support.

**upper** adj 1 (the upper shelf) higher. 2 (the upper ranks in the army) higher, superior, senior.

**upright** adj 1 (the upright posts in the fence) erect, vertical, perpendicular. 2 (He is an upright member of the community) honest, honorable, decent, respectable, lawabiding, upstanding.

**uproar** n (There was uproar when the referee made a dubious decision) disturbance, turmoil, tumult, commotion, pandemonium, bedlam, riot, rumpus.

**upset** vb 1 (His remarks upset her) hurt, distress, worry, bother. 2 (The animals were upset by the thunderstorm) agitate, alarm, frighten. 3 (He got a new job and upset our vacation plans) disorganize, disarrange, (inf) mess up. 4 (The child upset the pail of water) overturn, knock over, upend, capsize, tip over.

**upshot** n (The upshot of the quarrel was that he left) result, outcome, end, conclusion.

**up-to-date** adj (His ideas are very up-to-date) modern, current, contemporary, fashionable.

**urban** n (urban areas) city, town, metropolitan, inner city.

**urbane** adj (an urbane man whom women found charming) suave, smooth, sophisticated, elegant, cultivated, polished, refined, gracious, courteous.

**urge** vb 1 (urge the cows to the milking shed)

drive, propel, force, push, hurry. **2** (*We urged her to accept the-invitation*) advise, encourage, prompt, entreat, exhort. **3** (*The applause of the crowd urged the players on to greater effort*) spur, incite, stimulate, prod, goad, encourage, egg on.

**urge** *n* (*She had a sudden urge to laugh*) desire, compulsion, need, wish, impulse, longing.

**urgent** *adj* **1** (*It is urgent that we get him to hospital*) imperative, a matter of life or death, vital, crucial, critical, essential. **2** (*We have urgent matters to discuss*) important, crucial, vital, serious, grave, pressing.

**use** *n* **1** (*The lotion we bought at the drugstore is for external use only*) application, utilization, employment. **2** (*What use is this old chair?*) usefulness, good, benefit, service. **3** (*We have no use for this old bike*) need, purpose.

**use** *vb* **1** (*Do you know how to use this machine?*) make use of, utilize, work, operate, employ, wield. **2**-(*You will have to use tact*) exercise, employ, apply. **3** (*Have you used all the flour?*) consume, get through.

**used** *adj* (*a store selling used clothing*) second-hand, nearly new, cast-off.

**useful** *adj* (*This is a useful kitchen gadget*) of use, practical, of service, handy, convenient.

**usual** *adj* **1** (*the mailman's usual route*) regular, accustomed, customary, habitual, normal, routine, set, established. **2** (*The weather was usual for the time of year*) common, typical, standard, normal, average, run-of-the-mill.

**usually** *adv* (*We usually go out to lunch on Saturday*) generally, as a rule, normally, mostly, for the most part.

**utter** *vb* (*We heard him utter threats*) say, speak, voice, pronounce, express.

**utter** *adj* (*They are utter fools*) complete, absolute, total, thorough, outand-out, perfect.

**utterly** *adv* (*We were utterly delighted at the news*) absolutely, completely, totally, thoroughly, perfectly.

# V

**vacant** *adj* **1** (*The house is vacant*) empty, unoccupied, uninhabited, to let, deserted. **2** (*several vacant positions in the firm*) free, available, unfilled, unoccupied, empty. **3** (*look for a vacant seat*) empty, free, unoccupied, unused. **4** (*He wore a vacant look*) expressionless, blank, inexpressive, deadpan.

**vacation** *n* (*We have our bags packed ready for our summer vacation*) annual leave.

**vagrant** *n* (*vagrants begging for money for food*) tramp, transient, homeless person, hobo.

**vague** *adj* **1** (*She has only a vague idea about her duties in her new job*), hazy, imprecise, ill-defined, uncertain, nebulous. **2** (*Our vacation plans are still rather vague*) hazy, uncertain, undecided, indefinite, (*inf*) up in the air, doubtful. **3**-(*He gave rather a vague description of the person who attacked him*) imprecise, inexact, loose, hazy, wooly. **4** (*A vague shape loomed out-of the mist*) indistinct, indeterminate, shadowy, unclear, hazy, dim, fuzzy. **5** (*She is rather a vague person*) absentminded, dreamy, with one's head in the clouds.

**vain** *adj* **1** (*They made a vain attempt to save the drowning man*) unsuccessful, futile, useless, ineffective, abortive, unprofitable. **2** (*He is a very vain young man*) conceited, proud, arrogant, egotistical, narcissistic, cocky, (*inf*) big-headed.

**valiant** *adj* (*He made a valiant attempt to save his friend's life in the war*) brave, courageous, gallant, heroic, bold.

**valid** *adj* **1** (*The school regulation is still valid*) in force, effective, in effect, legal, lawful. **2** (*He has valid reasons for lodging an objection*) sound, well-founded, reasonable, justifiable, authentic.

**valuable** *adj* **1** (*The burglars took some valuable jewelry*) expensive, costly, high-priced, precious, priceless. **2** (*The old man gave them some valuable advice*) useful, helpful, beneficial, worthwhile.

**value** *n* **1** (*It is difficult to place a value on the antique table*) price, market price, cost. **2** (*She tried to convince the children of the value of a balanced diet*) worth, benefit, merit, advantage, gain, importance.

**value** *vb* **1** (*They asked him to value their house*) set a price on, price, place a value on. **2** (*She values the contribution that parents make to sports events*) appreciate, think highly of, rate highly, set store by.

**vanish** *vb* **1** (*The figure seemed to vanish into the mist*) disappear, fade, melt. **2** (*They were talking about a way of life that has now vanished*) go, die out, disappear, end, come to an end.

**vanquish** *vb* (*They vanquished the enemy army*) conquer, defeat, triumph over, overcome, crush, trounce.

**varied** *adj* (*a varied selection of magazines*) assorted, mixed, miscellaneous, diversified.

**variety** *n* **1** (*They tried to introduce some variety into the diet*) variation, diversity, diversification, change. **2**-(*A huge variety of flowers were on display*) assortment, miscellany, mixture, range, collection.

**various** *adj* **1** (*The dress comes in various colors*) varying, diverse, different, many, assorted. **2** (*For various reasons we are unable to attend the meeting*) numerous, several, many, varied.

**vary** *vb* **1** (*They tend to vary slightly in size*) differ, be different, be unlike, be dissimilar. **2** (*The temperature varies throughout the day*) change, alter. **3** (*try to vary your speed on a long journey*) change, alter, modify.

**vast** *adj* **1** (*the vast plains covered in ripe wheat*) extensive, immense, expansive, wide, sweeping. **2** (*A vast shape suddenly loomed out of the fog*) huge, enormous, massive, colossal, gigantic.

**vegetation** *n* (*an area of the world with little vegetation*) plant life, plants, greenery, flora.

**vehement** *adj* (*a vehement denial*) emphatic, vigorous, forceful, strong, fervent, passionate.

**vehicle** *n* **1** (*no parking for unauthorized vehicles*) conveyance, car, bus, truck, means of transportation. **2** (*They use the magazine simply as a vehicle for spreading their political views*) medium, means of expression, agency, instrument.

**veil** *n* (*The mountain peaks were hidden under a veil of mist/They moved the body under a veil of secrecy*) cover, covering, screen, curtain, blanket, cloak, mantle, mask, shroud, cloud.

**vein** *n* **1** (*Blood gushed from the vein*) blood vessel. **2** (*a vein of ore in the rocks*) seam, lode, stratum. **3** (*The marble fireplace had a pink vein in it*) streak, stripe, strip, line, thread. **4**-(*There was a vein of humor in her criticism*) streak, strain, dash, hint. **5**-(*The poem was in a serious vein*) mood, tone, tenor.

**vengeance** *n* (*They sought vengeance for the murder of their brother*) revenge, retaliation, reprisal, retribution, tit for tat.

**venom** *n* **1** (*find an antidote for the snake's venom*) poison, toxin. **2**-(*She spoke with venom about her fellow competitor*) spite, malice, ill will, animosity.

**venture** *n* (*a business venture*) enterprise, undertaking, project.

**verbal** *adj* (*asked to give a verbal account of the accident*) oral, spoken, in speech.

**verdict** *n* (*The jury delivered its verdict*) decision, findings, conclusion, judgment, ruling, opinion.

**verge** *n* (*the grass verge by the road*) edge, border, boundary.

**verify** *vb* (*He was asked to verify that he had been present*) confirm, corroborate, endorse, ratify.

**versatile** *adj* **1** (*a versatile kitchen gadget*) adaptable, multipurpose. **2**-(*She is a very versatile musician*) adaptable, adjustable, flexible, resourceful.

**version** *n* **1** (*She gave us her version of what happened in court*) account, story, report, side, interpretation. **2** (*There are several versions of that song around*) variant, variation, form.

**vertical** *n* (*hammer vertical posts into the ground to make a fence*) upright, erect, perpendicular.

**very** *adj* **1** (*Those were her very words*) actual, exact, precise. **2**-(*The beauty of the dress lay in its very simplicity*) sheer, utter, pure. **3**-(*He has been a member from the very beginning*) absolute.

**vessel** *n* **1** (*There was a foreign flag flying from the vessel*) ship, boat, craft. **2** (*We need some kind of vessel to give the dog a drink*) container, receptacle.

**veto** *vb* (*Some members vetoed his membership of the club*) ban, bar, place an embargo on, forbid, disallow, reject, turn down, give the thumbs down to.

**vex** *vb* (*Her mother was vexed by her refusal to come home for Christmas*) annoy, irritate, upset, put out, distress, (*inf*) peeve, (*inf*) miff.

**vibrate** *vb* **1** (*The music vibrated throughout the hall*) throb, pulsate, resonate, reverberate, ring, echo. **2** (*The whole bus vibrated as the driver tried to start the engine*) shudder, tremble, shake, quiver, shiver.

**vice** *n* **1** (*Vice seems to be on the increase in the modern world*) sin, sinfulness, evil, wickedness, badness, wrongdoing, iniquity. **2** (*one of his many vices*) sin, offense, misdeed, failing, flaw, defect.

**vicious** *adj* **1** (*The mailman was attacked by a vicious dog*) fierce, ferocious, savage, dangerous. **2** (*The attack on the old man was a particularly vicious one*) violent, savage, brutal, fierce, ferocious, inhuman.

**victim** *n* **1** (*They were victims of a-vicious attack*) casualty, sufferer. **2** (*tracking down their victims*) prey, quarry.

**victorious** *adj* (*the victorious army/the victorious team*) conquering, winning, triumphant, champion.

**victory** *n* (*We celebrated our victory*) win, success, conquest, triumph, achievement.

**view** *n* **1** (*The view from our balcony was beautiful*) outlook, prospect, panorama, vista. **2** (*A strange figure came into view*) sight, range of vision, eyeshot. **3** (*Our view is that he is dishonest*) opinion, point of view, viewpoint, belief, feeling, idea.

**vigorous** *adj* (*a vigorous attempt at winning the game*) strong, powerful, forceful, determined, enthusiastic, lively, energetic, strenuous.

**vile** *adj* (*What a vile thing to do*) nasty, foul, unpleasant, disagreeable, horrible, dreadful, disgusting, hateful, shocking.

**villain** *n* (*The police have caught the villains*) rogue, scoundrel, wrongdoer, ruffian, crook.

**violent** *adj* **1** (*a violent attack*) brutal, ferocious,

cruel, savage, vicious. **2** (*He has a violent temper*) uncontrollable, unrestrained, wild, passionate, forceful. **3** (*He took a violent dislike to her at first sight*) strong, great, intense, extreme, vehement.

**virtually** *adv* (*Traffic was virtually at a standstill*) more or less, nearly, practically, as good as, effectively, in effect, in essence, for all practical purposes.

**virtue** *n* **1** (*The church admires virtue and discourages vice*) goodness, righteousness, morality, integrity, uprightness, honesty, decency.

**visible** *adj* **1** (*The hilltops were scarcely visible in the mist*) in view, discernible, perceptible. **2** (*His unhappiness was visible to us all*) obvious, evident, apparent, noticeable, plain, clear, unmistakable.

**vision** *n* **1** (*Certain jobs call for good vision*) eyesight, sight. **2** (*He claims to have seen a vision in the graveyard*) apparition, ghost, specter. **3**-(*He saw his dead brother in a vision*) dream, hallucination. **4**-(*men of vision*) insight, perception, discernment, intuition.

**visit** *vb* (*He visits his aunt once a year*) pay a visit to, go to see, pay a call on, call on, drop in, drop by.

**vital** *adj* **1** (*It is vital that you attend the meeting*) imperative, essential, necessary, crucial. **2** (*hold vital discussions*) indispensable, urgent, essential, necessary, key. **3** (*She was a very vital person*) lively, energetic, vivacious.

**vitality** *n* (*well-nourished children full of vitality*) energy, liveliness, vigor, zest, vivacity.

**vivacious** *adj* (*She is so vivacious that everyone else seems dull beside her*) lively, animated, sparkling, scintillating, dynamic, vibrant.

**vivid** *adj* **1** (*vivid colors*) bright, brilliant, strong, intense. **2** (*a vivid description*) clear, graphic, powerful, dramatic.

**vocabulary** *n* (*the difficult vocabulary in the piece*) language, words.

**voice** *n* **1** (*She lost her voice when she had a cold*) speech. **2** (*They finally gave voice to their feelings*) expression, utterance. **3** (*governments refusing to listen to the voice of the people*) opinion, view, comment.

**volume** *n* **1** (*an encyclopedia in several volumes*) book. **2** (*measure the volume*) capacity, bulk. **3** (*the sheer volume of water pouring out*) amount, quantity, mass. **4** (*We asked them to turn down the volume of their radio*) loudness, sound.

**voluntary** *n* **1** (*Attendance at the meeting is entirely voluntary*) of one's own free will, optional, non-compulsory. **2** (*She is unemployed but does voluntary work*) unpaid, without payment, volunteer.

**vote** *vb* (*They are voting to elect a new president*) cast one's vote, go to the polls. **2**

(*She voted for the woman candidate*) elect, opt for, select.

**vote** *n* (*have a vote on who should lead the team*) ballot, poll, election.

**voucher** *n* (*a bundle of vouchers*) token, ticket, slip.

**vow** *n* (*marriage vows*) oath, promise, pledge.

**vow** *vb* (*He vowed to be true*) swear, promise, pledge, give one's word.

**vulgar** *adj* **1** (*They objected to his vulgar language*) rude, indecent, obscene, bawdy, smutty. **2** (*vulgar table manners*) rude, impolite, unmannerly, illmannered. **3** (*They thought her clothes were vulgar*) tasteless, flashy, gaudy, tawdry.

**vulnerable** *adj* (*They felt vulnerable camping out in that area*) exposed, unprotected, defenseless.

# W

**wad** *n* **1** (*The nurse used a wad of cotton to clean the wound*) lump, chunk, plug. **2** (*wads of dollar bills*) bundle, roll.

**waddle** *vb* (*The very fat lady waddled down the street*) wiggle, sway, totter.

**wade** *vb* **1** (*The children were wading in the pool in the park*) paddle, splash. **2** (*There was no bridge and they had to wade across the stream*) ford, cross.

**wag** *vb* **1** (*The dog's tail was wagging*) swing, sway, shake, twitch, quiver. **2** (*The teacher wagged her finger angrily at the children*) waggle, wiggle.

**wage** *vb* (*wage war*) carry on, conduct, engage in, undertake.

**wager** *n* (*He laid a wager that she would not win*) bet, gamble, stake.

**wager** *vb* (*She wagered that the horse would come first in the race*) bet, place a bet, lay a bet, lay odds, put money on, gamble.

**wages** *npl* (*She has asked for a rise in her wages*) pay, salary, earnings, income, remuneration.

**wail** *vb* (*The children were wailing because their mother would not give them candy*) cry, weep, sob, lament, howl, whine.

**wait** *vb* **1** (*The children were told to wait at the side of the road*) stay, remain, stop, halt. **2** (*She does not know if she has gotten the job—she will just have to wait and see*) be patient, stand by, mark time, (*inf*) sit tight. **3** (*They asked us to wait for them*) await, watch out for, expect. **4** (*They are employed to wait tables*) serve, be a waiter/waitress.

**wake** *vb* **1** (*He asked us to wake him early*) wake up, waken, rouse. **2** (*We woke at dawn*) awake, waken, wake up, get up, arise.

**walk** vb 1 (*We were able to walk to the mall*) go on foot. 2 (*The children were told to walk and not to run*) stroll, saunter, amble, march.

**walk** n 1 (*They went for a walk after lunch*) stroll, saunter, amble, ramble, hike. 2 (*I recognized him by his walk*) gait, step, stride.

**walker** n (*We passed a few walkers as we drove to the town*) pedestrian, hiker, rambler.

**wall** n 1 (*The garden had a wall around it*) enclosure, barrier. 2 (*We tore down a wall of the house to make two rooms into one*) partition. 3 (*tourists who went to visit the old city walls*) fortifications, ramparts, barricade, bulwark.

**wallet** n (*His wallet was stolen and he now has no money*) pocketbook.

**wallow** vb 1 (*The animals were wallowing in mud*) roll, splash, tumble. 2 (*She was wallowing in self-pity*) bask, luxuriate, revel, delight.

**wan** adj (*She looked wan after having had flu*) pale, white, pallid, peaked.

**wand** n (*The fairy godmother waved her wand*) stick, baton, rod.

**wander** vb 1 (*The child wandered off while his mother was shopping*) go off, get lost, stray, lose one's way. 2 (*They loved to wander over the hills when they were on vacation*) roam, ramble, rove, range. 3 (*The old man does not recognize his family and his mind has started to wander*) ramble, rave, babble.

**wane** vb 1 (*The moon is waning*) decrease, diminish, dwindle. 2 (*The power of ancient Greece waned*) decrease, decline, diminish, dwindle, fade, subside, dim, vanish, die out.

**want** vb 1 (*The children wanted some candy*) wish for, desire, demand, long for, crave, yearn for, hanker after. 2 (*poor people wanting food*) lack, be lacking in, be without, be devoid of, be short of.

**war** n 1 (*The war between the countries lasted many years*) warfare, fighting, conflict, struggle, hostilities, battles. 2 (*There was a state of war between the two nations*) conflict, strife, hostility, enmity, ill-will. 3 (*She took part in the war against poverty in the area*) battle, fight, crusade, campaign.

**ward** n 1 (*The hospital ward holds four beds*) room, cubicle, compartment. 2 (*Her parents are dead and she is a ward of her uncle*) charge, dependant.

**ward** vb 1 (*She succeeded in warding off his attack*) fend off, stave off, deflect, avert, rebuff. 2 (*They warded off the intruders*) drive back, repel, beat back.

**warden** n 1 (*He is a game warden in Africa*) keeper, custodian, guardian, guard. 2 (*The prisoners attacked a warden*) prison officer, guard, jailer.

**wardrobe** n (*She is buying a new wardrobe for her vacation*) clothes, trousseau.

**warehouse** n (*They collected the books from the warehouse*) depot, storehouse, stockroom.

**wares** npl (*There were many people selling their wares in the market*) goods, products, merchandise, stock, commodities.

**warlike** adj (*They encountered warlike tribes in the jungle*) belligerent, aggressive, pugnacious, hostile.

**warlock** n (*a story about a warlock*) wizard, sorcerer, magician, witch.

**warm** adj 1 (*She bathed the wound in warm water*) heated, tepid, lukewarm. 2 (*go for a swim on a warm day*) sunny, hot, close, sultry. 3 (*She has a warm heart*) kind, kindly, sympathetic, tender, loving, affectionate. 4 (*We received a warm welcome*) hearty, cordial, friendly, enthusiastic.

**warm** vb 1 (*The mother warmed the food for the baby*) heat, heat up. 2 (*The competitors warmed up for the race*) loosen up, limber up, exercise.

**warn** vb (*They were warned that they were entering a dangerous area*) advise, caution, make aware, notify, inform, (*inf*) tip off.

**warning** n 1 (*They had no warning of the terrible storm*) forewarning, notification, notice, information, indication, hint. 2 (*He was superstitious and regarded his experience as a warning of things to come*) omen, signal, threat.

**warrior** n (*a book about the deeds of ancient warriors*) fighter, combatant, champion, soldier, knight.

**wary** adj (*The children were taught to be wary of strangers*) cautious, careful, on one's guard, watchful, chary, suspicious, distrustful.

**wash** vb 1 (*They washed their hands before dinner*) clean, cleanse, scrub. 2 (*The children washed before going to bed*) have a wash, wash oneself, clean oneself, sponge oneself down. 3 (*They washed their clothes and hung them out to dry*) launder, clean. 4 (*waves washing against the boats*) splash, dash, beat.

**waste** vb 1 (*They waste a lot of money/Try not to waste time*) squander, fritter, misuse, misspend. 2 (*Because of his illness his limbs are wasting away*) grow weak, grow thin, wither, atrophy.

**waste** n 1 (*find a way of getting rid of the waste*) garbage, refuse, debris, trash. 2 (*doing research in the wastes of the Antarctic*) wasteland, wilderness, desert, vastness.

**wasteful** adj (*a wasteful use of money*) thriftless, extravagant, spendthrift, profligate, prodigal.

**watch** vb 1 (*We watched the sun going down*) look at, observe, view, contemplate, survey, stare at, gaze at. 2 (*If you watch what the teacher does you will be able to do the experiment yourself*) pay attention to, take notice of, to heed, concentrate on. 3 (*The police are watching him*) keep watch on, keep an eye on, keep under surveillance, follow, spy on. 4 (*Watch and don't get attacked in that area of the town*) take care, look out, take heed, beware, be alert. 5 (*She asked her mother to watch the children*) take care of, look after, keep an eye on, tend.

**watchman** n guard, caretaker, custodian, sentry, security.

**water** n 1 (*have a glass of water with the meal*) bottled water, mineral water. 2 (*children playing by the water*) pond, pool, lake, river, sea.

**watery** adj 1 (*The gravy was watery/The soup was watery*) thin, weak, diluted, runny, tasteless, flavorless. 2 (*watery eyes*) wet, moist, damp, tearful, weepy.

**wave** vb 1 (*flags waving in the breeze*) flutter, flap, ripple, shake, undulate. 2 (*He waved his sword angrily*) shake, swing, brandish. 3 (*He waved his hand to his friends*) flutter, waggle. 4 (*He waved to the driver*) gesture. 5 (*Her hair waves*) curl, kink, undulate.

**wave** n 1 (*The children were splashing in the waves*) breaker, swell, surf, billow. 2 (*the waves in her hair*) curl, kink, undulation. 3 (*a town hit by a crime wave*) upsurge, surge, rash, outbreak.

**waver** vb 1 (*His courage did not waver*) falter, vary, change. 2 (*We had been determined to go but then we began to waver*) hesitate, think twice, vacillate, shilly-shally, waffle. 3 (*lights wavering*) flicker, tremble, quiver.

**wax** vb (*The moon was waxing*) increase, enlarge.

**way** n 1 (*They asked which was the way to the police station*) road, route, direction. 2 (*She said that it was a long way to New York from there*) distance, journey. 3 (*They were taught the correct way to change the wheel of a car*) method, procedure, technique, system, manner, means. 4 (*The children laughed at the way the old lady dressed*) manner, fashion, style, mode. 5 (*They have old-fashioned ways*) habit, custom, practice, conduct, behavior. 6 (*His business affairs are in a bad way*) state, condition, situation. 7 (*In some ways I will miss them although mostly I am glad that they've gone*) respect, aspect, feature, detail, point.

**weak** adj 1 (*She felt very weak after her long illness*) weakly, frail, delicate, feeble, shaky, debilitated, tired. 2 (*Their leader was too weak to stand up to the enemy*) cowardly, timid, soft, spineless, powerless, wishy-washy. 3 (*She made a weak excuse for being* *late*) feeble, lame, pathetic, unconvincing, unsatisfactory. **4** (*The tea was too weak*) diluted, watery, tasteless.

**weaken** *vb* **1** (*The illness had obviously weakened her*) make weak, debilitate, tire, wear out. **2** (*Our chances of winning were weakened*) lessen, decrease, reduce, diminish, undermine. **3** (*Our parents refused to let us go but then they weakened*) relent, come round, give in.

**weakness** *n* **1** (*A tendency to lie is her major weakness*) fault, failing, flaw, defect, shortcoming, imperfection, foible. **2** (*She has a weakness for chocolate*) fondness, liking, love, soft spot, preference, penchant.

**wealth** *n* (*He shared his great wealth among his family*) riches, fortune, money, capital, assets.

**wealthy** *adj* (*an area of the town where wealthy people live*) affluent, rich, well-off, well-to-do, moneyed, (*inf*) well-heeled.

**wear** *vb* **1** (*The children were wearing warm coats*) be dressed in, be clothed in, have on. **2** (*She wore a gloomy expression*) have, show, display. **3** (*rocks worn away by water*) erode, eat away, rub away. **4** (*She was worn out by the long walk*) tire, fatigue, exhaust.

**weary** *adj* **1** (*The children were weary at the end of the long school day*) tired, fatigued, exhausted, worn out, (*inf*) deadbeat. **2** (*She is weary of her present job*) bored, discontented, jaded, (*inf*) fed up.

**weather** *n* (*What is the weather like there in August?*) climate.

**web** *n* (*a spider's web*) mesh, net, network, lattice.

**wedding** *n* wedding ceremony, marriage, marriage ceremony.

**wedge** *vb* **1** (*Since it was very hot they wedged the door open*) jam, secure. **2** (*Four of them were wedged in the back seat*) squeeze, jam, cram, pack.

**wedge** *n* (*a wedge of cheese*) chunk, hunk, lump.

**weep** *vb* (*The child wept when her mother went away*) cry, sob, shed tears.

**weight** *n* **1** (*estimate the weight of the cake*) heaviness. **2** (*A weight fell on his toe*) heavy object. **3**-(*When their daughter returned it was a weight off their minds*) burden, load, onus, worry, trouble. **4**-(*They attach a great deal of weight to his opinion*) importance, significance, value, substance.

**weird** *adj* **1** (*We heard weird noises in the cellar*) eerie, strange, queer, uncanny, creepy, ghostly, unearthly, (*inf*) spooky. **2** (*She always wears weird clothes*) strange, queer, odd, bizarre, eccentric, outlandish, offbeat.

**welcome** *vb* **1** (*They welcomed their guests at the door*) greet, receive, meet. **2** (*We welcomed the news*) be pleased with, be glad at.

**welfare** *n* (*She was worried about her children's welfare*) well-being, health, happiness.

**well** *adj* **1** (*She has been ill but is now quite well*) in good health, healthy, fit, strong. **2** (*They found that all was well*) all right, satisfactory, fine, (*inf*) OK.

**well** *adv* **1** (*He plays the piano well*) competently, skillfully, expertly. **2**-(*The children behaved well*) properly, correctly, suitably, satisfactorily. **3** (*They speak well of him*) highly, admiringly, approvingly, favorably. **4** (*They may well be right*) probably, likely, possibly.

**wet** *adj* **1** (*The ground was wet after the rain/Her clothes were wet*) damp, moist, soaked, drenched, saturated, sopping. **2** (*We had wet weather on vacation*) rainy, damp, showery.

**wet** *vb* **1** (*She wet the shirts before-ironing them*) dampen, moisten, sprinkle, spray. **2** (*The rain really wet them*) soak, drench, saturate.

**wharf** *vb* (*ships being unloaded at the wharf*) dock, quay, pier, jetty.

**wheeze** *vb* (*She had a bad cold and was wheezing*) pant, puff, gasp.

**whimper** *vb* (*The dog was sitting whimpering on the doorstep*) whine, cry.

**whine** *vb* (*The children were bored and began to whine*) wail, cry, whimper, complain, (*inf*) gripe.

**whip** *n* (*The jockey used his whip on the horse*) switch, crop, scourge, lash, horsewhip, cat-o'-nine-tails.

**whip** *vb* **1** (*They used to whip people who had done wrong*) lash, flog, scourge, birch, beat, thrash. **2** (*She whipped the cream*) beat, whisk, mix, blend. **3** (*He whipped his handkerchief from his pocket*) pull, yank, jerk, snatch, whisk.

**whirl** *vb* (*They watched the dancers whirling round the floor*) turn, spin, rotate, revolve, wheel, circle, twirl.

**whisper** *vb* (*She whispered to her friend at the back of the classroom*) murmur, mutter, breathe.

**white** *adj* **1** (*She was white with fear*) pale, wan, pallid, ashen, peaked. **2** (*Her hair is white with age*) gray, silver, snowy white.

**whole** *adj* **1** (*We asked her to tell us the whole story*) full, entire, complete, unabridged. **2** (*Not a single wine glass was left whole*) intact, in one piece, undamaged, unbroken.

**wholesome** *adj* (*wholesome food*) health-giving, healthy, nutritious, nourishing.

**wholly** *adv* **1** (*We are not wholly against the plan*) entirely, completely, fully, thoroughly, utterly. **2** (*The responsibility lies wholly with him*) only, solely, purely, exclusively.

**wicked** *adj* (*the wicked people who attacked and robbed the old man*) evil, bad, sinful, vicious, immoral, unethical, villainous, criminal.

**wide** *adj* **1** (*a city with wide streets*) broad, spacious. **2** (*A wide range of subjects is available at the school*) broad, large, extensive, comprehensive, wide-ranging. **3** (*He always wears very wide pants*) loose, baggy, roomy.

**widespread** *adj* (*There were widespread rumors of war*) general, common, universal, extensive, prevalent, rife.

**width** *n* **1** (*measure the width of the material*) wideness, breadth, broadness, span. **2** (*We admired the width of his knowledge*) wideness, breadth, scope, range, comprehensiveness.

**wield** *vb* **1** (*a knight wielding a sword*) brandish, flourish, wave, swing. **2** (*It is the deputy president who wields the power*) have, hold, exercise, exert.

**wife** *n* spouse, partner, (*inf*) better half.

**wild** *adj* **1** (*an area where wild animals roamed*) untamed, undomesticated, fierce, savage, ferocious. **2**-(*the wild flowers of the area*) uncultivated, native, indigenous. **3**-(*The ship sank in wild weather*) stormy, rough, blustery, turbulent, windy. **4** (*They had to travel across wild country*) rough, rugged, desolate, waste. **5** (*the wild behavior of the crowd*) rowdy, disorderly, unruly, violent, turbulent, uncontrolled.

**willful** *adj* **1** (*a nanny finding it difficult to cope with such willful children*) headstrong, strong-willed, obstinate, stubborn, determined, disobedient, contrary. **2** (*The jury decided that it was a case of willful murder*) deliberate, intentional, planned, premeditated, calculated.

**will** *n* **1** (*He seems to have lost the will to live*) desire, wish, inclination, determination, intention, volition. **2**-(*He died without making a will*) last will and testament, testament.

**will** *vb* **1** (*She willed it to happen*) desire, hope for. **2** (*He willed the house to his nephew*) bequeath, pass on, transfer.

**willing** *adj* **1** (*They had a lot of willing helpers at the church bazaar*) eager, keen, enthusiastic, avid. **2** (*There was no one willing to take responsibility for the organization of the event*) ready, prepared, disposed, agreeable, amenable.

**wilt** *vb* (*The flowers in the vase were wilting*) droop, wither, shrivel, dry up.

**wily** *adj* (*He was wily enough to convince the old lady that he was a representative of the church*) cunning, crafty, artful, scheming, sly, sharp.

**win** *vb* **1** (*We were not surprised when their team won*) be victorious, be the victor, come first, triumph. **2** (*She won first prize*) gain, get, achieve, attain, acquire, carry off.

**wince** *vb* (*She winced when they reminded her of her tactless remark*) grimace, flinch, cringe, recoil.

**wind** *n* (*The wind blew the papers all around the room*) breeze, gale, gust, blast, draft.

**wind** *vb* **1** (*Her grandmother asked her to wind her wool*) twist, twine, coil, roll. **2** (*The road winds up the mountain*) twist, twist and turn, curve, loop, zigzag, spiral, snake, meander.

**wing** *n* **1** (*The family occupy the west wing of the mansion*) side, annex. **2** (*They are on the right wing of the party*) section, side, group, segment.

**wink** *vb* **1** (*He winked an eye*) blink, flutter, bat. **2** (*lights winking on the water*) twinkle, flash, sparkle, glitter, gleam.

**winner** *n* (*They were the winners in the battle/ the winner in the tennis tournament*) victor, champion, conqueror, vanquisher.

**wipe** *vb* (*wipe the kitchen surfaces*) clean, sponge, mop, rub, brush.

**wisdom** *n* **1** (*admire their wisdom in getting out of the industry at the right time*) sense, common sense, prudence, good judgment, shrewdness, astuteness, smartness. **2** (*The young people benefited from the wisdom of their grandparents*) knowledge.

**wise** *adj* **1** (*We thought it wise to leave early when it began to snow*) sensible, well-advised, prudent, shrewd, astute, smart. **2** (*They asked the wise old men of the village for advice*) knowledgeable, learned, well-informed, enlightened, sage.

**wish** *vb* (*They could not have wished for friend-lier neighbors*) want, desire, long for, yearn for, covet, (*inf*) have a yen for.

**wish** *n* **1** (*They were supposed to obey the king's every wish*) want, desire, demand, request. **2** (*At last she was able to satisfy her wish to travel*) desire, longing, yearning, fancy, inclination, craving, (*inf*) yen.

**wistful** *adj* (*She had a wistful expression as she watched them leave*) yearning, longing, forlorn, sad, pathetic.

**wit** *n* **1** (*He did not have the wit to-realize that she was teasing him*) intelligence, brains, sense, common sense, shrewdness. **2** (*We had to admire his wit as he kept us all amused*) wittiness, humor.

**witch** *n* (*a story about a witch and her broom-stick*) enchantress, sorceress.

**withdraw** *vb* **1** (*She withdrew from the tennis match because of illness*) pull out, come out, retire. **2** (*They withdrew their son from the school*) remove, take away, pull out. **3** (*The troops withdrew when they were defeated*) pull back, fall back, move back, retreat, retire, depart.

**wither** *vb* (*The flowers in the vase had withered*) fade, dry up, dry out, shrivel, die.

**witness** *vb* (*They witnessed a terrible accident*) see, observe, look on at, watch, view, be present at.

**witness** *n* (*The police asked for witnesses at the scene of the accident*) eyewitness, onlooker, observer, spectator, bystander.

**witty** *adj* (*witty stories/witty people*) amusing, funny, humorous, comic, clever.

**wizard** *n* (*a fairy story about wizards*) warlock, sorcerer, magician, enchanter.

**wobble** *vb* **1** (*This table wobbles*) rock, teeter, shake. **2** (*wobble down the street on high-heeled shoes*) totter, teeter, sway, stagger, waddle. **3** (*Her voice wobbled and she began to cry*) shake, tremble, quiver.

**woe** *n* (*We listened to her tale of-woe*) misfor-tune, distress, suffering, trouble, misery, unhappiness.

**wonder** *n* **1** (*watched with wonder as the acro-bats performed*) amazement, astonish-ment, awe, bewilderment, curiosity. **2** (*The acrobats are a wonder*) marvel, mira-cle, prodigy, surprise.

**wonder** *vb* **1** (*wondering at the immensity of the sky*) admire, gape, marvel. **2** (*I won-der if they will marry*) conjecture, ponder, query, question, speculate.

**wonderful** *adj* **1** (*The church ceiling was a wonderful sight*) marvelous, remarkable, extraordinary, amazing, astonishing, fantastic. **2** (*She was a wonderful pianist*) superb, marvelous, brilliant, excellent, first-rate, outstanding.

**wood** *n* **1** (*houses made of wood*) timber. **2** (*go for a walk in the woods*) forest, copse, thicket.

**wooly** *adj* **1** (*buy the child a wooly toy*) fluffy, fleecy, furry. **2** (*wooly thoughts*) hazy, vague, muddled, confused, indefinite, uncertain.

**word** *n* **1** (*She was trying to think of another word for 'work'*) term, expression. **2** (*She gave him her word that she would be there*) promise, pledge, assurance, guarantee, undertaking. **3** (*They have had no word about their missing son*) news, informa-tion, communication.

**work** *n* **1** (*Making a doll's house for his daugh-ter involved a lot of work*) effort, exertion, labor, toil, trouble, elbow grease. **2** (*Her work involves meeting a great many people*) job, employment, occupation, profes-sion, trade.

**work** *vb* **1** (*He works in banking*) be employed, have a job. **2** (*The pupils will have to work at their studies to pass the exams*) exert one-self, apply oneself, make an effort, labor, toil. **3** (*Can you work this machine?*) oper-ate, use, control, handle. **4**-(*This machine does not work*) go, operate, function, run. **5** (*That idea will not work*) succeed, be suc-cessful, go well, be effective.

**world** *n* **1** (*the peoples of the world*) earth, globe, planet. **2** (*The world was shocked by the terrorist attack*) people, everyone, the public. **3** (*the medical world*) society, sec-tor, section, group.

**worry** *n* **1** (*His behavior caused her a lot of worry*) anxiety, trouble, bother, distress, disturbance, upset, uneasiness. **2** (*She was a real worry to her parents*) trouble, nuisance, pest, problem, trial, thorn in one's side.

**worsen** *vb* **1** (*The situation between workers and management has worsened*) get worse, take a turn for the worse, deteriorate, degenerate. **2**-(*His efforts to help simply worsened the situation*) make worse, aggra-vate, exacerbate, increase.

**worship** *vb* **1** (*go to church to worship God*) pray to, praise, glorify, pay homage to. **2** (*He simply worships his wife*) idolize, adore, be devoted to, cherish, dote on.

**worth** *n* **1** (*The jewelry is of little financial worth but is of sentimental value*) value. **2** (*We regarded his advice as being of little worth*) value, use, advantage, benefit, gain.

**worthy** *adj* **1** (*They were not worthy of respect*) deserving, meriting. **2**-(*the worthy people in the community*) good, decent, honor-able, upright, virtuous, admirable, com-mendable, deserving.

**wound** *n* **1** (*He got his wound dressed in hospi-tal*) injury, sore, cut, laceration, lesion. **2** (*Her remark was a wound to his pride*) blow, injury, hurt, damage, slight.

**wrap** *vb* **1** (*Wrap the child in a blanket and take him to a hospital*) cover, bundle up, swathe, enfold. **2** (*She wrapped the Christ-mas presents*) wrap up, parcel up, pack-age, tie up, gift wrap.

**wrath** *n* (*They had to face the wrath of the teacher when they played truant*) anger, rage, fury, indignation, annoyance.

**wreck** *vb* **1** (*He wrecked his father's car*) smash, demolish, ruin, damage. **2** (*His illness wrecked their vacation plans*) ruin, destroy, spoil, shatter.

**wrench** *vb* (*He wrenched the lid from the con-tainer*) twist, pull, tug, jerk, force.

**wretched** *adj* **1** (*She was feeling wretched about being away from home*) miser-able, depressed, unhappy, sad. **2** (*He felt wretched when he had flu*) ill, unwell, sick, (*inf*) under the weather. **3** (*He has a wretched cold*) nasty, unpleasant, dis-agreeable.

**wriggle** *vb* **1** (*children wriggling with impa-tience in their seats*) twist, squirm, writhe. **2** (*She tried to wriggle out of helping with the chores*) dodge, evade, avoid, duck.

**wring** *vb* **1** (*wring the clothes out*) squeeze, twist. **2** (*His enemies wrung the information from him*) extract, force, wrench.

**wrinkle** *n* (*She ironed her blouse to remove the wrinkles*) crease, pucker, fold, furrow.

**write** *vb* **1** (*write an essay*) compose, pen. **2**

(*She wrote down the names of the people present*) put down, note, list, record.

**writer** *n* (*He is a professional writer*) author, novelist, journalist.

**writing** *n* **1** (*She teaches children writing*) handwriting, penmanship, script. **2** (*a list of his writings*) work, book, publication.

**wrong** *adj* **1** (*It is wrong to steal*) bad, wicked, sinful, illegal, unlawful, criminal, crooked. **2** (*There is something wrong with the computer*) broken, faulty, defective, out of order. **3**-(*It was the wrong way to deal with the problem*) incorrect, improper, inappropriate, unsuitable. **4** (*She gave the wrong answer to the mathematical question*) incorrect, inaccurate, erroneous, mistaken.

**wrong** *n* **1** (*be taught right from wrong*) badness, evil, sin, sinfulness, unlawfulness. **2** (*He committed several wrongs*) misdeed, offense, crime.

# Y

**yearn** *vb* (*They yearned for some sunshine*) long, pine, crave, desire, covet, fancy, hanker after, (*inf*) have a yen for.

**yield** *vb* **1** (*They refuse to yield to the invading army*) submit, give in, surrender, concede defeat. **2** (*They finally yielded to his demands*) give in, comply with, consent to, grant. **3** (*investments which yield a good return*) bring in, earn, return, produce. **4** (*an area which yields heavy crops*) produce, give, bear, grow, supply.

**young** *adj* (*young people*) youthful, juvenile, adolescent.

# Z

**zealous** *adj* (*zealous followers of the sport/zealous in their efforts to gain support*) eager, keen, enthusiastic, passionate, fervent, earnest, fanatical.

**zenith** *n* (*when the Roman empire was at the zenith of its power*) peak, height, top, pinnacle, acme, apex.

**zero** *n* **1** (*How many zeroes are there when you write a million in figures?*) nothing. **2** (*We won absolutely zero*) nothing, nil, (*inf*) zilch.

**zest** *n* (*the old lady's zest for life*) enthusiasm, eagerness, relish, energy.

**zone** *n* (*a traffic-free zone*) area, sector, region.

# Appendix

All of us have problem words that cause spelling difficulties but there are some words that are generally misspelt. These include:

**A**

abbreviation
abscess
absence
abysmal
accelerator
accessible
accessories
accommodate
accompaniment
accumulate
accurate
accustomed
achieve
aching
acknowledge
acknowledgment
acquaint
acquaintance
acquiesce
acquiescence
acquire
acquit
acquittal
acreage
across
actual
additional
address
adequate
adieu
adjacent
admissible
admittance
adolescence
adolescent
advantageous
advertisement
advice
advise
aerate
aerial
affect
affiliation
afforestation
aggravate
aggravation
aggregate
aggression
aggressive
aghast
agnosticism
agoraphobia
agreeable
agreed
aisle
alcohol
alfresco
alibis
align
alignment
allege

allergic
alleys
alligator
allocate
allotment
allotted
almond
alms
alphabetically
already
although
aluminum
ambiguous
amethyst
ammunition
anachronism
analysis
analyze
anarchist
ancestor
ancestry
anemone
anesthetic
angrily
anguish
annihilate
annihilation
anniversary
announcement
annulled
annulment
anonymous
answered
Antarctic
antibiotic
antithesis
anxiety
apartheid
apologize
appalling
apparently
appearance
appendicitis
appreciate
approval
aquarium
aquiline
arbiter
arbitrary
arbitration
archeology
architectural
Arctic
arguably
arrangement
arrival
artichoke
ascend
ascent
asphalt
asphyxiate
asphyxiation
assassin

assassinate
assessment
assistance
associate
asthma
asthmatic
astrakhan
atheist
atrocious
attach
attendant
attitude
attorney
auburn
auctioneer
audible
aural
automatic
awful
awkward

**B**

bachelor
bagatelle
baggage
bailiff
ballast
ballerina
banana
banister
bankruptcy
banquet
barbecue
barometer
basically
basis
bassoon
battalion
bazaar
beautiful
befriend
beguile
behavior
beleaguer
belief
believe
belligerent
benefited
bequeath
berserk
besiege
bettered
beveled
bewitch
bias
bicycle
biennial
bigamous
bigoted
bilingual
biscuit
bivouacked
bizarre

blancmange
blasphemous
blasphemy
bleary
blitz
bodily
bonfire
bootee
borough
bouquet
bourgeois
boutique
bracketed
braille
brassiere
breadth
Breathalyzer
brief
broccoli
brochure
bronchitis
bruise
brusque
buccaneer
Buddhist
budding
budgerigar
budgeted
buffeted
bulletin
bumptious
bungalow
buoyancy
buoyant
bureau
bureaucracy
business
buttoned

**C**

cabbage
cafeteria
caffeine
camouflage
campaign
campaigner
cancellation
cancerous
candor
cannabis
cannibal
canvassing
capability
capillary
capitalist
caravan
carbohydrate
carburetor
career
caress
caries
carriage
cartoonist

cashier
cassette
castanets
casualty
catalog
catarrh
catechism
catering
cauliflower
cautious
ceiling
cellophane
cemetery
centenary
centiliter
centimeter
certainty
champagne
championed
chancellor
changeable
channeled
characteristic
chasm
chauffeur
cheetah
cherish
chief
chilblain
chintz
chiropody
chiseled
choreographer
choreography
chronically
chrysanthemum
cigarette
cinnamon
circuitous
cistern
civilian
claustrophobia
clientele
clique
coalesce
cocoa
coconut
coffee
cognac
coincidence
colander
collaborate
collapsible
colleague
colonel
colossal
comically
commandeer
commemorate
commencement
commentator
commercial
commiserate

commission
commitment
committal
committed
committee
communicate
commuter
companion
comparative
comparison
compatibility
compelled
competitive
computer
conceal
concealment
conceit
conceive
concession
concurrent
concussion
condemned
condescend
confectionery
conference
confetti
congeal
congratulations
conjunctivitis
conned
connoisseur
conscience
conscientious
conscious
consequently
consignment
consolation
conspicuous
constitute
consumer
contemptible
continent
continuous
contraception
contradictory
controlled
controller
controversial
convalesce
convenient
convertible
conveyed
convolvulus
coolly
cooperate
cooperative
coordinate
copying
coquette
corduroy
corespondent
coronary
correspondence

correspondent
corridor
corroborate
corrugated
cosmopolitan
cosseted
councilor
counseling
counterfeit
courageous
courteous
crèche
credible
credited
crematorium
creosote
crescent
crisis
criterion
crocheted
crocodile
croupier
crucial
crucifixion
cruelly
cruise
cryptic
cubicle
cupful
curable
curiosity
curious
currency
curriculum vitae
customary
cynic
cynicism
cynosure

**D**
dachshund
daffodil
dahlia
dais
damage
dandruff
darkened
debatable
debauched
debility
deceased
deceit
deceive
deciduous
decipher
decoyed
decrease
decreed
defamatory
defeat
defendant
defense
defied
definite
definitely
dehydrate
deign
deliberate
delicatessen
delicious
delinquent

delirious
demeanor
demonstrate
denouement
denunciation
dependence
depth
derailment
dermatitis
derogatory
descend
descendant
desiccate
desperate
detach
detachable
detergent
deterred
deterrent
deuce
develop
developed
development
diabetes
diagnosis
dialog
diametrically
diaphragm
diarrhea
difference
different
dilapidated
dilemma
dilettante
diminish
diminution
dinosaur
diphtheria
diphthong
disadvantageous
disagreeable
disagreed
disagreement
disappearance
disappeared
disappoint
disapproval
disastrous
disbelief
disbelieve
discipline
discotheque
discouraging
discourteous
discrepancy
discrimination
discussion
disease
disguise
disheveled
dishonorable
disillusion
disinfectant
disinherited
dismissal
disobeyed
disparage
dispelled
disposal
dispossess
dissatisfaction

dissatisfy
dissect
disseminate
dissent
dissimilar
dissipated
dissipation
dissociate
dissolute
dissuade
distilled
distillery
distinguish
distraught
disuse
divisible
documentary
doggerel
domineering
donate
doubt
drafty
dragooned
drastically
drooled
drooped
drunkenness
dubious
dumbfounded
dungarees
duress
dutiful
dynamite
dysentery
dyspepsia

**E**
eccentric
ecclesiastic
ecologically
economically
ecstasy
eczema
effective
effervescence
efficacious
efficient
effrontery
eightieth
elaborate
electrician
elevator
eligible
emancipate
embarrass
embarrassment
emergence
emergent
emolument
emotional
emphasize
employee
emptied
enable
encourage
encyclopedia
endeavor
endurance
energetically
enervate
engineer

enough
ensuing
entailed
enthusiasm
enumerate
epilepsy
equaled
equalize
equipped
erroneous
erudite
escalator
escapism
espionage
essence
essential
esthetic
estranged
etiquette
euthanasia
eventually
evidently
exaggerate
exaggeration
exalt
exasperate
exceed
exceedingly
excellent
excessive
exchequer
excommunicate
exercise
exhaust
exhibit
exhilarate
exorcise
explanation
exquisite
extinguish
extraneous
extravagant

**F**
fabulous
facetious
Fahrenheit
fallacious
fanatic
farcical
fascinate
fatigue
fatuous
February
feces
feeler
feign
ferocious
festooned
feud
feudal
fevered
fiasco
fiber
fictitious
fiend
fierce
fiery
filial
finesse
flabbergasted

flaccid
flammable
flannelette
fluent
fluoridate
fluoride
fluoridize
foliage
forcible
foreigner
forfeit
forthwith
fortieth
fortuitous
fortunately
frailty
frankincense
fraudulent
freedom
freight
frequency
friend
frolicked
fuchsia
fugitive
fulfill
fulfillment
fullness
fully
fulsome
furious
furniture
furthered

**G**
gaiety
galloped
garrison
garroted
gases
gateau
gauge
gazetteer
geisha
generator
genuine
gerbil
gesticulate
ghastly
ghetto
gigantic
gingham
giraffe
glamor
glamorous
glimpse
global
gluttonous
glycerin
gnarled
gnash
goiter
gossiped
government
graffiti
grammar
grandeur
gratefully
gratitude
gratuitous
greetings

gregarious
grief
grieve
groveled
gruesome
guarantee
guarantor
guard
guardian
guest
guillotine
guinea
guise
guitar
gymkhana
Gypsy

**H**
halcyon
hallucination
hammered
handfuls
handicapped
handkerchief
happened
harangue
harass
harlequin
haughty
hazard
hearse
height
heightened
heinous
heir
hemoglobin
hemorrhage
herbaceous
hereditary
heroism
hesitate
hiccup
hideous
hierarchy
hieroglyphics
hijack
hilarious
hindrance
hippopotamus
holiday
holocaust
homonym
honor
honorary
hooligan
horoscope
horrible
horticulture
hullabaloo
humor
humorous
hurricane
hurried
hygiene
hyphen
hypnosis
hypochondria
hypocrisy
hypotenuse
hypothesis
hypothetical

hysterical

**I**

icicle
ideological
idiosyncrasy
ignorance
illegible
illegitimate
illiberal
illiterate
imaginative
imitation
immaculate
immediate
immemorial
immoral
immovable
impasse
impeccable
imperative
imperceptible
imperious
impetuous
implacable
impresario
imprisoned
imprisonment
inaccessible
inadmissible
inappropriate
inaugural
incandescent
incessant
incipient
incognito
incommunicado
inconceivable
incongruous
incontrovertible
incorrigible
incredulous
incriminate
incubator
incurred
indefatigable
indefinable
indefinite
independence
independent
indescribable
indict
indictment
indigenous
indigestible
indomitable
indubitable
ineligible
inescapable
inexcusable
inexhaustible
infallible
infatuated
inferred
infinitive
inflamed
inflammable
inflationary
ingratiate
ingredient
inhabitant

inheritance
inhibition
iniquitous
initiate
initiative
innate
innocuous
innumerable
innumerate
inoculate
insecticide
inseparable
insincere
insistence
installment
instantaneous
intercept
interference
interior
intermediate
intermittent
interpret
interpretation
interrogate
interrupt
interview
intrigue
intrinsically
intuition
intuitive
invariably
inveigle
inveterate
involuntary
involvement
irascible
irrelevant
irreparable
irreplaceable
irresistible
irresponsible
irrevocable
irritable
italicize
itinerant
itinerary

**J**

jackal
Jacuzzi
jeopardize
jettisoned
jewelry
jodhpurs
juggernaut
jugular

**K**

kaleidoscopic
karate
keenness
khaki
kidnapped
kilometer
kiosk
kitchenette
kleptomania
knickknack
knowledgeable
kowtow

**L**

labeled
laboratory
labyrinth
lackadaisical
laddered
lager
language
languor
languorous
laryngitis
larynx
lassitude
latitude
laundered
launderette
layette
league
leanness
ledger
legendary
legible
legitimate
length
lengthened
leukemia
leveled
liaise
liaison
lieu
lieutenant
lilac
limousine
lineage
linen
lingerie
linguist
liqueur
liquor
liter
literature
livelihood
loneliness
loosened
loquacious
lorgnette
lucrative
lucre
lugubrious
luminous
luscious
luster
lustrous
luxurious
lyric

**M**

macabre
maelstrom
magician
magnanimous
mahogany
maintenance
malaise
malaria
malignant
manageable
management
maneuver
mannequin
mantelpiece

manually
margarine
marijuana
marquee
martyr
marvelous
marzipan
masochist
massacre
matinee
mayonnaise
meager
measurement
medallion
medieval
mediocre
melancholy
meningitis
meringue
messenger
meteorological
metropolitan
microphone
midday
migraine
milage
milieu
millionaire
mimicked
mimicry
miniature
miraculous
mirrored
miscellaneous
mischief
mischievous
misogynist
misshapen
misspell
misspent
modeled
modeling
morgue
mortgage
mosquito
mountaineer
multitudinous
muscle
museum
mustache
mysterious
mythical

**N**

naive
narrative
naughty
nausea
nautical
necessary
necessity
negligence
negligible
negotiate
neighborhood
neither
neurotic
neutral
niche
niece
ninetieth

ninth
nocturnal
nonentity
notably
noticeably
notoriety
nuance
numbered
numerate
numerous
nutrient
nutritious

**O**

obedient
obese
obituary
oblige
oblique
oblivious
obnoxious
obscene
obscenity
obsessive
obstetrician
occasion
occupancy
occupier
occupying
occurred
occurrence
octogenarian
odor
odorous
offense
offered
official
officious
ominous
omission
omitted
oneself
opaque
ophthalmic
opinion
opponent
opportunity
opposite
orchestra
ordinary
original
orthodox
orthopedic
oscillate
ostracize
outlying
outrageous
overdraft
overrate
overreach
overwrought
oxygen

**P**

pacifist
pageant
pajamas
pamphlet
panacea
panegyric
panicked

papered
parachute
paraffin
paragraph
paralysis
paralyze
paraphernalia
parceled
parliament
paroxysm
parquet
partially
participant
particle
partner
passenger
passers-by
pastime
patterned
pavilion
peaceable
peculiar
pejorative
penciled
penicillin
peppered
perceive
perennial
perilous
permissible
permitted
pernicious
perpetrate
persistence
personnel ·
persuasion
perusal
pessimism
pessimistically
pesticide
phantom
pharmacy
pharyngitis
pharynx
phenomenon
phial
phlegm
physician
picketed
picnic
picnicked
picturesque
pioneered
pious
piteous
pitiful
plaintiff
plausible
pleurisy
pneumonia
poignant
politician
pollution
polyethylene
porridge
portrait
portray
positive
possession
possibility
posthumous

| | | | | | |
|---|---|---|---|---|---|
| potatoes | recurrence | satellite | staccato | thief | vague |
| precede | redundant | scaffolding | staggered | thinness | vanilla |
| precedent | referee | scandalous | stammered | thirtieth | variegate |
| precinct | reference | scenic | statistics | thorough | vehement |
| precipice | referred | scepter | statutory | thoroughfare | vendetta |
| precocious | regatta | schedule | stealth | threshold | veneer |
| preference | regrettable | scheme | stereophonic | thrombosis | ventilator |
| preferred | regretted | schizophrenic | stirrup | throughout | veranda |
| prejudice | rehabilitation | schooner | storage | thwart | vermilion |
| preliminary | reign | sciatica | straitjacket | thyme | veterinarian |
| prepossessing | relevant | science | strait-laced | tightened | vetoes |
| prerequisite | relief | scissors | strategic | titivate | vice versa |
| prerogative | relieve | scruple | strength | tobacconist | vicissitude |
| prescription | reminisce | scrupulous | strenuous | toboggan | vigor |
| presence | reminiscence | scurrilous | stupor | toffee | vigorous |
| preservative | remuneration | scythe | suave | tomatoes | viscount |
| prestige | rendezvous | secretarial | subpoena | tomorrow | visibility |
| prestigious | repertoire | secretary | subtle | tonsillitis | vivacious |
| pretentious | repetitive | sedative | succeed | topsy-turvy | vociferous |
| prevalent | reprieve | sedentary | successful | tornadoes | voluminous |
| priest | reprisal | sensitive | successor | torpedoes | volunteered |
| primitive | requisite | separate | succinct | torpor | vulnerable |
| procedure | rescind | sergeant | succulent | tortoiseshell | |
| proceed | resemblance | serrated | succumb | tortuous | W |
| procession | reservoir | serviceable | suddenness | totaled | walkie-talkie |
| professional | resistance | serviette | suede | tourniquet | walloped |
| profiteering | resourceful | settee | sufficient | toweling | warrior |
| prohibit | responsibility | shampooed | suffocate | trafficked | wastage |
| promiscuous | restaurant | shattered | suicide | tragedy | watered |
| pronunciation | restaurateur | sheik | sullenness | traitorous | weakened |
| propeller | resurrection | sheriff | summoned | tranquilizer | wearisome |
| proposal | resuscitate | shield | supercilious | tranquilly | Wednesday |
| proprietor | retrieve | shoveled | superfluous | transcend | weight |
| prosecute | reunion | shuddered | supersede | transferable | weird |
| protagonist | reveille | siege | supervise | transferred | whereabouts |
| protein | revelry | significant | supervisor | transparent | wherewithal |
| provocation | revenue | silhouette | supplementary | traveled | widened |
| prowess | reversible | simply | surgeon | traveler | width |
| psalm | rhapsody | simultaneous | surveillance | tremor | wield |
| psyche | rheumatism | sincerely | surveyor | troublesome | wintry |
| psychiatric | rhododendron | sixtieth | susceptible | trousseau | witticism |
| psychic | rhomboid | skeleton | suspicious | truism | wizened |
| publicly | rhubarb | skillful | sweetener | trustee | woebegone |
| pursuit | rhyme | slanderous | sycamore | tsetse | wooden |
| putative | rhythm | slaughter | symmetry | tuberculosis | woolen |
| | ricochet | sleigh | sympathize | tumor | worsened |
| Q | righteous | sleight of hand | symphony | tunneled | worship |
| quarrelsome | rigor | sluice | synagogue | tureen | worshiped |
| questionnaire | rigorous | smattering | syndicate | turquoise | wrapper |
| quiche | risotto | smithereens | synonym | twelfth | wrath |
| quintet | riveted | sniveled | syringe | typhoon | wreak |
| | rogue | soccer | | tyranny | writhe |
| R | roughage | solemn | T | | |
| rabies | roulette | solicit | tableau | U | X |
| radioed | royalty | soliloquy | taciturn | unanimous | xylophone |
| radios | rucksack | soloist | taffeta | unconscious | |
| railing | ruinous | somber | tangerine | undoubted | Y |
| rancor | rummage | somersault | tangible | unduly | yield |
| ransack | rumor | sophisticated | tattoo | unequaled | yogurt |
| rapturous | | sovereign | technique | unique | |
| reassurance | S | spaghetti | teenager | unnecessary | Z |
| rebelled | sabotage | specter | televise | unremitting | zealous |
| rebellious | sacrilege | spherical | temperature | unrequited | zigzagged |
| recalcitrant | saddened | sphinx | tenuous | unrivaled | zucchini |
| receipt | salmon | sponsor | terrifically | upheaval | |
| receive | salvage | spontaneity | terrifying | uproarious | |
| recommend | sanctuary | spontaneous | territory | | |
| reconnaissance | sandwich | squabble | terrorist | V | |
| reconnoiter | sanitary | squandered | therapeutic | vaccinate | |
| recruitment | sapphire | squawk | therefore | vacuum | |